The Voluntary Sector

The voluntary sector is increasingly central to public policy debates, and is one of the fastest growing segments of the economy in the UK. Agencies situated between the market and the state are now portrayed by social commentators as the lifeblood of organized civil society. The expectation is that we should turn to this sector to address a raft of pressing societal problems, from social exclusion to environmental degradation.

This book is the first systematic attempt to examine whether these expectations are well founded through a detailed examination of the rhetoric and practice of voluntary sector action. A comparative approach is adopted throughout – in examining not only resource 'inputs', but also the character of the policy process, and the outcomes or consequences of voluntary organizations' activities. The book addresses the following questions:

- What is the contribution of the voluntary sector to the UK economy? How does it compare to the public and for-profit sectors in economic life?
- How and why have changing political conditions (including the accession to power of New Labour) and other factors come together to catapult these organizations into the public spotlight?
- How do voluntary sector 'impacts' (consequences) compare with those of the public and for-profit sectors? What are the strengths and weaknesses of each sector in responding to social needs and demands?
- What are the respective roles of the three sectors in particular policy fields: social housing, care and support for older people, and environmental protection? What can we conclude about comparative impacts in each case?

Jeremy Kendall is Research Fellow and lecturer in the Personal Social Services Research Unit (LSE Health and Social Care) and the Centre for Civil Society, Department of Social Policy, London School of Economics and Political Science.

The Voluntary Sector
Comparative perspectives in the UK

Jeremy Kendall

With a Foreword by Lord Dahrendorf

Routledge
Taylor & Francis Group

LONDON AND NEW YORK

First published 2003
by Routledge
11 New Fetter Lane, London EC4P 4EE

Simultaneously published in the USA and Canada
by Routledge
29 West 35th Street, New York, NY 10001

Routledge is an imprint of the Taylor & Francis Group

Typeset in Goudy by Exe Valley Dataset Ltd, Exeter
Printed and bound in Great Britain by Cromwell Press, Trowbridge, Wiltshire

British Library Cataloguing in Publication Data
A catalogue record for this book is available from the British Library

Library of Congress Cataloging in Publication Data
Kendall, Jeremy.
   The voluntary sector / by Jeremy Kendall. – 1st ed.
      p. cm.
   Simultaneously published in the USA and Canada.
   Incudes bibliographical references and index.
   1. Nonprofit oganizations–Great Britain.   2. Non-governmental
   organizations–Great Britain.   3. Great Britain–Social policy–1979–
   I. Title.
HD2845.K46 2003
338.7–dc21   2003007400

ISBN 0–415–30974–3 (hbk)
ISBN 0–415–30975–1 (pbk)

For Adelina

Contents

Illustrations

Figures

Boxes

Foreword

There was a time, not so long ago, when some of us felt that one should not even try to account for the contribution of the voluntary sector to the national economy. After all, we are talking about voluntary activity, immeasurable almost by definition, which contributes to well-being but not to the gross domestic product. However, this time of liberal scepticism is gone even in the United Kingdom with its non-statist tradition. At least since New Labour came to power in 1997, the voluntary sector has become part of the mainstream of public and political interest, and all its aspects warrant study and analysis.

Jeremy Kendall describes this change succinctly and clearly in the early chapters of his important book. In the last decade or so, the old conflict between advocates of public and private services has given way to thinking in terms of partnerships. Public–private partnerships were adopted at the beginning, not always successfully, but as an important new concept. Now public–voluntary sector partnerships have followed. In fact, increasingly all three – government, business and charities – join forces to regenerate communities and provide services generally.

Once this is the case, we want to know more about that new partner who came in from behind the veils of ignorance, the third or voluntary sector. In the United States, research on 'the sector' has long been significant and useful. By now, there are several institutions conducting such work in the UK and in other European countries as well. The London School of Economics has provided a home for more than one of them, and Jeremy Kendall belongs in their ambit. He was therefore well-placed to compare. Thus he could show that in purely quantitative terms – numbers employed, services provided – the UK voluntary sector is by no means as special in Europe as is sometimes assumed. Yet on closer inspection it remains further removed from both government and business than its counterparts in the rest of Europe. As with other socio-economic features, 'the UK voluntary sector does seem to resemble its US cousin more than its continental neighbours'.

This is but one of many insights arising from a study which combines quantitative analysis with historical description and socio-political theory in an exemplary manner, and in the process never loses sight of the 'unpredictability of the sector by virtue of its sheer diversity and complexity'. So does the sector contribute to the welfare of British – or indeed any other – society? With the help of his eclectic meta-analysis, Kendall disentangles research and rhetoric with respect to such claims as the innovation potential of the voluntary sector, its advocacy function, its contribution to leadership formation and community-building. The three special subjects of social housing, care and support for older people, and environmental policy provide instructive empirical support for Kendall's (in his own terms) 'contingent realism' which he holds against 'civic conservative pessimism', 'liberal scepticism' and 'social democratic optimism' alike.

In the final chapter of his book, Kendall counts me among those who have led him to his conclusions. But perhaps I have come to be yet more sceptical about the future of the voluntary sector than the author's account suggests. Increasingly it appears that 'the sector' is in fact two sectors: one genuinely voluntary, happily remote from government, hard-pressed to meet the charity tests of social usefulness – and the other linked to government as well as business, defined by its social objectives, subject to all sorts of controls and rules, and voluntary only in name. Sometimes the split runs right through the same organisation. Often, the old-style voluntary organisations feel neglected and even underprivileged, whereas their new-style colleagues wonder why they do not have civil-service privileges since they have become quasi-governmental organisations.

There is no doubt that the new partnerships between public, private and voluntary sectors add flexibility, a kind of looseness of the limbs of society, to our lives. But civil society thrives where even 'useless' clubs and organisations find their place. The foundation of civil society is laid by association – an old and beautiful word. These are freely formed combinations of people who share an interest in Lake District hiking or stamp collecting or playing New Orleans-style jazz. Their public benefit is the benefit for individuals who see themselves as citizens without having to ask the state for permission to do what they like doing. In the new world of partnerships it is important not to forget that life in a free society in some respects defies all organisational categories, and what has come to be called the voluntary sector is in fact a delightfully creative chaos.

Jeremy Kendall's splendid work provides food even for such unfashionable thoughts. It is a study which will greatly stimulate the topical debate while providing material for future research as well as policy.

RALF DAHRENDORF
May 2003

Acknowledgements

General interest in the subject matter of this book has recently escalated significantly. This is fortuitous for the author, whose curiosity about voluntary action has evolved over a long period of time. As an academic researcher, I have been privileged to pursue this interest in considerable depth, seeking to be constructively critical, realistic and sympathetic. All too often this sphere is either simply misunderstood, or shrouded in a mystifying haze, a situation which can all too readily provide opportunities for manipulation by the powerful. If this book helps to rectify some of those misunderstandings and clear some of that fog, then it will have been worthwhile.

I embarked upon the journey which ultimately led me to this book in 1989. Then, at the Personal Social Services Research Unit, University of Kent at Canterbury, I first became familiar with 'nonprofit sector' evidence and argument. With the enthusiastic guidance of Martin Knapp, I was given the opportunity to pursue this fascination within the framework of phase 1 of the Johns Hopkins Comparative Nonprofit Sector Project. I encountered the inspirational figures of Lester M. Salamon and Helmut K. Anheier, already long established as leading scholars in this field. Of course Martin, Lester and Helmut's collective knowledge was remarkable, but equally impressive was their genuine fascination with, and thirst for knowledge on, our chosen subject. Their enthusiasm was contagious, but also important was their recognition of the need to distil our emerging findings in timely fashion. One important outcome of this effort was the completion of a volume co-authored with Martin Knapp in 1996 (Kendall and Knapp, 1996).

That volume was well received, and this was important in providing some of the impetus for a second phase of this project in the UK, which had now expanded to include over twenty countries from a core of seven original participants. As will be clear in what follows, this book draws extensively on the work undertaken as part of that (now) huge international research endeavour, funded in the UK by Charities Aid Foundation and the Joseph Rowntree Foundation. Thus, I would like to thank the UK funders and the UK Advisory Group, chaired by Ian Bruce, and including Michael Brophy, Richard Corden, Paul Fredericks, Les Hems, Janet Novak, Cathy Pharoah and Roger Ward. Equally, this volume seeks to capitalise on other work undertaken independently in recent years. Funders for this work have included the National Council for Voluntary Organisations and the Department of Health (via the London School of Economics branch of PSSRU); while some policy analysis presented here has benefited from my part-time positioning at the Centre for Civil Society (also at LSE). Here, substance was discussed particularly with Professor Nicholas Deakin, Helmut K. Anheier and Sarabajaya Kumar, but importantly also with students on the Centre's M.Sc in Voluntary Sector Policy & Administration.

I owe a particular debt of gratitude to Steve Almond, who was extra-ordinarily efficient at processing and analysing the quantitative data that forms one important strand of this work. I am also grateful to Rachel Wigglesworth, who assisted with some of the early fieldwork and drafting that underpins the discussion of voluntary sector 'impacts' in the social housing and environmental fields in Part two of the book. I would also like to thank Chris Rootes, Liz Richardson and Rebecca Tunstall, both for sharing with me their extensive knowledge of the role of voluntary associations in the environmental and social housing fields, and for actively participating in the qualitative aspect of the research through helping to organise, and chair, focus groups. I am also grateful to those stakeholders from all sectors who were involved as interviewees, focus group participants and Delphi-style reviewers of chapter drafts.

The actual process of pulling these materials together into a single volume was made possible by a special grant from CAF over the summer of 2002. I would like to thank Cathy Pharoah once more for her support during this crucial period. Five other people also heroically reviewed the entire manuscript that autumn and offered me insightful suggestions: Perri 6, Richard Fries, Howard Glennerster, Peter Halfpenny and Stephen Osborne. Other insightful feedback on individual draft chapters which I would like to acknowledge was provided by Tessa Harding, Walter Holland, Richard Sandbrook, Marilyn Taylor, Anne Netten, David Mullins, Ted Marmor, Steve Rathgeb Smith, Justin Davis Smith and Stephen Young. As publishers, Routledge have proved to be a model mixture of efficiency, sensitivity and diplomacy: thanks in particular to Rachel Crookes and Francesca Poynter.

Most importantly, my wife Adelina Comas-Herrera has supported me throughout this endeavour. Naturally she is all too familiar with the trials and tribulations that unfolded in seeing this book through to completion! But of course, responsibility for any outstanding errors rests entirely with the author.

Finally, I would like to acknowledge the research department of the National Council for Voluntary Organizations for permission to reproduce Figure 4.1 from Jas *et al.* (2002) and for supplying unpublished expenditure data relating to 'general charities'; and the Policy Press for permission to reproduce parts of an article published in *Policy and Politics*, in Chapter 3.

JEREMY KENDALL
December 2002

1   Introduction

- **The voluntary sector in Britain currently commands more attention from policy makers than at any time since the heyday of Victorian charity and mutuality.**

- **The voluntary sector's contributions can be examined from a comparative perspective by asking: What resources does each sector command in economic life in Britain and abroad? What is distinctive about its involvement in the policy process?**

- **A further key question is: What are the 'impacts' of voluntary sector activity?**

1.1 High visibility, high expectations

In 2003, the voluntary, third or nonprofit sector occupies centre-stage in public policy discussions in the UK. Not since the late nineteenth century, when voluntary action was integral to contemporary concepts of citizenship, and the associated institutional infrastructure of charities and mutuals were the cause of considerable national pride, have organizations occupying the space between the market and the state commanded so much attention. The two largest political parties now give the sector high visibility in their aspirations, reflected in 2001, for example, by manifesto commitments of nurture and support.

The current New Labour administration's ongoing interest in this sector is demonstrated by its completion, as this book is finalized, of two major reviews from sources close to the centre of political power. The Strategy Unit, a policy development body servicing the Cabinet Office, has undertaken an assessment of the sector's policy situation, with an emphasis on legal structures and frameworks (Strategy Unit, 2002); while the Treasury has simultaneously reviewed 'the relationship between the voluntary sector and the government in service delivery, taking account of the key role the sector can play in strengthening civil society and building capacity in local communities' (HM Treasury, 2002a: 35). Think tanks of all political persuasions, who had previously conceptualized public policy approaches almost exclusively with reference to the market and the state – separately or in combination – have increasingly also reflected on the role of not-for-profits in their diagnoses of, and prescriptions for, an array of contemporary social problems. Theoretical and practical rationales for this line of thinking are discussed in detail in the pages that follow, but some of the factors which have fed into a more general aspiration to look beyond the two sector model include:

- Disillusionment with private market solutions, which often seem to engender a raft of difficulties and failings, particularly in social welfare and environmental policy domains. These include obvious limits to their capacity to meet the needs of citizens not endowed with economic resources; chronic vulnerability to the erratic movements of the economic cycle and financial markets; and, for some, psychological and philosophical objections to the sheer ubiquity of capitalist markets as a mechanism for allocating resources in modern developed societies (Hirshmann, 1986; Ware and Goodin, 1990; Ehrenberg, 1999).
- Mounting distrust in politician-dominated approaches, and scepticism from both Left and Right concerning the capacity of apparently overloaded, contradiction-riven, cash-starved, state-centred institutions to deliver public services able to match spiralling user expectations and increasingly diverse citizen aspirations (Klein, 1977; Offe, 1984; Olsen, 1982).[1]
- A positive endorsement of the actual and potential contribution of these organizations to the 'good society'. This is not just by offering choice and responsiveness in services (Knapp et al., 1990), but through providing opportunities for the generation of trust, civic virtue and 'social capital' via participation in community and public life (Putnam, 2000). This is increasingly seen not only as of intrinsic value in its own right, but as being deeply connected with local, national and international economic success, and – controversially – as even constituting a core ingredient of a 'third way' in the political domain (Blair, 1998; Giddens, 1998: 78–86).

In the mass media, coverage of the world of voluntarism has increased markedly, while specialist magazines, such as *Third Sector*, have witnessed considerable increases in circulation amongst practitioners and others with a stake in such organizations. In academia, a small body of specialist scholarship, with origins particularly in the late 1970s and 1980s, had already provided much of the impetus for new specialist academic journals founded and new degree courses at the start of the 1990s in Europe and the US. Most recently, traditional disciplinary journals from across the social sciences, spurred by a new wave of interest in civil society and social capital, have increasingly put these organizations on their analytic agenda.

Arguments from both the foundational literature and the more recent academic debate are drawn on extensively in this volume as and when conceptual and theoretical guidance is needed. We use these approaches to shed light on the sector's policy situation and on actors' beliefs about the voluntary sector and its strengths and weaknesses. But to give the reader an early taste of the most enduring theorizing in the field, Box 1.1 summarizes some of the key concepts from the foundational literature.

Box 1.1 Key approaches in international nonprofit sector theory

Prior to the 'rediscovery' of associations and the voluntary sector by civil society and social capital theorists, seven theoretical approaches had dominated scholarly debate on the role of voluntary organizations:

- Weisbrod (1975) portrayed the sector as a response to demands for *public goods* supplied by neither the market nor the state. The market 'fails' because of the free rider problem (resulting particularly from the market's undersupply of goods where nonpayers cannot be excluded); and the state 'fails' in the sense that electoral considerations are assumed to limit it to meeting the demands of the typical (median) voter.
- James (1987) argued that Weisbrod fails to take into account the supply side. She posited that the sector's capacity to deliver services will depend on the availability of *religious, ideological and political entrepreneurship*, as well as on the demands presented. The prototypical supplier is then a religious body or political or social movement, engaged in welfare services to shape the values of those it serves.
- Hansmann (1980) focused on the problem of meeting demand for goods when information is asymmetric, so that the potential consumer is vulnerable to supplier exploitation of superior knowledge about the service. He suggested that the voluntary sector's nondistribution constraint – preventing those in control of the organisation from benefiting from its activities – acts as a signal of *trustworthiness*. It provides assurance that the user will not be 'ripped off'.
- Ben-Ner and Van Hoomissen (1993) attempted a synthesis of the aforementioned theories, modelling voluntary sector suppliers as *coalitions of demand-side stakeholders*. Control over output quality is effectively said to be achieved by the integration within the organization of demand and supply: and because suppliers are also demanders, they lack incentives to skimp on quality.
- Salamon (1987) portrayed voluntary organizations as pioneers preceding state action in social domains, and therefore with 'first mover advantages' by virtue of sunk costs and acquired skills. Nevertheless, because they are prone to their own *voluntary failures* – different from state 'failures' – they often work closely with State agencies to get the 'best of both worlds'.

These accounts tend to portray the voluntary sector in a positive light. They see it as a response to the failures of other sectors, or as a collaborator with the State to overcome the failures of each. Two more politically sanguine approaches have also been developed:

- In regime theory, the voluntary sector's role in services as a response to political manoeuvring amongst class interests. Differences in state–voluntary sector relations between countries are said to reflect strategic constitutional settlements. Large voluntary sectors tend to emerge because this is in keeping with the ideology and interests of middle-class or landed political elites; while large public sectors tend to reflect a balance of power in favour of labour movements and allied forces (Salamon and Anheier, 1998, 2001).
- The voluntary sector is treated more straightforwardly as the instrument of capital in all liberal democratic countries in Marxist theory. Forms of welfare, whereby the state collaborates with the voluntary sector, are necessarily treated as an expression of social control (Wolch, 1990).

1.2 In the spotlight: some puzzling facts

An earlier study completed in 1995 charting the social, political and economic contribution of this sector, characterized this set of institutions as then beginning to move 'out of the shadows'. That study was the first to demonstrate the UK voluntary sector's overall scope and scale, and link that systematically to ongoing policy and research debates (Kendall and Knapp, 1996). Just 7 years after that research was completed, it can reasonably be argued that these organizations have not only consolidated their place on the public stage, but find themselves under a spotlight of unprecedented intensity. A position of relatively low policy visibility has been replaced by one of sustained scrutiny. This book aims to contribute to our understanding of this process and the challenges and opportunities that it raises.

The situation this book seeks to make sense of is certainly a complex one, and seems to involve a number of peculiarities or even contradictions:

- It is often claimed that the British voluntary sector is 'unique' or even a 'beacon' to other countries in Europe and in the world (for example, Home Office, 1993; Blair, 2002). Perhaps this assertion was accurate at the time of the Victorian heyday of philanthropy and mutualism (Prochaska, 1990; Morris, 1990). Yet as we shall see, at the end of the twentieth century, this sector turns out to be quantitatively smaller than in several other countries (and below the European average), and was also mobilizing fewer volunteers and members than many other countries (Gaskin and Davis Smith, 1995; Dekker and van den Broek, 1998).
- If there is a characteristic that sets the British voluntary sector clearly apart from equivalent organizations elsewhere, it is the sheer pace at which it has

had to adapt to both a turbulent policy environment and an expanded economic role. Other countries have witnessed new interest in this sphere but few if any have experienced quite such a step change in their situations in the past 5 years (Anheier and Kendall, 2001).

- The political party which took the lead in the late 1990s in courting the voluntary sector as a 'partner' – the Labour Party – is the party which has traditionally been thought of as least sympathetic to these organizations. For example, charities were often equated by the political Left with social backwardness and class divisiveness (Kendall and Knapp, 1996). Even mutual associations – whose solidaristic goals and working-class origins would *prima facie* seem to situate them well ideologically – were not included in the 1940s British welfare state architecture, unlike their counterparts in some areas of continental Europe.
- Nationally, rhetorical support for the voluntary sector is now ubiquitous – and the 2002 Strategy Unit and Treasury reviews bear witness to the aspiration to act on supportive beliefs; yet converting intentions into practice turns out to be a difficult, uneven and highly complex process
- The significance of the voluntary sector's presence compared with for-profit and government sector counterparts varies significantly by policy domain, having developed in distinctive ways at the level of individual fields such as those discussed in detail later in this volume – social housing, care for older people and environmental action.

Identifying how and why these situations have arisen, beginning to explore their consequences and attempting to reconcile these and a range of other apparently conflicting currents or trends are amongst the analytic challenges tackled during the course of this book. These *explananda* emerge in the process of pursuing the following objectives:

- Providing an up-to-date 'map' of the economic contribution of the voluntary sector, examining its resource base and identifying how and why some of its most important contours have changed over the past decade.
- Describing the voluntary sector's involvement in the policy process, identifying why the terms of its engagement with the state have changed so significantly, and highlighting how new ideas and institutions characterize the sector's policy environment at the start of the twenty-first century at both central and local government levels.
- Attempting to move beyond the examination of both the 'inputs' associated with the voluntary sector – the human and financial resources it mobilizes and deploys – and the institutional processes with which it is involved to focus also on the social consequences of these activities. The book therefore explores the sector's multifarious 'impacts', both as a way of revealing the sector's richness and variety, but also so as to be better able to compare it with the public and for-profit sectors.

1.3 Definitions and concepts

The 'default' definition of the voluntary sector used in this book is in keeping with the aforementioned study of Britain in international context (Kendall and Knapp, 1996). Included are organizations which are formal, nonprofit distributing, constitutionally independent of the state, self-governing and benefiting from voluntarism. These groups can be seen as comprising a 'broad voluntary sector' (BVS). At the same time, we also offer a 'narrow voluntary sector' (NVS) definition which is closer to what seems to be the typical, de facto understanding of what is, or should be, in scope in this country. Further details are provided in the next chapter. But for now the reader may be wondering why we have continued to adopt this unfashionable usage when other language – viz., voluntary and community sector, organized civil society, social economy, third sector or system, and so on – has apparently gained currency in recent years.[2] The Strategy Unit review further complicates matters by referring to a new construct, 'charities and the wider not-for-profit sector' (Strategy Unit, 2002).

First, these same definitions were used to conduct the statistical mapping in 1995 as in 1990, and to change the language while leaving the coverage unaltered would potentially cause confusion. Second, it seems that the shift in language has been largely an elite-led process, and has not really been adopted on the ground. Certainly in conducting fieldwork for this book, 'voluntary sector' was the single most commonly utilized collective noun, usually implicitly deploying our narrow definition. Third, it is worth underlining that, in using this as the default language for the particular purpose of this book, we are not making any claim that it should also be adopted by other studies with different intentions and priorities. For example, in examining how these organizations feature in European Union policies, the label 'third sector' seems to be an appropriate shorthand (Kendall and Anheier, 2001b); while if one is interested in accounting for informal, as well as formal, nonmarket and nonstate organizing processes across the world, the language of 'global civil society' is indispensable (Anheier *et al.*, 2001).

While the BVS and NVS concepts dominate, we will nevertheless necessarily depart from them at two points. First, in order to provide the most up to date statistical coverage possible, we have had to sacrifice full consistency in our usage over time. In reporting evidence up to 2000, we will need to rely on two alternative definitions, which are close to, but not coincident with, the NVS definition to which we have referred. Second, elasticity in the use of language has been an important hallmark of the rhetoric that is so pervasive in this area. We will see that even the relatively widely used and well-understood language of the 'voluntary *sector*' (as opposed to voluntary *action*) has a traceable pedigree of only 25 years, while in the past 10 years, 'voluntary and community sector' and 'civil society' have increasingly been adopted by policy-makers and politicians instead of or in addition to this received usage.

It is also worth being clear from the onset concerning what we mean by 'voluntary sector policy'. We use this as shorthand for 'public policy towards the narrow voluntary sector', where the latter is defined as above.[3] Simultaneously, we use a rather inclusive notion of policy, while at the same time placing relatively little emphasis on the charity law component. These emphases merit explanation at this point, because they make the ambit of the book rather distinctive. First, our approach to policy seeks to attend to those actions and institutions which are explicitly promoted by the British state as its current purposive or deliberate policy towards the voluntary sector. But it also involves taking into account aspects of public policy which de facto, affect the sector's situation in significant ways, even if not consciously framed as voluntary sector policy. This includes influences which 'spill over' to shape its policy environment, and were not intended to do so by their originators.

While this makes life much more complicated, there are good practical and theoretical reasons for such a broad canvass. Practically, the stuff of public policy as experienced by organizations in this sector are the relationships with, and resources received from, an incredibly complex and variegated state. Theoretically, it means thinking of these organizations' involvement in public policy as part of a 'path dependent' process that unfolds over time, and involves accident as well as design (see below). Taking into account how commitments and experiences from the past, as well as the latest policy pronouncements, jointly shape current policy possibilities, leads us to a more accurate and realistic appraisal of what it means to be a voluntary sector policy actor.

Second, and relatedly, the 'messiness' and complexity of policy is also a reflection of how it is constituted jointly by what we will refer to in this volume as 'horizontal' and 'vertical' components. Conceptually, an organization in the sector should be thought of as nested not only in a 'horizontal' policy environment by virtue of its sector of ownership (voluntary as opposed to public or private), but also as simultaneously inhabiting an 'industry' with its own specific 'vertical' policy environment which relate to the particular needs or problems being addressed. Apart from a relatively small number of specialist 'infrastructure' or 'intermediary' bodies, it is the 'vertical' ingredients which matter most. For example, social care policies tend to be more significant than tailored voluntary sector policies for many voluntary social care organizations. Although, as we shall see, the current Government has invested a large amount of resources in elaborating 'cross-cutting' – that is 'horizontal' – institutions, the most consequential drivers of change thus far have been 'vertical' in particular welfare fields, notably social care and social housing.

Third, in discussing the 'horizontal', the primary emphasis in this book is on aspects of the policy process other than those relating to legal structures and statuses for charities and other voluntary sector bodies. This legal dimension is considered at various points, but is not singled out with a separate chapter, or with separate sections within chapters, for example. There are two primary reasons for this. First, at the time of writing (2002) the broad parameters remain unchanged from those set out in an earlier volume and the situation set out there is still current (see Thomas and Kendall, 1996) – although if the recommendations of the Strategy Unit report are acted upon, the situation may be different quite soon (see especially Chapters 4–8 of Strategy Unit, 2002). Second, recent years have seen numerous other works published on this particular aspect of horizontality (for example, see Dunn 2000; Mitchell and Moody, 2001). It was felt that this book would make a greater contribution by focusing on other dimensions of cross-cutting policy. These other aspects have received relatively little attention in voluntary sector policy analyses. As we shall see, this is not least because, unlike the ancient laws of charity with its common law origins and professional infrastructure, they involve relatively new institutions.

1.4 Methodological and theoretical approaches

This book draws upon a range of methodologies and is eclectic in the use of theory. More detailed descriptions are provided in the chapters that follow as and when the need arises, but it is worth making some general remarks here to help locate the study in the third sector and policy literatures.

Some of the relevant parameters – including definitions and classifications for collecting and examining much of the data on both 'inputs' and 'impacts' – flow directly from the author's participation as the British national associate in an international study (cf. Salamon *et al.*, 1999; and see the Website listed at Comparative Nonprofit Sector Project, 2002). The quantitative data relating to economic change during the first half of the 1990s is in this category, and the implicit theory here reflects National Accounts assumptions and conventions (United Nations Statistical Division in co-operation with the Johns Hopkins Center for Civil Society Studies, 2002). The ongoing international study's emphasis on understanding 'impact' by (a) examining the sector's contribution at both a high level of generality, and in carefully selected policy fields; and (b) by relying heavily on interactively generated 'expert opinion' (with 'expertise' inclusively defined) in a Delphi-type of research design also provided the guiding framework for that part of the analysis (Salamon *et al.*, 2000a). More generally, that study's use of internationally developed 'third sector theory' to identify and conceptualize the British voluntary sector's potential strengths and weaknesses with reference to such constructs as 'market failure' and 'voluntary failure' (cf. Box 1.1) has also guided the British study where such formulations are helpful.

However, in addition, this volume also uses a number of other sources and approaches. First, to ensure that the 'map' is as up to date as possible, and to take us up to the new millennium, we draw upon further data analysis undertaken independently by the author with Steve Almond at the London School of Economics and Political Science during the period 1998–2000, and work undertaken by the National Council for Voluntary Organizations.

Second, the emphasis adopted in this book is distinctive in utilizing a number of analytic constructs to bring attention to aspects of the voluntary sector reality whose relevance was left unexplored, or underplayed in the US-led international study and the body of third sector theorizing upon which it draws.

One distinguishing feature of this book is to highlight the combined role of policy entrepreneurship, as well as broad political and institutional factors in jointly determining how 'horizontal' voluntary sector policy (to reiterate, policy specifically geared towards the voluntary sector per se) – is situated in the broader environment of public policy. Individual and corporate (organized) political actors – party political and otherwise, as well as more 'structural' changes – have all played significant roles in moving the sector into the policy limelight. Such actors have suggested the 'problems' to which its contributions can respond, and diagnosed its own internal problems or challenges.

Theoretically, recognizing these multiple factors involves drawing upon models from the public policy literature. For example, the 'multiple streams' approach to agenda setting of John W. Kingdon is used to explain the mainstreaming of 'horizontal' policy in Chapter 3 (Kingdon, 1995). But another distinctive emphasis is our examination of how policy legacies stretching back over decades, have critically shaped the voluntary sector's development and current situation. The underlying assumption is that in order to understand the present, we need to account for how inherited institutions shape current developments in significant ways. In the jargon of policy analysts, this involves taking seriously the 'path dependency' of the policy process, a notion whose theoretical bases are summarized in Box 1.2.

How does this emphasis relate to the approaches set out in Box 1.1 above? It is close conceptually to social origins theory, as applied for international third sector comparative purposes by Salamon and Anheier (1998) and Salamon *et al.* (2000b). That framework usefully recognized the relevance of path dependency for analysis in examining voluntary sector policy choice. The study's conclusion that the British 'regime' is a mixture of 'liberal' and 'social democratic' ingredients, reflecting past strategic welfare policy decisions, is a useful starting point.

However, this theory also has a number of limitations. It represents the British case in a way which seems insensitive to policy change over time; it is too reductionist in its uniform categorization of all sector relations in the UK as 'liberal' or mixed 'liberal–social democratic', and in not accounting for the importance of for-profit enterprise in policy choices. Moreover, as applied thus far, it has represented the relevant actors in policy development as essentially static class-based interests struggling for control over the welfare state apparatus. Policy is portrayed as instrumentally constructed by such interests, implicitly taken to be able and willing to act consistently across all relevant policy subfields. It seems to have little room for accident or happenstance, the initiative of independent interests not reducible to class categorization, variation between and within vertical policy fields, or factors which are not related to strategic welfare state design considerations.

In contrast, the more 'middle range' policy legacy effects identified in this book suggest a much more variegated picture involving unintended as well as intended consequences. The institutional environment which the voluntary sector inhabits varies significantly from field to field. Just as Pierson (1994) stressed that 'programmatic variation' is an integral feature of welfare state

Box 1.2 Path dependency and the theoretical significance of policy legacies

The most influential theoretical underpinnings for the idea that current choices over resource allocation are constrained by choices made at previous points in time were initially developed by economic historians interested in the evolution of complex, knowledge-intensive technologies. Four conditions under which prior decisions will tend to 'lock in' subsequent decisions have been suggested:

- High set-up or fixed costs, wherein strong incentives are created to continue to use the technology initially chosen, and expanding production using this existing technology will yield lower unit costs (economies of scale).
- Learning effects such that knowledge gained in the operation of the system leads to higher returns over time. Repetition allows individuals to find ways of using products more effectively.
- Co-ordination effects in which interdependence is a feature of the technology. In particular, if technologies embody positive network externalities, then a given technology becomes more attractive as more people use it.
- Adaptive expectations wherein individuals will tend to choose options which they expect others will also choose. This is in anticipation of co-ordination effects, so that estimates are made concerning what others are likely to choose and factored into current decisions in anticipation of benefiting from the associated externalities.

Why is this line of argument relevant to policy choice? First, North suggested that these conditions or features of complex technology are also to be found in social institutions (1990: Chapter 11). Second, Pierson (1994: Chapter 2) argued that one particular set of institutions where these effects are relevant are public policy, and especially social welfare policy, institutions. In social welfare policies as in complex technologies, the presence of these conditions does not predetermine future options, but it does tend to constrain them in significant ways.

Later work by Pierson (2000a, b) elaborated this analysis further by suggesting that yet other features of policy-making and political life make previous choices more salient to current choices than even the analogy with complex technologies would seem to suggest. These are identified and linked to the case of voluntary sector policy in Chapter 5, the introduction to Part II.

developmental trajectories, reflecting differently path-dependent state–society relationships within programmes, this book calls attention to vertical field level variation. Relatedly, policy actors are viewed as having motivations which reflect more than the static, social class-based values by which they might be categorized for more general purposes. Rather, to a significant degree, their beliefs and actions are shaped by the specific policy legacies that exist in particular fields, and the experiences and relationships they accrue while situated there. Significant commitments are acquired as a result of specializing in those particular policy domains, and potentially subject to revision over time as circumstances and evidence evolve within those fields (Sabatier and Jenkins-Smith, 1993; Levin, 1997). Moreover, as we will show in Part II of the book, this is not just a question of institutional classification. In examining developments at the level of particular vertical policy fields it is noted that such contrasting legacies seem to make for important differences in 'impacts', at least to the extent that those can be ascertained using current evidence (see below).

Close attention to this variety is important not just in order to understand each individual policy field in its own right, but also must be taken into account if we wish to make sense of the overall patterns change. The economic growth that we will identify in Chapter 2, for example, has reflected the aggregated effect of distinctive 'vertical' policies, unfolding under their own internal momentum, in social care and housing. It cannot be reduced to the deliberate cross-cutting policy efforts 'from above' by any one class or other interest. Each field has taken a particular developmental pathway, and the nature of the relevant voluntary sector, state sector, and for-profit sector contributions cannot be divorced from this context. The book seeks to begin to show how this is the case by diagnosing how stakeholders' attitudes and actions towards each sector are conditioned by field-specific policy legacies. It also does so by unpacking, to the extent that data allow, why and how the internal composition of the sector bears the imprint of history.

Finally, in seeking to address the question of what makes voluntary sector policy distinctive, this study will seek to attend to the role of rhetoric and persuasion in policy development (Majone, 1989). Rhetoric and persuasion are particularly significant in examining this sector. These organizations' voluntarism makes them an attractive proposition as allies for the state in the policy process, but also, we shall show, far less easy to engage than other sectors. They stand apart from commercial organizations, whose services can be straightforwardly bought with cash (assuming levels of funding allow profitability imperatives have been fulfilled). But they are also distinct in this regard from bodies directly controlled by the state, and from the actors involved in traditional corporatist arrangements, wherein participation is not on a voluntary basis.[4]

1.5 The book structure, comparative emphasis and value added

Throughout this book, the focus is on comparison, in a conscious attempt to differentiate the analysis here from much previous UK research. How processes, outputs and outcomes vary by sector is explored. A major, long-standing criticism of third sector research has been its lack of a comparative dimension (6, 1997a). A particular effort is therefore made in this book to set the voluntary sector in comparative context. This is done in a number of ways. First, in the first part of the book, inputs and activities are related to their equivalents in other sectors, and in the economy as a whole. Second, by including vertical field-level chapters in which the voluntary sector is considered alongside the public and for-profit sector actors also present, conscious comparisons are made. Finally, in using theory from the policy literature to guide the analysis at various points, the aspiration is to begin to ascertain what makes voluntary sector policy distinctive by comparison with other policy domains.

It is hoped that attempting a comparative approach makes this book more relevant and useful, especially for public policy commentators who have traditionally not devoted attention to this topic. In addition, the book draws upon the approaches outlined in the previous section in order to go beyond our earlier study (Kendall and Knapp, 1996) in several respects. Each goal will now be considered in turn, in the process both summarizing the structure of the book, and moving from the fairly abstract level of discussion thus far to identify some of the most significant real world institutions and policies that will be encountered in what follows.

First, the reasons why the unprecedented degree of interest in the voluntary sector as a horizontal 'policy actor' – that is, as an agenda setter, implementer and critic across public policy as a whole – has intensified so markedly in recent years are analysed. This is partly a reflection of the coming to power in 1997 of New Labour with its aspirations to differentiate itself from both Old Labour and the political Right at Westminster and Whitehall. But as Chapter 3 will examine, this development also reflects other factors at one remove from the world of high politics, drivers which are less a function of 'top-down' initiative and more to do with slower and less dramatic but nevertheless significant ongoing developments. An emphasis on the longer term is called for when it is recognized that New Labour has not developed its proposals in a historic vacuum, but within the context of inherited institutions and interests. It also emerges, setting the mapping evidence (Chapter 2) alongside our account of 'horizontal' policy mainstreaming, that the most rapid economic growth took place before New Labour came to office. As already noted, many of the significant policy developments for the voluntary sector in recent years cannot be 'read off' overarching political or economic preferences for voluntary organizations per se. Rather, they reflect significantly independent dynamics within policy fields, such as social care and housing. 'Vertical', policy field-specific analysis is therefore integral to the second part of the book (see below), and a crucial supplement to the 'horizontal' accounts offered in the third and fourth chapters.

Second, Chapter 4 seeks to show how the 'horizontal' process has been reflected in the development of an array of distinctive new institutions and practices at the national and local levels since 1997. Examples include the development of Compacts and Codes of good practice to frame the relations between the voluntary sector and the state; the initiation of an annual review of voluntary sector–government relations in Parliament; and the involvement of voluntary sector personnel in the units and teams established to address 'cross-cutting' or 'holistic' policy problems, and offer 'joined-up solutions' to them. These new initiatives have been grafted on to inherited arrangements, most obviously a significantly expanded unit with responsibility for the voluntary sector and volunteering at the Home Office – now labelled the Active Community Unit. An array of state-sponsored 'intermediary' or 'infrastructure' bodies, traditionally claiming to articulate the 'voice' of the voluntary sector, also represents continuity with the past, having been recognized and sponsored by the state for over 20 years at national and local levels (Wolfenden, 1978; Osborne, 2000).

All the signs are that this policy space will be broadened and deepened in future years. At the time of writing, brand new government policy statements list over 100 policy proposals for development. Some of these suggest the reform of institutions which long predate New Labour's interest, including the idea of restyling the Charity Commission as a 'charity regulation authority' (Strategy Unit, 2002); some would involve the strengthening of post-1997 settlement, as with the elaboration of Compact-related policies; while yet others would involve drawing into this domain extremely powerful but previously rather uninterested, state bodies. Significantly, the Treasury has given itself the leading role in designing a voluntary sector 'Futurebuilders' investment fund (HM Treasury, 2002a: 32).[5]

A third goal of this book is to subject the claims-making as to the voluntary sector's various contributions to critical scrutiny. Ample evidence now demonstrates the inputs the sector mobilizes in terms of financial and human resources, and the review of that material undertaken in the first part of the book is an important first step to a systematic portrayal of its economic role and institutional environment. But as awareness of the pervasiveness of this set of institutions grows, and the extent to which significant components of it are supported by public resources becomes clearer, there is an increasing thirst for information as to its impact: what difference does the sector make? In Part II, Chapter 6 first examines the research evidence that exists as to the sector's general comparative role: that is, at the level of actual practice, what do we know about whether the sector actually has the advantages and disadvantages posited for it in theory? Another important facet of Chapter 6 is an aspiration to systematically identify the rhetorical claims that have been put forward, and assess how those compare with the research evidence.

The remainder of Part II of the book focuses on the voluntary sector's role in three particular vertical policy fields: care for older people, social housing and environmental protection (Chapters 7–9). At this level of specific activities, it becomes more feasible – but still, as we shall see, highly complex – to begin to assess empirically the relative contribution of the sector. These areas have been chosen for closer examination in part on the basis of theoretical criteria laid down in the international research project's methodology. But the intention was also to choose areas where meaningful cross-sector comparisons were possible, at least to some degree. And as will become clear, our chosen fields were also obvious ones for the UK if further criteria to do with political, economic and policy relevance are considered.

The final chapter summarizes key findings from the study and their theoretical implications, and tries to stand back from vertical minutiae to reach tentative conclusions as to the nature of the voluntary sector as a policy actor. The diversity of the sector and the ambiguity in much of the comparative evidence means that this is a very difficult step to take. However, what it does seem possible to do is to be clearer about how the different 'models' that thus far have tended to guide thinking in this area seem to involve contrasting assumptions about each sector's overall importance and political situation. A number of the 'models' identified could plausibly be supported by drawing selectively on the different forms of evidence gathered together in this book. However, it is argued that an alternative, 'contingent realist' approach offers a more balanced way of doing justice to the current state of affairs, as suggested by this book's analysis.

Finally, a note on country coverage. The statistical data reported in Chapter 2 is UK wide. However, the remainder of the book strongly reflects an orientation towards the particular case of England. This is partly because of the author's institutional base; partly because of constraints on word length; and partly because much less is known about voluntary action outside England. However, there is now a healthy proliferation of research outside England (Plowden *et al.* 2001) and it seems clear that this widening of the knowledge base to systematically cover Britain as a whole will continue in years to come.

Notes

1 See Kendall and Anheier (2001a) for a theoretical discussion of how taking into account the voluntary sector's involvement in and around welfare systems can lead to modification in the alarmist conclusions of these and other 'welfare state crisis' theorists.

2 A range of developments have driven this newer usage, including theoretical concerns, interest in democratization processes in east central Europe and elsewhere, and the practice of European Union institutions; conceptually, see respectively Ehrenberg, 1999; Deakin, 2001; Kendall *et al.*, 2000; Kendall and Anheier, 2001b; Amin *et al.*, 2002. For details of the implications of different usage for statistical purposes, see CIRIEC, 2000; Hems, 2001.

3 Thus the comparative statistical material in Chapter 2 is inclusive, under the broad definition, of educational institutions, sports and social clubs, and trade unions and professional associations to allow for contrasts to be drawn with other countries. However, the impact of excluding these institutions on the grounds that they are not part of the 'narrow voluntary sector' is also demonstrated. In other parts of the book, including the discussions of policy and impact, the latter definition is generally taken to be appropriate.

4 One element of the classic definition of corporatism given by Schmitter refers to 'constituent units organized into a limited number of singular, compulsory, non-competitive, hierarchically ordered and functionally differentiated categories, recognized or licensed (if not created) by the state and granted a deliberate representational monopoly within their respective categories in exchange for observing certain controls on their selection of leaders and articulation of demands and supports' (Schmitter, 1979: 13). Kendall and 6 (1994: 33–4) argue that, *pace* Wilson and Butler (1985), this model is not an appropriate frame of reference for approaching the UK voluntary sector's involvement in policy.

5 Traditionally, the Treasury's active interest was reflected primarily through the existence of a single civil servant in the public expenditure department with part-time responsibility for the coordination of voluntary sector spending and taxation policy (Kendall and Knapp, 1996: 27). Under 'Futurebuilders', a one-off capital fund worth £125 million which significantly boosts the 'horizontal' resources available from central government (see Chapter 4, Box 4.1), the Treasury has taken a much deeper and proactive role. During the design phase (ongoing at the time of writing), it is running a secretariat which 'will coordinate the activities of task groups, service a reference group, undertake some policy analysis, draft papers and provide an information flow to the voluntary and community sector' (Compact Working Group, 2002).

Part I

Voluntary sector inputs and processes

2 The economic scope and scale of the UK voluntary sector in comparative perspective

- **The British voluntary sector is a major part of the monetary and nonmonetary economy.**

- **This sector in the UK has grown significantly from a comparative perspective.**

- **An important driver of this expansion has been financial support from central and local government.**

- **It is very difficult to classify the UK voluntary sector 'case'. It shares some similarities with both its US cousin and its European neighbours.**

2.1 Introduction

This chapter reviews empirical data on one very important aspect of the voluntary sector's role in British society: its growing, but at the same time changing, contribution to *economic* life as measured by the 'inputs' it mobilizes.[1] To this end, it updates and extends an earlier study which pioneered the comprehensive and systematic measurement of the UK sector's financial and human resources (Kendall and Knapp, 1996) within the context of an international study (Salamon *et al.*, 1999).

Two bases of comparison are offered. In Section 2.2, the overall size and composition of the sector in the mid-1990s are described, and how its composition and resource base changed over time during the period 1990–5 is demonstrated. (Appendix 1 summarizes the methodology used to construct these estimates.) This was a particularly dramatic time for British social policy, and de facto for those parts of the voluntary sector engaging directly with the state in human services, as it witnessed the implementation of a range of 'quasi-market' reforms (Le Grand and Bartlett, 1993). This involved the introduction of an institutional framework designed to heighten the role of market forces on the supply side – increasingly characterized, with the exception of acute health care, by greater diversity of ownership (public, voluntary and private (for-profit) sectors) – while retaining a leading purchasing and regulatory role for the public sector. The UK experience is also set in comparative context by showing how the sector here compares economically with the equivalent set of institutions in other parts of the world.

The data reviewed in Section 2.2 are now somewhat dated, as international comparative data are unfortunately not available after 1995. However, in section 2.3, we do bring the UK picture alone up to date to 2000, thus covering the end of the Conservative administration and the first part of New Labour's first term. This is an important period, because it was then that, as we shall see in Chapter 3, the voluntary sector was effectively 'mainstreamed', as far as public policy is concerned. In describing the sector's economic evolution during this period, available data allow us to attend to a different comparative element: in the case of paid employment at least, we are able to compare the voluntary sector directly with the private (for-profit) and public sectors within the UK. More generally, looking across the decade as a whole to the extent definitional complexities allow, our analysis suggests both change and continuity with regard to the voluntary sector's economic situation. Although indicating that the rate of change may have decelerated somewhat in the second half of the decade, by setting this in a comparative sector perspective, we can see that over the 5-year period as a whole, the voluntary sector still experienced proportionately greater growth in paid employment than either the public or for-profit sectors.

2.2 The voluntary sector's contribution to the UK economy, 1990–5

In order to compare the UK sector accurately with its counterparts abroad, while at the same time taking seriously the contested nature of the 'sector' idea (Kendall and Knapp, 1996: 16–20), in this section we have to use three different definitions. The coverage of each is outlined in Box 2.1.

In 1995, the UK Broad Nonprofit Sector (BNS) employed just under 1.5 million full time equivalent paid workers (Table 2.1). These employees accounted for just over 6 per cent of activity in the economy as a whole, meaning that the BNS was employing considerably more paid staff than the UK's largest single institutional employer, the National Health Service (NHS). This had 1.1 million workers in that year. In fact, for every four people employed directly by the public sector as a whole there was now one employee in the BNS. Even if a much narrower definition of the sector is used (NVS, see Box 2.1), we can see that over half a million people were employed by voluntary organizations, representing some 2.2 per cent of all paid employment, and with nearly one worker in the (narrow) sector for every two employed in the NHS.

While the sector's contribution to paid employment was therefore of considerable significance in 1995, our data show that volunteering remained the primary labour input for the sector as a whole. When all the hours of the BNS's 16 million volunteers are aggregated, this amounts to the equivalent of 1.7 million full-time voluntary employees, slightly more than its 1.5 million paid

---

Box 2.1 Definitions of 'the' voluntary sector used in Section 2.2

- *The Broad Nonprofit Sector* (BNS) includes all entities which are formal organizations having an institutionalized character; constitutionally independent of the state and self-governing; nonprofit-distributing; and involve some degree of voluntarism. This is a definition which has been reached through a process of consensus-building within the framework of the international project, is relevant for international comparisons, while representing a relatively inclusive definition compared to traditional UK usage.
- *The Broad Voluntary Sector* (BVS) includes all organizations in the BNS as identified above, other than political parties and religious congregations. This definition is the basis for broad comparisons between 1990 and 1995 in what follows, since statistical estimates relating to political parties and religious congregations are only available for 1995.
- *The Narrow Voluntary Sector* (NVS) includes all organizations in the BVS, less organizations not traditionally thought of as being part of the voluntary sector in the UK. This is primarily because they are seen as effectively being part of the state despite their constitutional status, and/or because they are thought not to be sufficiently altruistic or public-benefit oriented. Excluded on this basis are all universities, schools, sports and social clubs, and trade union and business associations.

---

employees (Table 2.1). And if we include these voluntary organizations' volunteers in our overall workforce calculations, the BNS emerges as providing some 12.3 per cent of the formal economy's human resources (where our comparator includes volunteering across all organizational sectors).

The sector's contribution to the economy can also be compared with the nation's gross domestic product (GDP). In total, the BNS expended £47.1 billion in 1995, some 6.6 per cent of GDP. However, this does not take into account the value of volunteering. The appropriate route to valuing this input in money terms is the subject of some dispute. But using reasonable assumptions would suggest that volunteering in the BNS generates a 'value added' equivalent to between £15.7 billion and £20.5 billion in monetary terms. (The former uses the median voluntary sector paid staff rate of pay to impute a lower bound estimate of the value to volunteer hours. The latter uses the mean, nonagricultural, nonpublic sector wage to generate an upper bound estimate.) If we compare this to GDP, in turn itself adjusted to include the value added of all informal and formal volunteering on a similar basis, the activities of the BNS emerge as representing 9.2 per cent of (volunteer-adjusted) GDP.

Table 2.1 The overall economic contribution of the UK voluntary sector in 1995

Economic indicator	BNS	NVS
Volunteer headcount ('000s)	16,311	7,852
FTE volunteers ('000s)	1,664	774
FTE paid employment ('000s)	1,473	503
Per cent of economy-wide paid employment	6.3	2.2
Total FTE paid and unpaid employment ('000s)	3,137	1,277
Per cent of economy wide employment,		
including volunteering (all formal sectors)	12.3	5.0
Total expenditure (TE)	£47.1 billion	£15.4 billion
TE as per cent of GDP	6.6	2.2
TE including volunteers[a]	£67.6 billion	£24.9 billion
As per cent of volunteer-adjusted GDP[a,b]	9.2	3.4

Sources: See Appendix 1.

Notes:
[a] Assuming volunteer hours can be valued using mean nonagricultural private sector wage.
[b] Denominator includes value of volunteering in all sectors (including private, public, third and informal).

2.2.1 Composition of the voluntary sector in 1995

Like the public and private (for-profit) sectors, the voluntary sector is character-ized by a staggering variety of organizational types, structures and activities (Kendall and Knapp, 1995). One helpful way of capturing some of this diversity, borrowed and adapted from the ways in which economic data on the former sectors are routinely analysed, is to break the voluntary sector's contributions down according to field of activity or 'industry'.[2] (This is in keeping also with the suggestion in Chapter 1 that policy be broken down systematically into 'vertical' elements.) Table 2.2 shows how both paid employees and unpaid volunteers are distributed across these different activities.

The analysis reveals that most paid employment in the sector under our broadest definition was concentrated in just three fields: education and research, culture and recreation, and social care (or personal social services – labelled 'social services' in the classificatory system), which collectively account for some three-quarters of BNS activity. These are the same three fields which dominated the sector economically in 1990 (see below). If we use the narrow approach, which excludes most of these categories by definition, then a different grouping comes to prominence: social services and development and housing together account for 58 per cent of all NVS employment, with other fields lagging some way behind.

If we also take into account volunteer inputs, the main outcomes are to push culture and recreation ahead of education and research, and bring into focus the relative significance of the religion field, in which the greatest concentration of volunteers is to be found. What emerges overall is a distinctive patterning by field according to the relative importance of volunteers:[3]

Table 2.2 Distribution of paid and unpaid employment by 'industry' UK BNS, thousands, 1995

Field of activity (ICNPO)[a]	FTE paid employment (%)	FTE volunteers (%)	Total employment (%)
Culture and recreation	347 (23.8)	351 (21.1)	698 (22.2)
Education and research	587 (44.3)	58 (3.5)	645 (20.6)
Health	60 (4.2)	143 (8.6)	203 (6.5)
Social services	185 (12.7)	221 (13.3)	406 (12.9)
Environment	18 (1.6)	44 (2.6)	62 (1.9)
Development and housing	108 (7.7)	210 (12.6)	318 (10.1)
Law, advocacy and politics	10 (0.7)	35 (2.1)	45 (1.4)
Philanthropic intermediaries	10 (0.7)	22 (1.3)	32 (1.0)
International activities	54 (3.7)	7 (0.4)	61 (1.9)
Religious congregations	58 (4.0)	544 (32.7)	602 (19.2)
Professional associations, trade unions, etc.	37 (2.6)	0 (0.0)	37 (1.2)
Not elsewhere classified	0 (0.0)	29 (1.8)	29 (0.9)
Total BNS	1,473 (100)	1,664 (100)	3,137 (100)

Sources: See Appendix 1.

Note:
[a] International Classification of Nonprofit Organizations (ICNPO); see references.

- Health, environment, community development, advocacy and religion are volunteer-rich, with unpaid workers heavily outnumbering their paid counterparts;
- In education and research, social housing, international activities (overseas development and relief) and professional associations and trade unions, paid staff are the dominant human resource; and
- In culture and recreation, and in social services, paid and unpaid employees are involved to a similar extent.

2.2.2 *The changing size and composition of the voluntary sector*

Not only was the sector making a major contribution to UK economic life in 1995: these data indicate that it also grew significantly during the first half of the 1990s. Figure 2.1 shows that between 1990 and 1995, the BVS's paid employment increased from accounting for 4.0 to 6.1 per cent of economy-wide full-time equivalent paid employment. As other, more narrowly based data confirm, much of this growth took place between 1990 and 1993, precisely when the UK economy was experiencing significant recessionary pressures (Hems and Passey, 1998).[4]

The extraordinarily high rate of change suggested by the data is in part explained by the transformation of educational institutions formerly directly controlled by local government into self-governing, nonprofit institutions

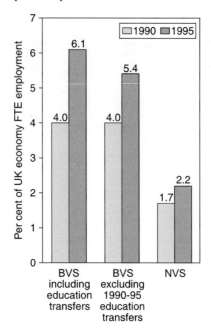

Figure 2.1 Growth in paid employment in the UK third sector.

Sources: See Appendix 1.

operating within the state system. Since this cannot be said to represent genuine growth, the figure also shows the effect of excluding these transfers. The result is still striking, with an increase of 33 per cent in absolute numbers employed. As a proportion of employment in the economy as a whole, the figure is slightly higher, at 35 per cent, because the UK labour force actually shrank over this period (Office for National Statistics, 1998).

Gauging the sector's overall size on the less inclusive NVS basis reveals a slightly lower growth rate, with employment increasing by 29 per cent from 390,000 to 503,000. This was similar to the growth rate of employment in the banking and insurance sector (Office for National Statistics, 1997). Until recent financial crises, this field was being routinely held up as one of the most dynamic areas of growth of the British economy, alongside computing and technology.

As the sector grew, its resource base changed. Figure 2.2 compares the funding sources for both the BVS and NVS in 1990 and 1995.[5] In both cases, we see a marked overall increase in reliance upon public sources. For the first time, the voluntary sector using both definitions now has income from the state as its most important single source of income. This includes all direct funding, through grants, contracts and service level agreements, but does not include the value of indirect support through tax advantages. Including the latter would further amplify the importance of state funding to the sector: increasing annual support by at least £1 billion at this time. (This estimate for the value of tax

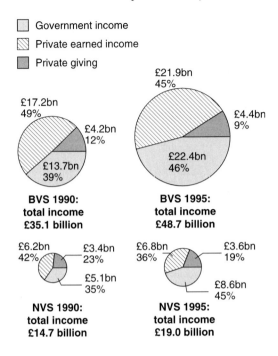

Figure 2.2 Sources of income, 1995 prices.

Sources: See Appendix 1.

relief in the mid-1990s (Williams, 1998) has subsequently been revised upwards. Including previously unaccounted-for concessions, a figure as high as £1.7 billion has been suggested for 1999/2000 (Jas *et al.*, 2002: 46)).

The figure also shows a decline in the relative importance of private giving for recipient organizations over this period. This is consistent with other evidence from the givers' side in the early 1990s. Most well charted was a fall off in donations from individuals, both in terms of the amount of resources given, and the rate of participation (Pharoah and Smerdon, 1998; Hems and Passey, 1998), although this still remains by far the most important single source of monetary private gifts for the sector. Our data suggest a slight real increase in the total receipts from donations for the BVS – at £2.7 billion in 1995 compared with £2.3 billion in 1990 (£2.5 billion compared with £2.1 billion for the NVS). However, because the sector has grown so rapidly in overall size, private giving from individuals represented a lower proportion of income than before, falling from 6.6 to 5.6 per cent of total BVS revenue (14.6 to 13.3 per cent of total NVS revenue). Corporate giving even fell in absolute terms according to our data, although this trend should be interpreted with caution, because of definitional complexities. The only source of donative income to keep pace with the sector's overall growth was revenue from grant-making trusts and foundations. This grew quickly enough to maintain its share of third sector total revenue (from 2.4 to 2.5 per cent for the BVS, growing from 3.4 to 4.0 per cent for the NVS).

Finally, our research provides evidence concerning the extent to which the UK voluntary sector has become more 'commercial' in the extent of its reliance to a much greater extent than previously on private earned income in the first part of the 1990s. This trend has been well documented in the US 'nonprofit' sector in recent years (Salamon, 1995; 2001). In the UK case, however, it appears that like private donations, private earned income (primarily accounted for by users' fees and sales, and income from investments) grew slightly in absolute terms – but only marginally increased (in the case of BVS and NVS fees and sales) or fell (in the case of BVS and NVS private earned income overall) as a proportion of total income to 1995. This is shown clearly in Figure 2.2.

2.2.3 Changes in composition over time

The overall trends described above mask significant differences between contrasting types of organization according to type, size and 'industry' (Kendall and Knapp, 1995; Hems and Passey, 1998). Distinguishing between 'industries' in assessing change over time is theoretically particularly important, because the vast bulk of financial and other resource relationships evolve at this level, developing in the context of particular 'vertical' policy domains in the sense we introduced in Chapter 1. The patterning of relevant state institutions and relationships they face will vary according to the activity in question (an aspect of diversity which is also central to the 'field specific' analysis presented in Part II of this volume).

Table 2.3 then contrasts the trends by 'industry' in terms of employment, while Figure 2.3 shows how sources of finance altered. The latter shows a remarkably consistent trend across most industries: the sector-wide trend in finance noted above – increased dependence on the state, and less recourse to private donations – was not the result of isolated trends in one or two dominant fields, but happened across broad swathes of the sector in this period.

However, there are important differences in the drivers for and character of change in each vertical industry. The largest absolute change in employment – accounting for over half of all employment growth – occurred in education and research. In large part, this growth reflected a redistribution by sector of ownership within this field. What we see here is primarily the outcome of 'migration' of institutions from direct state control to quasi-independent status within a state regulated and (largely) funded system. Box 2.2 (below) provides more details.

This growth at the definitional borders of the BVS was, then, unambiguously government-led. Focusing on the NVS, however, we find a more mixed picture. The personal social services as a whole has been the most rapidly growing component of the NVS during this time period. This was buoyed by a combination of government enthusiasm for, and the provision of resources to, independently provided (as opposed to local council owned) community-based care – in response to the ageing of the population, antipathy towards public

Table 2.3 Trends in UK BVS paid employment by 'industry', 1990–5

Field of activity	FTE 1990 (%)		FTE 1995 (%)		Absolute change
Culture and recreation	262	(27.7)	347	(24.6)	84[a]
Education and research	330	(34.9)	587	(41.6)	257
Health	43	(4.5)	60	(4.2)	17
Social services	146	(15.4)	185	(13.1)	39
Environment	17	(1.8)	18	(1.3)	1
Development & housing	74	(7.8)	108	(7.6)	34
Civic and advocacy	9	(1.0)	7	(0.5)	−2
Grant-making trusts	7	(0.7)	10	(0.7)	3
International activities	23	(2.4)	54	(3.8)	31
Professional associations, trade unions, etc.	35	(3.7)	37	(2.6)	2
Total BVS	946	(100)	1,412	(100)	467
Total BVS excluding 1990–5 education transfers and recreation		739		962	273

Sources: See Appendix 1.

Note:
[a] This trend should be treated with caution, as the 1990 estimate for recreation may be unreliable.

sector direct provision (hence, quasi-markets), and a host of other social, political and economic factors (to be discussed in more detail in Chapter 8). Figure 2.3 shows that this fed through into the development of a sector which became markedly more dependent upon state funding over this period. However, the main beneficiary of the combination of new public priority attached to social services and euthusiasm for quasi-markets in the 1990s was the private (for-profit) sector, populated mainly by small businesses (Wistow *et al.*, 1996). Particularly in the case of care for older people, which accounts for the lion's share of social care resources, the latter grew much more rapidly than the voluntary sector, first in residential care and more recently in the provision of home care services (Ware *et al.*, 2001). A similar pattern – that is, voluntary sector growth, but even greater expansion by private sector providers in absolute terms – can also be found in some other maturing welfare 'quasi-markets'. Health care, particularly mental health, and nursing care are perhaps the best examples.

The two other main areas of NVS growth shown in Table 2.3 were development and housing, and international activities. In the former case, expansion in this period built particularly upon an existing legacy of growth in the housing associations segment (as we will discuss in more detail in Chapter 7). Here, while there was competition within the sector between organizations, as a sector these organizations' market niche in publicly supported social housing remained institutionally insulated from private sector competition, by rules forbidding the latter's access to grants (although government financial support has itself become both more business-like and, since 1995, more scarce). In the latter case,

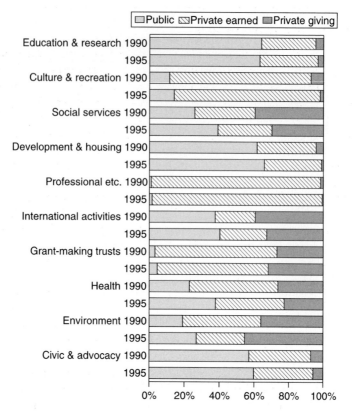

Figure 2.3 Changes in finance, 1990–5.

Sources: See Appendix 1.

European as well as domestic government funding has been an important catalyst for growth. British-based agencies are leading actors in the European Commission's overseas development policy community – a uniquely well-established field of EU–third sector joint working (Kendall and Anheier, 2001b). Furthermore, unlike most other fields, private earned income has increased significantly here too. We can speculate that this is connected to a range of interdependent economic, social and political factors often now grouped together under the banner of 'globalization' (Anheier *et al.*, 2001) and provides evidence that at least certain segments of the voluntary sector are no more immune to these multifarious influences than the Government and private sector.

Also noteworthy is that an area where we might have anticipated decline – the category covering trade unions – has instead witnessed stability or marginal growth. However, the headline trend conceals divergent trends within this field. Trade union activity did continue to decline in the UK in the early 1990s, following the well-documented existing trend – but a less well-known expansion of professional associations appears to have offset this effect.[6]

Box 2.2 Educational hybrids

Two waves of policy are relevant. First, the en masse transformation by central government mandate in 1993 of further, tertiary and other education colleges from local authority controlled institutions into self-governing charitable corporations. (This followed the much higher profile reconstitution of local authority controlled polytechnics as independent 'new universities', which had already taken place in 1989.) Second, the growth in the number of secondary, and to a much lesser extent, primary schools, which decided to 'opt out' of direct local authority control into the sector, following school-by-school parental ballots – an option presented to schools following government reforms of the education system in the late 1980s. Both broad types of reinvented 'hybrid' institution were consequently operating alongside the BVS's traditional nonprofit providers, the universities, maintained (state-funded) church and other voluntary schools, and charitable 'independent' (privately funded) schools (see also Box 2.5).

Under the New Labour administration from 1997 onwards, these broad changes in ownership have not been reversed, although some changes in governance requirements and the labelling of hybrid institutions has taken place. Most prominently, schools within the state regulatory and funding system have been redesignated as 'foundation schools'. We do not consider recent developments in education in the remainder of this volume, because these institutions are excluded by definition from the data available for the second half of the decade. Also, as noted in Chapter 1, in discussing policies and impacts we deploy the narrow definition.

2.2.4 The UK voluntary sector in international comparative context

Because the research reported thus far was undertaken using the common definitions and classifications developed in the Johns Hopkins project, the UK situation in 1995 can be directly compared with that prevailing in twenty-one other countries.[7] In this section, we identify three of the most striking findings from a British perspective (full details of the international project can be found in Salamon *et al.*, 1999).

The results of the international study, using paid employment as the basis for comparison, are set out in Figure 2.4. The definition for the numerator used here includes all organizations meeting the structural operational definition (what we have referred to above, in the UK case, as the BNS), other than religious congregations, for which data were not available for all participating countries. In addition, the denominator differs very slightly by excluding agricultural workers (a small adjustment in the British case, but a significant one in some other countries).

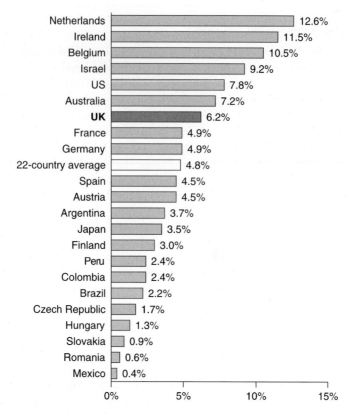

Figure 2.4 Nonprofit share of total paid employment by country, 1995.
Source: The Johns Hopkins Comparative Nonprofit Sector Project.

The UK voluntary sector turns out to be large from an international perspective, but relatively modest for a developed democracy. Figure 2.4 shows that the UK sector, at 6.2 per cent of all paid employment, is ranked seventh by overall size, accounting for slightly more than 1 per cent of economy-wide employment more than the 22-country average. Although the figure does not show it, if educational transfers are excluded this does not change the situation enough to alter this ranking, since this would reduce the UK figure to 5.3 per cent – still some distance ahead of France.

However, as the figure also shows, developing and newly democratic countries tend to have relatively small sectors by this measure, and developed democracies relatively large sectors (with the obvious exceptions being Finland and Japan). When we compare the UK to other EU and developing country averages – both 6.9 per cent – the UK third sector actually appears relatively limited in its scope.

These data also allow for the comparison of the UK's voluntary sector to those of other countries in terms of the composition of paid employment. Amongst a wide range of contrasts that could be drawn, three are particularly striking. First, the UK has one of the smallest independent nonprofit health sectors in relative terms. This of course reflects the continued dominance in the field of acute hospital provision of the public sector National Health Service (NHS), wherein acute hospitals are publicly owned and controlled.[8]

Second, one of the clearest contrasts with other EU countries is the relatively limited extent to which social services in the UK are provided in the voluntary sector. In this case, as we have already noted, in the UK it is the private (for-profit small business) sector which responded most rapidly to the expanding community care market and dominates core services for many priority needs, although the voluntary sector remains a significant actor within and outside the mainstream care system, and has indeed grown in absolute terms. In other parts of the EU, by contrast, the private sector appears to have had a relatively limited role to play to date, with care services instead dominated by the public, informal and – increasingly – the 'third' sector (Kendall *et al.*, 2003a).

Third, international activities is the single area in which the UK's voluntary sector is significantly larger, compared with other fields, than that of any other country on which data for this field are available. As we noted above, this is one of the fields in which the UK sector appears to have grown most significantly between 1990 and 1995.

In addition to providing a detailed map of the sector in 1995, the international comparative study also assembled time series data for 1990 to 1995 on employment trends in nine countries and revenue trends in seven. These data show that the growth in the UK has been more rapid than elsewhere – the 35 per cent growth over the 5-year period we have already noted (excluding education transfers) compares with a nine-country average of 23 per cent, and an EU average (for Belgium, Germany, France and the UK) of 24 per cent. Even if recreation is excluded (for which the UK's 1990 estimates must be treated with particular caution), with an increase in employment of 30 per cent, the UK sector grew at a faster rate than has been typical in the EU and other developing countries.

Finally, the previous section emphasized how the UK sector's growth has been accompanied by a dramatic shift in its resource base – most noticeably, a marked move towards reliance on public sector funding. Figure 2.5 shows how the UK compared in 1995 to the eighteen other countries participating in the study for which revenue data were available. Countries are grouped into two broad categories: those for which private earned income is the largest single source of income; and those for which public finance dominates.

The figure shows that the UK sector's reliance on the public sector as its primary source of funding is a pattern shared with just under half of these countries in 1995. Moreover, it is clear that this dependency is actually the dominant pattern for the EU. The key point on which the UK differs, however, from most or even all countries shown here is the extent to which this represents a new development. The UK is the only case in which the resource base has been transformed rapidly enough for it to move from primary reliance on private funding to public funding. The positions of other EU countries in the

Figure 2.5 Sources of nonprofit revenue by country, 1995 (22 countries).

Source: The Johns Hopkins Comparative Nonprofit Sector Project.

government-dominant group represent continuity with, rather than change from, the recent past.

2.3 Comparative sectoral trends within the UK after 1995

While international comparative data are unfortunately not available after 1995, more recent research within the UK can be used to update at least some of the key aspects of the full comparative mapping provided in the previous section from a 'domestic' perspective.[9]

This evidence allows us to partly update our map to the end of the decade. However, because of the bases for collecting these data, definitions are necessarily adopted which are narrower yet than those used for international comparison described previously in this chapter. These are specified in Box 2.3.

Box 2.3 QLFS definitions and 'general charities' definitions

- The Quarterly Labour Force Survey relies upon employee's own subjective definition of the sector of their employer. Respondents are initially asked if their employer is 'a private firm or business', a 'limited company' or 'some other kind of organization'. For those who choose the latter, they are then asked to choose between 'a public limited company'; a 'nationalized industry/state corporation'; 'local government or council'; a 'university or other grant funded education establishment'; a 'health authority or NHS trust'; a 'charity, voluntary organization or trust'; or 'some other kind of organization'. In this section we include as voluntary sector employees only respondents who categorized their employer as a 'charity, voluntary organization or trust' (see Almond and Kendall, 2000a, for more details).
- The 'general charities' definition is based on organizations, and has been developed for National Accounts purposes. It is a subset of all registered charities, excluding 'statutory' charities with close constitutional links to the British state (such as the British Council and the British Museum). Its coverage is similar to the 'narrow voluntary sector' referred to in the rest of this volume, except that the latter includes 'statutory' charities because of their independent legal status; and, also includes housing associations, which are typically not registered charities.

2.3.1 Comparative sector employment trends

Table 2.4 compares paid employment in each sector in 1995, 1998 and 2000. The accompanying figure (Figure 2.6) illustrates the absolute and proportionate rates of change in the three primary sectors over the 5-year period. Clearly, the most quantitatively significant developments in terms of volume of jobs from an economy-wide perspective have taken place outside the voluntary sector.

Using an inclusive headcount definition (incorporating self-employed workers and people classified as on government schemes), we see that in absolute terms the expansion of the paid labour force over the 5-year period overwhelmingly took place through a net increase in jobs in the private sector – now dominating the economy – accounting for three-quarters of all jobs. However, the other sectors were also growing as employers over the period as a whole. As far as the public sector is concerned, in 1998 as it ended its first year in office, New Labour had inherited a dwindling public sector workforce from the Conservative administration (Almond and Kendall, 2000b). But by 2000, this trend had been reversed. The net increase of 200,000 jobs over the full 5-year period was far less than in the private sector, but significant nonetheless. And if one focuses in the most recent period (1998–2000), these data suggest that by then there was a net

Table 2.4 Paid employment in three sectors, 1995, 1998 and 2000, thousands

Year	Private sector	Public sector	Voluntary sector
1995 Headcount	19,095.2	6,042.2	478.2
(FTE)	(16,418.8)	(4,979.9)	(372.0)
1998 Headcount	20,288.2	5,939.7	535.7
(FTE)	(17,391.6)	(5,138.1)	(386.2)
2000 Headcount	20,710.7	6,246.1	563.0
(FTE)	(16,201.5)	(5,240.9)	(442.6)

Source: Almond and Kendall (2002, Table 1).

Note:
FTE, Full-Time Equivalent, assuming 37½ hours per week is one full-time position.

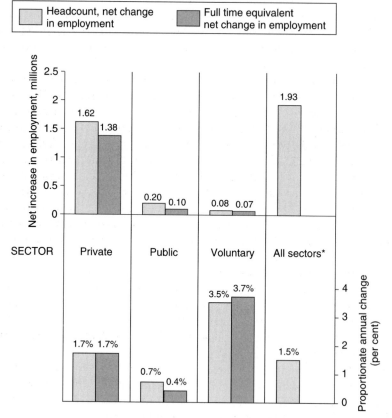

Figure 2.6 Net changes in total paid employment by sector, 1995–2000.

Source: Almond and Kendall (2002, Figure 1).

Note:
* Includes residual 'some other kind of organization' category.

increase of nearly as many jobs in the public sector as in the private sector (three in the former for every four in the latter).[10]

How does the voluntary sector compare? Focusing on absolute scale and change certainly suggests that these organizations' role in the labour market in terms of volume of jobs is not the leading one. These organizations' net contribution, at 85,000, was by comparison to the other sectors relatively modest in absolute terms. Yet as Figure 2.6 brings out, clearly the voluntary sector was growing *proportionally* faster than the private sector in employment terms. In comparison with the public sector, the proportionate growth of the voluntary sector is clearly even more marked over the period as a whole. At the same time, this obscures two different trends, before and after 1998. Up to 1998, the voluntary sector unambiguously witnessed a more rapid proportionate growth rate than the other two sectors. But in the 1998–2000 period of public sector employment 'recovery', the voluntary sector and public sector growth rate were broadly similar (2.5–2.6 per cent per annum).

In sum, the main conclusion is that employment in the voluntary sector (as defined in Box 2.3) grew significantly during the second half of the 1990s, and over the period as a whole, the sector experienced much faster proportionate change than the other sectors.

A second aspect of voluntary sector employment addressed earlier that we can update here to an extent, concerns its 'industrial' composition. This has to be a rather limited exercise, because the data source being used deploys the Standard Industrial Classification (1992 version) as a framework for categorizing workers' 'make or do' activities (in National Accounts jargon). Unfortunately, because this was designed with the worlds of private business and public sector services in mind, it does not allow for the same fine-tuned disaggregation of activities that the purpose-built ICNPO system described earlier. Nevertheless, even the SIC system's crude breakdowns are better than no breakdowns at all.

Table 2.5 reveals that some 84 per cent of the increase in paid employment in the voluntary sector between 1995 and 2000 is concentrated in the 'social work without accommodation' SIC92 category. This reflects the net outcome of a combination of ICNPO fields, because the SIC category implicitly conflates at least six major activities treated separately in that system. (These are part of group 4 (nonresidential social services); group 8 (philanthropic intermediaries); group 9 (international activities); subgroup 6200 (social, economic and community development); and parts of subgroups 3300 and 3400 (nonresidential health care activities for some client groups).)

It seems likely that this trend predominantly reflects trends in the social care field. We know that expenditure on formal care services in community settings has grown rapidly in both the private and voluntary sectors in recent years, and this will have fed through into greater employee numbers (see Royal Commission on Long Term Care, 1999; Laing and Buisson, 2002; Chapter 8 below).

Figure 2.7 illustrates the absolute and proportionate rate of change over 5 years in the three areas where voluntary sector growth has also been concentrated. We can see that, aside from 'social work activities', another area of

Table 2.5 Paid employment: industry distribution, 1995–2000, headcounts (per cent)

SIC category	Voluntary sector 1995	Voluntary sector 2000
'Social work without accommodation'	143.4 (29.9)	214.4 (38.1)
'Social work with accommodation'	59.7 (12.5)	57.2 (10.2)
All other SIC	275.1 (57.5)	291.4 (51.8)
Total	478.2 (100.0)	563.0 (100.0)

Source: Almond and Kendall (2002, Table 6).

growing importance reflected in the employment data is the development of social housing. This reflects the continuing efforts of many housing associations to broaden their property portfolios. As with social care, this represents cumulative growth building upon the early 1990s, and has been paralleled by a decline in direct public sector services (the shift away from council housing; for further discussion, see Chapter 7). Finally, we also see growth, from a relatively low base, in voluntary sector museum activities, alongside even more marked growth in both the other sectors. This is less well-charted territory from a comparative sector point of view.

2.3.2 Financial trends

Because, for those organizations that employ paid staff, the wage bill tends to be the largest single item of current expenditure, and because in the long run revenue and expenditure must move in the same direction, we would expect this employment growth to be mirrored in terms of total income within this sort of timeframe. This does indeed turn out to be the case. As Figure 2.8 (on p. 38) illustrates, the total income of 'general charities' increased significantly between 1995 and 2001, and this builds upon a longer growth trend from the early part of the 1990s (using this definition). The availability of this financial data over the full 10-year period is particularly useful, as we do not have employment data using a consistent definition for such a period of time. It suggests that, which-ever definition we employ, the following generalizations are sustainable:

- The voluntary sector grew economically, in terms of resource inputs, through-out the 1990s.
- This growth was uneven, being greatest in the first part of the 1990s, and slower towards the end of the decade.

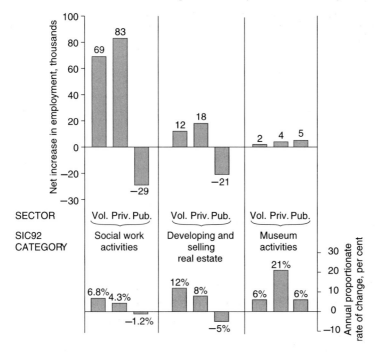

Figure 2.7 Major fields of voluntary sector growth, 1995–2000*

Source: Almond and Kendall (2002, Figure 4).

Note:
SIC92 fields now accounting for 2% or more of total voluntary sector paid employment and exhibiting growth of 30% or more over five years.

- This unevenness suggests that the voluntary sector's growth was counter-cyclical to a significant extent, since the early 1990s tended to be recessionary, while the late 1990s involved economic growth in the economy as a whole.

Finally, we argued earlier that to a significant extent, the sector's growth in the first part of the decade was fuelled by public expenditure. The 'general charities' data suggest that even for this narrower subset of organizations, reliance on the state for financial support has increased markedly across the whole decade. According to these data, income from Government increased by nearly 40 per cent between 1991 and 2001, outpacing total income growth of 32 per cent (Jas et al., 2002: Chapter 4). It was most marked (5.6 per cent per annum) at the time when the total income of 'general charities' was also growing most quickly in the recessionary early 1990s, while falling back (to an average of 1.6 per cent per annum) when total income growth tended to decelerate in the economically buoyant late 1990s. Interestingly, these data also

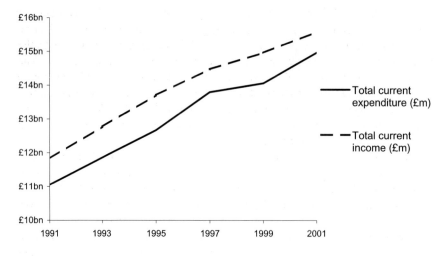

Figure 2.8 Trends in total income and expenditure for 'general charities'.

Source: Income trends from Jas *et al.*, 2002: 27, Figure 4.1. Expenditure trends from personal communication, National Council for Voluntary Organizations, 2002.

seem to suggest a slight recovery in private giving, dominated by individual donors, with annual growth at 3.9 per cent for 'general charities' in 2000/1. However, evidence from surveys of givers underline that a much longer-term trend of declining participation and lower average giving has not been reversed, with contemporary levels considerably below those that characterized the early 1990s (Pharoah, 2002).

We also suggested earlier that in the first part of the decade, increases in income could primarily be understood as a reflection of 'industry' level – or 'vertical' policies and developments. Unfortunately, time series data for the revenue of 'general charities' broken down by 'industry' are not available. However, surveys of government funders in the second half of the 1990s do imply that the two fields which were particularly significant in this regard using the narrow voluntary sector definition – social care and social housing – have remained in the forefront. Social Service Departments (local government) and the Housing Corporation (central government) continued as the leading funders over this period, as they had been in the earlier part of the decade.[11]

2.4 Conclusion

This chapter has considered evidence on employment trends and financial resources – the most readily measurable of the sector's inputs – and offered a glimpse of how the overall sector-wide picture can be disaggregated by different fields of activity. Unfortunately, complete up-to-date comparative data are not available. Undoubtedly the most troubling gap is the lack of time series data on volunteering for the second half of the 1990s. We saw that in the mid-1990s the sector as a whole was evenly balanced in the extent to which it relied upon paid workers and volunteers. Available data do not allow us to ascertain if the growth in paid employment that we described up to 2000 has altered that balance. It is to be hoped that ongoing and planned research led by the Home Office and independent researchers will allow us to develop a response to this situation, if not for that decade then for the next.[12]

However, despite the undoubted difficulties of working with different definitions and classifications, it has proved possible to outline how other resource inputs evolved in the 1990s with a reasonable degree of confidence. It has been shown that in recent years, the voluntary sector in the UK has relied increasingly on the public sector for its financial support. This will probably not surprise most of those involved with the voluntary sector. What is striking in the data, however, is the rate at which change has occurred. Moreover, it has been shown that this trend is not limited to a handful of fields of voluntary sector activity: it has happened systematically across most of the domains in which the voluntary sector operates. However, the most marked growth, confirmed by information from the expenditure side and extending across the decade as a whole, has been in social care and social housing.

Another key finding that emerges from considering the most recent data is that the increases in employment that have been made possible by this financial support appear small when set in the context of the absolute growth in the economy as a whole, and in the private (for-profit) and (most recently) public sectors. Yet the growth in the voluntary sector has tended to be *proportionately* more rapid. While much of this expansion may have been led by the very large organizations (Jas *et al.*, 2002), careful local case study research suggests that significant numbers of medium-sized and smaller agencies have also experienced the challenges of growth, some employing paid workers for the first time, and others significantly expanding small existing paid workforces (Russell *et al.*, 1995; Alcock *et al.*, 1999; Scott and Russell, 2000).

Some of the most important new insights that the research reported here can add derive from its positioning within a larger international study. The financial data underline the sheer pace of change in the UK from a comparative country perspective. In sum, all the evidence points to the extent to which the British voluntary sector has undergone exceptionally rapid economic change by both domestic and international standards.

Partly as a result, the UK voluntary sector certainly appears difficult to categorize. On the one hand, its positioning in the public sector-dominant funding category suggests the sector increasingly fits the model prevalent in western Europe. The UK sector clearly now differs sharply from the country with which it is often grouped – the US. One of the most important factors is that the UK sector has not had to respond to systemic public 'defunding' of welfare services by massively extending its reliance on fees and charges. Although some larger organizations have certainly seen the importance of private earned income rise in recent years (Jas *et al.*, 2002: 42), and some organizations may have taken this path in response to 'underfunding' or 'defunding' in particular programmes, overall the two countries seem to have moved in different directions as far as public welfare spending is concerned (compare Pierson, 1994; Evans *et al.*, 1998).

On the other hand, the UK voluntary sector in the 1990s was in no sense organized along 'corporatist' lines (cf. Chapter 1). It therefore seems to stand apart from what has been referred to as a 'corporatist model', which to a degree seems to typify the situation in continental Europe (Salamon and Anheier, 1998). This is both in terms of the historical legacies of voluntary sector–state relations which strongly condition the way these sectors interact; and second, in terms of the reality of the current environment.

Specifically, relations between the UK voluntary sector and Government have traditionally not been structured by any overarching principle. Most significantly, the concept of 'subsidiarity' promoted by the Catholic church and other religious bodies, traditionally so central to social policy arrangements in some parts of Europe, has been of only limited relevance in Britain. Box 2.4 explains the meaning and scope of the concept, while Box 2.5 refers to the one field where it has historically had some resonance in Britain, the primary and secondary education field.

Instead, links in Britain have developed in a pragmatic and ad hoc way, varying tremendously by field and subfield (as with client groups within the social care field). Relationships between state and voluntary sector seem to defy any overall labelling or be animated by any single organizing or 'institutional' principle. As we shall see in the following chapters, UK voluntary sector policy actors have very recently sought to consciously develop the notion of cross-cutting policy. However, rather than evoking a historic principle such as subsidiarity, 'horizontal' institutions have instead been developed *de novo*. That process is still at its formative stage, and of contested legitimacy. In this context, patterns of state–voluntary sector relations have basically continued to overwhelmingly reflect a jumble of 'vertical' policy legacies at national and local level, rather than the application of a single, uniform framework.

A further point worth highlighting is the extent to which conceptualizing the position and role of the voluntary sector in the UK purely in terms of relationships with the state is itself relatively misleading. Perhaps to a far greater extent than in other parts of Europe, the situation of the sector cannot be understood without taking into account the extent to which private, for profit provision has rapidly also come to occupy a pivotal role in welfare provision – both publicly funded and otherwise. In operating alongside, and sometimes competing directly with the private sector in a turbulent and competitive environment, the UK voluntary sector does seem to resemble its US cousin more than its continental neighbours.

Box 2.4 Subsidiarity and the voluntary sector in Germany and Europe

According to Anheier and Seibel (2001), subsidiarity is the 'institutional principle' which has been most significant in shaping the German non-profit sector's development across broad swathes of social policy in the twentieth century.

> The duality of public jurisdiction and private [voluntary sector] service provision [in the early twentieth century] represented a compromise between the republican ideals of an encompassing public responsibility for social affairs, shared primarily by the social democrats, and the interests of the two [Protestant and Catholic] Christian churches whose welfare associations were running the bulk of private charities. That compromise and the division of labour between public authorities and private nonprofit institutions was to become the strongest and most enduring pattern of government–nonprofit relationship in Germany: the principle of subsidiarity (p. 54).

> . . . the principle of subsidiarity means that the state takes on only those functions that the [voluntary] private sector cannot meet, and that larger units, such as central government, concern themselves only with tasks that are beyond the capabilities of smaller units, such as regional and local government, but also private units, such as the congregation and the family. Subsidiarity combines elements of decentralization and privatization of public functions . . . fit[ting] well into the German tradition of decentralisation and local self-governance. It emerged from the long-standing conflict between state and church, particularly Catholicism. In economic terms, however, subsidiarity appears as a fairly new engine underlying nonprofit sector growth in Germany, and achieving its full impact from the 1970s onward (p. 72).

Elsewhere, Salamon *et al.* note that 'subsidiarity . . . coupled with strong worker pressures for expanded social welfare protections, helped shape the evolution of social policy . . . this concept is especially influential in Germany, the Netherlands, Belgium, and to a lesser extent, Austria and Spain' (1999: 16).

These descriptions do not necessarily mean, however, that a general European subsidiarity-based corporatist 'model' of voluntary sector–state relations can be said to exist. This is because the principle has tended to be confined to certain parts of north and west Europe only; and within those countries where it has applied, it has been relevant to some social welfare services only. Even within countries where it has been relevant to social welfare services, it seems to have been interpreted very differently, evolved in meaning over time, and retained continued relevance to different degrees in the face of internal and external political and social pressures, according to field, subfield and client group.

Box 2.5 The dual system of schooling: a parallel with subsidiarity in Europe?

The only field of voluntary activity where the principle of subsidiarity could be argued to have decisively influenced policy towards the voluntary sector in the UK is in primary and secondary education, as realized in the 'dual system'. This was the accommodation between the central state, local state and Catholic and Anglican churches in place from the late nineteenth century until the education reforms of the late 1980s. However, even here, the notion of subsidiarity seems to have been implicit rather than explicit, and there are good reasons more generally to doubt the accuracy of portraying relations here as 'corporatist' (see Kendall and Knapp, 1996: Chapter 7, for a discussion).

Notes

1 This chapter draws heavily on work undertaken with my former colleague Steve Almond.

2 See Kendall and Knapp, 1996: 269–73 for more details concerning how the broad 'industry' groups and their subgroups are applied specifically to the UK voluntary sector. Salamon and Anheier (1997) provide an overview of the rationale for and application of this ICNPO system (the International Classification of Nonprofit Organizations).

3 As will become clearer in Part II, these very broad 'industry' patterns conceal considerable variation by 'activity' – that is at levels of disaggregation within industries. For example, in social services, in the residential care field, paid workers dominate with a limited, supplementary role for volunteers; however, in day care and low intensity care and support outside the mainstream social care system, volunteers play the leading role.

4 As Chapter 7 indicates, growth in the voluntary sector during this economic recession was not limited to the 'general charities' considered by Hems and Passey (1998): housing associations, excluded by definition from their data, expanded particularly rapidly over this period.

5 The classification of revenue sources used here was agreed by the participating countries in phase 1 of the Johns Hopkins study. For detailed discussion of the UK-specific interpretation of the revenue categories see Kendall and Knapp, 1996: Chapter 4. It is worth highlighting certain aspects of the conventions adopted for this study, to avoid confusion when comparing the findings generated using this system with other studies (which also differ very significantly because of the contrasting criteria used to a priori define organizations; Charities Aid Foundation, 2000; Jas et al., 2002; Caritasdata, 2001). First, public sector funding is taken to include not only direct funding, but also 'demand side' subsidies or quasi-vouchers which technically flow via the individual user. A significant example in the UK case is housing benefit paid to tenants of housing associations. Second, income 'earned' in delivering contracted services to Government is also treated as revenue from the

public sector, and added to other 'supply side' income from grants and service level agreements, as well as 'demand side' payments.

6 'Civic and advocacy' activity appears to have been the only 'industry' to experience negative growth during the early 1990s. However, the ICNPO system does not really capture the diversity of the sector's 'advocacy' or campaigning contribution. In the UK as elsewhere, as the field level impact study materials discussed later in this book will demonstrate (Chapters 7–9), advocacy tends to be conducted alongside service delivery and membership-oriented activities (Kendall and Knapp, 2000). It is thus implicitly included within other ICNPO fields, such as environment and health, rather than in the civic and advocacy 'industry'.

7 Other country data have been made available subsequently, albeit not always relating to 1995. See Comparative Nonprofit Sector Project (2002) for the most up-to-date information.

8 While providers in this area currently operate as self-governing 'trusts', unlike the education institutions, these are not charitable corporations, and their boards are appointed directly by the Secretary of State for Health, so they are excluded under our definition. This situation may change if proposals to offer some hospitals 'foundation', or 'public interest corporation' status allow them in future to operate as autonomous entities, and if they also involve voluntarism to a meaningful degree.

9 The analysis of paid employment data reported here was undertaken at the London School of Economics with the financial support of NCVO. Some of these findings have been reported in Jas *et al.* (2002), and Almond and Kendall (2002). The financial data here are based upon NCVO's own surveys of 'general charities', also published in Jas *et al.* (2002).

10 According to other evidence, public sector growth has even outdistanced the for-profit sector in recent years. Data from the Annual Employment Survey and Annual Business Inquiry Series (based on data collected from establishments rather than individual workers) imply that absolute employment growth was actually greater in the public sector than in the private sector in 1999 and 2000 (Hardwidge, 2002).

11 On Social Services Departments (SSDs) spending in the late 1990s, see Mocroft (2000). The full time series data on central government funding of the voluntary sector that were drawn upon in an earlier volume (Kendall and Knapp, 1996) was discontinued after 1994/5, but partial data have subsequently been assembled for the Home Office (Home Office, Research, Development and Statistics Directorate, 2001). This study shows the dominance of the Housing Corporation as a source of finance in the 1990s, in continuity with patterns that had been evident since data were first reported in 1982/3 (op. cit., Chapter 5). However, the Home Office report is incomplete, since it does not collate data on what our earlier study had shown were the second and third most significant sources of central government funding for the voluntary sector, expenditure on training programmes and urban regeneration.

12 The Home Office has already added a module on volunteering to the 2000 British Crime Survey, but the authors of a report on that survey emphasize that its findings cannot be compared with earlier studies of volunteering, including the Institute for Volunteering Research study which we drew upon earlier (Kristnamurthy *et al.*, 2001). However, a biannual Home Office Citizenship survey is now in progress; see also Citizen's Audit (2002) for further information on volunteering assembled as part of the ESRC's *Democracy and Participation* programme.

3 Mainstreaming the voluntary sector on to the UK policy agenda[1]

- **The New Labour Government has mainstreamed the voluntary sector as a policy actor.**

- **Influences have included the diagnoses of policy problems by specialist 'horizontal' institutions; New Labour's aspiration to differentiate itself from 'statist' Old Labour; and the promotional activities of policy entrepreneurs.**

- **Connections in policy and research are increasingly being made between the voluntary sector, social capital and social exclusion.**

3.1 Introduction

The previous chapter observed that, aside from the long-established legal and fiscal framework for charities, voluntary sector policy in Britain has traditionally been constituted almost entirely as the sum of its 'vertical' parts at the 'industry' level. However, in the second half of the 1990s and the first years of the twenty-first century, moves to alter that situation are taking shape. Attempts to seriously foster a 'horizontal' framework to operate over and above the legal system, on the one hand, and the myriad of inherited vertical structures and relationships, on the other, are beginning to evolve.

It has been in the context of the accession of a New Labour administration that the critical mass of political will necessary to pursue this agenda has come to fruition. Tony Blair's Government assumed public office in May 1997 after a landslide election victory, and within 2 years, three high-profile policy events with regard to the voluntary sector had occurred. First, the launch of a Compact between the new Government and groups claiming to represent the interests of the sector in England, in late 1998 (see Box 3.1).[2]

Second, a commitment made by Tony Blair in a speech in January 1999 to significantly upgrade and invest in the human and financial resources of the Government unit specifically charged with dealing with voluntary sector issues, the newly labelled Active Community Unit (formerly, the Voluntary and Community Unit, and Voluntary Services Unit).[3]

Third, the inclusion in Gordon Brown's first budget of a Treasury-led review of the tax situation. This 'Charity Tax Review' – and the more recent Strategy

---

Box 3.1 The Labour Government's Compact with the 'voluntary and community sector', 1998

Principles
- An independent and diverse voluntary and community sector is fundamental to the well-being of society.
- In the development and delivery of public policy and services, the Government and the sector have distinct but complementary roles.
- There is added value in working in partnership towards common aims and objectives.
- The Government and sector have different forms of accountability but common values of commitment to integrity, objectivity, openness, honesty and leadership.

Government's undertakings
- To recognize and support the voluntary sector's independence.
- On funding inter alia common, transparent arrangements for agreeing and evaluating objectives . . . [and] the use of long-term . . . funding to assist . . . stability.
- To consult the sector on issues which are likely to affect it.
- To promote mutually affective working relations.
- To review the operation of the Compact annually.

Voluntary sectors undertakings
- To maintain high standards of governance and accountability.
- To respect the law.
- To ensure users and other stakeholders are consulted in presenting a case to Government and developing management of activities.
- To promote mutually affective working relations.
- To review the operation of the Compact annually.

Source: Adapted from Home Office (1998).

Unit inquiry into legal structures which builds upon it – can be seen as the latest in a long line of inquiries into the fiscal and/or legal situation for charities, even if given initial momentum in response to concerns very particular to the late 1990s.[4] These concerns included the perceived fall in private giving,[5] and the wish to placate shareholding charities adversely caught in the crossfire of for-profit-oriented tax reforms (see Box 3.2).

However, unlike some other earlier reviews, the 1990s tax review quickly generated change, with a wide range of new and extended tax reliefs on private giving announced from November 1999 onwards by the Chancellor. These

---

Box 3.2   Caught in the crossfire: generic tax reform's impact on shareholding charities

The reform in question was the decision to modify traditional exemptions from Advance Corporation Tax payable on earnings from shares held in private (for-profit) companies. The move was designed to encourage private firms to invest operating profits rather than distribute them to institutional shareholders, important categories of which had not had to pay tax on their dividends. The principal target was the massively wealthy private pension funds, one of the largest groupings of institutional shareholders (Buckle and Thompson, 1996: Chapter 6). However, the Chancellor decided in advance of the budget that charities' holdings of shares should be treated in the same way. Efforts by intermediary bodies and tax pressure groups to secure a grant of equivalent value to make up for the lost revenue failed, and the agreement to have a review was in part a sop to lobbyists (Randall, 1998).

---

arguably mean that the UK now has one of the most favourable tax environments for the sector anywhere in the world (Walker and Pharoah, 2002 and references therein). It also paved the way to the 'cross-cutting' Treasury review to which we referred in Chapter 1 (HM Treasury, 2002; see also Chapters 4 and 6).

Moreover, the 'Compact' idea and its offshots were completely without precedent in this country or elsewhere, and represent an unparalleled step change in the positioning of the voluntary sector in public policy. The move to improve the resources of central government focused on the sector per se is also an important development. It is significant that this commitment was initially made by the New Labour Government at the start of its first term in office, when it was determined to demonstrate its ability to keep public expenditure tightly constrained with an eye to refuting its traditional 'tax and spend' reputation.

In effect, for the first time, in the last half of the 1990s, a purposive stance towards a voluntary sector per se has become mainstreamed into central government's public policy agenda, representing a major break from the past. Policy towards the sector prior to these development had been low key, piecemeal and ad hoc, with no serious commitment to unify it and give it meaning as an overall whole (see also Kendall and Knapp, 1996).

The purpose of this chapter is to ask: Why did this step change take place in the second half of the 1990s? How was it that the voluntary sector per se in the late 1990s becomes a 'hot' enough issue to claim the scarce resources of policy-shaper interest and time? And why was the voluntary sector policy agenda packaged as it was? Who and what was driving it?

3.2 A theoretical framework

This section will suggest that responding to the 'whys and wherefores' of voluntary sector policy demands attending to a range of factors at play in the worlds of politics and policy which, while evolving to a certain extent independently from one another and over very different timescales, came together at the end of the 1990s to generate change. The issue can be explored using the analytic framework developed by the US political scientist John W. Kingdon. Kingdon's influential 1984 book, *Agendas, Alternatives and Public Policies*, revised and reissued in 1995, seeks to offer a systematic account of the concepts we need to answer the questions 'How do subjects come to officials' attention? How are the alternatives from which they choose generated? How is the governmental agenda set? Why does an idea's time come when it comes?' (Kingdon, 1995: xi). The fields examined in considerable detail over a number of years by Kingdon were transport and health policy in the US, but the generic approach does seem to provide at least a starting vocabulary for examining the emergence of UK voluntary sector policy, as long as some important limitations and caveats, to be discussed below, are recognized. This approach is appropriate because it is one of the few frameworks for analysing policy which gives particular attention to the agenda-setting phase of the policy process, treats rather than takes for granted the question of issue awareness or salience, while also allowing for a low level of institutionalization – the aspect which, necessarily, we are dealing with in this case.[6]

Kingdon's framework starts by recognizing the potential role of a range of participants in agenda setting. In UK terms, these would include the major political parties holding central government office and, in opposition, civil servants, direct stakeholders – including those who see themselves as part of the third sector or undertake research upon it – and the general public and the media. These can all affect the positioning of voluntary sector policy in particular on the wider public policy agenda, and influence the way in which voluntary sector policy, as an agenda item, is framed and packaged.

Second, in Kingdon's approach, the policy process is portrayed as involving three 'largely independent streams': problems, policies and politics, and while the categories of participants referred to above can be involved in more than one stream, the streams themselves do involve different distinctive imperatives and dynamics (see Box 3.3).

According to Kingdon, the all-important coupling of these streams associated with the arrival of a policy option is most likely when:

> *Policy windows* – opportunities for pushing pet proposals or conceptions of problems – are open . . . windows are opened either by the appearance of compelling problems or by happenings in the political stream [while] alternatives are generated by the policy stream. *Policy entrepreneurs*, people who are willing to invest their resources in pushing their pet proposals . . . are responsible not only for prompting important people to pay attention,

> **Box 3.3 Multiple streams in Kingdon's approach**
>
> - The *problems stream* helps us grasp how and why states of affairs come to be considered problematic. It involves focusing events including crises and disasters, feedback from current programme operations, and indicator availability.
> - The *policy stream* is analogous to biological natural selection: ideas float around communities of specialists, and those proposals that meet criteria for survival – including value compatibility and technical feasibility – are the ones that persist.
> - The *politics stream* is defined to have party politics and electoral imperatives at its core. It is assumed to be affected by turnover of elected officials, since that determines the composition of the government. But it also involves swings in the 'national mood', and pressure from politically oriented interest groups.

but also for coupling solutions to problems and for coupling both problems and solutions to politics.

(p. 20, emphases added)

The evidence base for this analysis comes from two sources. First, a review of relevant literature and written sources, including a wide range of low visibility 'grey' literature generated from the voluntary sector itself from the 1970s onwards rarely accounted for in policy analysis. Second, more particularly a review of recent policy statements, as represented in official publications, think-tank literature, and scrutiny of unpublished speeches by relevant politicians. Third, a small number of 1–1.5 hour long interviews with those involved in the development of the field in general, and the Compact in particular, during late 1998 and early 1999, from the voluntary sector itself and its direct stakeholders, including government. The interviews had in common that they addressed the broad themes of this paper, but specific questions were tailored to reflect the particular role and positioning of the interviewee in the development of policies in this field.

3.3 The voluntary sector problem and policy streams

3.3.1 Origins of the language of 'sectors'

A necessary condition for it to be possible to talk of a purposive policy existing towards the voluntary sector per se – the 'horizontal' focus of this chapter – is for it to be a recognized category. That is, a critical mass of relevant stakeholders must believe that such a sector exists, or at least that it is useful shorthand for a meaningful institutional terrain before policy-soluble or policy-manageable 'problems' can be attached to it. Such a notion first came into usage amongst a small group of researchers and in the UK in the late 1970s with the publication of the Wolfenden Committee's report, *The Future of Voluntary Organisations*; prior to this a discrete 'sector' per se (6 and Leat, 1997) was not identified explicitly and directly as an actual or potential object of purposive public policy. In this report, the voluntary sector's role was sketched out in terms of a capacity to supplement and complement to what were then assumed to be the primary vehicles of social welfare – the state, and informal and family care. It was seen as a cost-effective provider, innovator and advocate operating as a 'partner' to the state, language which was to be developed in the coming years by those involved, and has subsequently provided a significant launch pad for thinking about 'impacts' in the UK (see Chapter 6).

In addition, a problem stream was developed by what were called 'intermediaries', organizations now sometimes referred to as 'infrastructure' or 'umbrella' bodies. Wolfenden (1978) had recommended the consolidation of such an infrastructure for the voluntary sector at the national and local levels to foster support for voluntarism, provide advice and raise awareness. For example, at the local level, Councils for Voluntary Service, Rural Community Councils and Volunteer Bureau were to be encouraged. The national level included the national associations of these agencies, as well as the National Council for Voluntary Organizations. Some of their concerns were around difficulties with legal definitions and frameworks, complaints of 'underfunding' by local government, and claims that more should be done to consult the sector and involve it in policy design. But for the time being, these fell largely on deaf ears.

3.3.2 Crises, feedback effects and indicators

Kingdon argues that three main mechanisms can bring conditions to the serious attention of policy-makers: focusing events, including crises and disasters,[7] feedback from the operation of existing programmes and indicator availability.

The low visibility (and audibility) of the voluntary sector, and limited interest in it from beyond the small community of 'intermediaries' and a low profile, understaffed Voluntary Services Unit (VSU) in the Home Office, can in part be understood as reflecting the fact that these 'prompts' for policy-makers' attentions were largely absent up until the mid-1990s. We will consider each in turn. Crises and disasters featured less prominently in the UK than in some other locales in terms of a perception that the sector itself was ever 'in crisis' (see also Kendall and Anheier, 2001a). For example, 'crises' have been linked with the sector on the international voluntary sector scene in three ways: opportunistic exploitation of loose regulatory regimes for personal gain, inappropriately high rewards for chief executives and abuse of vulnerable users of human service facilities run by voluntary sector organizations. While these were sometimes discussed in the media and the literature, they failed to generate more than sporadic, occasional interest in Britain. As isolated incidents, they cannot really be said to have been perceived as sufficiently pervasive, or to have been systematically enough linked to the 'sector' per se, to have justified a 'crisis' diagnosis (for more details, see Kendall, 2000; for international comparison, see Kendall and Anheier, 2001a).

Moving on to Kingdon's second category, feedback effects clearly did not make an impression at the sector level. There are perhaps three main reasons for this. First, a good deal of the public funding targeted specifically at fostering the voluntary sector during the 1980s and early 1990s was administered via grants regimes with vague, aspirational goals couched in terms of such hard-to-measure concepts as 'community development' and 'capacity building'. This would certainly seem to apply to the (then) VSU's funding for infrastructure, and with evaluations structured in this way it could be difficult to recognize success or failure.

Second, even if monitoring did generate mutually recognized problems they did not grasp senior officials' attention simply because the VSUs' sector-specific programmes were of low profile and status, and the small size of its budget meant it was of little interest to those seeking to control costs. Third, there were programmes which involved substantial commitments of public funding and involving tighter contractual arrangements with some readily digestible measures of achievement (however crude). The main examples during this period were training schemes designed to respond to unemployment, and the growth of contracts with social care providers in the 1990s (see Chapter 4). But these tended to be seen as 'owned' by bureaucrats in the relevant field (the Department of Employment and local government social services departments, respectively), and not matters for 'horizontal' sector specialists within or outside government.

Of Kingdon's categories, the one that seems to have had some role in 'problematizing' the general state of the voluntary sector, and effectively reached a critical mass for the first time in the mid-1990s, has been the existence of systematic, voluntary sector-relevant indicators. Pioneering work had been undertaken by John Posnett in the Economics Department at the University of York (Posnett, 1993). From the mid-1990s onwards, a wider and more robust range of evidence on precisely these matters came to the fore (Saxon-Harrold and Kendall, 1995; Hems and Passey, 1996; Kendall and Knapp, 1996; Hemmington Scott, 1994). This body of evidence and its offshoots was to feature prominently in the mid-1990s policy reviews. Kingdon suggests it is time trends data which are often most important in sparking interest among policy-makers. The reporting of an indicator going 'the wrong way' – declining private giving by individuals – is particularly relevant here. As early as 1993, the Conservative Government cited Charities Aid Foundation data suggesting that average giving was declining, and indicated it was 'concerned that the fall in typical giving should be arrested and reversed' (Home Office, 1993: 32). The Government went on to cite the various ad hoc simplifications of, and modific-ations to, the tax regime as representing its contribution to this addressing this trend. However, over and beyond this, the 'lead responsibility' was with 'volun-tary sector organizations themselves'. More recently, extant Family Expenditure Survey data, first systematically analysed with an eye to charitable giving in

1997, appeared to show a generational decline in donations (Banks and Tanner, 1997; 1999). Indeed, as we noted in the Introduction, the Charity Tax Review initiated under New Labour had explicitly had at the top of its agenda this problem of decline (HM Treasury, 1999: 1–2; more recently, see Pharoah and Walker, 2002).

As Kingdon, however, emphasizes, facts do not speak for themselves: it is the interpretation of facts that matters. To understand how and why these trends have come to be seen as matters of high salience, we need to consider developments in the policy and politics streams.

3.3.3 The policy reviews of the mid-1990s

The absence of sufficiently dramatic crises, feedback effects and a critical mass of indicators played an important part in ensuring that the self-defined voluntary sector policy stream was operating with low visibility for 15 years after Wolfenden. No major policy documents were developed during the 1980s, and the three major voluntary sector reviews to emerge in the 1990s were the CENTRIS, Demos and Deakin Commission reports.[8] Table 3.1 sets out their main elements.

The contribution of Demos, the left-leaning think tank with close connections to New Labour, is discussed in Section 3.4 below. Neither the CENTRIS report nor the Deakin Commission, at the time of their release, can be said to have made a direct and immediate influence on mainstream policy, but for very different reasons. We can understand each report's reception and eventual impact with reference to the criteria which Kingdon identifies as pertinent to ascertaining why some policy ideas do better than others: value acceptability, technical feasibility and anticipation of future constraints (where the latter is interpreted more broadly than in Kingdon's account).

First, the 1993 CENTRIS report dramatically violated the criterion of value acceptability, most importantly through its suggestion that the sector be split into a 'first force' arm of service providers competing for public contracts for whom tax benefits would be withdrawn, and a 'third force' of advocacy groups, continuing to lobby on behalf of socially excluded people and campaign for change. Putting on the agenda the withdrawal of tax advantages for some organizations while retaining them for others was effectively regarded from within the sector and outside it as breaching an article of faith: that an appropriate quid quo pro from the state for the sector's 'altruistic' contributions must be an entitlement or right to tax relief. The proposals also fell down on the criterion of technical feasibility. This was primarily on the grounds that many voluntary organizations develop both roles simultaneously, and that it would consequently be counterproductive or even impossible to segregate the sector along these lines (see also Part II of this volume for some supportive evidence of this claim). With these two criteria so clearly breached, it was politically important that the report as a package was immediately seen to be rejected.

Table 3.1 Voluntary sector policy reviews, 1993–6

Colloquial name, year published, lead author and institutional status	Funders	Style	Evidence base and orientation	Most significant recommendations	Most significant single clearly attributable impact to date
CENTRIS report (1993) Barry Knight Independent researcher	Coalition of charitable trusts and companies, some funding from the UK government (Home Office, Housing Corporation)	Idiosyncratic, iconoclastic, convictional, eclectic (pot pourri inspired by individual histories and other eclectic writers)	Varied primary quantitative empirical evidence gathered from local and national surveys; forward-speculation ('futurology')	Split the third sector between 'first force' (advocacy) and 'third force' (publicly funded service delivery agencies); withdraw tax relief for 'third force' agencies	None of recommendations adopted
Demos report (1995) Geoff Mulgan and Charles Landry New generic 'think tank'	Charities Aid Foundation, Joseph Rowntree Foundation	Faddish, self-consciously innovative, eclectic (disciplines: evolutionary psychology, political science, economics)	Secondary reporting of existing quantitative data: opinions and attitudes gleaned during agency visits, informal seminars and networking	Finance 'charity bank' and exploration of new loan and borrowing arrangements; abolish legal restrictions on charities' advocacy; 'models of public funding'; link tax benefits to activities not organizational form; encourage risk-taking in public funding	None in short term; arguable in long term (see text and Box 3.5)
Deakin Commission (1996) Chair: Nicholas Deakin 'Independent commission'	Esmee Fairbairn charitable trust, Joseph Rowntree Foundation, National Council for Voluntary Organizations	Deferential statesmanlike consensual ('civil society', reference points include Dahrendorf, Putnam)	Secondary reporting of existing quantitative evidence: extensive written submissions, informal submissions	Develop Concordat as 'core of good practice for future relations'; strengthen 'friend at court' for voluntary sector within government; establish task forces to develop Concordat, and to make specific actionable recommendations regarding tax issues, resource issues, business relations, quality assurance	Suggestion of Concordat between the state and the third sector recognizing the latter's independence and diversity (see Box 3.1)

For its part, the Deakin report's impact was very different: as a 'consensus document', built up by a team receiving the views and evidence from voluntary organizations, including the intermediaries, it was largely perceived as reflecting their priorities and concerns, as therefore avoided the value compatibility and technical feasibility difficulties that undermined the CENTRIS report. However, in one very important way, the Commission did go beyond the Wolfenden approach and the problem stream nurtured by the intermediary bodies: by recommending that partnership could actually be operationalized through a concordat between the voluntary sector and the state. In fact, the idea of such an agreement did not actually emerge from within the UK voluntary sector, or by looking at arrangements for the third sector overseas. Instead, it came from a concurrent research project upon which the Commission's chair had been working, dealing with the relationship between the Treasury and the central government spending departments which it funds: in this case, separate Concordats were being developed to lay down principles of operational agreement between these departments of state and the Treasury.

The idea was, however, rejected by the incumbent Conservative Government. In the official language of the Government's response:

> The government does not believe that, given the diverse nature of voluntary organizations and activity, a formal concordat is a sensible or usefully achievable objective.
>
> (Department of National Heritage, 1996: 2)

On the surface, the official response seems to amount to the rejection of two of Kingdon's criteria for the survival of policy ideas. First, not an achievable objective suggests the belief that such an arrangement is technically infeasible; and second, that it is neither 'sensible nor useful' is suggestive of a failure to achieve value acceptability from the perspective of the Government (even if it had achieved this goal as far as the sector's representatives were concerned). The Government also rejected the proposal that the VSU be strengthened in any tangible way. Instead, it referred only vaguely and noncommittally to 'raising awareness' (p. 2).

Because it largely reflected existing thinking within the voluntary sector's representative bodies, with the exception of the new 'Concordat' idea which at the time was rejected, and because as a package it received only lukewarm endorsement from the Government, commentators who wanted more than a voluntary sector 'consensus document' expressed some disappointment. However, it is also critical to interpret the Deakin Commission in dynamic political context: the style and content of the report to a large extent was framed not only with the relationship with the incumbent Conservative Government in mind, but in the knowledge that a general election was looming in the following year, with the likelihood of a Labour victory.

In sum, viewed against Kingdon's criteria of value acceptability and technical feasibility but interpreted in a dynamic and expansive sense – amounting to at the very least, a major modification of what Kingdon refers to as a distinct, third criteria of the 'anticipation of future [conditions]'[9] – the Commission's blend of timidity and innovation becomes more understandable, and can be regarded as ultimately successful, at least on its own terms. As a Deakin Commission insider remarked, it was not possible to 'cultivate' either the Conservatives when in office or the Labour Party too 'blatantly' without 'turning the other off'. And while we have seen that the former were largely passive and reactive to independent or voluntary sector initiatives, the latter were increasingly keen to nurture an active and sustained interest. It is to this development that we now turn in the following section.

3.4 The voluntary sector and the political stream

3.4.1 Party political developments

Surveying the main routes through which the Conservative Government supported the voluntary sector in the 1980s and early 1990s, it was concluded in an earlier study (Kendall and Knapp, 1996) that while tax treatments and legal frameworks were modified at the margin (Chapter 2), policies involving the sector in implementation tended to engage it in a disjointed, but also a somewhat abrasive and adversarial style (Kendall and Knapp, 1996: Chapter 5 and p. 159). While rhetorical support from some significant politicians was evident, it was quite sporadic and thin on the ground. Most of the claims concerning the sector's social importance emerged from the low profile group of policy actors discussed in the previous section, and neither in words nor actions did the Conservative administration of 1979–97 offer sustained commitment to the voluntary sector.

This lack of interest to a significant degree reflects the fact that throughout the 1980s and 1990s, the Conservative Government remained preoccupied with the dichotomy between the market and the state. Its ideological and policy formulation energies alike were channelled overwhelmingly into expanding the scale and scope of the former's operations. This was either in pure form through full-scale privatization, through a crusade to remove 'market distortions' (as with the measures taken to limit the powers of the trade unions in the labour market); or surreptitiously through using politically acceptable 'market-like' hybrid arrangements – as with those arrangements introduced into fields of social policy previously organized predominantly as publicly owned hierarchies (Bartlett and Le Grand, 1993). The world of formal organizations was viewed essentially with a two sector model. Box 3.4 discusses this claim in more detail.

For its part, the Labour Party spent the early 1980s challenging the Conservative Party on this territory – that is, as the champion of state solutions, and in principled opposition to the embrace of market forces. But from the late 1980s, as the reinvention of Labour as 'New Labour' began, this was to change (Driver and Martell, 1998). The party first began to distance itself from the 'dogma' of monothematic ideological attachment to the state with its policy review

---

Box 3.4 The Conservatives and the voluntary sector in the 1980s and 1990s

The evidence points to a lack of sustained or concentrated policy attention for the voluntary sector under the Conservative administrations of the 1980s and 1990s. This is not to claim that the Conservative Government and individual members of the party were not aware of the voluntary sector. For example, Mrs Thatcher lauded the 'volunteer movement', 'charitable activities' and 'charities' in several speeches and media interviews (Brenton, 1985; Green, 2002: 277–8, 289–90). And a reviewer of an earlier version of this chapter, who had been based at the VSU for part of her premiership, pointed out that she personally intervened to ensure that funding for the voluntary sector under one particular scheme was protected. Finally, a small number of Conservative thinkers did attend to charity in their philosophical treatises (Willetts, 1994; Green, 2002; see also Chapter 10). However, these are exceptions to the rule that the Conservative administrations did not systematically consider the voluntary sector as central to their priority policy objectives to the same extent that New Labour was to do in the late 1990s and early 2000s (see text). Supporting this interpretation, biographies of influential Conservative ministers rarely attend systematically to this domain, instead categorizing the world according to the state, the market, or the quasi-market in discussing what were seen as the most pressing policy issues problems.

---

between 1987 and 1992. This signalled a pragmatic endorsement of the advantages of markets in the economic sphere (where free markets were now understood as functioning well outside certain well-defined areas of market failure) and a commitment to retain many of the Conservative's reforms to trade union law. But, particularly with Tony Blair's assumption of the leadership in 1994, the party's emerging policies begin to take on a distinctly communitarian hue, influenced philosophically by writers such as John McMurray and Amitai Etzioni (Rentoul, 1995; Etzioni, 1995). Not only was a less traditional pro-state position increasingly adopted, but in a sustained and systematic way, references to and recognition of the voluntary sector began to appear.

Two steps seem particularly noteworthy, and are certainly without parallel in the Conservative Party – either when in government, or since moving into opposition. First, constitutional revision, as part of its 'revisionism' or 'moderniz-ation' strategy designed explicitly to secure the trust of the electorate in order to win public office. Clause IV, which epitomized the party's statism by placing public ownership at the heart of its formal identity was scrapped. 'Old Labour', uniquely for a European democratic socialist party, had seen 'common owner-ship of the means of production, distribution and exchange' as a necessary precondition for the achievement of socialist objectives. No mention was made of voluntary organizations. By contrast, for New Labour, one of the ways of achieving 'a community in which power, wealth and opportunity are in the hands of the many and not the few' was to be through 'working with trade unions, cooperative societies and other affiliated organizations, and also with voluntary organizations, consumer groups and other representative bodies' (see Riddell, 1997, for a detailed commentary).

Second, after a consultation exercise parallel to the Deakin Commission, the pre-election document *Building the Future Together* (Labour Party, 1997), deliberately distanced the party from 'statism'. (This exercise is discussed in more detail in Section 3.5 below.) In this and a subsequent series of documents and speeches, working closely with the sector was continually referred to as integral to the New Labour 'project'. For example, Tony Blair's Fabian Society short pamphlet *The Third Way: New Politics for the New Century*, printed just 2 months before the release of the Compact, finds significant room for the voluntary sector. 'Community' is linked deliberately with voluntary organizations and, thus coupled, is argued to be an integral part of the 'third way':

> Government must be acutely sensitive not to stifle worthwhile activity by local communities and the voluntary sector. The grievous twentieth century error of the fundamentalist left was the belief that the state could replace civil society and thereby advance freedom . . . a key challenge of progressive politics is to use the state as an enabling force, protecting effective communities and voluntary organizations and encouraging their growth to tackle new needs, in partnership as appropriate.
>
> (Blair, 1988: 4)

Thus, an important aspect of the 'newness' of Labour was its empathy with the voluntary sector. Moreover, what is unprecedented here was that so much space should be devoted to the voluntary sector in setting out what was a general statement of overall philosophy and policy, not just a lecture to a 'specialist' voluntary sector audience (as were Thatcher's and Major's most cited speeches on this topic in the 1980s and 1990s). At a philosophical level, what emerges strongly from these and other speeches was the communitarian character of New Labour's agenda – a communitarianism which was both moralistic and arguably even authoritarian (Driver and Martell, 1997). Such an 'emphasis on civil society [gave] New Labour the type of post-Thatcherite edge it wants' (Driver and Martell, 1997: 36).

3.4.2 *Other influences in the political stream*

The idea of sector-inclusive partnership came to the surface in the context of the party's internal debates in the early 1990s as it struggled to become more attractive to the electorate, as well as reflecting the philosophical predilections of its leadership. Outside the political parties themselves, but partly within the political stream and partly situated in the policy stream, are to be found the 'think tanks' and some of the more influential academic institutions.[10] We noted earlier how the think tank Demos produced one of a range of policy documents to emerge in the mid-1990s (Mulgan and Landry, 1995). We treat it as part of the political stream here because its co-founders had a long association with the political Left, its ideas have been more readily absorbed by New Labour than the Conservatives, and because Mulgan has now become a member of a powerful Policy Unit with the ear of the Prime Minister.

It therefore comes initially as something of a surprise that Demos's specific recommendations on the voluntary sector (Table 3.1) failed to make an immediate impact on New Labour's policy at this formative stage – although it arguably may have done so in the longer term (see Box 3.5).

In other relevant ways, however, Demos did exert a short-term influence, particularly if its claim of being a pivotal influence in providing both the theoretical underpinnings and practical tools for facilitating 'holistic' government is accurate (6, 1997b; 6 *et al.*, 1999). Demos and associated people do seem to have had at least some role in packaging and selling the idea of 'holism' in policy to the Government, even if the notion that many social problems require an interagency response has long been argued from outside the state, particularly by the voluntary sector itself.[11] Moreover, in the 1990s under the Major administration, there was a marked quickening in both the rhetoric of partnership, and the development of special programmes aiming to tackle needs which fell through the cracks of central and local government departmental and territorial divisions.

In spite of these obvious antecedents, dubbed 'joined-up' government by New Labour, the idea of systematic sectoral collaboration to meet complex needs was claimed to be one of its most significant new 'big ideas'. It has been tied in with the even wider 'modernization' agenda (see in particular Department of Environment, Transport and the Regions, 1998; Cabinet Office, 1999). The basic argument has been that many important social problems do not fall into neat functional categories corresponding to inherited government hierarchical structures, but are often experienced cumulatively, and require an integrated, co-ordinated and 'inclusive' response.

Box 3.5 The 1995 Demos report: long-term influence on New Labour?

While apparently not making a short-term impact, in the longer term, it could be argued that the Demos report has proved more influential. In particular, a number of the recommendations in the 2002 Strategy Unit report, such as the recommendation to make the legal environment more hospitable to the voluntary sector's campaigning role, move at least partially in the direction that had been proposed in 1995. However, the Demos report's *relative* importance in shaping the Strategy Unit's recommendations over such a long period of time is difficult to gauge. It is also difficult to separate any 'Demos effect' from the influence of its individual founder, Geoff Mulgan, now a powerful 'insider' as current director of the Strategy Unit.

However, more interesting for our purposes is not this idea in isolation, but its coupling with two newer discourses. First, the linking of partnership to the needs of a newly recognized category of people: those deemed to be 'socially excluded'. The emphasis on addressing the needs of those in poverty in the classical sense as well as those deprived of nonmonetary resources, drew upon wider European analytic approaches. The adoption of these ideas mirrored interest in them reflected in such influential and politically well-connected academic institutions as the London School of Economics (see Hills *et al.*, 2002).

Second, the search for 'joined-up solutions' was deemed to require institutional development beyond the piecemeal growth of special programmes, and to necessitate the insertion of a whole new layer of governance into the system (whose architecture is discussed in more detail in Chapter 4). A discourse analysis-based distinction between the 'old' and the 'emergent new' understood in this transcendent 'governance' sense are set out in Table 3.2, drawing out rhetorical contrasts (and tending to de-emphasize continuities) in terms of some of the most important dimensions (for more detail, see Newman, 2001b).

While 'social exclusion' and 'joined-up governance' are not the only components of New Labour's vocabulary which have tended to bring into policy focus the significance of the voluntary sector, Box 3.6 suggests that they are, for the moment, more pervasive and influential than other favoured constructs. It is therefore important to ask: Why the voluntary sector in particular as ally in fighting social exclusion and as partner in 'the new joined-up governance'?

First, this can be understood by the same logic as the general interpretation of the political stream developed in this chapter; by systematically seeking to define partners as not just the public sector and the private sector but voluntary organizations too, marked differentiation from the *status quo ante* was achieved.

Table 3.2 Rhetorical contrasts in public policy approaches

Dominant emphasis in public policy discourse	'Public management' (before New Labour)	'Modernization' (New Labour)
Strategic rationale for partnership	Achieve each partners' predetermined goals	Achieve 'superordinate' policy goals
Conception of 'performance'	Addressed partner by partner	Addressed through 'cross-cutting' measures
Primary catalyst for service improvement	Competition explicit, central targets downplayed	Shared central targets emphasized (competition implicit)
Response to failure to improve	Intensify market pressures	Intensify external regulation, direct intervention

Note:
Adapted from Newman (2001a).

Box 3.6 Mutualism and social enterprise

This book singles out for special attention the concepts of joined-up social exclusion and social capital as especially significant in the evolution of voluntay sector policy. However, these are not the only expressions from New Labour's conceptual armoury which seem to bring the role of the voluntary sector to the forefront of policy analysis: in particular, the language of 'mutualism' and 'social enterprise' have also entered the lexicon of the policy elite (Burchhall, 2001; Mayo and Moore, 2001). However, we choose to focus on the voluntary sector's affinity with joined-up government, social exclusion and social capital because these categories are more systematically integrated into the policy discourse; because they have featured as reference points in the process of 'horizontal' institution building described in the next chapter to a far greater degree; because they have been given greater recognition and resources within the state (for example, the new social enterprise unit at the Department for Trade and Industry is very small in comparison with the ACU, the SEU and other units dealing with social exclusion to be discussed in the next chapter); and because *prima facie* they appear to have a greater level of generality and are not tied to particular segments of the voluntary sector or its allies in the state apparatus.

Particular emphasis was now put on 'partnership' not just within policy fields or at problematic boundaries between them (as with the health and social care interface) where that had emerged as an issue from within particular vertical policy communities. It was elevated to the level of a general principle, 'superordinate', and supposedly cutting across all relevant vertical public policy fields.

Second and more practically, while the language of 'partnership' in the context of area-based policies had been frequent to the point of tedium before, voluntary organizations' actual involvement in special programmes was often felt to be ad hoc and marginal (for example, on the Urban Programme, see Kendall and Knapp, 1996: 147–8; on the Single Regeneration Budget, Taylor, 2001). Systematic institutional redesign could be presented as offering enhanced opportunities for more meaningful patterns of partnership to develop, and thus could be presented as a significant innovation (although, as we see in the next chapter, the early evidence from actual 'joined-up' implementation as far as the voluntary sector is concerned is limited, mixed and inconclusive).

Third, a connection emerges from the very act of redefining the policy problem of 'poverty' as one of 'social exclusion'. The framing of deprivation in this way focuses attention on a broader set of factors than the financial measures which had traditionally tended to preoccupy poverty analysts. This had naturally pointed towards state responsibility for solutions by virtue of its control of social security disbursements. Under the new formulation, nonmonetary aspects were being taken more seriously, and this brought into focus resources with which many voluntary organizations could be argued to be particularly well endowed: volunteers and community level relationships. In other words, connections could be made not only because of what voluntary organizations were perceived as not being – part of the state or the market – but also because of a more positive perception (or 'discovery') of the 'resources' which they had to offer.

This latter rationale now seems obvious with the benefit of hindsight, since clearer understandings of the meaning of social exclusion and careful discourse analyses have emerged in the new millennium (respectively, see Hills *et al.*, 2002; Newman, 2001a). However, we should not give the impression for the purposes of this chapter – explaining the late 1990s 'mainstreaming' – that a 'neat and tidy' theory of 'social exclusion' as problem and 'voluntary sector partner' as solution unfolded in a clear way as a driver of agenda change. It is more accurate to speak of a diffuse impression in the political stream, but also formed in large part as a result of personal experiences (see below). Put simply, it was taken to be self-evident that many voluntary organizations have been formed to meet the needs of those with cumulative problems in a diverse set of locales, and that they therefore could be assumed to have a wealth of experience and expertise to bring to the policy table.

It is thus interesting to note that the latterly influential formulations stressing voluntary organizations' economic and political productivity in terms of 'social capital' were *not* ingredients in the debate at this formative stage. These ideas, now being elaborated in and around the political stream by left leaning think tanks and in academia (see Chapter 6) certainly now help to provide a rationale for, and lend coherence to, a new 'horizontal' policy position. But it is note-worthy that these ideas only really entered the UK political lexicon some time after commitments were already being made by Labour towards the voluntary sector (when in Opposition), and vice versa. This simple fact suggests that the primary, initial, political impetus behind the new developments described in this section reflected political actors' very loosely defined goal of 'moving in a direction' towards a world in which the voluntary sector would have a greater part to play.[12] They were not acting at this point with a priori formulated, specific 'Keynesian' theoretical judgement.[13]

3.5 The role of policy entrepreneurs

While the developments in the policy and political streams outlined above make clear that a wide range of drivers appear to lie behind the mainstreaming of policy towards the voluntary sector, ultimately 'policy entrepreneurs' must step in to take advantage of the window of opportunity created by these trends. Interviews in the field revealed a belief amongst those involved in the process that, within this climate, two committed individuals simultaneously played this role.[14] First, with the financial and other support of NCVO, the chair of the independent 1995 Commission described in Section 3.3, Nicholas Deakin, a well-respected, centre-left social policy academic with a track record of working in, and analysing, the voluntary sector (see, for example, Deakin, 1995). While cautious (and for some, overcautious) in making recommendations that fitted closely with existing intermediary body (especially NCVO and CAF) thinking, Deakin injected a genuine element of innovation and surprise with the suggestion of a 'Concordat' between the state and the voluntary sector by looking laterally at research he happened to be undertaking on the relationship between Treasury and government spending departments.

Second, those interviewed were unambiguous that in the political stream Alun Michael MP was catalytic. Michael has been best known outside the sector for his difficult period as Wales' First Minister, and latterly for handling controversial fox hunting legislative proposals. However, his voluntary sector interests long preceded these roles. Michael led the Labour Party's review of relations with the voluntary sector between 1994 (when it was announced by Blair soon after assuming the party leadership) and 1997, and became minister with responsibility for the voluntary sector at the Home Office after the election that year, before moving to Wales to lead the Labour Party there under the new devolutionary settlement in 1998.[15] He authored the document *Building the Future Together* (see Box 3.7) which proposed the Compact in advance of the election remarkably similar to Deakin's Concordat in all but title (Labour Party, 1997). The revision of Clause IV of the Party's constitution, discussed above, was claimed throughout this period by Michael to be a crucial indication of its new-found endorsement of the importance of working with the third sector (Michael, 1995).

On taking charge in 1997 of what we have noted had been a traditionally weak unit within central government dealing specifically with voluntary sector issues, he managed to secure a doubling of resources and staffing. He was also instrumental in securing political resources for the unit. Civil servants within it claimed in interviews to be experiencing a completely unprecedented degree of 'prime ministerial backing', in large part as a direct result of his efforts. In fact,

---

Box 3.7 The Labour Party's *Building the Future Together* (March 1997)

After a 3-year consultation period, this pre-election document from Labour was authored by Alun Michael. It was released several months after the Deakin report, which was acknowledged as 'an invaluable contribution to debate . . . we agree with many of its conclusions' (p. 2). The document is most important for proposing the compact while Labour was still in opposition. It also thematizes the need to preserve the 'independence' of the sector; and suggests the importance of 'recognizing' the importance of volunteers.

Michael's enthusiasm for the sector seems to have reflected not only his Blairite political sensibilities, but also his personal experiences. Michael's background in community work in the 1960s and 1970s played a crucial role in convincing him that the voluntary sector had an important role to play (see Kendall, 2000a: 554).

The relationship between Deakin and Michael in the period 1995–6, while both consultation processes were ongoing, was deliberately one of ongoing dialogue and mutual account taking. As an insider revealed:

> They met frequently during that period and shared recommendations in advance . . . it wasn't exactly conspiratorial, but it was [seen to be important by both men] that there should be convergence. And that was consciously the objective of keeping in touch . . . the 'Compact theory' was simultaneously developed from different directions.

The similarity in the independent commission and Labour Party review recommendations were, therefore, not merely coincidental, but reflected deliberate syncopation by the entrepreneurs who led them.

Finally, reviewers of an earlier version of this chapter (including those who had been involved intimately in the Compact process, but who had not been consulted in the earlier research fieldwork) suggested the fundamental significance of a third individual, the career civil servant Sir Kenneth Stowe. Stowe – who the most erudite of commentators on Whitehall, Peter Hennessy, has singled out as one of the most skilful and influential officials of his generation (Hennessy, 2001: 660–2) – was involved with the independent commission. He acted as the 'indispensable facilitator of the Compact negotiation' (private information, 2002), and has subsequently provided continuity with implementation processes. Not only was he to chair the Compact Working Group, but in 2002 Stowe was also to chair the reference group overseeing the development of the Treasury's 'Futurebuilders' programme.

3.6 Conclusion

The announcement of the Compact between the Government and the voluntary sector in November 1998, Treasury-led reviews and the Prime Minister's announcement of a major upgrading of the unit within the central government responsible for the voluntary sector in January 1999 are all symptomatic of a step change in the relationship between the voluntary sector and UK central government. The development was a calculated attempt to establish for the first time a proactive and significant 'horizontal' policy position towards the sector per se, to extend beyond the inherited structures of support provided by the legal and fiscal system, and to supplement the 'vertical' policy arrangements in specific fields that have dominated in the past. 'Horizontal' policy over and above fiscal–legal concerns moved for the first time from the margins to the mainstream of the central state's agenda.

This chapter has sought to identify the main drivers for change in this process. The review suggests that this reflects the culmination of a number of developments in, to borrow from Kingdon (1995), the policy, problems and politics streams. Most obviously, perhaps, the Prime Minister's communitarian-inspired philosophical enthusiasm for the voluntary sector as an integral part of civil society has been an important ingredient in this development. But other political forces had also been at work. The Labour Party's revision of Clause IV was in part a 'revisionist' strategy in response to post-Thatcherite conditions, consciously engaged upon in order to persuade the electorate that they were dealing with *New* Labour. In this sense, the voluntary sector in the 1990s gained political salience on the basis of what it could claim not to be – neither the market not the state – rather than from what it was, or had actually achieved. The more positive endorsements associated with the sector's contributions to social capital and social inclusion were not explicit drivers at this early stage, but have now become important components of the policy discourse after the event.

These political developments, however, provide only one part of the story. Ultimately, the possibility of engaging with the voluntary sector has depended upon the 'invention' or 'discovery' of such a grouping. This originates in the UK in the late 1970s, when the language of sectoral 'partnership' was also introduced, but was used with any regularity and commitment by only a small community of low visibility voluntary sector intermediary bodies and relatively obscure public officials at the periphery of power.

The chapter described how this policy stream was developed during the 1990s. The availability of a critical mass of indicators on the voluntary sector's inputs seems to have been a crucial part of this process, and the chapter also sought to interpret the success or failure of the policy initiatives that drew upon them in terms of Kingdon's criteria for the survival of policy options. These include value acceptability, technical feasibility and anticipation of future constraints – or interpreting the latter more widely and appropriately, of future constraints and opportunities. In so doing, we have uncovered an apparently greater degree of connectedness between the policy and politics streams than suggested in Kingdon's formulation. That these streams were intimately intertwined is underscored by the way in which reviews were conducted in tandem, under the leadership of Deakin and Michael, in a conscious spirit of 'convergence'.

Remarkably, the Concordat/Compact idea was introduced completely *de novo* into the policy and politics bloodstream, and had become a significant element of government policy by November 1998 – just 28 months after the idea was initially floated by Deakin at the commission report's launch. It is hard to point to any other field in which such a major policy innovation has moved to the centre of public policy so rapidly. This can only reflect a unique combination of propitious political conditions, a new field of policy consequently remarkably permeable to new thinking, and the catalytic role of these entrepreneurs, and those supporting them. It is also worth underlining that the precedent of policy mainstreaming in the UK is remarkable from an inter-national perspective, as we hinted at the end of the previous chapter.

In the concluding chapter, we will return to this comparative aspect in seeking to respond to the question: 'What is distinctive about British voluntary sector policy?' However, to answer that question in as systematic a way as possible, we do also need to take into account what is beginning to emerge from the experience of putting this newly mainstreamed agenda into practice. The following chapter therefore offers a tentative sketch of early 'horizontal' developments since New Labour assumed political office.

Notes

1 This chapter draws heavily upon Kendall (2000a).
2 Compacts have also been developed in Scotland, Wales and Northern Ireland, which differ in terms of style and choreography, but also to an extent in content, from the English Compact. This chapter focuses only on the English case. See Vincent (1998) for a comparison of the content of the English and Scottish Commission reports which preceded the national Compacts; see Bloor (no date) for a comparison of the English, Scottish and Welsh Compacts themselves; and see also Plowden *et al.*, 2001, which includes an update on the Compact situation in each nation in 2001.
3 £25 million not allocated by the previous administration was initially made available in yearly tranches in the light of the comprehensive spending review. As we see in the next chapter, latterly the ACU has been expanded yet further.
4 Including the report of Lord Nathan in 1952, the work undertaken as part of the Radcliffe Commission review of taxation in 1955, the report of Lord Goodman in 1976 and various reviews and enquiries undertaken by House of Commons committees over the past 25 years: see Kendall and Knapp, 1996: Chapter 3.
5 The apparent fall in private giving in the 1990s was mentioned in Chapter 2, and the interpretation of this trend is discussed in more detail in Section 3.2. It has continued to make an imprint on the policy debate. In 2001 a 'giving campaign', jointly organized by the Government and interested parties from the voluntary sector, was launched, with the aim of reversing this downward trend (Pharoah, 2002: 2).
6 For theoretical comparison of this 'multiple streams' model with other approaches in the generic public policy literature, see Parsons (1995) and Sabatier (1999). Note that the claim here is that the approach is appropriate for examining the horizontal situation that developed in the late 1990s. This model is not used either to examine vertical field policy, or horizontal policy post-1998, cases which seem to involve different political conditions rendering the multiple streams approach less applicable. I am grateful to Perri 6 for pressing me to be explicit on this point.
7 Kingdon also considers that 'personal experiences of policy-makers' can act as 'focusing events'. However, in this this account, we will attend to personal experiences in the discussion of policy entrepreneurship (Section 3.5 below).
8 From within government, the generic New Public Management tool, the 'efficiency scrutiny' was used to evaluate central government funding schemes for the sector between 1989 and 1990 (Home Office, 1990). This is not discussed here because of its narrow terms of reference on finance, in comparison to the much more wide ranging character of the other reviews. None of our interviewees in 1998/9 mentioned this report.

9 It seems crucial to interpret this third criteria in a much more extensive way than suggested by Kingdon to accommodate the thinking of the actors involved. First, we interpret it to include expectations of changes in the identity of power-holders in the political stream, not just the future expectations of existing power-holders; and second, we regard future conditions as potentially providing not only constraints, but also opportunities (see Kendall, 2000a, for more discussion).

10 Kingdon identified two other primary factors in the political stream: the national mood and organized oppositional political forces. Neither of these seem to have been very significant in explaining developments in the 1990s. At this time, while surveys of public opinion undertaken by Charities Aid Foundation did examine views on such topics as normative sector responsibilities for public services and expenditure on fund raising, comparative evidence with regard to how the three sectors actually compared was not collected. For their part, right-wing opposition through think tanks and interest groups to the mainstreaming we discuss was emerging, but muted (see Whelan, 1996, 1999; Leach, 1999).

11 Community development discourse is an example, and will be mentioned as undergirding thinking about the voluntary sector's impact in 'community building' in Chapter 5.

12 The idea that much recent British social policy-making has been based upon 'moving in a direction, towards [an] aspired situation' rather than involving 'the attainment of a specified, clearly defined, goal or objective' is developed in Levin (1997; quotation from p. 225).

13 'Practical men, who believe themselves to be quite exempt from any intellectual influences, are usually the slaves of some defunct economist. Madmen in authority, who hear voices in the air, are distilling their frenzy from some academic scribbler a few year back' (Keynes, *General Theory*, 1947: Chapter 24).

14 The notion that policy actors can be 'committed' in this context is partly meant to indicate emotional attachment, but also rational pursuit of a goal, given that the individuals' reputations were at stake (see Levin, 1997, for an intriguing discussion of the significance of 'commitment' for policy analysis).

15 He later returned to Westminster, and took up a cabinet post as Minister for Rural Affairs. To further underline the point made about commitment, it is noteworthy that he has continued to be heavily involved in voluntary sector policy development since returning to Westminster, a role not self-evident from the nature of his ministerial appointment.

4 The horizontal voluntary sector agenda

Initial implementation experiences

A bigger role for the voluntary sector, in framing and delivering local services, is central to our vision

(Tony Blair, 'My Vision of Britain',
The Observer, Comment Extra, 10 November 2002)

- **New Labour has begun to implement the mainstreamed agenda.**

- **Evidence does not allow us to gauge the extent to which increased engagement with the voluntary sector has contributed to substantive policy outcomes for individual users or communities.**

- **Early impressions of the associated processes suggest mixed experiences from the perspective of those voluntary organisations who have been involved.**

- **The fraught experiences of actual implementation contrast with the smoothness of agenda setting.**

4.1 Introduction

What is known 5 years after New Labour came to power about the implementation of Tony Blair's 'vision' (see above)? This chapter begins to explore this question with a survey of what research can tell us about how 'horizontal' policy has developed in recent years, in the aftermath of the Compact, whose origins and *raison d'être* were analysed in Chapter 3.

At a minimum, the launch of the Compact was a symbolically important political act by the new administration designed to self-consciously differentiate itself from the policy *status quo ante*. While, as we shall see, it has proved extremely difficult to implement at national and subnational levels – and appears to be have difficulty competing with more specific social exclusion and urban regeneration agendas in many locales – the view is taken here that it is of enduring importance and worthy of research attention.[1] Not only has it acted as a sort of policy bridgehead, but it continues to act as a focal point for horizontal policy as far as national policy actors are concerned (and has generated considerable interest in other countries looking for 'models' in this policy domain). Tellingly, in the two major horizontal reviews released in 2002, the Compact features prominently in the forwards penned by Prime Minister Blair and Treasury Minister Boateng (Strategy Unit, 2002: 5; HM Treasury, 2002: 3). Both refer to the Compact to justify and underline the appropriateness of favoured policy problem diagnoses. Moreover, the Treasury review includes six specific recommendations relating to Compact awareness, implementation and scope (HM Treasury, 2002: 43–4); and a number of recommendations in both reports also reflect the agenda as packaged in the Compact and the process that generated it. It is therefore clear that powerful political actors are committed to the Compact and also to the institutions promoting it. This includes the ACU, despite the apparent existence of some rather negative views in parts of the sector concerning the latter's effectiveness (Plowden *et al.*, 2001; private information, 2002). Such psychological and institutional commitments are extremely important ingredients in explaining why social policies develop in certain directions and not in others (Levin, 1997).

This chapter proceeds by describing the Compact's policy progress as an important aspect of the policy scene in the early twenty-first century, but also considers a raft of other horizontal developments. This account is necessarily short and descriptive because evaluative evidence is still yet to emerge (Section 4.2). What recent research does also allow us to do, however, is to examine voluntary sector policy experiences from a more 'bottom-up' perspective. This is through attending to diverse evidence concerning how the voluntary sector had been involved as a policy 'partner' in the initial phase of designing and implementing one of New Labour's flagship policies, the New Deal for young unemployed people (Section 4.3); and through an examination of recent evidence on how voluntary sector organizations, in general, are engaging with local government in England (Section 4.4).

It is noted that the 'horizontal' policy environment for voluntary organizations has changed significantly since 1997. It is difficult to draw general conclusions, because the nature of the policy legacies and institutional linkages vary so markedly, depending upon the aspect of horizontality addressed. Overall, however, we find some evidence of mutually advantageous learning, but also report tensions and problems suggesting that horizontal voluntary sector policy implementation faces particular challenges, and is proving to be significantly more complex and demanding than anticipated by its supporters.

4.2 The Compact and allied new institutions

A range of new national bodies have now been set in place as part of the institutionalization of the policy agenda whose origins were explored in the previous chapter. Some are a direct and obvious follow through to the Compact *per se*. Increases in horizontal funding from government more generally have also been announced. These resources are still small in scale by comparison with the vertical flows which dominate relations between the sector and the state as charted in Chapter 2 (compare the size of the budgets noted in Box 4.1 with the

Box 4.1 Horizontal central government funding for the voluntary sector

Direct central government 'horizontal' funding flows are hard to log. First, there is no agreed definition of what constitutes cross-cutting support. Second, because the Government tends to announce, re-announce and re-announce again the same funding in different contexts, and refers to 'extras' and 'increases' without being clear on the base reference point, it is not straightforward to settle on a definitive figure even if a definition is settled.

The most common figure recited in speeches and reported in the voluntary sector and wider media is £300 million, as referred to by the Chancellor of the Exchequer Gordon Brown in announcing the funds made available through the comprehensive spending review for 2001–4. The BBC, for example, reported these funds as available for 'supporting and expanding the voluntary sector' (BBC News online, 11 January 2001). However, much of this funding (£120 million) is in support of volunteering undertaken in the public sector, not the voluntary sector, and funding for a specific 'vertical' policy field, being limited to a very particular group in society, children The Children's Fund, while allowing a significant part of its budget – £70 million – to be administered to local community groups via a 'community foundation network' in collaboration with local intermediary bodies and grant-making trusts is specifically in support of the Government's 'children out of poverty' strategy. To this end it complements another centrally initiated initiative, Sure Start, which is also seeking to benefit children oriented groups in particular.

If public sector volunteering and CFN-mediated funding are considered out of scope, a residual figure of £110 million for dedicated 'horizontal funding' over 2001–4 emerges. This is comprised of two elements:

- £60 million for 'modernizing infrastructure and the Active Community Unit', which builds on the earlier commitment to expand the ACU made in 1999; and
- £50 million via a 'community chest' to 'permit an organization or a committed individual to make a contribution to his or her community'.

In addition, subsequently announced:

- £36 million in a 'Community Empowerment Fund' to support the voluntary sector's involvement in Local Strategic Partnerships (see Deakin, 2002).

The allocation of the 'community chest' and the 'Community Empower-ment Fund' are now guided by the Neighbourhood Renewal Unit's National Strategic Action Plan. However, whether aggregated on the basis of baseline budgeting or new allocations under the review, the Active Community Unit emerges as the largest single source of ongoing direct horizontal funding. The ACU's most recent total budget for the current year (2002/3) totalled £56.8 million, or £53.6 million net of the civil servant administrators' wage bill and other internal costs. It is comprised of the following four elements:

- Main grants programme: £29.2 million*
- Community support grant: £5.9 million
- 'Active Community':   £18.5 million
- Volunteering matched funding: £15.0 million

Source: Active Community Unit, 2002.
Note: *Includes funding for intermediary or 'infrastructure' bodies.

An additional 'horizontal' funding source was proposed in the 2002 Treasury review: a one-off 'Futurebuilders' grant, worth £125 million over 3 years, to allow voluntary organizations to 'modernize'. It is stated that 'the Treasury will lead in setting up this fund' (HM Treasury, 2002: 32), but details have yet to be formulated at the time of writing.

Finally, it is important to note that this direct financial support of a purpose-fully sector-wide, 'horizontal' nature is small compared to the value of 'tax expenditures' (see Chapter 2). It is also limited compared to the Com-munity Fund's channelling of grants for 'good causes' funded by net profits from the National Lottery/Lotto – with grants made valued at some £351 million in 2001/2. However, it is not clear if the latter funding source can or should be seen as 'central government funding' (because of how it was raised and the legal independence of the Fund's governance) or horizontal (because of the specificity of most of the spending in terms of beneficiary categories). (Other Lottery distributors would also be considered out of scope here, because access is not limited to the voluntary sector, and because funding is geared towards specific vertical spending priorities.)

financial allocations discussed in that chapter). But these flows are nonetheless significant here, because they are specifically targeted on the sector, and associ-ated with the self-conscious attempt to build voluntary sector policy per se.

The wider institutional architecture of the central state has also been reformed in a way that is a reflection of the new aspirations for 'joined-up' policy-making and an 'opening up' of the policy process to new actors (Chapter 3; cf. Mulgan, 1999). We know that such new generalist institutions as the Strategy Unit, the Social Exclusion Unit (SEU) and (since 2001) the Neighbourhood Renewal Unit (NRU) – part of the core Executive through being part of the Cabinet Office answering directly to the Prime Minister – have undertaken consultation to a 'mighty' extent (Timmins, 2001: Chapter 21). These have engaged individuals with backgrounds in the voluntary sector in developing diagnoses of 'cross-cutting' problems and suggestions for policy redesign and implementation reform, tending to focus on issues subject area by area. Individuals with voluntary sector backgrounds have deliberately been targeted for involvement in the numerous ad hoc policy reviews that have taken place, including those involving 'task forces' and policy action teams (up to 300 initiated in the first 3 years of the administration).[2]

Moreover, voluntary organizations have been involved in actual implementation on the ground, especially where area-based initiatives involve neighbourhood level delivery (see below). What we can not ascertain using existing data is the overall relative participation rate of each sector in these new structures (as measured, for example, by proportion of partners from each sector represented in design and/or implementation processes). Nor is there apparently systematic evidence on the difference that the voluntary sector has actually made to these processes, or their ultimate outcomes.[3]

In the absence of evidence on the relative impact of voluntary sector involvement in these new institutions, the remainder of this section has modest aims. It simply maps how the most important institutions to have emerged as a direct result of the follow through to the Deakin–Michael agenda have been set in place, and notes how the substance of that agenda has taken shape. We see that while this agenda is to a significant degree concerned with the direct follow through to the Compact, it also reflects concerns that are emerging for voluntary organizations involved in addressing social exclusion, and which relate to local level service implementation (to be considered in more detail under Section 4.4 below).

4.2.1 Implementing the Deakin–Michael agenda

The most tangible way in which the Deakin–Michael agenda has been manifested has been through the initiation of an annual review in the House of Commons of relations between ministers (accompanied by civil servants), 'representatives' of the voluntary sector,[4] and a local government representative or representatives (at two of the three meetings so far undertaken). Five themes have tended to dominate these meetings (and subsequently have been strongly reflected in the Treasury review; HM Treasury, 2002a):

- The variable extent to which the national Compact is actually being complied with by Whitehall departments and other central government bodies. Most systematically, an independent consultant's report on the situation, presented at the 3rd Annual Review, reports 'slow and patchy' progress and low visibility outside a small core of 'enthusiasts'. A wide range of administrative and political difficulties were identified, and diagnosed as stemming from the low status, level of authority and resource capacity of implementing officers within departments, and of the functions associated therewith (Carrington, 2002).[5]

- Progress reporting (initially on the development, and latterly to trace implementation) on 'codes of good practice' (see Box 4.2) – again, with a mixed picture regarding awareness levels and implementation thus far.
- Discussion of whether and how to develop institutional mechanisms for any mediation or dispute resolution regarding the Compact and codes.
- Reporting on the extent of adoption of local and regional versions of Compacts; uneven and slow progress emerges as a source of considerable frustration on the part of politicians in particular. There was also an annoyance that the professional body representing local government was not 'proactive enough' in the process (and no representative had come to one of the meetings, or offered apologies).
- Discussion of the development of voluntary sector – public sector 'partnership' and 'service delivery' relationships more generally at local level, with a strong emphasis on how these were fitting – or failing to fit – with the broader new institutional architecture of joined-up governance.

The monitoring evidence used to track local Compact developments (the fourth theme) has in part come from the Compact Working Group itself and the

---

Box 4.2 Compact codes of good practice

At the time of writing, four codes of good practice have been produced by special subgroups of the Compact Working Group, amounting to just under 100 pages of text:

- A 39-page code on 'funding' effectively seeking the application of Compact general principles into financial relationships and arguing for more long-term funding and support for 'infrastructure'.
- A 19-page code for 'black and minority ethnic' voluntary organizations seeking to involve them more in all respects, and a joint commitment to race equality.
- A 16-page code for 'volunteering'.
- A 15-page code for 'consultation and policy appraisal', urging more systematic involvement throughout the policy process and the offering of 'enough time to be clear about purpose' on the part of government.

Local Government Association, but richer independent research has been important in allowing a more detailed picture to be painted (Craig *et al.*, 2002). The main lessons to emerge from that research have been, first, that the process is time-consuming and depends upon mutual trust between sectors; it could not be rushed, and suggesting fixed timetables was even 'pointless'. Second, there were tensions around the 'fit' and prioritization regarding local Compacts and other new joined-up institutional architecture in many places, particularly 'local strategic partnerships' (see Box 4.3).

Third, these difficulties could be reinforced not only by the disinterest of many 'unconvinced' or 'sceptical' local politicians, but in some locales by active hostility. This stemmed from concerns that Compact development was part of a wider process threatening the power base of local government, and therefore representative democracy.

Finally, 'solutions' were argued to require nurturing by Compact 'champions' within local government, more resources from the state to develop the local voluntary sector's 'capacity', and more inclusivity with regard to the full range of interests at local level (Craig *et al.* 2002: 27–30).[6]

In sum, the process of institution building has developed from early discussions of policy design to a focus on implementation, and a difficult struggle to convert highly general principles into practice has taken shape. This is proving to be a complex, challenging and apparently frustrating process. Not only is there the difficulty for 'enthusiasts', by definition led by those who regularly attend the annual meetings, of winning over the indifferent and the hostile. The process of implementation is also bringing to the surface differences in

---

Box 4.3 Local strategic partnerships and local Compacts

Local strategic partnerships were introduced in 2001 in an attempt to strengthen the new 'joined-up' architecture. Central guidance requires all sectors to be involved in local and neighbourhood level regeneration efforts. The (uneven) voluntary sector participation in this process that was emerging, with encouragement from central government funding via the Community Empowerment Fund in some locales (see Box 4.1; Deakin, 2002) was welcomed by Compact enthusiasts, but at the same time, they argued the LSPs could crowd out attention which might otherwise have been devoted to Compact processes. LSP 'accreditation' procedures have therefore been introduced, to counteract this possibility by requiring local Compact development as a prior condition for the release of central government funds to the LSPs. However, the wording of the requirement is vague to the extent that funds could be released even if Compact development is 'tokenistic', according to at least some protagonists.

interpretation between enthusiasts concerning how, and at what pace, to proceed. The balance between priorities within the agenda is also a contentious point. An emphasis on developing services for those defined by the Government as suffering particularly from social exclusion – in practice, area-based policies in a small number of deprived urban neighbourhoods – has competed for agenda space with priority for less geographically-specific and service-specific Compact and allied issues.

4.3 The New Deal for young unemployed people

A separate body of evidence has also emerged on the design and implement-ation processes concerning another central government policy which has 'horizontal' character: the New Deal for young people (aged 18–24; NDYP henceforth).[7] This is the most significant of a number of 'new deals' for people who have been out of the job market for prolonged periods (6 months on job seeker's allowance in this case). As with the Compact itself, voluntary sector involvement had been discussed prior to the election with national generalist intermediary bodies. There were also pre-election discussions with voluntary sector specialists in training, particularly for people with special needs. It was championed by Gordon Brown as government policy in a blaze of publicity as fundamental to New Labour's 'welfare to work' agenda, with piloting and implementation unfolding from early 1998 onwards.

The NDYP is a useful case to examine not least because, unlike the Compact, it has a clear precedent, and thus a basis for comparison over time: the voluntary sector's extensive involvement in employment and training schemes in the 1980s and 1990s (Moon and Richardson, 1984; Kendall and Knapp, 1996: 143–6). Second, research has examined both the policy design stage and the implementation stage of NDYP as it has affected the voluntary sector.

Unfortunately, as with the wider institutional architecture referred to earlier, available evidence does not allow us to draw substantive conclusions regarding how the voluntary sector option and other options have compared in practice in terms of outcomes, including the perspectives or welfare of 'new dealers' (Prince's Trust and Employment Policy Institute, 1998; Dewson and Eccles, 2000). However, data are available on 'throughput'. The goal specified in New Labour's manifesto pledges was to 'get 250,000 off benefit into work'. This was achieved ahead of time in 2000, and by March 2002, some 283,680 young 'new dealers' were in 'sustained jobs' (Department for Work and Pensions, 2002). There is no consensus as to the specific marginal impact of this scheme (since there is disagreement as to how many of these jobs would have been offered in the absence of the NDYP). Yet its aspiration towards 'holistic' processes involving 'partners' with relevant expertise providing personally focused and sustained attention was widely welcomed by most independent analysts.

For their part, voluntary sector commentators have tended to interpret the new policy emphasis as evidence that the public sector was now more willing to learn from the voluntary sector's own best practice, as it had indeed claimed.

There were several instances where rules and procedures were modified during consultations on the programme's design, and these were welcomed (unpublished research, nd). While the voluntary sector was also deeply implicated in the job creation bureaucracies of the 1970s and 1980s (Addy and Scott, 1987), what was seen to be different about the NDYP in principle was a greater willingness to offer opportunities for agencies to contribute at all stages of the policy process.

Qualitative research on the views of those voluntary agencies most involved, with these actors tending to initially believe that the new regime was an entirely new departure (unpublished research, nd; Patel and Elgar, 1999; Patel, 1999; Cooke, 2000). There was also evidence on the state side that some of the public sector officials with key roles in implementation were developing constructive relationships with the sector in certain locales despite perceived difficulties with 'rigidities' at the regional level of the Employment Service (Dewson and Eccles, 2000).

However, the limited research available also points to serious difficulties. Despite the emphasis commentators have tended to put on change under New Labour, some problems experienced by providers clearly resonate with prior adverse experiences of voluntary organizations in delivering training to government. There were also parallels with well-rehearsed dilemmas associated with local government-led 'contract culture' (to be discussed in the next section). First, smaller groups, particularly those claiming to have expert knowledge about particular local community needs but lacking financial infrastructure, apparently failed to become extensively part of the process. The various adjustments to rules and regulations meant to foster inclusion in the early years were apparently insufficient to allow many of these groups to become involved. A more general, routine complaint not confined to smaller organizations was of 'excessive bureaucracy and paperwork', whatever the claims of the Government to have improved the situation in that regard (Cook, 2000: 11–12).

Second, it was claimed that 'insufficient' financial resources have been made available. The funding entitlement tied to each voluntary sector placement tends to be less than the 'going rate'. In order to pay trainees a 'proper wage', many providers found themselves cross-subsidizing the state, sometimes apparently illegally, given their constitutions (Cartwright and Morris, 2001).[8] Moreover, the appropriateness of the mechanism for provider remuneration was a point of contention. Not only had part of the 'output related funding' formula used to reward voluntary sector providers for 'performance' been linked to a measure of achievement which seemed excessively narrow, but this element was actually given greater emphasis – by fiat – as political imperatives dictated. As the 2001 general election loomed, this was experienced as intensifying pressure to demonstrate that people were quickly moving into jobs, regardless of those individuals' needs. The top-down manner of this adjustment, as much as the poor outcome (trainees in temporary, unsatisfactory jobs inconsistent with enhancing their long-term employability) was widely interpreted as going against the grain of holism. For many organizations, it created a disabling sense that the Government was arbitrarily 'moving the goal posts'. Some claimed they were more vulnerable or strained by this situation than providers in the for-profit sector. This was in part because their implied greater commitment to individuals' needs made it harder for them to 'short change' trainees by inappropriate placement, or discontinuing their involvement. But it was also in part because they were less likely to have the resources to sue the Government for any perceived breach of contract (Cook, 2000: 10–11).

Other difficulties stemmed precisely from the changed context and the climate of very high expectations associated with it. Unpublished research has suggested that particularly in the early stages and despite a myriad of events and fora, significant numbers of voluntary organizations had their expectations dashed regarding the 'openness' of the process. Some felt that a misleading impression had been created at the onset as to what elements of NDYP would be 'negotiable' and what predetermined by central fiat, so that the initiative had been rhetorically portrayed as much less centralized than turned out to be the case in practice.

For their part, politicians and public officials, while impressed by national intermediaries' apparently wide-ranging consultative reach and capacity to raise awareness, seem to have been disappointed by their inability to persuade larger numbers of local members or affiliates, let alone the sector as a whole, to become involved in the 'crusade'. Why was this the case? Some voluntary agencies were simply legally unable to participate (due to their missions), but there were major reservations about the scheme amongst agencies who could have chosen to become involved, but did not. Many of these had been deterred because they expected bureaucratic and funding difficulties – correctly as it turned out, perhaps in some cases having had their fingers burnt under the previous regime and expecting that a change in party political control would not prevent a repeat performance. In addition, several were reportedly unhappy in principle with the scheme's use of sanctions against 'new dealers', even as a last resort, and so were refusing to sign up for philosopical or ideological reasons.

More generally, that the sector was in fact fragmented, tremendously variable at the local level, and not based on hierarchical authority and readily mobilized at speed for national policy implementation seems to have surprised and frustrated many in the public sector. This may have partly been because of simple misunderstanding of the 'loose and baggy' nature of the sector, but it could also have reflected broader political imperatives. Those representing the voluntary sector certainly had an incentive to stress the sector's capabilities, and downplay doubts about the sector's capacity to 'deliver', because this might have jeopardized the wider aspiration to gain status with, and attention from, the state.

4.4 Local governance

In an earlier overview (Kendall and Knapp, 1996), it was possible to examine public policy development regarding the voluntary sector by looking at different tiers of the state in turn, finishing with local government as the pre-eminent point of engagement. However, the insertion of a new layer of institutional architecture by central government to encourage 'joined-up action' oriented towards combating social exclusion has meant that a widening range of policies delivered locally, now increasingly involve local government as one partner amongst many. Significantly, textbooks on local public services increasingly speak of 'local governance' rather than 'local government' (for example, Leach and Percy Smith, 2001). This section therefore attends to both aspects.

4.4.1 Implementing national social exclusion policies locally

In one 'horizontal' domain – area based social exclusion-oriented policy – local government's dominant position has been eroded, and we have seen ever greater interest from central government. Indeed, this has proceeded so far that it now no longer makes sense to think of the locally elected tier of the state as the dominant level of state engagement in many deprived urban locales. The national strategy for neighbourhood renewal now lead by the NRU, the New Deal for Communities, Sure Start and the development of 'action zones' in education, health and employment are all symptomatic of this reconfiguration of power.

While we stressed in Section 4.2 that it is currently not possible to quantify and evaluate the voluntary sector's overall comparative contribution to these processes, researchers have begun to piece together impressions of how this new policy environment has been experienced by local community groups (as opposed to the voluntary sector more generally). Analysts sympathetic to these organizations have tended to welcome the new programmes as further widening opportunities for participation that were already developing in the 1990s under urban policy initiatives, although their sheer number and complexity are said to have generated confusion, 'initiative-itis' and consultation fatigue.

Parallels with the more mixed NDYP actual experiences of involvement are also striking. Despite some notable achievements in meeting headline objectives and the effusive rhetorical encouragement from central government, persistent problems of implementation with adverse effects for the sector have been reported. Aside from some local government actors hostile to change as a threat to their role, blame for this is often laid at the door of self-interested lead departments at both levels of government lacking the incentives, resources or ability to co-operate ('persistent departmentalism'). Claims of 'excessive' burdens of bureaucracy, whereby middle or lower tier 'street level' officials are portrayed as frustrating higher intentions, have been rife. And the familiar criticism of 'tokenism' has repeatedly recurred. Some groups have had the impression that they had been involved only for 'cosmetic' purposes. Relatedly, the output or outcome targets that matter (including those that trigger financial resources) were still apparently typically imposed, not negotiated. They were not developed in such a way as to reflect learning processes at the community level, even with those policies which had claimed to do precisely this (see Taylor, 2001: 99–103; Newman, 2001b).

4.4.2 Implementing statutory local government service responsibilities

While as part of the 'partnership' approach to urban social inclusion oriented policy local government may have lost its dominant position, there remain two local domains in which this tier of the state has continued to act as the policy focal point. In these cases, while ultimately funded in part by central government and only able to act according to the latter's legislative provisions, local government has continued as the dominant actor as far as public resource allocation decisions and steering local policy implementation are concerned.

Most obviously relevant here is the delivery of public services for which local government has retained the lead statutory responsibility. Critical in shaping the current general scope and scale of relations is the national policy legacy bequeathed by the previous Conservative administration in terms of the specific content of local government responsibilities. Of particular importance was the decision to situate lead responsibility for financing and shaping – but not providing – 'community care' more systematically than heretofore at the local government level. As a direct result of this national policy decision and the consequent expansion of local contracting out that followed from it, social services department spending, and funding through contracts, now accounts for more than half of all local authority expenditure on the voluntary sector (cf. Chapter 2). Therefore the set of concerns associated with this particular relationship, which lay at the core of debates on the so-called 'contract culture' during the 1990s, are still salient (see Box 4.4).

Now overlaying and seeking to steer this inheritance, New Labour has introduced changes in the generic mechanisms by which local government is required to discharge these duties, including most significantly a 'Best Value' regime. This has required councils to demonstrate not only economy and efficiency narrowly defined (as applied under the competitive tendering CCT regime of the previous administration in some policy fields), but also 'quality' and compliance with national standards. Challenge, comparison, consultation and competition are the four principles by which local authorities are required to implement this policy (Martin, 2000). This 'Best Value' agenda as implemented at local level is clearly highly relevant to voluntary organizations supported by local government (Blackmore, 2000). Unlike CCT, this is meant to cover all local government services. But, remarkably, its strategic relevance to the voluntary sector has only very recently been recognized from the centre (HM Treasury, 2002: 37), and there is virtually no research specifically addressing its impact on voluntary sector delivery of the public services for which local government is responsible.[9]

4.4.3 'Local democratic renewal'

Local democratic political participation is the other main domain in which local government has remained the critical tier of the state. One of the stockpile of 'big ideas' with which New Labour approached local government was the notion

Box 4.4 The 'contract culture' and the voluntary sector: enduring issues?

'Contract culture' is a somewhat clumsy label for summarizing important aspects of the situation faced by many voluntary organizations involved in delivering local public services in the mid 1990s. Most evidence is available on social care and related services in the aftermath of the 1990 NHS and Community Care Act. The label refers to a cluster of concerns around the increased use of formal contracts and other institutions to govern funding flows and relationships between sectors, and the competitive environment associated with this shift. While New Labour sometimes rhetorically replaces 'competition' with 'partnership', this seems to clash with the requirement of competition as the fourth 'C' under the Best Value regime (see text). Indeed, more generally, the implementation of 'modernization' seems not, in fact, to have involved the sorts of unambiguous rejection of past approaches the rhetoric implies (Newman, 2001, 2001b). We have also seen (Section 4.2) that the Compact, which in one sense was framed in order to 'protect the sector' in this evolving situation, has so far made little impact in local implementation terms.

Concerns from the mid-1990s are therefore of enduring relevance. These include:

- *Formalization*, which can involve potentially the erosion of trust-based relationships, new administrative burdens, and 'over bureaucratization'. However, offsetting potential benefits include higher standards, greater transparency, more predictability, greater realism in expectations and desirable adjustments in status and recognition.
- *Inappropriate regulation*, whereby technical feasibility, economic or political pressures lead to an undue concentration on easily measurable inputs and services, to the potential detriment of valued but intangible or hard to measure outputs and outcomes.
- *Threats to autonomy and goal distortion* where funded organizations are said to face a loss of control over their own operations as a result of getting 'too close' to the state. This could not only compromise the spirit, if not the letter, of their modus operandi, but directly or indirectly influence their willingness or ability to represent important interests to the state. It could also therefore alienate important contributors, including members, volunteers and private funders.
- *Excessive financial insecurity* when contracts and other financial arrangements do not fairly distribute risk between purchasers and providers, and are not designed so as to reflect actual costs of delivery over the lifetime of the service.
- *Erosion of comparative advantage* if the process generates disproportionate transaction costs, and limits agencies' ability to undertake the

range of innovative and participative benefits attributed to them in the literature (see also Chapter 6).

See Kendall and Knapp (1996: 227–35) for sources and more detail. More recent research has continued to examine how these and related policies have been experienced by individual voluntary organizations (Scott *et al.*, 2000; Alcock *et al.*, 1999; Morris, 2000). Overall, the evidence on the actual prevalence of these hypothesised effects tends to be mixed and somewhat inconclusive.

that 'democratic renewal' should be nurtured by developing a much wider range of participative processes than periodic voting alone.

How is this related to the other reforms reviewed, and to the voluntary sector at the local level? An emphasis on democratic participation via the medium of voluntary associations could theoretically have evolved through local Compact negotiation processes. However, we have seen that Compact adoption has been very limited thus far, and in those cases where they have been adopted, it is not clear that this has been a priority. What of the other components of the new horizontal architecture surveyed earlier in this chapter? The encouragement of community group participation as part of the 'joined-up' agenda for addressing social exclusion has been limited to those geographical areas benefiting from area-based programmes, and has essentially acted as a means to the end of improving local services and environments. Moreover, we have seen that participation here, even if it could have involved some political dimension, has been limited.[10]

What about the relevance of the 'democratic renewal' policy itself? It seems that the guidelines for specifically implementing this policy across the country as a whole have spoken essentially to the encouragement of individual citizen involvement rather than voluntary group activities. According to the leading UK researchers on political participation, this emphasis has been 'partly out of [central government's] desire to redress past imbalances, and partly out of a distrust of narrowly focused lobby groups' (Lowndes and Wilson, 2001: 635).

In this context, the extent to which voluntary organizations have been involved in efforts to foster local democracy per se probably therefore still tend to heavily reflect local conditions and inherited local policy legacies, rather than centrally set priorities. How have local authorities used their discretion? A recent attempt to survey the overall political and philosophical approaches of local authorities to the voluntary sector – with fieldwork in the Midlands around the time that New Labour were coming into office – argued that three existing 'viewpoints' could be ascertained (more comprehensive but less up to date is Taylor and Lansley, 1992). Most local authorities' engagement was either incremental and 'ad hoc', involving no explicit policies, or involved accounting for voluntary groups purely to the extent they could contribute particular services. Only a minority had a 'participative/democratic ethos' where there was

> perceived to be value in the very existence of voluntary and community
> organizations which are seen as essential . . . the capacity to provide services
> [was] likely to be a secondary consideration. Many voluntary organizations
> [were] supported because the Council [valued] what they [were] trying to do
> in terms of community representation or development.
>
> (Leach and Wilson, 1998: 8)

Where this ethos prevailed, support for community representation and development could involve deliberate attempts to foster campaigning through grants as a deliberate counterpoint to balance the shift towards service delivery through contracts (cf. Box 4.4); favouring groups with elected committees; and facilitation of access to any enabling networks and funding opportunities available from other tiers of the state (Lowndes and Wilson, 2001: 634).

In practice, the deliberate nurturing of a 'community development' infrastructure involving the appointment of specialist workers, and the creation of consultative fora have often tended to be the most concrete way in which local authorities have pursued this agenda.[11] In some locales, intermediary bodies have also received support from local government to foster networks, and to discharge a 'representative' role. But research suggests this has been controversial. This is partly a reflection of perceived 'narrowness' (intermediaries' lack of capacity to channel relevant expertise and interests), but also because the provision of support for a single voice is seen by some as a cynical means for local government to avoid meaningful general consultation (see Osborne, 2000: 37–9).

4.4.4 The cumulative picture

The distinctions we have tried to make in this section in describing relevant elements of the local policy implementation environment – that is, distinguishing between the 'new generation' of 'joined-up' policies, relationships around local government statutory service responsibilities, and political participation aspects in turn – are a useful starting point. Yet in so doing, we have implicitly followed a 'top-down' logic, cataloguing developments using the categories of government.

In practice, the roles which these policies are seeking to develop separately are often intertwined within voluntary organizations (a theme to which we return in Part II of this volume), which can often mean involvement in multiple policy initiatives. This complex interdependency is a facet of the policy process which needs to be taken into account in any mapping of the reality of policy implementation per se.

Any reasonably complete account therefore needs to examine how the voluntary sector is currently experiencing this cascade of change 'from below' not discretely (programme by programme), but in terms of the combined, cumulative effect. New evidence is becoming available on this topic. As part of a wider programme of ongoing research seeking to examine perceptions of voluntary organizations' contribution to democracy ('willing partners?'), Taylor and colleagues are beginning to paint a composite picture of precisely how these multiple pressures play out. They emphasize variety – by policy field, locality and type and size of organization. However, they do feel able to generalize to a certain degree, and to this extent their findings become relevant to our 'horizontal' account (Taylor *et al.*, 2001a, b; Craig and Warburton, 2001). Some of the themes are summarized in Box 4.5.

4.5 Conclusion

This chapter has reviewed evidence on the implementation of policies which include at least an element of 'horizontality' in the sense of cutting across, and having relevance to, broad swathes of the voluntary sector. Nationally within the voluntary sector, clearly most affected have been 'intermediary bodies'; organizations whose interests have coincided with the 'thematic' approach taken by an array of centrally instigated task forces and policy action teams; and those involved with the delivery of central government priorities via various tiers of the state in order to implement specific national programmes with a significant element of 'horizontality' – such as the New Deal for young people. At the local level the impact is clearly uneven. Horizontal policy may still be perceived as essentially a nonissue in places which are not on the map for area-based social exclusion and regeneration policies, where local Compacts have not been adopted, and where policy pro-activity on the part of local authorities is absent. In other places, however, these policies have multiplied to such an extent that a primary concern is to find ways of making them gel with one another, and avoiding the fatigue associated with 'initiativ-itis'.

Box 4.5 The cumulative picture for local voluntary organizations

Positively, Taylor *et al.* suggest that local policy environments are now often experienced by voluntary agencies as more 'open' than in previous years, and the latter have adopted sophisticated strategies in response to this new situation. Consequently, most organizations feel themselves to be involved in a dynamic ongoing process of adaption and change. However, they also report 'consultation fatigue' and 'lack of real change' to be significant problems. The latter perhaps suggests the persistence of familiar 'contract culture' concerns inherited from the previous administration (cf. Box 4.4). Moreover, in terms of wider democratic processes, Taylor *et al.* argue that the situation is evolving 'creatively' only 'in some pockets' (Taylor *et al.*, 2001b: 26). This seems to confirm our earlier suggestion that a 'participatory democratic' ethos at local level has continued to be the exception rather than the rule in recent years.

What can we conclude from this evidence taken as a collective corpus? Research able to ascertain the social outcomes or consequences that flow from these investments of money and energy has yet to be undertaken. Our conclusions, therefore, are limited to remarks on the process of implementation. In this regard, even at this early stage, implementation looks like a success in some respects. The Prime Minister's vision of a 'bigger' role seems to be unfolding. In aggregate, it seems likely that the scale of voluntary sector participation in horizontal processes in unprecedented – although we cannot gauge its relative contribution, compared with that of other participants, on the basis of existing evidence. The increase of financial flows into the sector specifically for 'horizontal' purposes from central government, as a measure of input, is also significant.

However, bigger is not necessarily better. Implementation has clearly thrown up difficulties from the perspective of involved organizations, some of which seem to be continuities with those experienced under the previous administration. In particular, with regard to relations with central government, we have seen that some problems familiar from the old job creation and training regimes have recurred under the New Deal arrangements. There are continuities at the local government level too. Existing tensions associated with discharging the 'contract culture' and democratic roles in particular have tended to persist 'uncreatively', in Taylor *et al.*'s terminology, for local voluntary organizations. And as far as the *de novo* institutions are concerned, central government 'enthusiasts' have shown signs of frustration, particularly at the slow pace of Compact recognition and adoption both across Whitehall departments and at the local level. Both politicians and bureaucrats seem to have been somewhat surprised and disappointed by the lack of policy engagement evident outside the immediate network of intermediary bodies and other organizations with whom New Labour had already worked in setting the initial agenda.

How, then, is voluntary sector policy distinctive? General aspects of the distinctiveness that seems to flow from the sector's voluntarism – drawing from the material reviewed in this chapter, but also relevant discussion of 'vertical' components of policy covered in later chapters – will be drawn out in Chapter 10. For now, we narrow the issue to explaining one particular sense in which voluntary sector policy, in its horizontal guise, in Britain is perhaps unique. This is the astonishing contrast between the unambiguous and rapid success in agenda-setting experiences reviewed in the previous chapter, and the apparently fraught and drawn out process of implementation charted here. Given the evident shared interests so successfully articulated in the Deakin Commission and the *Getting it Right Together* reviews, and the climate of optimism apparently associated with the launch of the Compact, why is the record some 4 years later so mixed, and why are even the 'enthusiastic' protagonists so much more circumspect now?

Four factors seem to be important. One is simply the broader range of stakeholders involved in implementation. Agenda-setting in the late 1990s involved a self-selecting sample of 'enthusiasts' from the government in waiting and the voluntary sector alike, by definition interested enough to be involved in, and willing to contribute expansively to, that process. Implementation has involved relying on a much wider range of actors. Within government, this has included civil servants from national and regional offices, local officers of local government and local politicians, some of whom have evidently been benignly predisposed towards these policies but many who have not. To a significant degree, antipathy, particularly at the local level, has reflected attitudinal factors, relating to ideology and a perception of interests and roles under threat. Moreover, even those already sympathetic to the values and aspirations espoused – or perhaps in some cases, convinced by the persuasive efforts of the Compact Working Group or others 'enthusiasts' – have faced various institutional barriers, most notably internal 'departmentalism' and associated issues of territoriality. It might be added that the pace of change required just to comply with the raft of centrally mandated objectives has limited the policy space for local government discretionary initiative. Even 'enthusiastic' local government actors wishing to engage with voluntary actors as partners in democracy per se will have found it difficult to promote such efforts. Consultation fatigue can involve both consulters and consultees.

Within the voluntary sector, the process of implementation has involved attempts to engage constructively with organizations, some of whom may have shared the initial enthusiasm of those 'intermediary bodies' who had invested in developing the idea of voluntary sector policy for so long, but some of whom clearly did not. There are a number of reasons for this. Implementation is much more demanding of time and energy. While we saw in Chapter 3 that the consultation exercise associated with agenda design did include a range of events involving quite large numbers of organizations, their 'sunk cost' investment of time and effort was far less extensive than that of intermediaries, and there could thus have been less psychological commitment to the process (Levin, 1997; Jones and Cullis, 2000). For others not involved at all in the agenda-setting phase, pragmatic 'wait and see' attitudes often seem to have prevailed. Some of the early problems of implementation we have reviewed may have been sufficient to put these organizations off, or lead them to withdraw even if their agendas theoretically coincided with the Government's (whereas a higher level of a priori commitment might have seen them persist for longer).

A second factor is the existence of tensions regarding the substance of the agenda which only begin to bite once the details of implementation start to be fleshed out, and decisions regarding priorities made. The most obvious contrast here is between constituting voluntary sector policy as essentially concerned with nationwide support for the sector as a whole; and more specific support, geared towards addressing social exclusion, defined in spatial – essentially local and urban regeneration policy terms. At present, the 'horizontal' agenda appears to be reasonably able to loosely accommodate both strands and the tension is more implicit than explicit. But this latent tension will conceivably come more to the fore as implementation moves forward, and yet more detailed decisions have to be made about competing financial priorities, particularly if public funding largesse contracts in times of fiscal austerity.

A third source of difficulty is that the development of concrete strategies for putting agreed concepts into timely practice has thrown into stark relief contrasts in understandings of policy feasibility, appropriate levels of bureaucracy and differing interpretations of respective roles and responsibilities. To an extent, this may be a reflection of political positioning. For example, ministers' evident aspiration to accelerate local Compact coverage relatively rapidly would be in keeping with essentially political imperatives – the short time-frame of the electoral cycle – and less of a direct concern for the career civil servants, intermediary bodies and researchers who seem to have favoured a longer period.[12] A good example of different understandings of 'responsibilities' which has emerged in implementation is provided by the experiences of the NDYP. The voluntary organizations involved felt misled regarding the extent to which key aspects of policy were negotiable at the design and piloting stage, and were aggrieved that a crucial shift in remuneration procedures occurred without consultation. For their part, politicians and civil servants may have felt that they were legitimately exercising prerogatives to develop responsive policy in the light of changing circumstance, even if this was not popular with this particular set of providers.

Finally, and closely related to the preceding points, we seem to have witnessed widespread unrealistic expectations. 'Enthusiasts' in each sector may have overestimated the capacity of the other to 'carry' their own 'constituents' in actual implementation. For example, the voluntary sector may have attributed too many of its traditional problems in dealing with the state to the political party in control, rather than to the bureaucratic institutions within it. The difficulty and complexity of addressing some of the attitudinal and institutional barriers mentioned earlier may have been given insufficient weight by many voluntary organizations, particularly those who had only ever operated under a Conservative administration.

For its part, there certainly seem to have been 'over-optimistic' expectations on the part of the Government concerning local government's willingness to comply with its aspirations. Many actors at this level seem to feel under siege, on the one hand overrun with an array of new local initiatives, while on the other hand jealous of their power base and with a deeply ingrained suspicion of the centre.

As far as the voluntary sector is concerned, the Government was clearly too quick to take the enthusiasm of intermediary and lead bodies as 'representative' of sector-wide attitudes towards its horizontal policies. The voluntary sectors' horizontal specialists, for whom the opportunity to develop these initiatives has been a major source of legitimacy, were always going to be much more committed for reasons of self-interest than organizations in the sector at large. But the situation also seems to reflect a general underestimation on the part of both Government and horizontal voluntary sector, of the unpredictability of the sector by virtue of its sheer diversity and complexity. This fundamental fact is one to which the book returns in the final chapter.

Notes

1   Some reviewers of an earlier version of this book took the view that devoting any attention to the Compact at all in 2002 was inappropriate because of this 'crowd out'

effect. I am grateful to these critics for pushing me to be more explicit concerning why the Compact is worth analysing.

2 Most recently, the Strategy Unit's (2002) *Private Action, Public Benefit* report focused specifically on the 'charities and wider not-for-profit' sector. Prior to this, as far as new ad hoc committees are concerned, three reviews had focused directly on the voluntary sector and related activities per se: the report of the Better Regulation Task Force on charities, and the reports of Policy Action Team 9 and Lord Warner on 'active community' issues. Other reviews have been of concern for the voluntary sector by virtue of their particular policy topic, such as homelessness, special needs education or welfare to work. The sector's involvement in the latter reviews is therefore 'horizontal' more in terms of the institutional mechanism than in terms of the subject matter or topic.

3 An evaluation of the overall impact of these new initiatives per se is beyond the scope of this chapter. Moreover, it is still too early in the implementation process to reach conclusions. At an ESRC seminar on the 'third way' in 2001, there was no agreement between experts concerning the net impact of New Deal and Social Exclusion programmes. However, see Richards and Smith, 2001: 148–54; Timmins, 2001; and Hennessy, 2001, for respectively broadly negative and positive early assessments, despite the paucity of evidence, on the processes concerned.

4 Typically, 'representatives' have included those involved in a 'Compact Working Group' (funded by the Home Office, and with a small secretariat at NCVO), interested other mainstream intermediary bodies, and a few less well-established groups. Significantly, as noted in the previous chapter, Sir Kenneth Stowe has taken the chair of the Compact Working Group.

5 Others have more broadly diagnosed this situation as a problem of low *political* status. Unlike the Strategy Unit, SEU and NRU, the Active Community Unit is not linked directly to the Cabinet Office. For some, this helps to explain the ACU's reputation for ineffectiveness in recent years, as mentioned in Section 4.1.

6 More recently, Hems (2002) has also argued that progress in Compact development at the local level has compared poorly with the national level, particularly in terms of the development of codes of good practice. His positive portrayal of the national Compact is in marked contrast with Carrington (2002), although to an extent this seems to reflect the different foci of the studies. In particular, Hems (2002) gives particular weight to the 'mainstreaming' achievements in terms of agenda-setting as discussed in Chapter 3, while Carrington (2002) attends essentially to subsequent implementation process.

7 The NYDP could be considered 'horizontal' in three senses. First, 'holistic' design through attempting to 'join up' the inputs of various central government departments. Second, the process of designing and evaluating the New Deal has involved engaging generalist intermediary or infrastructure organizations, as well as specialist training providers. Third, in delivery, as with training schemes developed under previous administrations, the involved organizations have included not only training and unemployment specialists, but other organizations which have diversified into this field from outside, including social care and environmental groups.

8 Research has also attributed funding difficulties to a problem with unscrupulous administrators (apparently tending to be in the for-profit sector) actually completely withholding the placement fees due to voluntary providers. Although an innovation fund and other grants have been made available within NDYP partly as a response to these concerns, they were felt to be insufficient (Cooke, 2000).

9 The 'Best Value' agenda is also being applied to social housing, and thus involves central government responsibilities too. Exceptionally, in this one case, national research specifically on how the voluntary sector 'performs' compared to council-owned housing is now available, and is drawn upon in Chapter 7.

10 The difference between participation in tackling social exclusion via 'joined-up' policy at the local level, and more wide-ranging political participation as discussed here is problematic. This is because the definition of 'political' is contested (Maier, 1987). However, participation as part of area-based social exclusion policy seems to be necessarily narrower, because it presupposes an agenda focused on spatial deprivation, and rules out wider political concerns which cannot be accommodated within that frame of reference.

11 Birmingham City Council seems to have been the best researched example of such an approach in recent years (see Maloney *et al.*, 2000, 2001; more generally see Mayo, 1994; Broady and Hedley, 1989).

12 Commenting on an earlier draft of this chapter, Howard Glennerster suggested that this tension between short-term political imperatives and longer-term 'apolitical' concerns has also been evident in the development of health action zones, the area-based policy programmes jointly focusing on health and social exclusion.

Part II

Voluntary sector impacts and outcomes

5 Introduction to Part II

- **This part of the book is concerned with the 'impact' or socio-economic and political consequences of voluntary sector activity.**
- **International third sector theory, suggesting the sector's 'functions'/strengths and 'failures'/weaknesses, guides the approach.**
- **It also is important to situate these understandings against the evolving political and policy background. Policy legacies are a significant component of this context.**

5.1 From inputs and processes to consequences

The first part of this volume focused on the most important 'input' resources, and cross-cutting or 'horizontal' policy processes, relating to the voluntary sector in Britain. The overall scope and scale of the UK voluntary sector was examined, set it in comparative context internationally (with reference to the third sector abroad) and domestically (compared with the for-profit and public sectors), noting the significant changes that took place during the course of the 1990s. The book then addressed how and why, at the 'horizontal' level, voluntary sector policy has come to the fore in recent years, and looked at the somewhat piecemeal evidence that has become available on the nature and effects of relevant institution-building processes that has been associated with that development.

This part of the book goes beyond such description and offers a preliminary and tentative account of the actual and claimed consequences or 'impacts' of voluntary sector activities. This is a difficult and controversial step to take. Voluntary organizations are often attempting to meet social needs which are ill-defined, hard to measure, of long gestation and high complexity. Many of these problems and needs involve 'fuzzy technology' with contested understandings of the very nature of 'production' (Kendall and Knapp, 1999, 2000). These can include what have become known as the 'wicked issues', recently given so much emphasis in social exclusion debates (Newman, 2001b; Leach and Percy-Smith, 2001), and where resonance with voluntary sector interests is clear (Billis, 2001). But the sector is also trying to meet a multiplicity of needs which do not involve such a clear overlap with Government priorities, as with many social problems which are not spatially concentrated in poor neighbourhoods. For example, special needs confined to a few individuals, which have not been recognized as public policy prerogatives or been prioritized for public funding purposes.

While problematic, intensifying demands for evidence on 'impacts' will not go away, as witnessed by references to the issue of 'value added' in the recent Treasury review (HM Treasury, 2002). Realization of the sheer scale of inputs naturally raises such questions as: 'So what? What difference does it make? How does the voluntary sector compare with other sectors?' While the 1990s agenda development phase apparently proved possible without answering these questions in a systematic way, high-profile 'horizontal' implementation has raised the stakes. Both funders and recipients alike are looking for a firmer rationale for the new 'horizontal' public sector investment of money and time described in the previous chapters, as well as the inherited 'vertical' flows within specific policy fields. There is an aspiration to underpin with evidence the general sense that the sector, pace Hobson (1999), is not just another growth 'industry' but is indeed making particular and distinctive contributions to society.

How can such a variegated and complex landscape be approached? While inputs can be summarized in monetary terms, and were indeed aggregated to construct the statistical profile offered in Chapter 2, attaching monetary values to the actual 'products' of the voluntary sector, while having enormous advantages in terms of simplicity, is much more difficult to justify theoretically and methodologically.[1] Foster *et al.* (2001) offer a brave attempt to apply such an approach, but in the process side step rather than address a whole raft of fundamental questions. This includes the debate over whether it is appropriate to interpret the value of the sector purely in terms of willingness (backed by ability) of donors and recipients to pay if criteria other than allocative efficiency are also relevant to decision-making (see below). Even if such a narrow approach is accepted, perhaps on the pragmatic grounds that it is one approach to one dimension of a complex problem, 'technical' problems remain. These include the issue of whose values to include when information asymmetry problems are rife, and in circumstances when actions are not predicated on well-formed, a priori 'consumer' preferences (see Weisbrod, 1996).[2]

Alternative analytic approaches include those also within the 'positivist' social science tradition, but measuring benefits in a wider way while not attempting to attach monetary values; and 'social constructionist' perspectives which seek to explicate the multiple meanings of inputs and outputs developed by different stakeholders, rather than reach an overall assessment. A theoretical framework for taking the first route has been developed in the UK, but not applied (Kendall and Knapp, 2000), while some work in the second tradition has been undertaken in North America (see Kendall and Knapp, 1999, for a review, and more recently see Cutt and Murray, 2000). There are also burgeoning literatures on evaluation from within management science and allied traditions (see Paton, 2003), and tailor-made approaches for setting financial alongside activity data are increasingly being proposed by accounting and finance specialists in Britain and overseas (Palmer and Randall, 2002).

The approach in this part of the book is of a different order from these studies, and can be thought of as eclectic meta-analysis, rather than evaluation within a specific disciplinary frame of reference. It is meta-analysis in the sense that it considers a range of evidence as collected and interpreted by others, using international third sector theory as a frame of reference; and it is eclectic because an attempt is made to attend to the role of institutions and the political discourse associated therewith as 'productive' ingredients in a long-term cumulative process, as well as drawing on the discrete 'snap shots' provided by particular social science research studies, as and when those are useful in assessing particular aspects of impact.

As mentioned in Chapter 1, the following chapters then seek to explore the question of consequences in a number of ways, drawing on both the approaches suggested by the 'impact' component of the international comparative non-profit sector project, and wider policy theoretic considerations. The former tends to abstract from the political process and essentially approaches the topic in a static way:

- What are the claimed and actual contributions of the voluntary sector (Chapter 6)?
- What are its drawbacks (Chapter 6)?
- How are these strengths and weaknesses assumed to be, or demonstrably realized or otherwise at the level of particular fields (Chapters 7–9)?

The latter, policy theoretic concerns guide us towards consideration of the voluntary sector's political situation. Rather than simply abstracting from the context of policy and politics in which voluntary action takes place, this dimension, specific to the UK study, deliberately focuses upon it. It considers how that context seems to shape understandings and possibilities, and the extent to which changes within it have consequences for the voluntary sector. This book recognizes and seeks to take into account how perceptions of, and attitudes towards voluntary sector roles vary as policy environments vary. It seeks to address:

- Why and how do continuities and changes in understandings of roles reflect wider rhetorical debates and concomitant political developments (Chapter 6)?
- At the level of particular fields of activity, how do contrasting vertical policy legacies shape the way in which contributions and weaknesses are currently understood and evolving (Chapters 7–9)?

The remainder of this introduction first describes how the international comparative study was used to approach the subject. We then outline the general policy theoretic concerns which prompted the addressing of the two additional questions posed above. These considerations were important in providing the motivation for the book to incorporate a more 'critical', political dimension.

5.2 The comparative nonprofit sector project impact study methodology

Once countries had been selected for this part of the study,[3] there were a number of steps to the international project's impact evaluation, as summarized in Table 5.1.

Most of these countries, including the UK, did not, however, undertake the final 'case study' element of the project, in part because of prevailing resource constraints. Therefore, there were essentially three steps in these countries, which are briefly considered in turn.

5.2.1 *Identifying contributions and drawbacks*

This and the following step approached the 'impact' question regarding what we referred to as a 'horizontal' basis in earlier chapters. Thus, the unit of analysis was the voluntary sector as a whole, and 'the underlying hypothesis was that the nonprofit form creates certain propensities or possibilities that encourage or allow these organizations to perform particular social roles, but also make them prone to particular weaknesses, more regularly than other types of institutions, such as businesses or state agencies' (Salamon *et al.*, 2000a: 4). The mode of analysis in this first step was a US-based literature review of the third sector theoretical literature, complemented by inputs from other participating countries including the UK. 'Widely cited potential contributions and drawbacks' were:

* A **service role** geared particularly towards production in spheres of economic activity where markets and governments 'fail' because of a combination of public good properties and trust dependency (see Chapter 1, Box 1.1), but also the inability to pay of some individuals in need. Even where sectors

Table 5.1 Impact analysis steps

Task		Unit of analysis	Mode of analysis
I	Site selection	Countries	Data analysis
II	Identity contributions and drawbacks	Sector	Literature review/interviews
III	Validate contributions and drawbacks	Country	Literature review/interviews
IV	Measure contributions and drawbacks	Policy field	Literature review, expert interviews, focus groups
V	Explore contributions and drawbacks	Agency	Case study inquiries

Source: Adapted from Salamon *et al.*, 2000a, Table 1.

apparently co-exist in providing the 'same' services, the literature predicts differences below the surface. The more positive aspects[4] could include 'higher quality' because of the absence of financial incentives to cut corners (suggested by Hansmann's (1980) 'contract failure' approach), or positive opportunities for 'stakeholder control' (Ben-Ner and Van Hoomissen, 1993); greater 'equity' or, perhaps more specifically, 'responsiveness to need' because of constitutional goals, self-selection of more 'sympathetic' management into this sector, or access to voluntarism; lower cost, theoretically associated particularly with voluntarism; and capacity to specialize due to hypothesized 'community embeddedness'.

Three other roles were crystallized and elegantly stated, particularly in the pioneering international comparative studies of Ralph Kramer (1981, 1993), although in general the reason why the voluntary sector should have a comparative advantage over other sectors in each case is less clearly articulated than in the case of the above:

- An innovation role wherein the voluntary sector is anticipated 'to fulfil in the public sphere the same kind of innovative role that small businesses play in the private sphere [through a combination of absence of the profit motive and because compared to the public sector it is] more able to take risks and available to anyone with an idea' (Salamon *et al.*, 2000: 6).
- An advocacy role in which voluntary organizations link individuals to the broader political process (embracing 'campaigning' and user-level advocacy in British parlance).
- An expressive and leadership development role involving, following Kramer, 'acting as a value guardian of voluntaristic, particularistic and sectarian values, a voluntary agency is expected to promote citizen participation, develop leadership, protect interests of social, religious, cultural or other minority groups' (Kramer, 1981: 9).

A final role has come to prominence particularly as a result of the work of Robert Putnam, first in Italy and then the US (Putnam, 1993, 2000) although it also has precedents in extant strands of the international third sector literature:

- A community-building role, whereby the sector is claimed to contribute not just to diversity reinforcement, but to social and political integration too. This involves the generation of 'social capital'. In Putnam's increasingly influential formulations, this is said to involve the fostering of trust between people either with similar backgrounds and values ('bonding social capital') or cutting across such divisions ('bridging social capital'); the creation of habits of reciprocity; and the reinforcement of socially productive norms.

The hypothesized drawbacks, basically as originally formulated by Salamon (1987) in a widely read contribution to the literature, include:

- Particularism, whereby responsiveness to group concerns can have the downside of also being discriminatory or exclusionary.

- Paternalism, whereby the lack of rights-based resource allocation can potentially leave service recipients with a sense of dependency.
- Excessive amateurism or professionalism either because 'over-reliance' on volunteers or on paid staff means that the appropriate skills mix cannot be realized for a given level of output, and/or because the requisite labour is by its very nature less easy to steer with either monetary rewards or public sanction. The theoretical result could be that the 'scaling up' to an efficient size can be difficult or impossible.
- Resource insufficiency, generalizing the problem of amateurism to other inputs. This may also be linked to the 'free rider' problem which emerges because of the public good properties of the outputs being considered (cf. Chapter 1, Box 1.1). A connection to the broader macro-economy can also be made: to the extent the sector relies on private contributions, it would be anticipated to suffer from an inability to handle economic cycles.
- Problematic accountability involves the most explicit comparative perspective in the literature as far as weaknesses are concerned. It is argued that there are no strong mechanisms to match the disciplines provided by pressures to maximize shareholder value in the for-profit sector, on the one hand, and the democratic accountability mechanism provided by Parliament and public scrutiny committees in the public sector, on the other.

5.2.2 'Validating' and 'measuring' contributions and drawbacks

The second and third steps required national researchers, first to review the evidence in their country regarding whether 'the hypothesised roles and vulnerabilities . . . were recognizable as expectations of the nonprofit sector, and if so how widely recognised they were' (Step II, Table 5.1); and second to 'determine whether nonprofit organizations actually deliver them' (Step III, Table 5.1). The pursuit of these questions in the UK constitutes an important part of Chapters 6–9 in this volume.

Step IV then involved the selection of particular (vertical) fields on the grounds of task manageability, and

> to ensure that the results were not biased towards a particular role, the choice of fields was deliberately constrained so that each country identified a field to correspond to the following orientations:
>
> - traditional human services;
> - promotion of economic rights and opportunity;
> - promotion of human rights or free expression.
>
> (Salamon *et al.*, 2000a: 10)

Thus, the unit of analysis was the field or 'subfield'. The mode of analysis was a combination of literature review, analysis of available data, personal interviews and focus group sessions. Table 5.2 shows how these choices were made in particular countries.

Table 5.2 Country selection: impact study fields

Traditional human services			Economic opportunity				Expression and rights		
Education	Health	Social care	Micro-enterprise	Community development	Social housing	Other	Environment	Culture and arts	Other
Colombia	Argentina	Japan	Colombia	Ireland	Netherlands	Argentina	Colombia	France	Ireland
US		Ireland	Japan	Israel	**UK**	Australia	Japan	Australia	Israel
Netherlands		Israel		Romania		France	Netherlands		Romania
		Australia		US			**UK**		
		Romania							
		France							
		UK							

Source: Adapted from Salamon *et al.*, 2000a.

In the UK case, the chosen fields were:

- social housing as a promoter of economic opportunity;
- care and support for older people as a traditional human service;
- environmental activity as a promoter of expression/rights.

These choices were motivated by a combination of pragmatism, theoretical interest and policy salience. First, in all three cases, either the author was already involved in relevant research, or benefited from sustained assistance from other leading researchers on the particular fields in question. Thus, the mixed economy of care for older people was a longstanding research interest of the author; while colleagues at LSE housing, and the Centre for the Study of Social and Political Movements at the University of Kent at Canterbury contributed at all stages of the research process in the social housing and environmental field cases respectively. This ranged from the desk-based literature review, through fieldwork (including identification of appropriate stakeholders and carrying out focus groups) to acting as participants in the quasi-Delphi reviewing of chapter drafts. Appendix 2 summarizes the balance of stakeholder categories and the timing and process for the primary qualitative element of data gathering which applied in each field.

Second, theoretically, we were particularly interested to gather evidence and arguments concerning the comparative contribution of the voluntary sector with reference to the public and for-profit sectors. In these three fields, all three sectors co-exist, at least in terms of some of their more measurable activities, such as discharging the service provision role. While this emphasis tended to make the research more demanding – and in many ways much more complex, and also less 'consensual' in its conclusions than it might have been had the issue been sidestepped – it also connected our findings more readily to the international third sector theoretical literature. As Chapter 1 (Box 1.1) noted, much of this literature seeks to portray the sector with reference to other sectors. Moreover, framing the issues as far as possible in this way was not just a theoretical curiosity: it was also in keeping with the current aspiration of policy-makers to find ways of gauging the 'added value' of the voluntary sector, a consequence at least in part of the policy mainstreaming described in Chapter 3 (Blackmore, 2002; HM Treasury, 2002a).

Third, these fields have been amongst the most fascinating in 'vertical' policy terms in recent years. As Chapter 2 already noted, social housing and social care (which includes care and support for older people) have been particularly dynamic areas of economic growth in the voluntary sector in recent years. While paid employment has not grown quite so spectacularly in the environmental field, as Chapter 9 will show, its membership base has expanded quite dramatically, and this area now accounts for more members than almost all other associational fields. Getting below the surface of these shared growth trends reveal very different policy situations, however. Central government legislative from the mid-1970s onwards have been catalytic in the social care and housing cases, but with contrasting institutional arrangements in each case, not least in terms of the tiers of the state involved, the character of sectoral relationships, and the timing, forms and routes taken by public expenditure. In the environmental field, by contrast, the voluntary sector, while increasingly involved in policy delivery, has had a particularly high profile in actually constructing and shaping an agenda which had previously simply not existed. At the same time it has been particularly prominent too in shaping international and European policy debates and policy choices, as well as national and subnational policies. These policy inheritances are not merely historical curiosities, but shape the current character and capacities of the sector in each case, an issue whose theoretical relevance the next section addresses.

5.3 Accounting for political context: policy theoretic considerations

At an early stage of exploring the literature on the voluntary sector's roles at both the sector ('horizontal') and field ('vertical') levels, it became clear that understandings of these contributions in terms of both 'expectations' (the focus of stage III) and actual delivery (the focus of stage IV) were bound up with the political process. Discourse in this area has clearly developed not only because social science and social policy evidence was slowly accumulating over time, gradually being reflected in more sophisticated research accounts. There was also change in the approaches of politicians and practitioners, as reflected in rhetoric and practice, which have co-evolved with research. It was therefore decided to explore how understanding of the voluntary sector's consequences may be linked to rhetoric, as well as discussing comparative research evidence.

In part, this follows directly from the logic of Part I. We have seen that the voluntary sector 'horizontal' policy agenda in the 1990s was driven by developments in the 'political stream' in combination with research evidence. The political beliefs that lie behind this trend, as expressed in rhetoric, were important components of the policy environment within which voluntary organizations were and are embedded. In discussing the catalysts of policy mainstreaming and experiences of implementation, we have already referred to the relevance of ideology. What we seek to do here is to make such linkages more explicit in terms of protagonists' understandings of outcomes, as opposed to processes. Can we recognize a shared understanding of the voluntary sector's impacts in the political domain? How does this relate to the research evidence? Has political understanding evolved to reflect the ideological and political factors identified in Part I?

But does rhetoric actually matter? Is it not only actions that count? After all, talk is cheap. Rhetoric is only one part of the picture, not least because, as we have seen in the previous chapter, the actors who make rhetorical claims are not necessarily in a position to fully implement their aspirations. Or perhaps rhetoric could be dismissed as having a deliberate function – but a purely manipulative one, masking the 'real' intentions of policies, and seeking to give the impression that 'something is being done' with what are in reality inherently insoluble problems (Seibel, 1990)? Indeed, in our earlier study (Kendall and Knapp, 1996) we argued that precisely this seemed to be the case with the voluntary sector's involvement in employment and training schemes in the 1980s and early 1990s.

5.3.1 Why talk isn't cheap (now)

However, there is good reason to believe that rhetoric is significant – and needs to be analysed if processes and consequences are to be understood in a reasonably rounded way. First, Seibel's 'shunting yard' theory, at least in this crude form involving exploitative politicians, naive recipients and a duped public at large, does not seem tenable at the current time. The sheer scale of the economic investment in the relationship between the two sectors suggests that there must be more to it than this: resources are flowing not predominantly to low political priority areas, but to a range of mainstream social welfare services in a context in which public expectations are high, and known to be high by politicians. [5]

Second, one of the consequences of the mainstreaming of horizontal voluntary sector policy is precisely that talk is no longer 'cheap' in this aspect of policy – in a political sense. As long as political discourse was essentially an argument about the relative merits of the state and the market, this may have been the case. But New Labour's very identity is, as we have seen, now bound up with its relationship with the voluntary sector, and its politicians choose to refer to the importance of its role in major speeches concerning the party's 'project'.[6] If very obvious gaps were to become apparent between the claims made in such speeches and the actual development of policy, this could be seized upon as evidence that the party was failing to live up to its electoral promises on a fundamental point of principle.

In addition, there are other reasons for examining rhetoric, which are not just a consequence of the current high-stakes situation that has arisen as a result of New Labour's aspirations at this particular moment in time. They follow from the recognition that rhetoric plays a key role in policy argumentation in general relating to evaluative claims in public policy. Particularly when we are dealing with contested definitions and initial problem diagnoses, high complexity in the measuring outcomes and opaque 'technologies' (the process of turning inputs into outputs) – precisely the conditions we have noted tend to prevail in this field – social science evaluative evidence is never going to be definitive. The issues are 'trans-scientific', since they are:

> neither purely technical nor purely political . . . questions of fact that can be stated in the language of science but are, in principle or practice, unanswerable [or at least, not definitively answerable] by science.
>
> (Weinberg, 1972, cited in Majone, 1989: 3)

This applies particularly in the case of efforts to gauge the comparative worth of different sectors. There will always be room for argument concerning claims reached by evaluative research of this kind. This can be demonstrated by a theoretical example. Suppose an evaluation reached the conclusion that sector A was 'performing' better than sector B on some criterion, say cost-effectiveness, in a particular local public service activity. One might *prima facie* expect that, in a policy environment geared towards such a goal – and a high premium on this criterion is certainly characteristic of the current 'Best Value' agenda (cf. Chapter 4) – a policy which favoured B directly or indirectly might be reconsidered. For example, opening up a grants regime previously open only to sector B to be accessible to sector A would seem to be a policy option for increasing that local public service's cost-effectiveness.

However, even if such a study passed some basic 'quality threshold' in terms of 'scientific' robustness and validity, it is hard to envisage circumstances in which a credible argument could not be made that the results were somehow 'misleading' for policy purposes. Perhaps the claim would be made that the 'wrong' definition of sectors had been used and the starting assumptions of the evaluation inappropriate; that the results were 'not transferable' outside the particular context in which they had been undertaken; that they were 'out of date' and circumstances had now changed, rendering them 'irrelevant'; that there were dimensions of effectiveness that were intangible or difficult to measure, and so had to be excluded – but which if included, would have altered the results; that the time frame of the study was too short, and that a longer period of evaluation would have reversed the result, and so on. In situations like these, the role of persuasion, including a rhetorical element not reducible to a 'scientific evidence base' alone, is central (Majone, 1989).

5.3.2 *Policy legacies, path dependencies and the voluntary sector*

If the foregoing considerations suggest that attending to rhetoric should be a necessary condition for understanding the way in which voluntary sector impacts should be understood, this is not sufficient. At any one point in time, the policy environment in which understandings of impacts are situated is constituted not just by the content and implications of the rhetorical claims of 'political' actors – including voluntary sector stakeholders themselves in our case – but also by the repertoire of discourse, institutions and resource commitments inherited from the past.

It was stressed in Part I that the recent and current policy situation of voluntary sector policy in the late 1990s is not just a reflection of New Labour initiative. It was also constituted by the institutional 'groundwork' laid down by 'horizontal' actors from the late 1970s to the early 1990s (Chapter 3), and the legacy of evolving relationships between the different tiers of the state (Chapter 4). What is being claimed here is an extension of that claim from the policy processes already discussed to outputs or outcomes. That is to say, contemporary understandings concerning the voluntary sector's impact involve both current rhetoric and argument, as well as being shaped in significant ways by commitments made, and institutions established, both recently and at previous points in historical time.

This will be as important in particular fields as in sector-wide analysis. Indeed, as suggested in Chapter 1, the stuff of policy for most voluntary organizations flows predominantly from their particular ('field-specific') interests and concerns. These proximate policy legacies shape attitudes and beliefs about such basic facets of each sector as their comparative trustworthiness and capabilities on the demand side; they underpin particular patterns of supply within and across sectors; and they feed into culture as reflected in the shared understandings and assumptive worlds that exist in sectoral relationships.

Why is this the case? The ubiquity of path dependencies is now well recognized across broad swathes of the economy and social policy domains (see Chapter 1, Box 1.2). But are there reasons to believe they might be especially prevalent where the voluntary sector is involved? Pierson (2000a,b) has recently claimed that the impacts of path dependencies are particularly significant in political and public policy life in general, and two of his three arguments for why this is so seem of particular relevance to voluntary sector policy.[7] First, as with political life and state institutions in general, public and quasi-public actions and services are involved. Such services necessarily involve, partly as a corollary of their nonexcludability and nonrivalry properties (Chapter 1, Box 1), high set-up costs. There are thus de facto barriers to movement in and out of the field. In the absence of coercion, reliance must typically be placed heavily on voice (rather than exit, or a balanced combination of exit and voice) to engineer change in institutions (Hirschman, 1970). This line of argument also ties in with the earlier point concerning the significance of persuasion and rhetoric here.

Second, Pierson argues that 'complexity and murkiness' characterizes state policy institutions, and these would also seem to apply in the voluntary sector policy case. Chapter 1 noted how third sector theory has diagnosed problems of asymmetric information as typically characteristic of the fields of activity where voluntary organizations operate, and the issues of fuzzy technology and 'wicked issue' opacity in policy terms were mentioned earlier. Precisely when such conditions apply, Pierson argues that individual policy actors are 'heavily biased in the way they filter information into existing mental maps. Confirming information tends to be incorporated, while disconfirming information is filtered out' (2000a: 79). This would include beliefs concerning which institutions facilitate the generation of trust which the complexity of the situation demands.

Both ingredients point to the durability of voluntary sector policy institutions. Entry and exit from policy fields involving established voluntary organizations may tend to be less frequent than would have been the case if the relevant services were simple and private. On the supply side, high levels of diversity could be expected to result, as any new entrants that are able to organize would tend to add to, rather than supercede, incumbents' provision. In the case of charities, legal conventions would seem to further reinforce tendencies towards stability and co-existence by making it difficult for organizations to cease their operations. By also suggesting that potential new entrants to a given field of human need should not seek to compete with other charities or 'duplicate' their services, charity law also seems to attenuate competitive pressures (Kendall and 6, 1994; Leat, 1993).

In total, not only are rhetorical claims of some significance, but there is a bias towards policy adjustment through voice and persuasion rather than exit or competition seemingly build into the system. The chapters in this part of the book try to reflect these policy theoretic considerations in three major ways. First, in the following chapter, the static description of horizontal impacts is supplemented by an examination of how political rhetoric concerning those impacts has evolved in recent years, and show how new research has been geared towards these considerations. Methodologically, the evidence base for this section has been an analysis of how the content of the political discourse and complementary recent research has changed over the past decade. Second, in the two 'field-specific' chapters where policy is relatively 'mature' (social care and housing) we offer an initial account of the 'policy legacy' that has constituted the context within which arguments concerning impacts have developed, look at how beliefs about each sector's roles and capabilities have evolved, while also being shaped by historical policy events, and show how this has tended to bequeath an extraordinarily diverse set of organizations in each case. As the chapters proceed, functions and weaknesses are discussed following the 'generalizing' logic of the international comparative project, but conscious also of the enduring relevance of policy legacies, we try to attend to supply side diversity to the extent space constraints allow.

These chapters also seek to reflect the 'trans-scientific' nature of the field by exposing, rather than suppressing contrasts in understanding evident in the literature, and differences in the perspectives of our 'experts' or 'policy insiders' (to the extent these differences are 'political', we are thus attending to 'low politics' in these chapters).

Notes

1 As we noted in Chapter 2, attaching a monetary value to volunteers as 'inputs' is controversial too. This is in part because it is believed either to be inappropriate to use such 'reductionist' language at all or because this language is accepted, but volunteering is argued to be an output or outcome rather than an input. See Kendall and Knapp (2000) for further discussion.

2 The difficult problems of principle and design in the Foster *et al.* (2001) study are aggravated by the limited nature of the primary data which the researchers utilized to construct estimates in their empirical application. To generate a national estimate, they were forced to deploy some truly 'heroic' assumptions, most notably that hostel services for homeless people could be taken as representative of all activities in the voluntary sector. Despite these and other limitations, this clearly deserves to be seen as a pioneering, unique and under-recognized study.

3 At the time of writing, eleven countries had undertaken some or all of the impact study. However, it is expected that 'at least thirty countries' will eventually apply this approach (Salamon *et al.*, 2000: 3).

4 The negative aspects of service provision suggested by third sector theory are identified below in discussing 'hypothesized drawbacks'.

5 Seibel's original example was homes for victims of domestic violence – a pressing social need, but not on the same scale and thus of the political significance of the most important policy fields discussed in this book.
6 In opposition, the Conservatives are now also trying to 'recreate' themselves in a more voluntary sector friendly vein. In an attempt to distance themselves from too harsh a Thatcherite image, one aspect of 'caring' which they have chosen to develop has been ideological support for voluntary sector interests (Hague, 2000).
7 The third of Pierson's rationales for the pervasiveness of path dependencies in political life does not apply, at least in principle, to voluntary sector policy: the use of political authority to completely foreclose exit. Voluntary sector policy is in fact different from classic state policy precisely in being underpinned by voluntarism rather than fiat.

6 Overall voluntary sector impacts
Research and rhetoric in the UK

- **The functions or strengths attributed to the third sector in the international theoretical literature are familiar claims in the UK. But some of these claims do not always stand up to critical scrutiny.**
- **Recognition of failures or weaknesses are also evident in the British case.**
- **Political rhetoric in recent years has been selective in drawing upon the body of research evidence. There is therefore a 'motherhood and apple pie' flavour to much contemporary political debate.**

6.1 Introduction

This chapter has two main aims. First, to offer a broad overview of the overall consequences that have been associated with the voluntary sector in general in the UK, guided by the framework provided by stage 1 of the comparative nonprofit sector project 'impact study'. Here, the theoretical frame of reference is nonprofit or third sector theory as developed in the international literature that has emerged over the past 30 or so years (as referred to initially in Chapter 1, and whose relevance to impacts was highlighted in the introduction to this part of the book). The project's emphasis has been on enabling a static comparison between countries at one moment in time, the second half of the 1990s. Sections 6.2 and 6.3 therefore diagnose how the UK situation 'fitted' in terms of the comparative international framework applied in that study at that time, implicitly focusing on continuities and abstracting from political context.

However, as stressed in earlier chapters, evidence and argument on the voluntary sector's situation is politically embedded, and has evolved as political conditions have changed. Accordingly, Section 6.4 addresses the second main aim of the chapter: it tries to show how recent political rhetoric on 'impacts' is related to the more 'objective' understanding that emerges from the research materials reviewed. Both the content of general parliamentary debate, and the particular position of the most powerful New Labour figures are considered. We see that political rhetoric has drawn selectively and with changing emphases over time – since 1996 – on the accumulated stock of concepts and evidence identified in Sections 6.2 and 6.3. It is also underlined that this is a dialectic, two-way process, with political priorities feeding back into academic research, as exhibited most obviously with the new-found enthusiasm in voluntary sector circles for the concept of social capital.

6.2 Functions of the UK voluntary sector: research understandings

There is a fairly straightforward 'fit' between the British material presented in this and the following section, and the international framework presented in the introduction to Part II (Chapter 5). In particular, most of the 'functions' presented there are familiar to voluntary sector policy and research audiences in Britain. This is no accident. Research on social welfare or 'human services' by UK scholars (Wolfenden, 1978; Knapp *et al.*, 1990; Billis and Glennerster, 1998) and research by American scholars taking Britain as a 'case' for comparative study (Kramer, 1981, 1993; Wolch, 1990) has been foundational in specifying current understandings of the voluntary sector in the international literature on this topic. Other studies which have been particularly relevant in this area include the general policy reviews discussed in Chapter 3, and a government-sponsored 'efficiency scrutiny' in 1989 (see Lewis, 1999) – although these studies' quantitative evidence bases were essentially concerned with inputs, with consequences discussed discursively.

An exception in terms to this general rule of well-established recognition might be the 'expressive' and 'leadership development' functions, in the sense that this language has been less systematically used in Britain. But as will be seen below, the former notion does now capture well a strand of scholarship which might otherwise have been overlooked (and which, we will show in Section 6.4, has also subsequently received more interest and attention in rhetorical debates).

This and the following subsection therefore use the international framework as an organizing device for considering the evidence and argument from the British research discourse. In so doing, not only is an attempt made to demonstrate these contributions' relevance by introducing specificity and content, but as mooted in Chapter 1, there is a particular concern to bring to the fore materials which speak to the comparative situation of the voluntary sector compared with the public and for-profit sectors. This proves to be difficult, but feasible with some of the 'functions' identified in the international third sector literature; it proves to be generally much harder to do this in the case of the 'weaknesses' reviewed.

6.2.1 The service-provision function

This function was implicitly emphasized in Chapter 2, wherein the 'industry' or field composition of the voluntary sector as an economic actor was surveyed. It has been routinely acknowledged in the foundational research accounts. For example, the Wolfenden committee (1978; see Chapter 3) viewed the social welfare voluntary sector as currently ranked third behind the state and the informal sector (family, and wider kinship and friendship support networks) whose services it was deemed to 'complement, supplement, extend and influence'.

Since Wolfenden's formulation, the 'extension' role has continued – but as Chapter 4 has already underlined, the character of the state has altered dramatically at the local level, a process latterly associated with the shift from 'government' to 'governance'. As we also already noted, the state's own direct provider role was over a longer period significantly cut back as 'contracting out' was expanded (6 and Kendall, 1997). But in another sense the state grew through the massive expansion of its regulatory and auditing capacity (Power, 1997; Newman, 2001a). The other change unanticipated by Wolfenden has been the extent to which for-profit provision has expanded dramatically, with ideological support during the New Right hegemony of the 1980s and early 1990s (Kendall and Knapp, 1996).

In sum, as will be seen in more detail in later chapters, the voluntary sector by the mid-1990s had in its services portfolio 'mainstream' as well as 'extending', complementary services. Alongside the for-profit sector, in that capacity it has been heavily regulated in delivering many services which were previously under local state ownership and control.

How do these activities relate to international third sector theoretical constructs? Both the complementary and mainstream public services that the voluntary sector offers generate 'externalities' and/or are 'public goods'. This is in the economic sense that the welfare of society at large and not just direct users is affected by – in this case, benefits from – their delivery. But many are 'public' too in the (related) legal sense. Provided the relevant purposes are delivered independently of the state, and with recognized 'public purposes' rather than financial gain as the institutionally dominant motive, the system allows them to be recognized as 'charities' with concomitant privileges and responsibilities (Thomas and Kendall, 1996). They are also often 'trust goods' in the sense in which legal-economic third sector scholarship has applied that concept (cf. Anheier and Kendall, 2002). That is, they involve vulnerable users or beneficiaries who might suffer if profit-oriented providers were to exploit, for monetary reward, their clients' inability to exercise 'voice' or 'exit' (Hirschmann, 1970).

Indeed, many of the voluntary sector's most well-known welfare services in the UK combine these properties, such as the social care and education provided for children with special needs, or hostel accommodation for adults with mental health problems. In each case, the users are clearly vulnerable, and the externalities at stake include protection for society, 'caring externalities' associated with compassion or sympathy and, in the latter case, 'option demand' (like an insurance policy, or more fatalistically on a 'there but for the grace of God' logic).

Two other aspects of service provision are worth emphasizing. First, it is noteworthy that many of the services provided are 'niche' services or specialist forms of care. For example, in the cases cited, the voluntary sector provides care for many clients who have particularly acute behavioural problems, or relatively rare conditions. Presented needs have not generated sufficient demand for markets in the conventional sense to develop locally, and local government direct service provision would not be economic (see Box 6.1).

Second, some of services are geared towards beneficiaries whom society has tended to stigmatize or blame for their condition. Billis and Glennerster (1998: 88) refer to this category as the 'societally disadvantaged'. These authors suggested that in the late 1990s, voluntary sector services for people with HIV/AIDS and drug problems without the resources to pay high for-profit clinic fees, and for whom public sector services, including the NHS, have been characterized by 'general failure', are examples.

Chapter 5 also paraphrased the international literature as suggesting that in industries where there is co-existence with the for-profit and government sectors – as we have noted, an increasingly frequent scenario in the UK – the voluntary sector's services are likely to be distinguished by relatively greater equity (defined as willingness and ability to 'serve those in greatest need'), lower cost and/or higher quality. We will consider each in turn.

There are at least three possible meanings to the first element considered here (a fourth aspect, 'wage equity' is considered later in the section). The pursuit of 'equity' as that notion is usually understood is in fact rarely linked with the voluntary sector in the UK, but rather with the public sector, or at least publicly-funded services (Box 6.2).

Yet if 'equity' is recast as micro-level responsiveness and proximity to external societal need then there is considerably more resonance with UK

Box 6.1 The economic logic of voluntary sector national provision as a response to local government service responsibilities

The 'contract culture' literature stresses the growth of contracting between local authority funders and voluntary sector providers in providing mainstream services in the 1990s (Chapter 4). However, contractual relationships involving voluntary sector regional or national specialists and diverse local authorities seeking to meet local special needs have been much longer established. These relationships have often evolved where the number of clients in each locale is so small that it is economically not worthwhile for local government to develop its own services. Local government then typically contracts with established national or regional voluntary sector service providers to secure the lower unit costs associated with provision on a larger scale. This is an interesting counter-example to the 'scaling-up' problem discussed under the 'weaknesses' later in this chapter.

Box 6.2 The public sector and equity concerns

Public authorities alone have access to the resources needed to pursue macro-redistribution strategies. For example, the public sector's largest employer, the National Health Service, has access according to need regardless of ability to pay as its founding principle. One of the primary reasons this system replaced the existing network of voluntary hospitals was because the latter were deemed to lead to inequity of access. Moreover, the formulae deployed in the intragovernmental transfer of taxpayers' funds towards both central government health care and local government education and social services have as a primary objective the matching of resources to geographically defined need. The capacity and expertise to organize and affect redistributive transfers is typically seen as one of the most significant distinguishing features of the national state.

---

discourse. It is widely understood that voluntary organizations are not subject to a variety of bureaucratic constraints which necessarily characterize government agencies at all levels, a distinction also important in understanding the 'innovation' function discussed below (for a useful theoretical treatment of these issues, see Douglas, 1983). However, Knapp *et al.* (1990) caution that it is very difficult to find robust empirical evidence to substantiate the former claim from a comparative perspective.

Finally, 'equality' is sometimes also suggested to be a distinctive internal operating norm within voluntary organizations. Yet here again, there is mixed evidence concerning these claims' relationship with actual practice. Diana Leat's exploratory study of managers who experienced organizational life in both the voluntary and for-profit sectors reported a belief that a greater commitment to equal opportunities did seem to be evident in the former setting. At the same time, however, there were 'doubts about what it really meant . . . the phrase double talk was frequently used here' (Leat, 1995: 19; and see discussion of 'wage equity' and 'amateurism' in Section 6.3).

The UK evidence on the other two properties theoretically linked to the service delivery function is yet more controversial and complex. As far as cost is concerned, the Wolfenden committee suggested some tendencies and hazarded a number of causal connections. Based on some rather limited research comparing voluntary provision to local authority services, its report argued that the former was less costly if it made 'substantial use of volunteers'; could be more responsive if smaller; and 'in the light of evidence we have about services relying on paid staff, it seems that voluntary organizations are certainly not less cost-effective than statutory ones, and on one or two points may have some advantage over statutory services' (pp. 155–6). The committee tentatively linked this to three points: lower wages, smaller overheads and the presence of more committed staff.

More recently, Knapp and colleagues critically reviewed Wolfenden's argument and other academic research evidence that had accumulated on the questions of relative cost-effectiveness and flexibility in the UK and US by the end of the 1980s. This included examination of Wolfenden's rationales, and the so-called 'multiplier effect' cost-effectiveness gains which are claimed to arise when charitable funds as well as volunteer inputs accompany public financial inputs. Their conclusion was much more equivocal than Wolfenden's. These claims and those about quality (which were considered under the rubric of cost-effectiveness) were found 'not to stand up to close scrutiny. A number of [social science comparative] investigations have been undertaken. The most sensible generalisation to make about the evidence is that it is impossible to generalise about the presence or direction of any cost-effectiveness difference between the sectors' (1990: 204–6). Inefficiency is discussed further in the context of employment and organizational practices below.

Later work by Knapp also stressed that involving volunteers in public service delivery involved a range of administrative, organization and congestion costs as well as any benefits secured, and the former could potentially outweigh the latter (Knapp, 1990). Contrariwise, a Government 'efficiency scrutiny' of public funding with a very different methodology – including 'an examination of central government grants programmes, visits and written evidence', considered on that basis that the state at least did achieve 'value for money' (Home Office, 1990). There was no explicit sector comparison here, and the assumption (presumably underpinned by qualitative field evidence) was de facto being made that the advantages of the involvement of volunteers (assumed to be a net benefit to services) and the 'levering in' of nonstatutory funds necessarily outweighed any comparative inefficiencies which might have been evident if other sectors had simultaneously been examined.

A final source of comparative evidence of relevance here relates to paid workers. This is an important question in considering quality because of most voluntary sector services' labour-intensity, and in considering costs because salaries tend to be the most important item of expenditure in labour-intensive welfare services. Although the Deakin Commission had claimed that the voluntary sector's 'ability to motivate staff is the envy of the other sectors' (Commission on the Future of the Voluntary Sector, 1996: 104, para 4.3.9), its evidence base was not clear. More recently, Almond and Kendall (2000b, 2001a,b) examined comparative rates of pay for paid workers in all three sectors using data collected from employee (as opposed to organization) respondents. They validated Wolfenden's suggestion that wages were lower in the voluntary sector than the public sector, both in terms of average rates of pay and lower prevalence of low pay. However, they also found that voluntary sector average rates of pay tended to be higher than the for-profit sector (not discussed by Wolfenden) and low pay less prevalent also, where comparisons were meaningful (at the occupation and field level). This differential was to a significant degree driven by higher pay for care assistants, and 'intermediate workers', which includes traditionally low status professionals or quasi-professionals such as social workers, youth workers and child care workers. In contrast, the socio-economic group 'professionals', a category including 'managers' and the 'classic' high status professions, such as medics and teachers, typically received lower pay if employed in the voluntary sector. One result is that the wage distribution within the voluntary sector is more compressed than in either the public or for-profit sectors.

What are the overall implications for costs and quality? In situations where sector cost differentials are driven by wage differences, these findings point towards both voluntary sector and for-profit sector provision being less costly than public sector provision. Outside the state, however, whether the voluntary sector or the for-profit sector is more economical would clearly depend upon the distribution of workers employed. Where pay for 'intermediate workers' and care workers dominate labour costs, the for-profit sector would emerge as the cheaper option; while if managers and high-status professionals account for the lion's share of spending, then the voluntary sector would tend to emerge as the provider with lower costs.

The implications for quality (and efficiency, appropriately defined to account for the ratio of quality-adjusted service to cost) are unclear. For example, it could be claimed that high-quality services could best be delivered in sectors where a given level of expenditure secures the maximum number of resource inputs. Quality of service differences could then be directly inferred, as straightforwardly related to the cost differences identified, and the voluntary sector option would tend to be higher quality for services where manager/high-status professionals dominate. Contrariwise, it could be argued that high rates of pay tend to induce greater motivation and commitment (the 'efficiency wage' argument conventionally made by public sector trade unions). If we make this inference, then the relationship is reversed, and it would be intermediate worker-intense activities in which a quality advantage would belong to the voluntary sector over for-profits.

The implications of the sectoral wage compression mentioned is also open to more than one interpretation. For example, narrower differentials could be read as supportive of employee motivation, and hence service quality, by suggesting recognition of staffs' collective intrinsic commitment, and fostering an ethos of solidaristic dedication to service (Almond and Kendall, 2001b). On the other hand, the situation could be read as a consequence of 'unhealthy' constraints on employers' ability to appropriately reward high-performing employees – a view apparently taken by some managers who have moved from the for-profit to the voluntary sector (Leat, 1995). In sum, comparative research in Britain has been unable to progress beyond Knapp *et al.*'s (1990) necessarily inconclusive conclusions on this issue.[1]

6.2.2 The innovation function

Innovation may be defined as the introduction of change in production. To distinguish it from 'mere' service development, it can be added that it involves the adoption of observable discontinuities in service design (6, 1993; Osborne, 1998). The three key varieties are 'product innovation' involving wholly new goods and services, differentiation from existing outputs or in terms of users; 'process innovation' involving a new technology for a given set of outputs; or 'organizational innovation' involving a new internal structure or the adoption of new external relationships.

The body of the 1978 Wolfenden Committee report, and evidence submitted to it by the Government, was quick to recognize the voluntary sector's role as 'pioneer' (cf. Owen, 1964; Chesterman, 1979). Knight (1993: Chapter 8) interpreted evidence collected in his national and local studies in housing, community businesses, women's groups and parents' and children's groups as demonstrating instances of innovation. Osborne (1998) compares and contrasts organizations within the voluntary sector. Most recently, this theme has been developed by think tanks. Following the lead of Demos (Mulgan and Landry, 1995: 50–7; Leadbetter, 1997), these have presented numerous case studies of 'social entrepreneurship' in and around the voluntary sector stressing the catalytic role of committed and strong-willed 'hero entrepreneurs' and/or of an effectively fostered ethos of mutualism.

Large numbers of historical and current examples of innovative activity can readily be found in the voluntary sector. Yet it does not follow that the voluntary sector is necessarily systematically relatively more innovative than other sectors. A priori, while the 'categorical constraint' that is a corollary of the state's imperative to provide services universally and evenly would seem to position it poorly in this regard (see above), it clearly has retained some innovatory capacity. Budgetary conditions permitting, this can occur through creative local interpretations of specific statutory responsibilities, or through the imaginative use of more general powers. Knapp *et al.*'s (1990) literature review provides numerous examples of challenges to the 'legend' which stress the extent to which innovations in Britain and the US have been public sector led, involving both public sector finance and provision, or public finance and voluntary delivery.

No empirical comparisons with for-profit organizations in terms of innovatory potential or actual performance seem to be available. This would seem to be a major blind spot, given that this is one of the classic benefits claimed for the private market place. Certainly, the theoretical case that the profit motive under competitive conditions provides a major spur to innovation has been clearly articulated in the field of political economy at least from Adam Smith onwards. Interestingly, while his own evidence is confined to comparisons within the voluntary sector, Osborne (1998) makes the case that 'institutional forces' perform the role in that sector that the profit motive plays in the competitive market. Explicitly rejecting the 'hero entrepreneur' explanation (see also Scott *et al.*, 2000), he stresses external influence, noting that voluntary organizations in his sample tended to 'be innovative' when special grants are made available for that purpose by public agencies. For-profits tend to be either irrelevant because the state did not allow them access to such grants, or because the activities in question would appear to have been unlikely to generate sufficient profit to justify involvement. Ultimately, then, we rely in part on the leading role of the public sector noted earlier, and in part on the uneconomic nature of the activity in question. In other words, the voluntary sector may be relatively innovative not as a general rule, but under particular conditions.

6.2.3 *The advocacy function*

As with the innovation function, it is incontrovertible that this takes place in the British voluntary sector, but comparative evidence is unavailable. The accounts of Kramer (Kramer, 1981; Kramer *et al.*, 1993) and Knapp *et al.*'s (1987, 1990) comprehensive review of the literature both highlight this role and provide details of forms and types. Theoretically, Wolch (1990) was particularly interested in the sector's role as a dramatic catalyst for social change, and gave this dimension of actual or potential 'output' as much prominence as service delivery in her model (see also Evers, 1995). More practically, Brenton's seminal contribution argued that the 'watchdog role' was the most important of all the sector's functions (Brenton, 1985: 220–2) and more recently, the campaigning contribution was recognized, and indeed emphasized, as essential for a 'healthy democracy' in the Deakin report. On paper at least, protection for this role has subsequently been included as part of the Compact and the associated codes of conduct (see Chapters 3 and 4; see also Plowden, 2001: 28 and 36–8).

However, empirical research has shown that only a small minority of voluntary organizations actually undertake campaigning per se (Knight, 1993; Shore *et al.*, 1994). This is either because many do not wish to exert political influence, or because they feel they can best achieve change through pursuing the other functions discussed in this section. (Moreover, the later 'vertical' chapters that follow will reveal rather sophisticated repertoires for exerting influence which are not easily reducible to the 'campaigning' label.) Further, for those organizations that do pursue this, there are doubts concerning its effectiveness, even in terms of self-reported impressions. The report *Cause and Effect* suggested that the sector had higher expectations of its lobbying activity that it was currently realizing, although the interpretation of the data – particularly the 'gap analysis' – is methodologically controversial (NCVO, 1990).[2]

A much fuller picture of the character and extent of this function will become available when the final results of Taylor *et al.*'s research are available (see Chapter 4). But early findings from that research already provide a rare hint of at least the subjective impressions of the comparative influence of the voluntary compared to the for-profit sectors on the state. Many local voluntary organizations reported to these researchers that their counterparts in the business world 'had the ear' of the state, and there was a perception that private companies ultimately exerted more influence than they did (Taylor *et al.*, 2001a).

6.2.4 *The expressive function*

As noted in the opening section, an 'expressive function' per se is the role which *prima facie* has had less resonance with the traditional mainstream UK voluntary sector discourse, certainly until relatively recently. This might simply have been because it has been implicitly assumed to be part and parcel of other functions. A second possibility is that the literature has tended to concentrate on those fields of activity where the instrumental meeting of social needs has been seen as the dominant concern. Certainly, research focused on the voluntary sector per se has tended to look to social welfare activities, rather than such fields as culture, recreation and environment, where this function could be more obviously of core salience.[3]

Another possibility, from a liberal perspective, could be that the value of freedom of expression, whether individually or through collective action, has tended to be taken for granted as a self-evident good. Particularly since J.S. Mill famously argued the case for both personal and corporate or associational 'individuality' over 150 years ago (Mill, 1867 [1985]), it may have been so deeply embedded in British culture and value systems that there may have been little perceived need to broach it explicitly.[4]

However, at the end of the period considered in this section, developments outside the British voluntary sector research community were belatedly beginning to push this role explicitly into the limelight. This new awareness was partly linked to the transformation of the political landscape in east central Europe. What we are referring to as the expressive function had been systematically denied by formal institutions under the former communist regimes (see Kendall *et al.*, 2000). The relish with which citizens in those countries seemed to greet their new-found opportunities to practise freedom of expression reawakened awareness in the west, including Britain, of its value. This awareness was reflected most obviously in the Deakin Commission report, which consciously styled the voluntary sector's contribution as a crucial ingredient to 'civil society' – drawing directly on Ralph Dahrendorf's metaphor of healthy pluralism through 'creative chaos' (Commission on the Future of the Voluntary Sector, 1996: 22; see next section).

6.2.5 *The community-building function*

The general significance of community-building – community development in British usage – has long been widely discussed as a central role for voluntary organizations, being recognized from Wolfenden (1978) to Deakin (1996) and given particular prominence in Knight (1993).

The notions of 'community' and 'community development' are even more difficult and complex to define and examine than the other functions reviewed here: as Mayo surmises, 'it is not just that the term has been used ambiguously; it has been contested, fought over and appropriated for different uses and interests to justify different politics, policies and practices' (Mayo, 1994: 48). Approaches share the notion that participation by local citizens in voluntary groups could foster 'personal development', improve social relationships, give people 'control over their own lives', and thus make society operate more 'healthily'. However, because there are different understandings of what types of development and relationships ultimately constitute a 'healthy' society, and what 'taking control' can and should mean in terms of the resultant outcomes, different emphases seem to be implied on the types of voluntary organization whose contribution is to be prized. More 'radical' thinkers tended to see aggressive campaigning groups oriented towards the consolidation of social rights and societal transformation as prototypically significant; while for more reformist observers, apolitical self-help groups and those lifting individuals into conventional labour market opportunities have been particularly valued.

Despite these definitional difficulties and ideological fault lines, claims have still been made in a general way (that is, implicitly or explicitly suggesting that community development-oriented organizations could 'add value' wherever they might be situated in terms of their ultimate goals and political or apolitical outcomes). This is because it is argued that the process of involvement could be deemed of value in its own right, particularly where the people concerned have had to live in 'difficult' neighbourhoods – especially the notorious 'sink' council housing estates – and where their ethnicity and other characteristics meant they have experienced systematic discrimination. For such communities, involvement in the sector through either volunteering, membership or employment (and often a combination, where one leads to the other) could be claimed to potentially engender an 'upward spiral' at both individual participant and group levels. In what is emphasized to be a fragile and painstaking process (Knight, 1993; Mayo, 1994; Power, 1993) – and over and above the effects in terms of services delivered or actual campaign outcomes – the following claimed advantages have been mooted:

- Confidence, growing as experience of successful collective action is gained;
- Skills acquired, of relevance for economic, social or political life;
- Individuals' self-esteem and communities' reputation fostered;
- A sense of control over life regained, bolstered or enhanced; and
- More generally, fatalism or 'poverty of expectations' replaced by more positive attitudes and perspectives.

As Chapter 4 has already implied, in practice these or allied ideas traditionally received some rather limited support in the explicit policies and financial commitments of local government (cf. Broady and Hedley, 1989; Mayo, 1994). At the same time, while often accused of 'underfunding', central government was implicitly taking some of these factors into account in urban policy. For example, support for voluntary organizations, volunteer participation and 'capacity building' were treated as legitimate 'outputs' of the Single Regeneration Budget Challenge Fund (DETR, 1998, Annex J, glossary). The Community Development Foundation, funded by the Home Office, has also been active nationally in presenting these activities as urban regeneration 'outputs', alongside those associated with service delivery per se.

But why the voluntary sector rather than other sectors? The comparative aspect is rarely made explicit. Of course, if volunteering per se were always to be seen as of net benefit – either because it could be assumed to lead to the sorts of 'process' effects listed above, or perhaps because it were otherwise intrinsically valued, for example on the 'expressive' rationale discussed above – then the voluntary sector would necessarily have a quantitative advantage over other formal sectors. Otherwise, a rare example of an explicit attempt in the literature to diagnose the comparative advantage of the voluntary sector in cases of 'community disadvantage' is made by Billis and Glennerster, who stress the combination of the community function with the service function. They ask if there are particular social conditions or 'states of disadvantage' under which the voluntary sector might be expected to play a more significant role than others. It is argued that, as well as the case of 'personal disadvantage' and 'societal disadvantage' mentioned under the service provision function above, the voluntary sector fills a gap when it comes to 'community disadvantage'. Here, they have in mind deprived local neighbourhoods, in which a for-profit presence is missing because of lack of opportunities to trade for financial gain. For its part, the public sector is portrayed as narrowly focused on median voter preferences, short-termist and in possession of a poor track record (Billis and Glennerster, 1998: 93). The 'structural' attributes in terms of ambiguity and hybrid character which are claimed to give the voluntary sector this advantage are noted in Box 6.3.

Other 'failures' to which voluntary organizations can potentially be seen as a response are evident in the literature, even if not stated in those terms – and if typically assumed rather than demonstrated. First, for-profits are involved, but selectively, and often in property development rather than retail. Where this activity has been speculative and oriented towards short-term profit accumulation for external owners (and there is some evidence in the literature that these orientations have dominated; Deakin and Edwards, 1993), the free market will have channelled resources outside communities which could otherwise have aided 'community-building'. In terms of the labour market, the pure profit motive is indifferent to the domicile of the worker (what matters is his or her productivity), so employment opportunities created by for-profit enterprise in retail, property development or any other activity might not be geared towards the needs of local people. In each case, to the extent they re-invest surpluses and seek to employ people from the neighbourhood, voluntary groups would be well situated from a comparative perspective. Finally, to the extent the latter give those with direct experience of local problems more of a voice in diagnosing solutions to them, they would be better equipped epistemologically to respond to those needs.[5]

This is one function for which it is also particularly important to acknowledge the rapidity of recent change in research, although the international research framework does not attend to this, as noted earlier. Overlaying the received discourse set out above, the concept of social capital has recently been catapulted

---

Box 6.3 'Structural' rationales for voluntary agencies' comparative advantage

Billis and Glennerster's (1998) analysis seeks to go beyond the foundational accounts of the voluntary sector's role introduced in Chapter 1 (Box 1.1). The core ideas of voluntary agencies as involving multiple stakeholding and internal relational ambiguity are perhaps not as original as the authors seem to imply. However, the link made with particular categories of socially excluded people is undoubtedly innovative – and timely in the light of this Government's policy focus on disadvantage understood in this way (see Chapters 3 and 4).

Billis and Glennerster claim that complex multiple stakeholding interests – involving trustees, paid staff, volunteers and users – can be contrasted with the relatively straightforward dominance of shareholder and median voter interests in the for-profit and public sectors respectively. Ambiguity arises because stakeholding in voluntary agencies tends not to involve clear-cut divisions of labour, but 'overlapping roles', with a lack of clarity regarding responsibilities for key organizational functions. The authors interpret this situation as potentially able to lessen gaps of knowledge and interest between each of the stakeholder categories. Particularly when users are stigmatized or powerless to leave deprived communities, and are therefore not positioned to exercise choice as sovereign consumers, the proximity that follows from the need to negotiate ambiguous role boundaries on an ongoing basis can be a significant advantage. Such contact can, it is claimed, bring greater sensitivity to need at the 'street level', potentially in contrast to the principal–agent problems that they stress tend to characterize both public sector and for-profit sector bureaucracies.

---

into the public policy debate in the UK. It now provides a fashionable and politically resonant conceptual focal point for discussions of the voluntary sector's actual and potential contributions to social 'infrastructure' and 'social cohesion' through fostering community level relationships and building trust. As Box 6.4 suggests, there are differences of opinion in the research community regarding both its theoretical utility as a concept, and how to interpret the emerging body of empirical evidence on its pervasiveness and relevance.

As with other functions, it therefore has to be concluded that the jury is still out on the comparative impact of the voluntary sector in community-building. There is a rich collection of anecdotes and arguments available, with practitioners and policy analysts pointing to credible examples and suggesting plausible lines of reasoning in support of the voluntary sector's contributions. But it is hard to claim on the basis of the burgeoning empirical social science

Box 6.4 The voluntary sector and social capital in Britain: a contentious new debate

The claim that the voluntary sector can contribute to 'community-building' by fostering an 'upward spiral' of trust and confidence amongst active volunteers or members – particularly within deprived geographical communities – has long been recognized in Britain (see Section 6.4). However, American political scientist Robert Putnam's suggestion that such activities could be understood as generating 'social capital' with broader positive micro- and macro-economic and political consequences has dramatically intensified political interest in this argument over the past 5 years. Moreover, because his formulation has involved framing this claim in a language which connects it with mainstream social science, it has caught the imagination of a range of academic political scientists and economists, and more recently think tanks, who had traditionally been relatively uninterested in the voluntary sector per se. As a result, the community-building function is really the only function of those discussed in Section 6.2 to have been examined in an extensive way at the sector level since around 2000. The debate seems to divide into two broad camps – optimists and sceptics.

Optimistically, an associate of Putnam, Peter A. Hall, examined membership trends on selected organizations (and other data), and concluded that, unlike the American case, in Britain there had been 'no erosion' of social capital. He suggested that a range of educational reforms, government policies and changes in class structure had prevented it (Hall, 1999; see also Johnston, 2001). Regression models have shown association membership to exert an independent influence on regional economic development (Casey, nd), and variation in involvement in political life can be partly explained statistically by voluntary group involvement (Pattie *et al.*, 2002). In-depth qualitative research examining the role of associations in deprived neighbourhoods has begun to suggest in a rich and balanced way the social mechanisms and processes whereby involvement can painstakingly foster concrete changes in attitudes and behaviour (Richardson and Mumford, 2002). Political scientists examining local authority–voluntary sector relations in one locale show that both parties believed mutual trust was important for the 'health' of their city, revealed high levels of intravoluntary sector trust, and found that most of those organizations which were closely involved with local government characterized that relationship as one of high trust – although 'outsiders' held very different perspectives (Maloney *et al.*, 2000). Finally, public opinion surveys have suggested that most of the general public tend to believe that charities or voluntary organizations are relatively trustworthy compared to government or private companies (most recently, see Saxton, 2002).

Sceptically, problems of circularity and tautology with basic concepts and opacity on assumptions and reasoning have been diagnosed (Newton, 1997; Anheier and Kendall, 2002); empirically, the relevance of Hall's findings have been challenged because the rather limited organizational membership data on which he relies are dominated by passive not active membership (Cameron, 2001). The assumption that population-wide, relatively stable membership trends in Britain are in any case always reflecting voluntary sector membership is erroneous, because some of the growth in recreation and leisure is certainly accounted for by for-profit club membership. In addition, European Values Survey comparative data on time trends in Britain suggest a more complex and contingent relationship between trust and membership than other time trends data (Grenier and Wright, 2001). Membership also seems to have the same class correlates as volunteering. For this and related reasons, associational membership often seems to involve 'bonding' or 'strong tie' relationships (exclusive or 'club'-like, suggesting 'particularism' in this chapter's language) – rather than 'bridging' (inclusive or more 'public') links, with their more obvious social and dynamic 'weak tie' economic benefits (6, 1997; Aldridge *et al.*, 2002). Moreover, case studies, building upon common observations from the community development literature, have suggested other 'failures' or recurring breakdown tendencies at the neighbourhood level: financial and organizational 'insufficiency' are common problems, and also the quite frequent problems of antipathy, resentment, jealousy and rivalry between members and nonmembers. These issues all suggest the enormous practical difficulties of postulating social capital through associations as a ready response to social exclusion problems in deprived neighbourhoods (Richardson and Mumford, 2002). Finally, focus group research has suggested that the public's apparent tendency to vest greater trust in the voluntary sector than other sectors is premised on its capacity to retain characteristics which the policy environment may increasingly be undermining. These include voluntarism and separateness from both the state and the market (Tonkiss and Passey, 1999).

literature that the voluntary sector per se is necessarily 'better' either in general (or under particular well-defined conditions) than other formal sectors (or informal organizing) in building social capital.

6.3 Weaknesses of the UK voluntary sector: research understandings

The weaknesses suggested by Salamon (1987) presented in the introduction to this part of the book have long been implicit in much of the 1980s British literature (in particular, the Wolfenden research and Brenton, 1985). They were explicitly argued to be relevant to the UK by Knapp *et al.* (1987, 1990), although not explored in detail. We consider each in turn.

6.3.1 Philanthropic insufficiency

The extent to which voluntary activity has remained patchy and uneven since the consolidation of the welfare state in the mid-twentieth century has long been recognized in Britain, particularly in social care. Here the state, as with most other countries, never took extensive responsibility for finance and provision as it did in other welfare areas, and a distinctly mixed economy has remained, in which the voluntary sector is prominent (Kendall *et al.*, 2003). Exploratory research for the Wolfenden Committee's report recognized and demonstrated geographical variability. In discussing the 'distribution of voluntary activity' in the main report, the Committee effectively put a version of 'insufficiency' on the agenda, arguing that people from lower socio-economic groups were less involved in formal voluntary action, and recognizing the existence and extent of geographical variation (by comparing a small number of locales).

The assertion that volunteering is associated primarily with middle-class people – particularly white women – is widely made (Brenton, 1985; Leat, 1993). This conventional wisdom has been confirmed by a relatively sophisticated econometric model. Knapp *et al.*'s (1995, 1996) probit multivariate model (simultaneously taking into account the full variety of factors affecting the decision to volunteer) leads overall to the validation of this view. This study also established that, overall, women were more likely to formally volunteer than men, and people from ethnic minorities were less likely to formally volunteer. The extensiveness of geographical variation posited by Wolfenden – both in terms of the presence of voluntary organizations, and extensiveness of participation by volunteers – has also been demonstrated empirically with new studies undertaken in the early 1990s, although the measurement attempts thus far have been relatively crude (Knight, 1993; Marshall *et al.*, 1997).

Evidence concerning the relationship between macro-economic performance, social need and the voluntary sector's ability to respond to it is mixed. Based upon a small survey during the early 1990s recession, Taylor-Gooby (1994) concluded that, while charities were usually acutely aware of intensified social needs at such times, most were simply unable to cope as they were experiencing real falls in total income. Data on the resources provided by some of the stakeholders on whom the voluntary sector relies, including individual givers and companies, appeared to reinforce this gloomy picture (Halfpenny and Lowe, 1994; Banks and Tanner, 1997; Lane, 1993).

Yet, as has been shown in Chapter 2, the voluntary sector as a whole was actually growing rapidly over the period 1990–5. These findings can be reconciled in part to the extent that the sector recovered significantly after 1993/94, when the recession came to an end. But there were also internal differences within the sector during the first part of the period: different parts of the sector, and organizations dependent on different resource flows, were affected in contrasting ways. In particular, small local organizations (which Taylor-Gooby's sample included) seem to have been much more vulnerable than larger organizations to recessionary pressures (Hems and Passey, 1998); and public expenditures in the leading growth policy subfields, social care and housing, were evidently counter-cyclical (see Chapters 7 and 8).

6.3.2 Philanthropic particularism

The manifestation of particularism which has received most attention in Britain is the high correlation between social class and participation referred to earlier. Box 6.5 suggests some of the ways in which the two seem to be linked. One further factor which could be at play is deliberate discrimination or institutional barriers erected by established organizations. The 'particularism' of this sort which has been most recognized as a problem in the literature is that relating to people from black and minority ethnic groups. For example, it has been argued that 'black people wishing to volunteer in mainstream organizations may face particular difficulties with bureaucratic ways of working, a clash of cultures, tokenism and racism' (Mayo, 1994).

Whatever the ultimate causes of low participation, Brenton (1985) and Hedley (1995) have been among the commentators who bemoaned the extent to which 'established' organizations have failed to involve black people, and thus not benefited from what this section of the community has to offer. Moreover, NCVO's *On Trust* research report on the composition of management

---

Box 6.5 Higher socio-economic groups and particularism

People from higher socio-economic groups may participate more in voluntary activity than others for a variety of reasons, including:

- The tendency for people from higher socio-economic groups to be relatively time-rich.
- Superior access to the variety of financial and social resources needed to form organizations in the first place (Ben-Ner and Van Hommissen, 1993).
- A higher willingness to volunteer as a result of greater awareness of the potential benefits (perhaps linked to education levels).
- A greater tendency to be embedded in the social networks which are closely associated with formal volunteering.
- A cultural preference for volunteering through formal organization rather than through informal networks.

committees (NCVO, 1992) certainly showed just how few people from minority ethnic groups more generally were involved in governance. In terms of paid employment, however, there appears not to be such an obvious overall pattern of exclusion, with considerable variations between different minority ethnic subcategories (Almond and Kendall, 2000). Evidence on these aspects of particularism is therefore mixed, and existing research does not really allow us to weight the relative importance of the different factors which seem to be relevant.

A rather different consequence of particularism, according to Salamon (1987), could be 'wasteful duplication'. It is hard to identify the sort of objective evidence which would either confirm or reject this claim: activities regarded as 'healthy competition' from one perspective or legitimate expressions of different values could be seen as inefficient overlap from another. However, subjective beliefs on the issue can be identified, and it was already suggested in the previous chapter that the legal environment seems to tend towards the 'wasteful duplication' interpretation. Thus, the majority of donors to charity apparently believed that this was a problem in Britain in the early 1990s (Halfpenny and Lowe, 1994); the Charity Commission has veered towards a hierarchical interpretation of duplication (or competition) in advising potential founders of charities; and local government has often encouraged voluntary bodies to reach agreements on mutually exclusive 'catchment areas' for some of the services they fund (Kendall and 6, 1994); while nationally, politicians seem to be divided on this issue (see Section 6.4 below).[6]

6.3.3 Philanthropic paternalism

Elitism, and the paternalism it implied, were seen as cause for celebration not condemnation by traditional conservatives, and there have been traces of these views in local government's voluntary sector stance in some locales (Obler, 1981; and Chapter 4, this volume). However, politically, in Britain and elsewhere the growth of the new social movements from the 1960s, and user movements particularly from the 1980s, challenging the influence of both 'the great and the good' and service professionals, has helped to make these views less acceptable. New organizations were formed specifically to pursue this agenda, but also many users tried to affect change from within more 'traditional' or 'established' charities, whose operating philosophies had continued to reflect conservative interpretations of their founding missions, often consolidated in practice over long periods of time.

Yet paternalistic attitudes and institutions have remained more than historical curiosities. As recently as the early 1980s, Gerard (1983: 162) classified over three-quarters of the respondents to his survey of national charities as characterized by 'moral and spiritual values, conservatism, stability and services to those in need' (more recently, see also Knight, 1993). That this is still seen as a problem for the voluntary sector is implied by the apparently limited extent to which the user movement has secured changes in governance as a route towards combating inappropriate paternalism (cf. Brenton, 1985). Most recently, Robson *et al.* (1997) reported that while three-quarters of their sample of organizations 'attempted' to increase user participation, only just over half actually had users on their boards, and only a quarter had a policy or programme on this issue.

6.3.4 Philanthropic amateurism and accountability lapses

It is fitting to finish this account of weaknesses by drawing upon the work of Ralph Kramer, whom we have noted was a pioneer of cross-national voluntary sector comparative work. His portrait of 'inefficiency', which he diagnosed as a feature of at least some social service agencies in England that he examined, bears citation:

> it involves insularity, low accountability, a casual, muddling, and bumbling style of operation, and other administrative deficiencies. The managerial inefficiencies of voluntary agencies is rooted in the context of a charity market, dominated by a spirit of independence and laissez-faire ... Some voluntary organisations never develop beyond this initial, fumbling stage, while others that do remain on a plateau and fail to achieve its organisational capacity.
>
> (Kramer, 1981: 267)

Leat's exploratory study of the perspectives of for-profit managers who transferred to the voluntary sector found ample evidence that many believed their organizations to be of this sort (Leat, 1995); while Knight (1993) also presented some suggestive evidence, and the Commission on the Future of the Voluntary Sector (1996) acknowledged the existence of perceptions that inefficiencies were significant. However, existing evidence does not allow us to identify the extent to which these practices or styles were relevant then, and certainly not to generalize about the situation since the late 1990s.

Kramer probably primarily had in mind the 'failures to achieve organizational capacity' resulting from unsatisfactory deployment and skills acquisition of both volunteers and paid workers. The development of 'human resource management' perspectives on the voluntary sector by management scientists provide further clues as to the ways in which 'amateurism' may be manifested in UK voluntary organizations. Batsleer (1992: 234–7) provides an excellent summary of the issues at stake, and we quote extensively from his survey in Box 6.6 (see also Cunningham, 1999, 2000; Patel *et al.*, 1999).

6.4 Rhetorical accounts: themes and emphases

This section examines the political rhetoric that has developed in recent years regarding the claimed 'impacts' of the voluntary sector as part of this book's general attempt to situate the voluntary sector politically. The content of recent parliamentary debates, and key speeches by ministers are noted in order to identify both shared understandings and differences regarding the sector's roles,

---

Box 6.6 'Amateurism' in voluntary sector human resource management

- 'Voluntary trustees and management committees have rarely been competent to handle quite complex roles and responsibilities as employers or supervisors ... the vagaries of short-term nature of much funding has meant that many small and medium-sized organizations have lacked the capacity to develop the personel functions which have begun to emerge in larger organizations ...'
- '... the "professionalization" of the voluntary sector has not really been a process of infiltrating a single-minded cohort of highly paid, career-oriented staff. It has been a conscientious attempt to create flexible, responsive and entrepreneurial patterns of work in circumstances which have often born the hallmarks of casual labour rather than classic professionalism ...'
- '... the issue of equal opportunities (EOs) has been a persistent preoccupation, for many organizations seen as being the most appropriate way of giving practical expression to the distinctive value-based of the voluntary sector ... [but] whether a decade and a half of EOs has significantly altered the profile of the sector is a matter of considerable debate. There has been much turmoil and acrimony, some spectacular conflicts ... and persistent claims of thoroughly bad practice and procedures masquerading as "good practice" ...'

Source: Batsleer, 1995: 234–7.

---

and to assess how these relate to the research evidence and argument presented in Sections 6.2 and 6.3.

6.4.1 Parliamentary discussion

One development closely associated with the mainstreaming diagnosed in Chapter 3 has been the increased frequency of parliamentary debate on the subject. Prior to 1996, the previous full debate had been nearly 50 years earlier, at the time of the release of Lord Beveridge's *Voluntary Action* (1948). But between 1996 and 2000, four debates in the House of Commons and the House of Lords took place.

An important first point that emerges from across these discussions is the existence of cross party consensus at Westminster concerning the desirability of: a 'healthy' civil society and voluntary sector; extensive volunteering; the importance of protection and growth in the sector's various sources of funding;

and the promotion of 'partnership' between the state and the voluntary sector. Over the past few years, debates in the Houses of Commons and Lords have involved almost universal agreement on the importance of all these goals. Thus, while it took a New Labour Government to mainstream voluntary sector policy (in 1996, they had initiated the first debate while still in Opposition), all national high political actors in the parliamentary arena seem to share recognition of its contribution.

Second, a review of these debates also shows how the speakers in question articulate beliefs that the voluntary sector performs one or more of the roles we have identified in Section 6.2. Box 6.7 reports on recent statements which both speak to one or more of these roles and include some comparative component, or imply a gap left by other sectors (a much longer list would have been included if assertions without a sector comparison had been included). They underline that all the functions we reviewed from a research perspective have been recognized in rhetorical terms.

Rhetoric from New Labour enthusiasts can reflect follow through to the specific ideological and political agenda and situation discussed in earlier chapters. More generally amongst Parliamentarians, a mixture of influences is

---

Box 6.7 Parliamentary rhetoric on the voluntary sector's functions

Service provision
'Voluntary organisations are run on a leanness that would make many public bodies gasp and with a return on public investment with which any private sector industry would be pleased' (Addison, Lords Hansard 96, col 318).

'Normally voluntary organisations are very cost-effective. Many of them are very professional in their approach. They provide an effective combination of professional paid staff and volunteers' (Dubs, Lords Hansard 96, col 336).

'Charities can often provide small-scale, specialised services, particularly in the field of personal care, which would be technically more difficult, and thus uneconomic, for public sector social services to provide. They can also respond rapidly to changing social conditions in a way that governments sometimes cannot' (Masham, Lords Hansard 98, col 1261).

Innovation
'The voluntary sector is innovative and often based very firmly in the local community. And it has the ability to respond quickly to new needs. That is not a characteristic shared with central or local government, which tends to respond more slowly' (Dubs, Lords Hansard 96 , col 336).

'Charities . . . certainly show greater creativity than the public sector, and greater flexibility to respond to challenges and changing needs' (Young, Lords Hansard 98, col 1217).

'Charities pioneer. They operate in smaller fields than some huge [public sector] ministry and can thus identify small areas of need. [And] they can act more rapidly than can a government' (Quinton, Lords Hansard 98, col 1251).

'We, as politicians and members of society, value voluntary organisations' independence and their ability to innovate, experiment and engage with the particular circumstances of an individual or local case. That approach is not available to government officials, who have to abide by the Whitehall rule book' (Lidington, Commons Hansard 00, col 280WH).

Advocacy

'Some have suggested that the voice of charities be stilled. In a democratic society, how can government seek to silence a voluntary organisation working for the good of principles set out in charitable objects, if paid lobbying by those who have a commercial interest continues unabated? If the Alzheimer's disease society cannot speak for sufferers and their carers, who can?' (Michael, Commons Hansard 96, col 213).

Expressive

'Charities are of course very driven by their values. They allow people to give expression to the values that have brought them into existence' (Young, Lords Hansard 98, col 1217).

Community-Building

'At this time of year, many of us find ourselves attending fetes and other such events, which raise funds for good causes and are usually a celebration of neighbourhood identity. That is something of value that the voluntary organisations bring to this country, which no government agency, however well intentioned can reproduce in the same way' (Lidington, Commons Hansard 00, col 279WH).

'There is a great range of innovation . . . [and] tradition [is] the other side of that coin. I share the view that . . . faith-based voluntary organisations need to be encouraged and nurtured. The church is often the only professionally led organisation still in existence in some of our most deprived communities and run-down areas' (Michael, Commons Hansard 00, col 294WH).

Sources: Commons debate 'voluntary sector' 23 July 1996; Lords debate 'voluntary work' 27 November 1996; Lords debate 'charities' 4 March 1998'; Commons debate 'voluntary sector' 15 June 2000.

relevant. First, personal experiences are clearly important. Most obviously, this has included members' involvement as trustees in particular charities and views presented to them by voluntary organizations active in their constituencies, or which have lobbied them at Westminster.

Also relevant has been research evidence – but usually 'at one remove'. With the notable exception of Lord Dahrendorf, who refers to various scholarly debates which implicitly touch on 'functions' (even if not articulated as such), the primary sense in which research evidence penetrated this domain was indirectly through sympathetic reactions to the Deakin report's portrayal of its roles. This is scarcely surprising, as awareness of the 'technical' minutiae we have reviewed would scarcely be expected of generalist politicians.

A third and related point to emerge from these debates is that, overall, the voluntary sector's strengths are discussed more extensively that its weaknesses, a symptom of rhetorical selectiveness. Where weaknesses are addressed, they have usually been presented not primarily as an intrinsic failure for which the sector should be 'blamed', but as a potential problem for society to which 'partnership' with the state is a legitimate response. For example, trends in individual giving – which could be thought of as an intensification over time of 'philanthropic insufficiency' – are presented as potentially requiring a public policy response (see Chapter 3). Another prominent example is 'particularism' in the form of low levels of involvement by the black and minority ethnic community, where there is agreement on the need to intensify state financial support for black-led support organizations. Something of an exception is the other meaning of 'particularism' in the sense of 'wasteful duplication', which we will return to below.

Thus, in many ways the political discussion of the voluntary sector's roles has been marked by nonpartisan discussion with a somewhat 'motherhood and apple pie' flavour which almost ritualistically emphases strengths and avoids examination of weaknesses. However, there are two primary and related senses in which ideological 'fault lines' are evident, even if tending to be articulated in a low key and nonconfrontational way.

First, there are different views concerning the desirability of the processes and institutions that we described in Chapter 4, and these suggest fundamental differences in belief concerning what the state can and should do to nurture the voluntary sector's nonservice delivery 'functions'. The focal point for this discourse has been the Compact. At the start of the period in which these debates took place, the Conservative administration was still in place, and as we have seen in Chapter 3, it initially resisted the Concordat/Compact proposal. At the same time, while not positioning himself as entirely rejecting the proposal outright, in the House of Lords, Dahrendorf articulated concerns as a liberal intellectual with principled distrust for the state that, to the extent that it represented state encroachment on 'liberty', it could threaten the 'creative chaos' of the voluntary sector. From 1998 onwards, while cautious Conservatives and Liberal politicians (or Lords cross-benchers) have not argued for the dismantling of the Compact and the institutions it has spawned,[7] they have tended not to be amongst their most enthusiastic supporters. For his part, Dahrendorf has continued to take the liberal intellectual lead, being prominent in expressing deep concerns that, whatever its benign intentions and claims to protect the sector's 'independence', the Compact and its offshoots may tend to 'rigidity' undermining much prized spontaneity and voluntary freedom of action. Different interpretations of voluntary sector 'health' and 'partnership' were clearly at stake.

The second discernible difference is less clearly focused on a particular policy initiative or process, but does seem to involve a conflict of basic values. There are those who tend to give weight to the voluntary sector's role as an efficient provider of services and see 'duplication' as a pressing concern to be 'tidied up' through partnership or co-operation. This echoes the dominant view of the public at large, and the perspective of the Charity Commission and much of local government, as we noted in Section 6.3 when discussing particularism. In contrast, there are those who attach particular importance to the expressive function, and emphasize their tolerance of particularism – even if apparently 'inefficient' or 'failing' – as a price worth paying in order that the expressive role be granted political and social space to play itself out.[8] Box 6.8 compares these positions. In the language being used here, contrasting positions are evident in terms of the relative importance attached to the efficient discharge of the service provision function, on the one hand, and the expressive function, on the other; and associated differences in how to think about 'amateurism' and 'wasteful duplication' (an aspect of 'particularism'). While the language is carefully hedged with caveats and conditions, there is an undeniable difference in emphasis between speakers on these points.

6.4.2 The emerging New Labour analysis

The act of instigating a cross-cutting review of the sector's involvement in public services in 2001 – the most recent manifestation of the heightened Treasury interest identified in Part I – underlines the political importance attached by New Labour to the service delivery function. However, the chapter on 'value added', accounting for just three of the report's 52 pages, is rather brief (HM Treasury, 2002). Each summarizes just a small proportion of the extensive body of evidence and argument reviewed in Section 6.2. Presumably reflecting its politically determined frame of reference, the main report chapter finds no real room for a discussion of the sector's actual or potential weaknesses.[9]

The most significant features of the Treasury document are probably therefore, first, simply its existence, and second, its positive emphasis, rather than any specific details in its content. We therefore need to retain a focus on purely political statements for a fuller sense of this administration's latest thinking on 'impacts'.

It will be recalled from Chapter 3 that a broad affinity was apparent from the mid-1990s onwards between the New Labour 'project' and enthusiasm for the

---

Box 6.8　Contrasting emphases on the service provision and expressive functions

Greater weight to the service provision function/the pursuit of efficiency

'In my view, voluntary bodies need to pull together more effectively than they often do, not to speak with one voice, but to speak more nearly with one voice on certain questions that they have often been able to do . . . partnership needs to come from within the sector as well as from outside it. There is a need for more co-operation at all levels, wherever it is appropriate and wherever different voluntary bodies gather together to pursue a common purpose' (Dartington, Lords Hansard 96, col 330).

'There are too many charities carrying out almost the same activities. There should be more amalgamation of charities doing similar work' (Westbury, Lords Hansard 98, col 1237).

Greater weight to the expressive function

'The whole point of voluntary and charitable activity is that it can be idiosyncratic in purpose, amateurish in organisation, prone to make mistakes, and even fail in its objectives. It is indeed – and it should be – a creative chaos, within the law . . . none of the drive for competitiveness must detract from the moral texture of our lives, from social cohesion' (Dahrendorf, Lords Hansard 96, cols 315 and 317).

'Tidiness is not a virtue in this sector. The idea that we should have mergers to avoid duplication or that small struggling organisations should disappear flies in the face of the importance of local, individual, value-driven personal effort. Let us celebrate the glorious diversity of the charity sector and defend the loose and baggy monster' (Young, Lords Hansard 98, col 1217).

---

voluntary sector, for philosophical (broadly, 'communitarian'), political and electoral reasons. Yet the statements of the late 1990s cited there tended to be rather vague. From 2000 onwards, a little more specificity has at least begun to emerge. Box 6.9 summarizes the relevant claims regarding contributions made in the most important speeches from the most powerful government ministers.[10]

For our purposes, it is noteworthy that ministers' rhetoric speaks to the full range of the sector's functions, but there is a particularly strong emphasis on the local level 'community-building', social capital and as part of that, the voluntary sector's role in fostering trust. Underlining this orientation within the policy-making machinery, the new apparatus of 'joined-up governance' discussed in Chapter 4 (Section 4.2) has recently been geared towards the production of two reports whose commissioning and terms of reference and commissioning were

Box 6.9 Ministerial rhetoric on voluntary sector 'functions'

Tony Blair: Community-building

'We have always said that human capital is the core of the new economy. But increasingly it is also social capital that matters too – the capacity to get things done, to cooperate, the magic ingredient that makes all the difference. Too often in the past government programmes damaged social capital – sending in the experts but ignoring community organisations, investing in bricks and mortar but not people. In the future we will need to invest in social capital as surely as we invest in skills and buildings. The voluntary sector is – I believe – showing the way, making the link between rebuilding communities and rebuilding economic opportunity' (Speech at NCVO annual conference, July 1999, p. 4).

Gordon Brown: Community-building, innovation and 'personalized' services

'voluntary action has four great practical strengths – (1) its local character . . . on the ground knowledge and engagement bridges not just the gap of size between neighbourhood and state, but also the gap of knowledge and perhaps too the gap of trust . . . (2) its greater flexibility to innovate . . . resting not just on the freedom and the flexibility of voluntary initiative, but on its diversity as well . . . (3) its individual, personal approach, capacity especially to offer help to those pushed to the margins of poverty, who are often mistrustful of the sort of authority that the state or any other forms of authority represents . . . it is about being there . . . and (4) its capacity to strengthen citizenship . . . by participating in our community, we learn about the world beyond our front doors and garden gates, and our citizenship is stronger as a result. It is our own constructive contribution to the forging of good social relations and the rich civic society on which we all depend. It is a contribution that the state cannot make in our place' (Brown, 2000: 20–5).

Lord Falconer: Community-building: local responsiveness to social exclusion

There are many goods neither the state not the market provide: unprofitable services, and where public problems are unwieldy . . . three strengths of the voluntary sector include (1) its ability to respond to the social exclusion agenda; (2) its sensitivity and local level of activity, closer to communities and to the issues unlike remote bureaucracies, it can innovate more freely...there can be a virtuous circle of trust and improved outcomes; (3) provides experience, should not only be seen as a response to social exclusion (Author's notes from speech at Centre for the Open Society and Social Market Foundation, March 2001).

David Blunkett: Community-building

'We must recognise the importance of social capital – the informal norms of trust and co-operation that are strengthened and created by voluntary association in civil society. Rather than government and voluntarism being opposed, the legitimacy of public institutions and the vitality of civil association seem to improve and decline in tandem . . . volunteering and voluntary activity are vital to the renewal of our democracy. The processes of formal participation and practical engagement cannot be separated. For this reason, volunteering and voluntary activity are vital to the renewal of our democracy. People who engage . . . in clubs, church groups and voluntary organisations – are more likely to care about the well-being of the community as a whole. As members of associations and participants in voluntary activities, they develop the skills, habits and casts of mind necessary for democratic participation' (Blunkett, 2001: 17 and 25).

themselves suggestive of the particular importance attached to 'community-building' priorities.[11] This shows that ministerial rhetoric, like broader parliamentary political rhetoric, is in effect selectively focusing on the favourable aspects of the limited evidence that is available.

6.5 Conclusion

The functions and weaknesses associated with the voluntary sector in the international third sector theoretical literature are familiar in the British context, and often recognized in policy practices. More sophisticated accounts of how these are expressed and fit together have evolved with the publication of certain landmark 'consolidating' papers, including research for the Wolfenden Committee, and the work of individual scholars such as Ralph Kramer, Martin Knapp, David Billis and Howard Glennerster. A possible exception until fairly recently has been the case of the 'expressive function' and its 'leadership development' corollary, which per se have arguably received less systematic prominence in the foundational research literature.

However, it has been shown that more recently the expressive role has come to the fore, at least in part as developments overseas have raised awareness of a contribution that otherwise tended to be taken for granted. In addition, a second function, 'community-building' has come to much greater prominence very recently. This reflects – and is reflected in – the increased popularity of the concept of 'social capital' in both academic and political circles. As Section 6.4 underlined, community-building and social capital have been given particular weight in Government rhetoric over the past 2–3 years.

Comparative research evidence and argument is, however, both limited and ambiguous. In some situations, no meaningful sector comparison is possible; but when the sectors do co-exist, it is not clear that the sector has fulfilled these functions to a greater extent than the other sectors. If voluntarism is taken to be intrinsically valuable, or its benefits can be assumed to outweigh its costs (an assumption made in the Treasury review of 2001–2) then the fact that volunteers are concentrated in this sector implies a voluntary sector advantage in this respect as a *fait accompli*. Otherwise, however, a range of interpretations of the available evidence are theoretically possible.

Against this inconclusive backdrop, the rhetoric on the voluntary sector's consequences has filtered the research evidence and supplemented it with pre-determined 'mental maps' involving ideology, personal experience and anec-dote, being 'selective' as policy process theory would predict (Majone, 1989; Hood, 1998; Pierson, 2000a, b). As with all rhetoric, the goal has been to present plausible story-lines which fit with the agenda that the speakers wish to promote. Politically, this has worked in a number of ways. First, in interpreting individual functions where the research evidence is actually inconclusive or ambiguous, rhetoricians have, consciously or otherwise, pursued lines of argument which are favourable to the voluntary sector. Second, rhetoric has drawn attention to functions rather than weaknesses, and where it has recognized the latter, these are often seen as matters of joint sectoral responsibility, rather than as the 'fault' of the voluntary sector itself. Third, the 'community-building' function has received particular recognition by ministers most recently. Although the Government claims to be open to discussion on the voluntary sector's 'added value', with respect to its functions, the rhetoric developed suggests that beliefs and assumptions favourable to the sector are already well developed. This emphasis in terms of impacts ties in with the policy emphases and institution-building efforts, and ultimately therefore the communitarian agenda, discussed in Chapters 3 and 4.

These developments have been accompanied by more general and diffuse recognition in high politics more generally. The two main political parties both express appreciation of the sector's beneficial consequences. Yet if there is a consensual 'motherhood and apple pie' flavour to much of the rhetoric, there are also two 'fault lines' evident in terms of emphases and priorities. First, while all rhetoricians express the belief that the state should be 'supportive' of a 'healthy' voluntary sector and civil society, there are different emphases on the role the state could and should play to this end. The current administration differs from other Parliamentarians, and opinions expressed outside Parliament, in believing that ongoing institutional reforms are conducive to the sector's health – a theme to which we shall return theoretically in Chapter 10. Second, parliamentary rhetoricians differ in the weight they seem attach to the 'service delivery' function and the 'expressive' function, and some have stated a clear preference for one over the other in situations where they conflict (Box 6.8). Ministers thus far have pointedly avoided aligning themselves on this point. The New Labour slogan 'modernization' now introduced in the context of the Treasury review's 'Futurebuilders' does not help here, because the meaning of that concept is itself ambiguous (Hood, 1998).

In this context, it will be important for research to retain as critical and rounded an edge as is possible. A balanced account seeking to steer clear of a priori commitments to any particular political agenda would certainly point to at least the following features of reality which tend to be downplayed in the rhetorical perspectives reviewed:

- The enormous difficulties of generalization.
- The possibility that (under some reasonable weighting system reflecting widely accepted values) the voluntary sector's 'weaknesses' could be more extensive that its 'advantages' in at least some situations or circumstances.
- The need to underline and analyse rather than ignore or underplay the apparently ambiguous (neither purely negative nor purely positive) effects of policies of the type discussed in the preceding chapter in terms of fostering, or providing space for, the fulfilment of the sector's 'functions'.
- The possibility that, in practice, trade-offs exist between 'functions', and 'functions' cannot always be uncoupled from 'weaknesses'. In particular, it has been suggested that a tension could be present between enhancement of the sector's role as an efficient service provider and its expressive role – since the 'price' of the latter could include technical inefficiency, amateurism and duplicative particularism.

Not least because of the very diversity and complexity of the voluntary sector, research on its 'impacts' has been markedly prone to indeterminacy. However, even as scholarship becomes more developed, disputes will not be 'closed', but will simply become more sophisticated. A theoretical example of this was presented in the introduction to this part of the book, when it was noted how a *prima facie* conclusive statement on the sector's comparative 'under-performance' with regard to service provision could plausibly be challenged. The ambiguities over how to interpret the comparative evidence on such 'functions' as service quality, and the dispute over social capital currently ongoing are good, real-world examples of how the research evidence and its interpretation is still evolving and contested. In the latter case, more or less optimistic views now vie with sceptical perspectives which challenge this enthusiasm on theoretical, empirical and methodological grounds (cf. Box 6.4). This represents just the beginning of what will undoubtedly be a long running and vibrant discussion.

The final chapter to this book will suggest a hopefully constructive way to think about the sector's consequences in broader political and institutional context. However, in the meantime, the following three chapters seek to go at least some way towards addressing the topic 'objectively', on the basis of meta-analysis of existing research.

By examining the voluntary sector's situation at the level of three policy subfields, the chapters aim to develop a more systematic and balanced account than would be the case if we relied on 'horizontal' evidence alone. Significantly, the criteria for selection were not based upon a political or rhetorical pre-disposition to emphasize advantages at the expense of disadvantages. Rather, the international project's decision rules as specified in the introduction to Part II were followed, selecting fields which it was thought would allow the hypothesized 'functions' to be represented, independent of any associated negative effects.

Notes

1 Almond and Kendall (2001b) also compare and contrast employment across the three sectors in terms of a range of other aspects of employment conditions and circumstances. Some of their evidence could be interpreted as suggestive of a different, if not necessarily higher, quality in the voluntary sector paid work situation which could have distinctive implications for cost or service quality. Inter alia, they found that unpaid overtime was more prevalent, training opportunities were more extensive, and workplace flexibilities and 'family friendliness' were often more evident. However, see also the discussion of amateurism in voluntary sector human resource management in Section 6.3.

2 As with Osborne's evidence on innovation, this study unfortunately relied completely on voluntary organizations' self-reporting, and there was no external validation of these impressions. This clearly limits the extent to which conclusions as to 'effectiveness' can be drawn from a positivist, objective standpoint, and this is indeed a more general problem with the social movement literature (Kendall and Knapp, 2000: 112)

3 However, there were a number of works in, and in parallel to, the specialist voluntary sector literature which arguably speak to aspects of this function, even if this particular label is not used; compare Paton, 1992; Knapp *et al.*, 1995; Ware, 1989; Hirst, 1994; and Barker, 1993.

4 Radical theorists would take issue with this claim, arguing that the structures of British society have systematically and deliberately denied those outside the political elite the opportunity to express their values by virtue of invidious manipulation of agendas and ideological conditions. (For neo-Marxist materials specifically on the voluntary sector as a vehicle for imposing elite values in the UK case, see Wolch, 1990; Beckford, 1991.)

5 In theory, however, this advantage could accrue to any sector which took seriously the advice of experienced local people or community workers. David Donnison has outlined the 'scientific principle' behind the latter approach. This is 'the recurring observation that we do not fully understand human problems, and cannot therefore formulate fully effective responses to them if we do not give the people who experience them a voice both in the analysis of the problems and in the formulation of the solutions. Other voices must be heard too. But a study of the needs . . . which does not give a voice to those people will – to some degree at least – get it wrong' (Donnison, 1991, cited in Mayo, 1994: 149–50).

6 A further problem of 'particularism' can emerge in service delivery to the extent organizations used their autonomy to systematically 'cream skim' or 'cherry pick' low cost or 'difficult' clients. We will return to this issue in examining the evidence in particular policy fields, as little can be said at the level of generality with which this chapter is concerned.

7 However, outside Parliament, think tanks and other organizations linked to the Conservative party have argued for precisely this. See the discussion of 'other

influences in the political stream' in Chapter 3; and the summary of 'civic conservatism' contained in Chapter 10.

8   In the person of Dahrendorf, this position is articulated as part of a broader world
view, a clear liberal-expressive orientation. We return to this issue in the concluding
chapter.

9   However, the accompanying 'technical report', in its summary 'case studies', is rather
more balanced, acknowledging failures at least implicitly with its euphemistic
references to 'challenges', 'problems' and the suggested 'need to evaluate new schemes'
(HM Treasury, 2002b).

10   The selection of speeches by the Prime Minister and Chancellor of the Exchequer
are self-evidently from the most powerful sources. Falconer has also been included as
particularly significant, both because of his close and long-standing personal
connections to, and influence on, the Prime Minister (Hennessy, 2000) and his one-
time responsibility for volunteering as Minister of State at the Cabinet Office.
Blunkett (2001), for his part, while according to Hennessy not as influential at the
very centre, has been particularly active promoting the 'civil society' agenda in the
Cabinet, and his account is relatively well developed.

11   The process of implementing these particular reports (Policy Action Team 9, 1999;
Warner, 1999) were not discussed in Chapter 4 because it is not clear how they are
being taken forward. This is in part because of their very long-term aspirations, but
also because, according to Plowden *et al.* (2001), the Government has been far
slower than expected to make progress on the initial steps suggested by their agendas.

7 The impact of voluntary sector social housing

- **The voluntary sector's growing prominence in social housing can partly be explained by the perceived limitations and failures of other sectors.**

- **The attractiveness of the voluntary sector's housing portfolio significantly reflects its situation as a 'late starter' compared to other sectors in delivering mainstream housing.**

- **On average this sector can be compared favourably with other sectors in the delivery of social housing services in certain significant respects.**

- **Regarding 'weaknesses', a remarkable recent feature of voluntary sector social housing has been its freedom from resource insufficiency.**

7.1 Introduction

This chapter is the first of the impact studies at the level of the vertical policy field.[1] The area of social housing in England was chosen as the UK example of a field in which the voluntary sector contributes to society in the sense of 'improving economic opportunity'. Adequate housing – in the British policy discourse, involving 'decent' conditions – meets a primary human need, providing the security and stability upon which participation in economic and social life can build. Social housing in the voluntary sector is delivered by 'housing associations' (since 1996, technically 'registered social landlords') required by law to be 'nonprofit', whose boards are volunteers and from whose activities excess surpluses (profits) must by law be reinvested in housing activities.[2]

This is of particular interest because, as we noted in Chapter 2, it has been one of the most prominent areas of economic growth in the voluntary sector during the 1990s. This dynamism can also be demonstrated by considering the evolution of sector market shares within the housing field, and the availability of long-range, time-series data allow us to set these developments in a longer term, and historical context. Table 7.1 shows how these organizations' prominence is both a very recent and, albeit more limitedly, a very old phenomenon: the sector entered the twentieth century as second only to the market as an allocator of housing resources. It was not until the second quarter of that century that the public sector (primarily local government) grew sufficiently quickly to push it into third place. This ranking of ownership types has then held to the present, but as the table shows, the pendulum has gradually swung back towards voluntary organizations at the expense of local government.[3]

The field's current role as a leading area of growth within the voluntary sector, and its intriguing historical trajectory, are important reasons for focusing upon it. Its historical and current participation in a 'mixed economy' means that a comparative perspective can be attempted. Other reasons for focusing on social housing included the existence of a significant, consolidated body of literature upon which this chapter has drawn heavily (particularly useful overviews are offered by Power, 1993, 1997; Hills, 1998; Malpass and Murie, 1999; Cope, 1999; and, historically, Mullins, 2000 and Malpass, 2000). Literature was supplemented with appropriate 'expert' interviewees, and an 'expert' focus group was also undertaken (see Appendix 2). These fed into an initial report, which was then taken forward by a quasi-Delphi review process. Thus, the first draft was circulated for reaction to 'experts', and a revised version was published in 2000 incorporating this feedback (Wigglesworth and Kendall, 2000). This chapter draws on the latter, but integrates insights gleaned from a further review of the rapidly evolving literature and additional expert feedback.

Section 7.2 reviews the historical trajectory of the sector's relations with the state, not as an end in itself, but to bring into focus those past developments which continue to shape the present situation. It is clear that each sector's portfolio of social housing reflects the cumulative outcome of both

Table 7.1 Long-term trends in housing stock and tenure in England and Wales, and in England only (%)

Year	Owner-occupied	Public sector rented	Voluntary sector rented	Private (for-profit) sector rented
England and Wales				
1914	10	0.3	0.6	90
1939	33	10	(57 – combined figure)	
1961	44	24	(31 – combined figure)	
1971	52	28	0.9	19
1979	57	29	2.0	12
1989	68	21	2.8	7
England only				
1988	66	23	2	9
1991	68	20	3	9
1995/6	68	18	5	10
1998/9	69	16	5	10
2001/2	70	14	6	10

Sources: Data for England and Wales, 1914–89 from Power (1993); data for England from 1988–2001/2 from Office of the Deputy Prime Minister (2002).

deliberate policy decisions, the timing of events beyond the control of policy-makers, and the legacy of evolving beliefs about sectoral capabilities informed by both evidence and ideology. Sections 7.3 and 7.4 then review the functions and weaknesses introduced at the start of this part of the book, in turn. Section 7.5 is a summary conclusion underpinning the enduring relevance of strategic state policy decisions and the dynamics of central–local government relations. It points to a balance of evidence which seems to cast housing associations in a favourable light. But it also cautions that any overall con-clusion masks considerable intrasectoral variation, and involves major caveats and lacunae which must be kept to the fore in any assessment of each sector's impact.

7.2 The legacy of history

In the case of social housing, the imprint of history is incontrovertible. Most obviously, housing designs and layouts tend to be 'creatures of their time', reflecting the values and aspirations prevalent when they were constructed, and involving features which may often be costly to alter or replace if they fall out of favour. British housing policy has bequeathed a legacy unique in Europe in terms of the nature of the housing stock supplied in each sector.

The hand of history clearly constrains the 'demand-side' in social housing too, most obviously as expressed collectively via the outcome of state-funding decisions. In formulating beliefs about the potential role of the public and for-profit sectors, twentieth-century British political elites tended to rely largely on ideology and beliefs concerning contemporary public opinion. Accordingly, Labour administrations tended to limit market freedoms, for example via elaborating private rent controls, and spending more generously on council housing. For their part, Conservative administrations tended to develop policy measures to encourage the market (relaxation of rent controls, tax breaks for small businesses) and limit the state by the means that were politically feasible (Hills, 1998; Timmins, 2001).

Less conspicuously, twentieth-century policy-makers' preferences for the voluntary sector at central government level initially developed less directly from ideologically underpinned high politics, but more pragmatically and incrementally according to evolving perceptions of its practical capacities. In the early twentieth century, this pragmatism initially generated a dismissive attitude towards this sector. This was informed by contemporary impressions of the actual and potential roles of existing providers, which then ranged from twelfth-century almshouses to nineteenth-century housing trust estates, including those in the capital. Civil servants believed that the voluntary sector's track record of 'underperformance' in response to encouraging 1919 legislation suggested its role must necessarily be extremely limited (Malpass, 2000: 81 and 89, Chapter 5). Politicians followed their advice on what was, for them at that time, a secondary matter of policy compared with the grander issue of municipal versus market responsibility.

The voluntary sector remained as a low visibility provider on the 'outer edge' of mainstream policy in the 1940s and 1950s in the aftermath of war. This was the moment when Aneurin Bevan famously rejected for-profit involvement in social housing as fundamentally flawed. It was dismissed as 'unplannable' by virtue of the assumed speculative tendencies of private builders. Instead, in line with its statist sympathies, Labour placed great faith in local government as the appropriate vehicle for a massive expansion of social housing following large-scale slum clearance. The voluntary sector, in those socialist quarters which gave it much attention, at this time tended to see it in negative terms, as characterized by 'failures' rather than 'functions'. That is, it was seen as undemocratic, unaccountable, conservative and middle class, and where defined more positively, was seen strictly as a residual 'complement not substitute' to directly controlled council housing (Malpass, 2000: 132). The Conservative administration of the 1950s – a more natural ally, to the extent these existing bodies' traditional and elitist style was ideologically resonant – for its part was too busy trying to enhance the for-profit market, and control council housing growth, to develop a supportive orientation.

However, during the 1960s, the limits of the other 'primary' sectors were becoming more apparent as evidence on actual patterns of provision was generated by policy review and research. This awareness prompted renewed interest in developing a much more expansive voluntary sector complementary role. Local authorities' slum clearance and mass housing estate consolidation policies had proceeded at an incredible rate, and were now beginning to have extensive negative side-effects. These were recognized by some councils who chose to support new associations specifically to help tackle these 'spillover' problems. (Having consolidated their own dominant positions in this field, they found it easier to be sympathetic towards others from a position of power.) The for-profit rented sector was increasingly under attack, at both elite and popular levels, and the anger of some lead them to establish a new generation of voluntary housing bodies (Box 7.1). Central government for its part chose to experiment with the encouragement of co-operative ownership and cost-rent schemes. Although these did not take off as expected because the new organizations had problems raising capital, it helped to get off the ground what is now referred to as the 'modern British housing movement'. This was, then, a set of organizations with 1960s and 1970s roots, which saw itself as radically different from the earlier 'conservative' generations of providers mentioned above.[4]

By the mid-1970s, the general housing policy emphasis had shifted from mass estate construction to rehabilitation and selective rebuilding, and area-based urban policy in inner cities was developing fast. This timing is of critical importance for our purposes, because it was also at just this moment that the voluntary sector moved unambiguously from its earlier peripheral policy situation to a more mainstream, state-sponsored position. Because it was only a 'late comer' to mainstream housing policy by European standards, the sector in Britain had not taken on the running of mass housing estates. That role had

---

Box 7.1   The negative imagery of for-profit rented housing in the 1960s

The Millner Holland Report exposed 'twilight' areas of private renting, involving landlord exploitation – not just through exorbitant rent levels, but via 'harrassment, extortion and colour bars' and 'winkling' – coercion to move protected tenants (Power, 1993: 206 and 208). Negative folk memories of profiteering landlordism in rented accommodation going back for decades were reinforced by the infamous activities of Rachman, and Labour criticism of these practices were a key factor in helping Labour win the 1964 election (see Timmins, 2001: 189–91). The evocative televised drama *Cathy Come Home*, portraying victims of profiteering landlordism, directly provoked the formation of the homeless campaign organization Shelter. This in turn spawned a number of new housing associations in the late 1960s, and now supports a large network of advice and support for tenants (see discussion of 'advocacy' below).

---

already been taken by local government as a 'natural' corollary to its slum clearance role and its assumed centrality to local public services.[5] Rather, it developed initially on a more humane and small scale, not just because that was in keeping with its own ('supply-side') aspirations, but because that was the thrust of policy at this time. As such, it can be readily contrasted with both the 'independent nonprofit' sector in Europe and the council-owned sector in Britain. Unlike British housing associations, these were both now working with the legacy of mass housing from the expansionary 1960–75 period. In sum, for the voluntary sector, at this critical moment, there was a fortuitous coincidence between intensifying policy interest and the rejection of 'mass' models.

According to Malpass (2000), this new interest in the voluntary sector was not a Damascene conversion from the sceptical attitudes on 'capacity' that had prevailed earlier in the century. Rather, initially policy-makers' attention was captured 'despite doubts' generated by earlier historical experiences, because of an intensified awareness of the failures of other sectors.[6] During this period, extensive and generous central state support was forthcoming, providing unprecedented capital resources – whose absence had been critical in preventing growth earlier in the century – and producing a 'golden era' of extensive publicly backed 'risk-free' investment (Mullins, 2000). This support powered much of the growth in market share shown in Table 7.1, and provided a firm base for further development, even after a less generous regime had been adopted in 1988 (see below). The 1974 Housing Act was the launch pad, strengthening the Housing Corporation, whose enhanced capital funding of the sector was now accompanied by the elaboration of an increasingly dense regulatory regime. It tightly controlled the pattern of new development, aiming to ensure economic and efficiency in management, and alignment with broader national social policy objectives. Particular 'priority groups' were singled out as in need of housing association accommodation, including those whose needs were thought to be unmet in the market or via council housing.

Into the early Thatcher era, the voluntary housing sector emerging as the major beneficiary of that regime's aspiration to take away the power and influence of local government. Existing doubts about the latter were elevated to a partisan ideological assault from 1979 onwards (Kendall and Knapp, 1996), and council housing was starved of capital support by central government's funding settlements. For its part, the voluntary sector prospered. State encouragement came via supply-side stimulus provided by the Corporation's developmental grants – only available for registered 'nonprofit' providers. Simultaneously, demand-side means-tested housing benefit funded by the state put low-income tenants in a position to pay rent. This made the sector doubly reliant on state funding.

The situation also changed with the 1988 Housing Act, which initiated a revolution in the system of housing finance. Spurred by a desire to stimulate 'efficiency', the new financial framework required housing associations to raise funds from their own reserves or private lenders to supplement the public subsidy, for which they now had to bid on a competitive basis. The ongoing gradual shift in market share towards the voluntary sector accelerated in the mid-1980s, as cash-starved local government increasingly transferred property to housing associations after tenant ballots, a trend encouraged by central government (Malpass and Mullins, 2002). These major 1980 policy shifts, were broadly retained by the New Labour administration from 1997. However, there was a switch in emphasis, away from the raw unit cost competition of the mid-1990s towards a supposedly moderated, quality controlled allocation in the process of bidding for public capital subsidies.

Four points of enduring relevance emerge from this review. First, the growth and character of housing associations as policy actors can be understood from a comparative perspective principally by reference to perceptions of the limitations and failures of other rental sectors. As will be seen below, there was considerable awareness amongst contemporary experts of a range of positive contributions. But it was initially what it was not – not for profit, and not part of the local state – that were the initial drivers of recognition and encouragement. Evidence-based doubts about the state at the local level gathering pace in the 1960s and early 1970s were reinforced by ideological hostility from 1979 onwards, injecting huge momentum into a political process of 'demunicipalization' in which housing associations played a leading role.

Second, as a result of an unforeseen, unplanned sequence of events, the voluntary sector was 'in the right place at the right time'. Its property portfolio (more recent mass housing transfers notwithstanding) has been on a relatively small and humane scale, to a large degree because it had been a 'late starter' as a mainstream policy actor by European standards. Had it already been at the centre of social housing development by the 1960s, it would presumably have had to cope with a much greater proportion of the problematic 'mass' housing stock with which councils were saddled.

Third, central government has been critical in shaping the sector's develop-ment. It was its decision in the early 1970s to develop a deliberate policy response to the voluntary sector's 'capital constraint' problem (initially diag-nosed several decades earlier) which allowed the sector to 'take off'. This catapulted some organizations, primarily with 1960s and 1970s origins, into an economic 'superleague', with many now operating on a regional or national scale.

Fourth, while the 'modern British housing movement' is prominent, it should be underlined that supply-side diversity reflects historical origins more generally too. The sector also comprises, albeit on a more limited scale, a very wide range of older organizations too (Mullins, 2000).

7.3 Functions of the voluntary sector in social housing

7.3.1 *Service provision: the primary role*

Certainly as far as its leading public sponsor – the Housing Corporation – is concerned, service provision is the most important rationale for supporting the 2,000 housing associations that it now funds. While tremendously varied in their origins, size and scale, the shared purpose identified in the Housing Corporation's official literature is to provide accommodation for those who are inadequately housed or homeless, and for whom suitable housing is not available at prices within their means, or elsewhere in the local market. At the same time, housing associations also undertake other, housing-related activities, prominently including social care, training schemes (including New Deals since 1997) and urban regeneration (NHF, 1995; Mullins *et al.*, 2001). This diversity in terms of activity is taken into account in discussing other functions in what follows (while Chapter 8 also attends to housing associations incidentally as an import-ant part of the mixed economy of social care for older people).

There is diversity in client group and accommodation forms, as well as origins and size. The view that the *raison d'être* for nonprofit social housing is peoples' limited ability to rely on the market due to personal financial constraints and social vulnerabilities has in practice embraced a multitude of tenants including homeless people, older people, people with mental health problems, young people at risk, people with drug and alcohol abuse problems, women at risk from domestic violence, refugees and ex-offenders. Accommodation forms range from sheltered housing to short-term provision in self-contained units, group accom-modation and hostels, as well as general housing. With the transfer of former local government housing stock to housing associations, the portfolio of the sector now also includes an increased proportion of general housing for low-income groups, including many more unemployed people.

The 'practitioners' definition' involves explicit recognition of the market's inability to provide sufficient housing for significant numbers of people in need, reinforcing the extent to which the voluntary sector is defined primarily as a response to 'market failure'. The market mechanism, through owner occupation or renting, is taken to be the 'normal' method for allocating housing, and there can be intervention while not supplanting private property rights directly. Rent controls, and the use of demand-side compensation by means-tested 'vouchers' effectively redeemable in any sector – as with housing benefit – means low ability to pay has not necessarily precluded for-profit supply. Strategic rent capping has been widely deployed, while the state rent subsidy/for-profit supply combination does now account for a significant (but unknown) proportion of for-profit rented – de facto social – provision.

However, the state has not chosen to directly invest in the for-profit sector in the same way that it has supported housing associations via the Housing Corporation, or state housing via council housing.[7] This undoubtedly partly reflects a perception that public opinion, conditioned by memories of for-profit landlords' exploitation and abuse at times of housing shortage (Box 7.1), would be hostile to such an initiative, and the success of active lobbying by the voluntary sector's representative body to prevent such a policy (see discussion of 'advocacy'). Essentially technical arguments concerning 'market failure', which could have been relevant, only go so far, since they seem unclear as to why voluntary sector provision is necessarily preferable to regulated for-profit provision or public sector provision (see Box 7.2).

Some evidence has been accumulated on the quality and relative *costs* of the provider sectors over the past 20 years. As far as quality of housing stock is concerned, Hills (1998) has reviewed comparative evidence from the English Housing Conditions and General Household Surveys of the late 1980s and early 1990s, and shown that on most (but not all) measures, housing associations

---

Box 7.2 'Market failure' and social housing

In orthodox economic theory, proactive public policy can be justified on the grounds that housing is a 'merit good' to which society believes everyone 'should' have access. The capital intense character of housing makes its supply highly inelastic, so shortages in which considerable monopoly power accrues to providers for long periods will mean the state interventions to curb profit-seeking will be economically beneficial for society. There are also widespread 'imperfections' in the capital market. However, a preference for the nonprofit form is only one possible 'solution'. Publicly funded 'vouchers', rent regulation and public owner- ship are others. It is not clear that economic theory can match each of these potential 'solutions' to clearly defined conditions under which each (or some combination of the three) is to be preferred on grounds of efficiency or equity (see Hills, 1998; Le Grand *et al.*, 1992: Chapter 4).

have the best record for rented accommodation, and on no measure have the worst record.[8]

More recent research from the Housing Corporation does confirm that housing association provision on average currently seems to involve less overcrowding and higher bedroom standards than either public or private sector social rented housing (London Research Centre, 1998). There is also some limited evidence that housing associations have tended to offer better 'front-line' services, employing staff in a more decentralized way – a relative advantage retained despite a number of decentralization initiatives within the state sector from the 1970s onwards (Power, 1993, 1997). In addition, and most systematic-ally, recent 'Best Value' comparisons suggest that differences between each sector's 'performance' suggested in 1980s and 1990s research hold now, at least in some domains, and in spite of possibly narrowing over time. Putting to one side some complications in terms of comparability, in 2000/1 it is now known that housing associations were 'performing' markedly better in terms of emergency repair response and reletting times, although only slightly better than their council housing counterparts as measured by average tenant satisfaction and the handling of rent arrears (Murie and Walker, 2002).

In terms of both the nature of stock and current services, expressed opinion in our interviews and focus group was certainly that on average housing associ-ations provide a higher quality service than their public sector counterparts. However, this tendency conceals marked intrasectoral variation, linked inter alia to widely varying management approaches, costs and employees' situations – a state of affairs whose complexity had been emphasized in pioneering comparative research undertaken at the end of the 1980s (Centre for Housing Research, 1989, cited in Malpass and Murie, 1999: Chapter 11).

Three important factors thought to lie behind the observed patterns were singled out by experts. First, as emphasized in Section 7.2, the historically inherited housing portfolios of the sectors were directly relevant. Problematic, undercapitalized and poor quality (sometimes bleak, alienating and dangerous) 'mass' estates and high-rise properties were concentrated in the public sector (notwithstanding some recent LSVT transfers of estates of this sort to the voluntary sector). Second, the extent to which voluntary organizations have traditionally been housing specialists able to focus completely on this activity with a single purpose, often with well-developed systems of management control. This was in marked contrast to local authority providers tied directly into local government systems with diffuse responsibilities and inherently bureaucratic, complex and cross-cutting professional and administrative procedures (Power, 1993: Chapter 20). In the words of one focus group participant, public ownership therefore tended to involve 'balancing a whole basket of tasks, some of which are not easily compatible'. Third, better resourcing of maintenance programmes made possible better performance in terms of repairs, not least a legacy of the relatively generous Housing Corporation funding settlements of earlier years.

The latter two factors noted above echo the argument of Page (1993), who in common with other commentators in the literature also draws attention to two further factors. First, quantitatively superior paid staff to tenant ratios, in terms particularly of a 'front-line' presence (see also Bines *et al.*, 1993; the comparative quality of staffing is considered in discussion of 'community-building'). Second, compared to the public sector, a lack of direct political control, aggravating the more 'technical' difficulties associated with public ownership already mentioned.

Why might direct political control be worth avoiding in social housing? An OECD study diagnosed short-termism and 'policy swings' following from the electoral cycle as problematic, because by its very nature, housing requires long-term frames of sustained investment. In addition, locally, rents could be kept 'too low' in order to win votes in the short term, with possible sacrifices in maintenance and investment (OECD, 1988, cited in Power, 1993: 371). Power (1997: 43) goes so far as to argue that there is a straightforward trade-off to be made between 'political control' and 'service to tenants, the repair and maintenance of the social housing stock . . . public housing systems are prone to acute funding crises, low standards of repair and poor management because the nature of politics is vastly different from the nature of housing management'.

Moreover, in Britain, at a macro-political level, Conservative administrations in particular have been systematically unwilling to provide local government with sufficient resources to develop its own high-quality social housing (Timmins, 2001). It is conceivable that had they been working with housing associations rather than councils as the primary suppliers, these administrations might have been more generous, because destructive party political or ideological tensions could have been avoided. Finally, on the ground it may be easier to cultivate trust with community members of provision is at one remove from the political process (see also discussion of social capital under 'community-building' below).

Regarding costs, a Centre for Housing Research study (1989) emphasized that housing management costs were 'average' for national or regional housing associations, but 'high' for local associations (compared to 'low' for district council housing and 'average' for metropolitan council housing). However, it is unclear whether this was a reflection of weaker management control, other technical inefficiencies, differences in stock characteristics and geographical situations, or simply lack of access to scale economies in the case of local housing associations. A more recent examination of the causes of variation in average managements costs suggests the scale economies are less important in explaining variation than whether stock is situated in London, and whether it involves flats rather than houses (both inflating costs for obvious reasons). Utilizing new 'Best Value' data, this new study also reported that unadjusted average management costs were very similar in each sector when compared crudely. But since the multivariate analysis later suggested that a 'London effect' was particularly significant, and since housing associations have a higher proportion of property in London than councils, this might suggest that controlling for the London effect would reveal lower costs in the former sector.[9]

Comparisons of the single most important recurrent housing costs as far as tenants are concerned – rents payable – have also been attempted. Housing association rents tend to be set, on average, at higher levels than local authority but lower level than private sector equivalent property (Wilcox and Rhodes, 1998; DTZ Consulting, 1998). It might be that this difference reflects a 'London effect' (see above), but it might also imply higher average net revenue, another underlying reason why housing associations may have been positioned to deliver superior quality compared to local councils. Higher rent receipts could help fund the more generous staffing and extensive repairs activities referred to above, or allow for the accumulation of surpluses for reinvestment.

Finally, it is worth noting that accounts of costs and quality in direct housing services rarely allude to the significance of volunteers. This is unsurprising to the extent that volunteers' role is primarily confined to governance, via management committee memberships, in the case of housing associations. Hills (1989: 264) has referred to the 'enthusiasm and experience of large numbers of voluntary management committee members' as underpinning these organizations' 'good reputation for innovation and good management'. However, their limited 'front-line' delivery role makes them of less direct significance in this field than in other areas of voluntary direct services, although they clearly do play a part in discharging other functions (see below).[10]

7.3.2 Advocacy

Box 7.3 refers to the voluntary sector's role in 'client level advocacy'. The remainder of this section focuses instead on public policy advocacy, and in this aspect a mixed picture emerges as to the achievements of housing associations and others. Implicit in a debate in the housing literature about whether housing associations are basically part of the state apparatus (Malpass and Murie, 1999; Malpass, 2000) or exercise a meaningful and productive amount of autonomy (Mullins and Riseborough, 2001; Mullins, 2000), are more negative and positive understandings of this role respectively. Less ambiguously, a long-term political success of the voluntary sector's representative body in this field (now the National Housing Federation, NHF) has undoubtedly been its ability to create, and politically sell, a sense of distinctiveness from the for-profit sector, despite the incredible internal diversity within the voluntary sector. Most consequentially, this body successfully argued at key moments of strategic policy design (including various housing acts) – and sometimes in the face of considerable scepticism on the part of civil servants – that nonprofit status should be a prerequisite for access to state capital funding.[11]

Finally, on a more day-to-day basis, respondents in our interviews and focus groups tended to feel that the NHF and its predecessors could have done more to keep social housing high on the generic public policy agenda in the second half of the 1990s. However, it was acknowledged that this was difficult because the obvious competitors for agenda space – education, health and social security – were of more interest to the general public, the media and politicians because all voters had a much more obvious stake in these fields. Yet more tangibly, the sector had been successful in securing funding for, and implementing discrete

---

Box 7.3 Client level advocacy: housing advice

Many housing associations provide management, training or advisory services for other housing groups in addition to operating their own accommodation. The voluntary sector also contributes to housing advocacy through the operation of local specialist housing advice agencies, as well as through the advice on housing which forms an important part of the activities of generalist advice agencies. Highest profile of all is the national homeless charity Shelter, mentioned earlier, which now helps more than 100,000 people a year. Its fifty-four housing aid centres exemplify many of the advice-giving activities also undertaken by more local organizations and some housing associations, including helping people avoid losing their homes to begin with; finding places to sleep at night; informing people of their legal rights; representing people in court or presenting their case to lenders or public authorities; and through assistance in drafting letters to landlords and bank managers.

While the public sector also provides housing advice, individual recipients of voluntary sector advice services may perceive the latter to be more approachable and less 'bureaucratic', in part because they are less preoccupied with meeting statutory duties. Moreoever, Shelter and others give strong emphasis to the 'unofficial', independent, nonjudgemental nature of their advice. This means that potentially beneficial courses of action can be pursued on behalf of public sector tenant beneficiaries in particular which might not be encouraged by local authorities' own staff. A final distinction between advice offered by the voluntary sector and other sectors is that the former is often delivered by volunteers. While knowledge of this status may generate worries that the adviser does not possess appropriate expertise and professionalism, suitable training can overcome this; moreover, it may reassure clients that their adviser is motivated to act in their interests, and be more likely, as a lay person, to see matters from their perspective.

---

central government programmes such as the *Rough Sleepers Initiative*, achievement which it was suggested resulted from strong, ethical leadership.

7.3.3 *Innovation*

The primary research undertaken for this study suggested six key areas of innovation (see also Walker *et al.*, 2001). Two of these were essentially generic innovations – that is, not specific to the sector: changes in technology in a narrow, technical sense, in terms of the use of alarm systems, teleworking, close circuit TV and call centres; and improvements in infrastructure quality made possible by using sustainable products. Two others, tenant participation and area regeneration, are discussed under 'community-building' below.

The other two innovations identified, which seemed to be particularly associated with housing associations, and which cut across their functions were organizational responses to the new housing association financial regime (by definition confined to housing associations); and extensive and creative patterns of diversification. Concerning the former, in the aftermath of the 1988 Act, it was explained in an interview how 'the government didn't come along and say "this is how to do it", it was left to us to innovate, and there are a whole range of things that have evolved'. However, this was not undertaken by housing associations in isolation. In particular, the Housing Corporation and the NHF played an important role in developing new schemes and procedures to provide a route whereby housing associations could secure the requisite private finance. One important example of collaboration between these two agencies was the founding and functioning of the Housing Finance Corporation (THFC), which has raised some £1 billion of the £12 billion private funds secured since the Act.

Mullins and Riseborough (1997) and Mullins *et al.* (2001) have described in detail how housing associations have diversified within and outside of their core housing services. Some of their examples within housing could be labelled market differentiation – including the provision of housing to new groups of users, such as people with learning difficulties or low-income first-time buyers; others involve organizational innovation in the sense of developing new sets of external relationships. A key example here is the growth of intersectoral consortia or partnerships involving housing associations with statutory health (NHS) and social care agencies, particularly in the provision of accommodation and care for vulnerable people discharged into the community from long stay hospitals (see also Chapter 8). Housing associations' widespread diversification into social and community care services would be an example of radical product innovation in the sense of extending themselves beyond their traditional housing brief as would be their involvement in a range of new training schemes, foyer schemes and crime prevention initiatives.

It appears to be exceptionally hard to pin down the origins of both the generic and more sector-specific innovations that we have described. On one hand, it should be noted that since 1996 the Housing Corporation has explicitly sought to encourage 'novel approaches and replicable good practice' (Evans, 1998a) with a ring-fenced budget for that purpose. On the other, some of our experts felt that the wider regulatory activities of the Corporation and charity law jointly served to limit housing associations' ability to innovate. In fact, the Corporation's perspective on what is or is not legitimate innovation has varied over time. At the end of the 1990s, it was expressing concerns about the risks inherent in diversification beyond housing into 'noncore' activities, issuing plans to 'regulate diversity' for the first time (*Housing Today*, 121, 18 February 1999). However, in part as a response to housing associations' lobbying on their concerns that this did not recognize certain activities which were in fact central to their portfolios, the 'core' was redefined to include most of the other activities discussed in this chapter (Mullins *et al.*, 2001: 14–16).

7.3.4 *The expressive and leadership development function*

A number of developments to which we have already referred seem to imply recognition of the expressive role, even if not usually articulated with this language in this field:

- The policy aspiration of diversity and choice in forms of tenure, evident since the 1960s. At this time, worries about councils' tendency towards 'monopoly' and the 'standardized' and 'mass' nature of much of their new building, were first coming to the fore (Section 7.2).
- The increased differentiation of categories of need and recognition of an expanding range of 'priority groups' by the Housing Corporation (see description of current service provision orientation).
- The latter's willingness to support innovation in some of the ways outlined.

Implicit in all these initiatives is an assumption that uniform, undifferentiated supply will by its very nature be an insufficient outlet for the variety of needs and aspirations of a heterogeneous and changing society. A concrete example, which also allows us to make an explicit sector comparison, is suggested by the case of ethnic minority led and managed housing associations. Numerous failures of other forms of tenure to which these can partly be seen as a small, but significant response, are readily apparent from the literature. People newly entering Britain from the black commonwealth in the 1950s and 1960s were some of the most prominent victims of profiteering landlordism (Box 7.1). Usually lacking the economic wherewithal to purchase property, the first wave of immigrants found that private renting was often characterized by either blatant prejudice or involved barely affordable but appallingly inadequate accommodation. The arrival of many also coincided with the construction of some of the worst council mass housing. In the 1960s in particular, these people were arbitrarily excluded from access by prejudiced housing officials, in the context of what would now be referred to as an 'institutionally discriminating system' (Henderson and Karn, 1985, 1987).

The situation has now changed significantly. Economic success for some people from ethnic minorities has been associated with much higher levels of owner-occupation in the 1990s (Hills, 1998: 155). In addition, legislative action against racial prejudice and urban regeneration initiatives in some locales with high concentrations of minority ethnic tenants began to address some of the most glaring needs from the second half the of 1970s onwards. At the same time, the problem of exceptionally low local election voter turnout in these communities would suggest that one of the theoretical advantages of council housing – responsiveness to voter needs – would tend to break down, making generic housing associations potentially a relatively attractive option.

Yet these mainstream solutions were not adequate for all. Where economic resources have been too limited to enable market participation, and conventional housing associations did not provide sufficient opportunities for the expression of particular cultural needs, targeted state assistance has been available, allowing ethnically specialist associations to provide an alternative. Some sixty were in operation by 1995, purposefully constituted to cater for distinctive cultures. Benefits have not been limited to tenants, since their approaches have influenced general housing practice, encouraging more awareness of the needs associated with cultural diversity (Harrison *et al.*, 1996). Their influence has also been broad through some joint working with mainstream associations and local authorities. Part of the impetus for their growth has been the Housing Corporation itself, which since 1986 has sought to implement developmental strategies. According to Leeds University Race and Public Policy Research Unit, these have been 'remarkably successful and have had very few counterparts in other "Western" countries' (see Harrison, 1998).

Leadership development was included as a function in our study to reflect the way in which many countries in the broader international study claimed that the third sector often acted as an incubator for civic skills which later equipped individuals to act more effectively in the public sector, or as leaders in the world of business. In the case of English housing associations this formulation has most resonance with the 1960s and 1970s, when a number of individuals active in the modern housing movement became involved in state finance and regulation via employment at the Housing Corporation. Yet, more recently, a flow in the opposite direction has been more evident: we found a number of examples of individuals who had moved from the public sector – having been officers with responsibility for council housing – to become housing association chief executives. This reflects the peculiarly British legacy of the late 1970s onwards, involving first a gradual change in the balance of sectoral responsibility for social housing, and then the more dramatic 'residualization' of the late 1980s and 1990s.

'Reverse' cross-sectoral influence also emerged in the sense that the effect of the for-profit sector on housing associations, rather than the other way round, was thought to be increasingly pervasive amongst our respondents. The changing nature of the housing association financial environment, particularly since private institutional borrowing was catalysed by the 1988 Housing Act, increased the perceived importance of business acumen. This lead to the recruitment of more volunteer board members positioned to advise on funding and accounting matters. Some respondents suggested that this involvement of corporate expertise in governance was a mixed blessing. By narrowing the sense in which they are perceived to be different from business, such inward migration from for-profits could threaten housing associations' social credibility and orientation (see also Section 7.4 below).

7.3.5 Community-building function

Community-building implies activity with durable and long-term consequences. It can therefore be helpful to think of this function as reflecting those activities which involve housing association investment – either in physical, human or social capital. In the late 1990s, these resonated with the Housing Corporation's *Housing Plus* agenda, 'emphasis[ing] ways in which housing investment can reduce social exclusion, improve environmental sustainability and meet tenants' growing social needs' (Evans, 1998b: v). These aspirations build on what were seen as productive existing approaches already pioneered for decades by housing associations at the local level, particularly in urban neighbourhoods, and in some cases constituting their *raison d'être*. These efforts have been supported from the state on a significant scale in deprived urban communities since the 1960s through a range of area-based policies.

Generally, housing association's fortuitous legacy – and apparently superior achievements – in terms of the timing of state-support for physical investment in accommodation in comparison to councils have been discussed above. Moreover, the diversification out of housing noted under 'innovation' has involved investment in physical infrastructure other than accommodation, typically involving work pursued jointly with partners from other sectors as part of coordinated ('joined-up', in the jargon noted in Chapter 4) urban regeneration efforts. Many housing associations have used their resources to improve the environments of rundown neighbourhoods through contributing financially to, for example, community centres, child care and doctors' surgeries.

As far as human capital is concerned, evidence on the quality of housing staff is relevant. There is some evidence of superior qualifications amongst staff in housing associations compared to council housing (Centre for Housing Research, 1989; Bines *et al.*, 1993). In addition, to the extent they have diversified, housing association's have promoted a wide range of training opportunities. This ranges from the training which constitutes part of the *raison d'être* of foyer schemes to on the job training for care assistants and community workers. Others support local businesses through the provision of sites and information as an indirect way of improving the local labour market. Of course, these non-housing activities are undertaken in all sectors, but there seems to be no evidence on how they compare in terms of resource inputs or outcomes. However, one feature of human capital development that may be specific to some parts of the voluntary sector is its purposive local orientation. Some associations have developed employment practices in a distinctive way through the use of local labour clauses, limiting job opportunities to local people. This possibility is legally prohibited to local government, and theoretically is unlikely to be prominent amongst for-profit organizations (Box 7.4).

Finally, housing associations have contributed to the building of social capital in inter-related ways. We can say this has occurred 'vertically' when relatively high levels of trust between providers and individual direct users are to be found. One interviewee claimed housing associations scored relatively highly in

> **Box 7.4 The theory of for-profit housing and local labour clauses**
>
> According to orthodox economic theory, a for-profit supplier should be indifferent between employing locally based workers and others: the choice would be based purely on productivity criteria. This could be problematic to the extent productivity is interpreted with a short-term time frame, which is arguably the case for quoted companies in Britain. The stock market-dependent component of the for-profit sector may be peculiarly myopic by international standards (Hutton, 1995) and would actually therefore be expected to maximize financial gain only in the short run. This could work against employing local people in deprived areas who might need longer-term opportunities to realize their potential and demonstrate their worth.

this regard because of their distance from party politics: 'Because we are not subject to party political control at the local level we are able to work in a much more trusting way with local people.' Another thought trust was more easily nurtured in housing associations because they were not tainted by the 'stigma' which characterized services owned by local authorities. In line with traditional community development thinking, one interviewee claimed that such participation could markedly increase the confidence and self-esteem of individual tenants – providing their efforts were seen to have been successful, 'they go from being poor and downtrodden to saying "hang on, we have achieved something, we have become someone again"'.

However, another view was that it was tenant's active participation in the development and running of activities which mattered, regardless of whether the assets were owned by housing associations or local government (see Price Waterhouse, 1995; since the 1970s, there has been increasing tendency, encouraged by central government, to give tenants more control over these affairs in *all* social housing settings: see Power, 1993).

In fact, strictly speaking and now adopting a narrower interpretation of the idea that was adopted in the previous chapter, social capital refers not to individual sentiments or attitudes, but to the perceived quality of relationships between people. Evans' evaluation of *Housing Plus* initiatives found that the extent to which tenants reported that a 'sense of community' was present actually varied a good deal between housing associations in each of the six locales studied. In addition to the promotion of tenant participation, good physical infrastructure, and the use of local labour clauses (see above) to 'encourage a sense of ownership', he identifies four other factors which 'promote social cohesion . . . by promoting informal social controls and helping to cement community ties', albeit without detailing how or why. These are shown in Box 7.5. As far as some of these are

---

Box 7.5 Factors associated with the successful promotion of 'social cohesion' by housing associations

- Designing estate layouts and densities to promote community safety, especially involving the 'incorporation of defensible space'.
- Ensuring a balanced social mix on estates which matches that of surrounding areas.
- Minimizing disruption to social networks by sensitive allocation procedures, the provision of lifetime homes and a range of accommodation . . . in locations well served by public transport.
- Maximizing local income retention through energy efficiency, welfare advice, exploring scope for cheap finance and bulk discount schemes.

Source: Adapted from Evans, 1998b: 7 and 56.

---

concerned – in particular, physical infrastructure, and estate layouts and densities (the first 'factor' in the box) – we should also note that housing associations will tend to be better placed than council housing for the historic reasons discussed in earlier parts of this section.

7.4 Weaknesses of the voluntary sector in social housing

7.4.1 *Chronic resource problems*

As a direct consequence of the enabling provisions of the 1974 Housing Act, this 'weakness' is of debatable salience in this field. We know (Section 7.2) that a number of 'expansionist' associations managed to build up quite significant levels of reserves during the 'golden age' of 'risk-free' capital allocations between 1974 and 1988, and by taking advantage of some of the other factors in their favour noted earlier. This situation was seen positively by our experts. For them, it had legitimately provided the organizations which had grasped such opportunities with deserved scope for growth. The statistics of significant expansion in the early 1990s also testify to the voluntary sector's capacity in this case to avoid the adverse effects of the economic cycle in this case. We noted in Chapter 2 that during this recessionary period, housing growth accounted for a significant part of the voluntary sector's overall expansion, and this is underlined from a comparative sector perspective within the field by the data in Table 7.1.

At the same time, there were qualifications and anxieties. First, the concern expressed by some writers that the growth set in train by the 1970s legislation has tended to involve a loss of local accountability and 'over-professionalization' as its corollary (see below). Second, a worry that the raw intravoluntary sector competition of the early 1990s, when competitive bidding for capital allocations from the Housing Corporation had intensified dramatically, had been counterproductive. Rather than succumbing to a 'free for all', some respondents felt that housing associations should have advocated collectively to secure a more favourable, less commercially oriented regime in the first place, or at least acted in a less cut-throat downward spiral of bidding once it was in place. However, one large housing association interviewee candidly referred to 'housing association schizophrenia, there were lots of complaints about the introduction of private finance, and then behind the scenes they competed furiously which actually drove the grant rates down further. There are some paradoxes between the so-called voluntary sector ethos and their [actual] behaviour!'

However, overall the positive perspective was reinforced when our fieldwork respondents came to set housing associations' overall experience in comparative context. Relative to capital-starved council housing, it was seen as having been tremendously fortunate in recent years; while as stressed earlier, the for-profit sector had by law been denied access to developmental funding from central government under the Housing Corporation programme. The housing association sector also suffers from potentially less 'insufficiency' than the for-profit sector when operating in deprived neighbourhoods by virtue of being able to draw on financial opportunities not available to for-profit operators. Examples of such schemes of which diversifying housing associations have taken considerable advantage include the Community Fund and community development funding from some local authorities.

7.4.2 Particularism

This 'weakness' had some resonance in the case of housing associations – but was interpreted as a strength too, in the sense of often representing a desirable degree of specialization. Where it was interpreted negatively, it was in the sense that housing associations were thought to be too specialized in providing only for particular categories of need, activity or people. One of our focus group participants felt that overall, housing associations had erred through 'housing exclusively those in greatest need, with estate environments created with little or no socio-economic mix from day one with all their inherent management problems'. This criticism is equivalent to suggesting that such housing has tended not to strike the right balance in the sense identified by Evans noted above, although it is not clear how the sectors now compare in this regard.

At a less broad brush level, some of our interviewees referred to situations in which a major mismatch between housing association-led supply and local authorities' housing priorities arose. Some local housing associations' 'narrowness' in making available places only for people strictly of a particular age, gender or ethnicity could be frustrating for local government housing officials in these situations. A concrete example we were given involved an Irish housing association which would inform the housing department of vacancies, but if the latter was unable to find someone of the correct ethnicity, the place would not be made available, however severe the housing need on other criteria. However, it is not clear how typical this situation has been. In theory at least, there is a legal duty requiring associations to 'co-operate to a reasonable extent' with local authorities, and 'nomination agreements' developed to govern relations between the sectors should help to limit overt conflicts of this kind. Much will depend upon how 'reasonable' is interpreted by those involved.

7.4.3 Paternalism

The most outspoken comment on this weakness came from our for-profit sector interviewee who dismissively remarked that 'housing associations do nothing to find out what tenants want, they tell the tenants what's good for them!' Considerable evidence from the literature points to this problem historically (Emsley, 1986; Malpass, 2000). It is most likely still to be found in some of the older charitable trusts and antecedents to the modern housing movement. Here, patronizing and insensitive attitudes towards tenants undoubtedly persist. At the same time, however, a number of interviewees were quick to add that the problem could also be found, historically and currently, in council housing. Moreover, it was claimed that *across* sectors, the problem had increasingly been recognized and was being addressed: the growth of tenant participation models, such as those mentioned above in the context of community-building, often proactively supported by housing associations, was seen as a part of a wider movement away from paternalistic attitudes (see also Wigglesworth and Kendall, 2000, on the tenants' participation movement).

7.4.4 Excessive amateurism or professionalism

One of our housing association focus group participants summed up this widely recognized dilemma for housing associations in remarking that 'it is [a question of] getting the balance right between acting in a business-like way, and having business objectives'. Amateurism is often associated with the inappropriate use of volunteers. And because, unlike some other parts of the voluntary sector, most volunteer involvement in housing associations is in governance rather than direct services, it was examples of amateurism here which were most readily identified: poorly structured consultation with tenants, failure to follow basic protocols in convening and conducting board meetings, and poor attendance were all mentioned.

Three of our interviewees also pointed to another aspect of 'amateurism' – limits to the capabilities of paid staff. It was argued here that smaller organizations in particular were not well positioned to tempt the best quality staff, and subsequently their 'performance' suffered in comparison with larger organizations. This claim seems to be consistent with the findings on low levels of qualifications in the staff of local housing associations noted in our earlier discussion of human capital.

In discussing how 'excessive professionalism' might be manifested, the issue of securing managerial and financial expertise for boards to allow them to handle the new financial environment was sometimes seen as a challenging one in our discussions. Particularly if this expertise could only be mobilized by involving people from outside the local community with little or no experience or knowledge of local problems and conditions, organizations stood to lose sensitivity to the situation of the local people they were meant to be supporting. By implication, actual and potential contributions to fostering the local dimension of human capital, and the social capital aspects of community building, would be under threat here.

Relatedly, Peter Malpass is perhaps the most prominent amongst those who point to the shifting balance within the housing association sector away from locally based associations, towards regional and national bodies, and has lamented this process's apparent encouragement by the Housing Corporation. Mergers and acquisitions designed to reap presumed economies of scale and increase organizational capacity more generally, and the penetration by regional and national associations into local markets previously dominated by local associations, have been greeted with horror when they have involved a loss of local presence and hence accountability (Malpass, 2000: 253; for a less polemical account, see Mullins, 1999).

7.4.5 Problematic accountability

The issue of specifically local accountability has already emerged as potentially problematic in our discussion of political control, and of professionalism. More generally in all housing associations, unlike publicly owned services, there is no automatic link to the electorate at large with the power to vote those running the services out of office. In fact, putting the special cases of endowed trusts and recent voluntary transfers to one side, voluntary sector governance arrangements in this field have been more akin to the for-profit sector than those which prevail in other policy fields, since their members can be shareholders, albeit with strictly limited financial return rights. Malpass and Murie (1999: 209–10 citing the survey research of Crooks (1985) and Kearns (1990) and their own unpublished research) contrast them unfavourably with the elected members of local government: they refer to housing associations' boards as 'self perpetuating oligarchies', and are sceptical about the supposedly beneficial effects of tenants' increasing level involvement with some committees.

In the absence of electoral control, housing association accountability is currently dealt with via three essentially technocratic routes. First, there are the relatively limited requirements for registered charitable providers to submit reports and accounts to the Charity Commission and similar requirements for housing associations registered as industrial and provident societies with the Registry of Friendly Societies.

Second, and much more demanding, are the requirements for public accountability applied to publicly funded housing associations by the Housing Corporation through the intense regulatory and financial regime to which we referred in previous sections. In addition to the annual submission of reports and accounts and information on activity in terms of units developed and maintained, financial measures and indicators of tenant composition along a number of dimensions – to enable measurement against the Housing Corporation's policy objectives – are also submitted. Housing associations are further required to report the scale and scope of their innovatory and good practice activities, again, to enable the Housing Corporation to gauge the extent to which national policy goals in these domains are being achieved. In each case, the Housing Corporation has formulated national minimum standards which housing associations are required to meet. Furthermore, unlike other areas of public service involving voluntary organizations, the 'Best Value' regime (see Chapter 4) has already lead to the development of national 'performance benchmarking' (in aggregate, generating some of the recent comparative data we were able to draw upon in discussing the service function).

Third, housing associations in membership of the NHF are required to adhere to a 'code of governance' concerning the behaviour and propriety of board members, and a range of other, voluntary codes have also been produced on such procedural issues as whistle blowing, integrity at work, and equal opportunities, issues coming to the top of the agenda partly in response to the Nolan inquiry (see below). The NHF has also developed a model of 'stakeholder accountability' which seeks to provide guidelines on how those with an interest in housing associations might exert influence.

The extent to which these existing and ongoing efforts to secure accountability are sufficient is a difficult and highly complex issue: Malpass and Murie's critique seems to have some currency, but was rather overstated from the perspective of our fieldwork participants. In defence of the status quo, most of our focus group participants and interviewees including the representatives of central and local government, felt that overall levels of accountability was not a central weakness, especially in relative terms. First, it was suggested that the old model of public sector accountability secured through elections was very far from accurate in the case of municipal housing. This was because the mechanism of voting through periodic local elections was too crude and irregular a means of transmitting voter preferences (particularly true of minority ethnic people, as noted earlier); and because 'not many people vote for a local authority on the basis of the housing they provide'. Second, it was claimed that housing associations could achieve and were achieving representativeness of their communities, even if they were not directly controlled by elected politicians. Third, there was another, pragmatic argument that under the existing regime, 'when you make a complaint something will happen'.

However, other commentators have harboured serious anxieties about accountability in housing. This reflects a view that however accountable to and closely monitored they are by the Housing Corporation and the NHF, there could and should be high profile, transparent and enforceable mechanisms to secure 'bottom up' accountability to the local communities in which they operate (see Riseborough, 1995; Evans, 1998b: 47–8). The 1995/6 Nolan inquiries into *Standards in Public Life*, by treating housing associations as 'local public spending bodies' within the scope of its inquiry alongside public-owned services, may have been a turning point. The review suggested that the activities of housing associations should be more open to critical local scrutiny. At the broadest level, this suggested that because they were part of 'public life', housing associations' governance should be characterized by selflessness, integrity, accountability, openness, honesty and leadership. One prominent researcher in this field has argued that the Nolan critique 'hit the sector hard', suggesting that problematic accountability was perhaps 'the key area of perceived weakness' for the sector. At the same time, he argued that, notwithstanding the Malpass and Murie (1999) critique of the reality of tenant participation on boards, that aspect of formal accountability has been less problematic in social housing than other fields. That is, tenants as users of services in housing have tended to account for a relatively high proportion of all board memberships than do equivalent 'users' in the voluntary sector more generally (Mullins, 2002; and see Chapter 8 regarding the care for older people situation).

7.5 Conclusion

Unlike local government, English housing associations were in the right place at the right time to build up relatively attractive property portfolios, and benefit from central state largesse. They became involved in policy in this field to a significant degree at just the moment when mass housing models were being rejected, which coincided with policy-makers' increasing turn towards approaches at a distance from the for-profit and public sectors. The problem of inadequate capital, which had traditionally limited the sector's ability to develop, was addressed on relatively generous terms by central government, which from 1979 was simultaneously deliberately starving local government of capital, predominantly for ideological reasons. A combination of effective 'trade body' lobbying and a discrediting climate as far as the for-profit and public sector alternatives were concerned helped to create a protected niche for the sector within the public housing system in which it has been able to thrive.

Our review of functions and weaknesses has reflected how deeply this current situation reflects a peculiarly British historical legacy of strategic political and policy decisions. In other parts of Europe, the nature and sequencing of political decision-making seems to have been less favourable, and some of the contrasts we have been able to make would probably not apply.

Wherever possible, an aspiration has been to gauge the housing association sector in relative terms by comparing its contributions to those of the public and private sector, and to establish why any differences might have arisen. This proved to be most feasible in a concrete and systematic way in the case of the 'service delivery' function. The sector emerged with an impressive comparative record, around which there was a marked, supportive consensus, although by concentrating on averages and tendencies, we have inevitably barely scratched the surface of the incredible diversity within the sector. 'Weaknesses' are evident, but they seem to be less pervasive than in the sector as a whole, and as the next two chapters will show, in other vertical policy fields too. Most markedly in contrast with those cases is the extent to which 'resource insufficiency' is clearly not ubiquitous in either a quantitative or a qualitative sense.

Caution is apposite, however. The evidence here does not constitute an unambiguous case that the voluntary sector is 'better' than the public or for-profit sectors. First, to the extent there is 'superiority' in some service provision aspects of performance in the voluntary sector compared with the council sector, this partly reflects the costs of the traditional model of local democratic control deployed in the latter. For those whose values lead them to place particular weight on this as a matter of principle, those costs are simply worth paying – although we have seen considerable scepticism on this point amongst the 'experts' whose views we canvassed. But it should be acknowledged that at stake is a political choice which cannot be answered by purely technical considerations.

Second, it should be stressed that over and above the question of local democracy, there is in any case an 'attribution' issue. Because the relationship between the public and voluntary sectors has been symbiotic, it is difficult to find examples were the fulfillment of functions or exhibition of 'weaknesses' can unambiguously be said to have originated in, or have been 'caused by', any one sector. Certainly, broad generalizations as to sectoral capabilities and achievements based upon factors which are in some sense intrinsic to each sector are impossible here. Rather, what seems to emerge as most significant from this review are the combination of historical legacy in terms of stock – a history not controlled by any one interest, and involving unanticipated twists and turns; situational/geographical considerations, again not necessarily linked to organizations in any one sector; and sensitivity to local community relationships and aspirations. The latter seems to emerge from commitment and expertise in building up well-functioning networks between sectors and individuals, rather than being associated uniquely with, or dominated by, any one form of ownership.

Notes

1 This chapter draws on an earlier preliminary paper co-authored with Rachel Wigglesworth (Wigglesworth and Kendall, 2000).
2 Some strictly regulated distribution of returns to external private individual investors is permitted with some contemporary forms of housing association. But capital is now raised primarily via two routes: state investment and interest paying 'private finance' from banks and other private sector lending institutions.
3 Because of the recent acceleration of the 'large-scale voluntary transfers' (LSVT) programme, it is possible that the council sector will soon own less stock than housing associations, if transfers from the former to the latter were to be included as part of the sector. However, unless otherwise stated, these 'hybrid' bodies are not included in the chapter, in part because of space constraints (they would have had to have been treated as a 'case apart'); in part because the evidence on impacts we are able to draw upon seems mostly not to include them (with some exceptions such as Murie and Walker, 2002); and because they seem to have been spontaneously 'defined out' from the perspective of our 'experts'. Objectively, it is particularly unclear whether these entities are sufficiently independent from local government to be treated as part of the voluntary sector as defined in this study (see Chapter 1). At the same time, it must be acknowledged that it was not possible to systematically

exclude the pure transfer component of the sector from the data reported in Chapter 2 on trends between 1990 and 1995.

4 The 1960s were also foundational for the field because the Housing Act 1964 established the Housing Corporation which has loomed large as statutory funder and regulator ever since (see following text).

5 Britain and Ireland were exceptional in choosing the local state as the primary means of ownership for new social housing in the 1960–75 period, when 'the bulk of the very large and difficult estates appeared . . . virtually simultaneously in all countries' (Power, 1997: 39).

6 As far as for-profit housing was concerned, rent controls and economic conditions were not conducive to profitable activities in those local areas which were most evidently in need; and there was consensus around 'a growing dissatisfaction with the performance of local [state] housing authorities and a corresponding feeling that it was necessary to foster variety of ownership of rented housing' (Malpass, 2000: 157).

7 There has been another route by which for-profits have developed a limited role in social housing: the 1992 Housing Act required local authority white collar housing functions to be subject to compulsory competitive tender, with all sector's theoretically eligible to bid. However, through a combination of local authority resistance and for-profit disinterest, only a handful of public housing management contracts involve for-profits, primarily situated in London boroughs. One of the few contracted for-profit providers was amongst the interviewees for this study.

8 For example, data on all three rental sectors were available for proportion of unfit properties and proportion of dwellings 'needing most repair'. Housing associations had the best record in both cases, most clearly superior to council housing in the case of repairs record, but considerably better than for-profit renting on both counts. In terms of 'crowded conditions', GHS data show housing associations superior to for-profit renting, although slightly inferior to the council sector, while central heating was less likely to be absent in housing associations than in other forms of rented tenure. The 1986 English Housing Condition survey found that housing association and for-profit tenants were much less likely than council tenants to experience difficulties in getting repairs done, while the 1994/5 survey found housing associations had the best record of all in terms of satisfaction with repairs and maintenance. Another useful measure is 'overall satisfaction'; statistics for 1994/5 again show housing associations on average perform better, with 10 per cent dissatisfaction, compared with 12 per cent in the for-profit sector and 14 per cent in the council sector. For full details and discussion, see Hills (1998).

9 None of the analyses reported here seem to have accounted for differences in tenant mix by sector. If housing associations on average tend to have less 'difficult' tenants than councils – taking into account this different 'case mix' to compare like with like could work in the opposite direction to the London effect noted.

10 Housing Corporation data, adjusted for nonresponse, suggested that in 1995 there were some 69,000 full time equivalent employees in housing associations, compared to 23,000 part-time volunteer committee members, and just 8,000 'other volunteers'. These returns may not be picking up all relevant unpaid contributions, but they are suggestive of orders of magnitude.

11 This situation is far from a foregone conclusion. The Conservative Government of the mid-1990s was reputedly becoming increasingly unconvinced by the NHF's position. Had it won the 1997 election, the requirement that recipients of Housing Corporation funding be 'nonprofit' would have been abolished.

8 The impact of voluntary sector social care and support for older people

- **The policy environment which organizations in this field inhabit has evolved in a particularly complex and piecemeal way since the mid-twentieth century.**

- **The evidence that is available on comparative economy and quality of care in mainstream service delivery is inconclusive.**

- **In low-intensity social care and support activities, the advantages of voluntarism have long been recognized by policy-makers.**

- **A wide range of failures or 'weaknesses' are evident. However, it is difficult to distinguish between problems attributable to the field, and those attributable to the voluntary sector within it.**

8.1 Introduction

The focus of this chapter is the social care and support for older people provided by the voluntary sector. This was chosen as the example of a case in which the sector contributes to society by its involvement in a 'traditional social welfare field'. There are a number of demographic, economic and social reasons why this field has already increased, and will increase further in policy salience in years to come. The ageing of the world's population, accompanied by increases in the proportion of older people living alone (linked to rises in divorce/separation and remarriage rates), and continued increases in female labour market participation rates are all likely to limit the capacity of the informal sector to meet social care needs. Caring responsibilities will necessarily shift to formal organizations (Pickard *et al.*, 2000; Wittenberg *et al.*, 2001).

Voluntary organizations' contribution to social care, like the housing associations discussed in Chapter 7 (fields which sometimes overlap, as we shall see), has very deep historical roots. They antedate the emergence of 'personal social services' as a recognized public policy field. Prior to the growth of local government owned and controlled social care in the aftermath of the formative welfare legislation in the 1940s (and since the early 1980s, the rapid expansion of the for-profit sector), voluntary agencies were the leading formally organized source of care and support. Their role has sometimes been underplayed by social policy analysts, who have often concentrated on the harsh and punitive state institutions of the Poor Law in tracing key historic social care trends. However, institutional innovation was much evident in the voluntary sector, with the formation of associative voluntary societies supplementing already long-established almshouses and local endowed trusts with pre-modern origins (Thane, 2000). Linked to the religious denominations, occupational, professional and trade groups, whose general growth was characteristic of this era (Perkin, 1989) were elaborate networks of welfare institutions geared to meeting the needs of their constituencies – including age-related needs. Thus, for those with the 'right' associational affiliations, the poor house, labour market participation or informal support were not the only care options as they became vulnerable through old age. 'Community-based' activities such as visiting, and 'institutional care', including convalescent, retirement and rest homes were provided under voluntary sector auspices (Prochaska, 1990: 374; Morris, 1990: 441).

Pre-1940s voluntary organizations are still major actors in social care, and to a greater degree than in the social housing field. This extraordinary historical richness was itself an important rationale for focusing on this field for this chapter. A second reason was the availability of evidence on how the voluntary sector compares, in at least some important respects, to the public sector and the for-profit sector. Given the aspiration of this study to build as much of a comparative element as possible, this was an important consideration. As Figures 8.1–3 show, all three sectors co-exist in residential care, domiciliary care and day care.[1]

Another reason for selecting this field was that there have been a number of published academic studies exploring the comparative aspect upon which it was possible to draw, including research done at the Personal Social Services Research

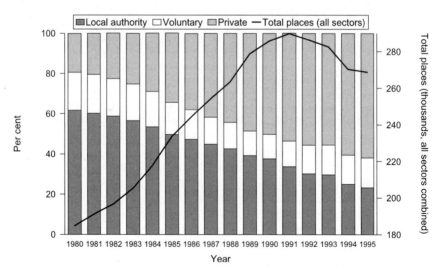

Figure 8.1 Percentage by sector and total residential places for older and younger physically handicapped people.

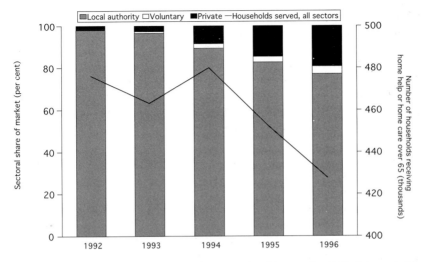

Figure 8.2 Local authority funded domiciliary care for older people, 1992–6: households
served.

Source: Data from DH Statistical Bulletin 1997/8.

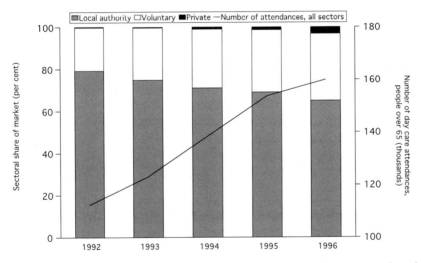

Figure 8.3 Local authority funded day care for older people, 1992–6: average number of
attendances.

Source: Data from DH Statistical Bulletin 1994/5 and 1997/8.

Unit, much of which involved the author. Moreover, the discourse of the 'mixed
economy' involving all three formal sectors, plus the informal sector, is well
established amongst stakeholders, as will be clear in what follows. As anticipated,
our primary 'expert' informants (see Appendix 2) found it easier in this field
than in the others to make direct comparisons.

8.2 The policy legacy

As part of the 'welfare state settlement' (Thane, 1986), the 1946 National Assistance Act conferred certain social care responsibilities on local government for the first time, including responsibility for the welfare of older people. But, for a variety of political and social reasons, this policy field in the UK, as in other developed countries, tended to be a relatively low-spending priority in the years after the war (see Kendall *et al.*, 2003a). Certainly in Britain, compared with health and income support (nationalized by central government), or housing (where we have seen that local government was taking a very strong lead with central support), initial public investment in this area was relatively limited, with no wholesale public sector 'takeover' or high-profile political drive for the expansion of public ownership and control. Instead, in a low-key way, local authorities were empowered to meet older people's needs both through building up their own portfolio of services, and by funding voluntary organizations to do so (Brenton, 1985).

At the same time, social care for older people was given added impetus from within the sector between the 1930s and the 1970s with the formation of new national specialist voluntary organizations and federations, that is, agencies geared specifically towards vulnerable older people. Agencies such as Age Concern, Help the Aged and the Abbeyfield Society were distinguishable from established providers by their founding orientation towards older people in general, of all religious and occupational backgrounds, and provided social care and accommodation alongside an awareness-raising role.

At the national level, civil servants interacted particularly with these new older people-specific national organizations. The Women's Voluntary Service (now the WRVS) and the British Red Cross Society, with whom close links had developed as a result of joint responses to wartime contingencies, were also influential in setting and implementing the national agenda. The patchiness and uneven coverage of existing voluntary sector services, especially in terms of care for people in their own homes (home care or domiciliary care) was evidenced in surveys (Means and Smith, 1998a). In the pro-state 'optimistic' climate of the time (George, 1996), this was seen as providing a rationale for the expansion not just of state intervention, but of services directly managed and owned by the state. Local authorities, whose responsibilities in this field were lead by Social Services Departments (SSDS) from the late 1960s onwards, came into their own as the major employers of paid care workers.

For their part, voluntary organizations now tended to see their roles, as the public sector saw them more generally: as essentially pioneers, supplementers and niche market specialists, often only temporarily acting as providers for local services which had become, or were becoming, 'mainstream' responsibilities of the state, as with residential care and home care.[2] Yet because services identified as core public responsibilities were still actually quite limited compared with the full range of needs being met de facto in the community, the sector was never marginalized in this field as it had been in health, social housing and social security. In particular, to the extent voluntary contributions shaded into the informal sector and mobilized otherwise unavailable community networks, volunteers and other support (in a style that resonated with dominant contemporary social work discourses and professional norms), the sector was recognized as having a legitimate and enduring role (see Box 8.1).

8.2.1 Unplanned policy developments

The most conspicuous policy shift in the 1970s and early 1980s involved the public sector's growth trajectory. In the prevailing climate of 'welfare pessimism', the general pattern of incremental local government growth of ownership and control was decelerated, and public sector social care was amongst the services affected (George, 1996; Evandrou *et al.*, 1990).

In this context, it was other sectors which took the strain of meeting need – and in a fashion that was largely unplanned and unintended by either central government social care policy-makers or local government actors. In an apparently reactive and ad hoc way, social security offices responded to lobbying by voluntary organizations in a number of locales to cover the cost of outstanding fees for residential care which would otherwise not have been paid. In 1982, local practices were *ex post* joined up to constitute a 'national policy' of social security financial responsibility for care home funding, and generalized to cover the costs of both voluntary and for-profit delivery.

The Registered Homes Act 1984 followed, reflecting a desire to regulate the increasing numbers of older residents in what was now referred to as the 'independent sector', referring to services not owned by the local state.

While this national policy was initially thought of as to a relatively inconsequential adjustment to public administrative law (Timmins, 2001:

Box 8.1 Policy recognition for voluntarism in social care

Voluntary organizations, and especially volunteers, have received myriad endorsements in official policy statements in social care as:

- Facilitators of mutual aid.
- Providers of support for independent living in the community.
- A source of community development.

This contrasts markedly with other welfare policy fields, where voluntarism, while sometimes acknowledged, was not so systematically prominent and lauded in the policy discourse.

(See Seebohm, 1968; DHSS, 1981; Barclay, 1982; Brenton, 1985; Bulmer, 1987; and Webb and Wistow, 1987; for a recent summary re-statement, see ADSS and NCV, 2001.)

414), its repercussions for public expenditure were vast. Most of the 'unwitting' (Timmins, 2001: 414) massive expansion of social security-backed supply that was to follow was forthcoming from the for-profit, and not the voluntary, sector. Aggregate voluntary sector residential provision grew only marginally, and thus accounted for a dwindling share of a rapidly expanding market (see Figure 8.1). Masked by this overall trend, there was, however, some growth in the scale of national specialist provision, and also the emergence of what might be referred to as new, public funding-backed 'nonprofit social entrepreneurship'. The latter was often expressed in the context of 'consortia' or other mixed organizational forms initiated at the interstices of a variety of tiers and fields of the central and local state. The harsh fiscal climate alluded to above was experienced unevenly in publicly funded services, and not all fields suffered the retrenchment experienced by local government social service departments. Creative packaging of service options could exploit money from not only local government and social security but other public budgets, where service responsibilities were blurred, problematic or perceived to be shared, for social care ends (see Box 8.2).

8.2.2 *Policy makers reassert control*

The 1990 National Health Service and Community Care Act involved the most sweeping legislative reforms in the field since the 1940s. In an effort to

---

Box 8.2 'Spillover' from adjacent public budgets into the social care field

Public expenditure on health care remained buoyant in the 1980s. As Chapter 7 has already noted, housing associations, many of which were geared towards older people at this time (Malpass, 2000), were enjoying a major period of growth under the impetus of Housing Corporation financial support only available to voluntary organizations. A significant segment of the limited expansion of voluntary sector residential care activity that did take place in the 1980s and early 1990s involved joint mobilization of funds from these central government budgets rather than the coffers of local government (Renshaw *et al.*, 1988; Kendall and Knapp, 1996: Chapter 5).

A more limited parallel seems to have taken place in domiciliary care: some new purpose-built providers, as well as existing national specialists, were able to access health budgets or new joint SSD–NHS arrangements to promote community care through home care schemes (Ferlie *et al.*, 1989). Many also took advantage of the funds that were becoming available in the 1980s from central government's job creation and training programmes to boost their workforce capabilities.

regain control of public expenditure and rectify 'perverse incentives', local authority SSDs were allocated the social security funds which had previously fuelled residential care growth, and charged with managing their local 'mixed economies of care' so as to rebalance them towards community-based care options. As part of this process, they were given high powered incentives to limit the scope of their own services and to enhance the role of both the for-profit and voluntary sectors in mainstream services. This was to be through the deployment of contractual and quasi-contractual agreements for residential and nonresidential care, and through the creation of 'not-for-profit' providers to manage floated off services formerly directly run by local authorities.[3]

The economic growth of voluntary sector social care in the 1990s presented in Chapter 2 was largely a reflection of its response to the opportunities presented in this SSD-led 'contract culture' environment (see also Chapter 4). There was also some continued development fuelled by 'spill over' from (still more generous) adjacent housing and health care budgets. Increased engagement between local authorities and the voluntary sector was also mandated by the requirement that councils develop annual community care plans (see Lewis and Glennerster, 1996; Nuffield Institute for Health, 1998).

8.2.3 New Labour: continuity and change

With the arrival of the New Labour administration in 1997, broad contours of the situation at the local level – in terms of the separation of purchasing from provision, and the location of financial responsibility at SSD level – remained. That fundamental fact aside, there has been more policy proactivity under the new administration here than in either of the other fields considered in this book, in terms of the sheer scope and scale of new initiatives, legislation, institution-building and regulatory elaboration. First, the new government's more general pursuit of 'joined-up government' (see Chapter 4) and enthusiasm for volunteering was reflected in new national initiatives specifically for older people (for example, see Cabinet Office Performance and Innovation Unit, 2000; BGOP Steering Committee, 2000). Second, a Royal Commission on Long-Term Care reported and made recommendations. The voluntary sector's national 'age-specific specialists' such as Age Concern England contributed enthusiastically with evidence and argument, but were to disapprove vocally of the Westminster Government's unwillingness to take up proposals for free 'personal care' in England and Wales (Royal Commission on Long-Term Care, 1999; Department of Health, 1999).

Third, the most significant change for voluntary sector service providers at the local level has been changes in registration requirements and inspection arrangements pursuant to the Care Regulations Act 2000. With the establishment of a new National Care Standards Commission, the relatively loose regulatory structures inherited from the mid-1980s have been replaced in residential (and nursing) care with much more demanding and wider ranging institutions. Mandatory regulation of home care is being introduced for the first time in 2003. Fourth, and more indirectly, changing relationships *within* the state are altering the policy environment in which these organizations operate. The central state's direct influence has been intensified through a growing panoply of monitoring activities, including a rapidly expanding role for the Audit Commission and Social Services Inspectorate (SSI), accompanied by target setting as part of Whitehall's increasingly elaborate intelligence gathering. Box 8.3 shows how social care commentators have taken contrasting views on the desirability of some aspects of these developments as a package.

The foregoing account of the policy legacy is relevant to understanding the current impact of the sector in this field in three primary ways. First, despite the fact that statutory responsibilities for social care are still situated formally at local government level, it makes clear the increasingly conspicuous role of central government in this domain. The policy environment in social care is jointly shaped by both tiers of the state.[4] Second, the somewhat uncontrolled and 'messy' nature of policy-making in this field has tended to leave room for an extremely diverse set of organizations. Yet while this historical record may be suggestive of daunting variety, it also suggests the existence of identifiable broad

---

Box 8.3 Initial evaluations of social care reforms

Initial normative evaluations of the net impact of the most recent round of social care reforms seem to fall into two broad camps, and these are worth briefly elaborating as background for the following section. *Optimists* point to increased public funding, clearer planning horizons and a new era of collaboration between central and local government to replace the antagonisms of earlier periods, contributing to a constructive atmosphere in which the third sector can more readily participate with confidence. There is some evidence from the SSD level of increasing sophistication in contracting practices, involving increased sensitivity to providers' conditions, and a willingness to favour active market management and more 'relational' styles of working over 'macho' purchasing and adversarialism (Knapp *et al.*, 2000). *Sceptics*, however, still argue that historic 'underfunding' has not been sufficiently tackled, nor future needs taken into account; and are worried by the elaborate apparatus of 'central command and surveillance' put in place under the new regime (see Hudson, 2000). Taken together, the resultant combination of fiscal austerity and top-down style could push local authority purchasers into an unsympathetic and defensive approach towards contractual negotiations. In support of this more depressing picture, there is also local authority level evidence of immature purchasing, and failure to understand, or engage with, providers. At the same time, time-consuming and costly information and auditing demands are at an unprecedented level.

classes of organization in this field. The typology in Box 8.4 tries to capture this.[5] We will find it useful to refer back to this in what follows, since it provides a basis for qualifying what would otherwise be inappropriate generalizations, as far as the claims of our 'experts' are concerned.[6]

Third, the policy legacy and the typology which ties in with it, are crucial to bear in mind even when interpreting evidence gleaned from large sample surveys, upon which we also draw in this chapter. This is because in different types of care, the various types of organization are present to varying degrees. For example, in the case of residential care, the voluntary sector is dominated by what we refer to in the typology as social care generalists, social entrepreneurs and not-for-profit trusts. While in the publicly funded domiciliary and day care on which most survey evidence is available, it is local affiliates of national specialists which are more prominent. So the 'typical' organization in each case tends to have different historical roots, relations with the state and resource characteristics.

8.3 Functions of the voluntary sector in care and support for older people

8.3.1 *The service provision function: mainstream services*

According to the OECD, social care concerns 'assistance with the normal activities of daily life, including personal functioning, domestic maintenance and social activities'. It involves social control, societal protection and social integration (Evandrou and Falkingham, 1998), and in the economic jargon, can therefore be seen as a quasi-public good: its processes or outcomes generate 'caring externalities' from which society at large, and not just individual users, collectively benefits (Knapp, 1984). In the UK, the most significant forms of social care service for older people have traditionally been residential care (old people's homes); domiciliary care (provided by visiting people in their own homes); and day care (where people are transported for the day to a facility in which they can congregate socially, and receive food and support services). (Other categories of care, such as 'intermediate care', are now increasingly complicating the situation.) As Figure 8.1 underlined, in the first two forms of care, the voluntary sector is significant, but with a smaller market share than both the public sector and the for-profit sector; while with day care, its contribution is smaller than that of the public sector, but much larger than the for-profit sector.

In fact, only 1 per cent of older people in Britain were seeing a 'helper from a voluntary organization' in 1998 (Bridgewood, 2000). But a much more significant proportion of the minority of those older people who are vulnerable enough to need formal care are in receipt of voluntary sector contributions which are not necessarily easily captured in such surveys' statistical categories. Particularly prominent in delivering such social care and related support in the community for amongst the most dependent older people are the churches ('social care generalists'), age-specific specialists and housing association wardens (Bauld *et al.*, 2000: 253, Table 8.3 and 259–61).

Box 8.4 Major types of providers of care and support for older people within the voluntary sector

- *Traditional generalist social service agencies* with services for older people operating alongside services for other people in need. Typically with pre-Second World War origins, these tend to be either directly or indirectly connected to religious denominations or based around occupational, trade or professional groupings with a wide variety of structures. Mixed funding, often including substantial income earned on historically inherited assets and accumulated financial reserves.

- *Specialist social care and support groups for older people*, or groups de facto oriented to older people, typically founded from around the Second World War onwards, and often with federal structures. Mixed funding, with much variety between local affiliates (in the case of federations) in terms of scope, scale and activity emphases. Some specialize in services, some in information, advocacy and policy issues, while some undertake both.

- *Pensioners' groups* typically established to lobby for state pensions from the Second World War onwards, but now engaging to a significant degree with SSDs to promote the interests of older people as current or future users of social care services.

- *Nonprofit social entrepreneurship organizations* founded and/or expanded from the 1960s onwards, but most extensively in the 1980s, in direct response to the availability of public funds, particularly for community care, training and housing programmes. These may or may not specialize in providing care for older people, can develop national structures from typically local or regional origins, and often remain heavily reliant on public funding and user contributions.

- *Community care fora and networks* established specifically to influence the planning and implementation of local social care services, particularly from the early 1990s onwards. More generally, senior citizens and older people's forums have developed from the late 1990s.

- *Self-help and community groups* (geographical, ethnicity or interest-based) not covered in the above categories. Mixed funding.

- *Not-for-profit trusts* operating homes formerly run directly by local authorities from whom they have been 'floated off'. Typically funded almost entirely by direct authority funding (usually block contracts) and user contributions.*

---

* Like the 'voluntary transfers' identified in social housing, unless otherwise stated we do not consider these bodies within scope in this part of the book. A key exception is that we have no option but to include them when we draw upon survey data which does not distinguish internally between providers of each type.

How does the economic character of services differ by sector? The available empirical evidence on costs paints a mixed picture, and as with social housing, conceals very significant intra-sector variation. Domiciliary care is more costly on average under voluntary than for-profit sector auspices (Matosevic *et al.*, 2001), but residential and day care are more economical in the voluntary sector than in other sectors. This is even after controlling for the cost-relevant effects of differences in user dependency. Domiciliary care's relative costliness in the voluntary sector is probably largely driven by the higher average rates of pay these organizations tend to pay front-line care workers (cf. Chapter 6). The lower costs of the voluntary sector in other settings seems to involve different combinations of factors. In day care, volunteers' labour contributions to local affiliates of national specialists (economizing on production costs; Knapp and Missiakoulis, 1982), and capital grant-makers' preferences for the voluntary sector in a relatively unregulated and politically risky environment (as a way of economizing on transaction costs) are relevant (see Box 8.5). In residential care, by contrast, where relatively large traditional generalists and nonprofit social entrepreneurs dominate, technical economies of scale and scope, cross-subsidy from other current activities outside social care, and historically accumulated reserves allow voluntary organizations to be less costly and/or charge lower fees than their predominantly small business for-profit counterparts. On average, these 'technical' efficiency advantages seem to more than outweigh any off-

---

Box 8.5 Preferential access to capital grants to the voluntary sector

One of our national specialist interviewees argued that eligibility for public sector capital grants was a significant advantage for the voluntary sector over the for-profit sector in day care:

> One of my favourite areas of our comparative advantage is if we want to build new premises for the delivery of day care, we don't actually have to go to the market to borrow the money at existing rates to do it – although that may well be part of it. We can go to either public sector sources for capital grants, we have trusts, the Lottery for capital too, or we can go out and raise the money from the public. [As far as capital funding under the Department of Health's general grant scheme of the 1968 Act is concerned] the for-profit sector is not eligible. I know of no statutory power which would enable a body to make a grant to a private sector organization for a property which would in the long term be an asset of that organization. There would be parliamentary questions, a major public row.

setting comparative cost-raising factors in this form of care. For example, as with domiciliary care, front-line care workers may on average be paid more, inflating employment costs; while a for-profit interviewee argued that organizational slack, management limitations and x-inefficiencies were more prevalent in voluntary sector than for-profit care homes.

What about outputs or outcomes? The quality of social care is widely understood to be intimately bound up with the quality of the staff that provide it, and the continuity of care they are able to facilitate (Kendall *et al.*, 2003). The higher average pay for front-line staff already mentioned, coupled with lower prevalence of low pay (Almond and Kendall, 2001a), and lower staff turnover rates (LGMB, 1997) compared to the for-profit sector could be suggestive, therefore, of higher quality.

However, consideration of social care quality should ideally involve taking into account care outcomes or proxies for such outcomes too. Accordingly, it is less straightforward to measure than costs. Indeed, in practice public decision-makers tend to rely on informal information, trust and reputation as a basis for assessing quality (Mannion and Smith, 1998). Allen *et al.* (1992) reported that field-level SSD staff point to advantages in terms of 'ethos', 'care environments' as well as the access to local networks associated with voluntarism, resonating with the policy discourse more generally (cf. Box 8.1). At a more strategic level, SSD directors have sometimes had ideological preferences for the sector simply because it does not explicitly involve profit-seeking. However, the use of crude distinctions by sector has faded as the influence of market-hostile doctrines have waned, and as awareness that nominally 'for profit' organizations are typically not purely motivated by profit maximization objective has grown (Kendall, 2001; Kendall *et al.*, 2003)

At the same time, recognition of the voluntary sector's benign intentions have sometimes been offset by worries about the capabilities or competence of some, particularly in coping with the increasingly competitive contractual environment of the late 1990s (Wistow *et al.*, 1996; Knapp *et al.*, 2001; Kendall *et al.*, 2003b). In addition, severe doubts about the voluntary sector have been evident as far as the majority of older people themselves are concerned. In fact, this sector is only endorsed as the care option of choice by a small minority for the mainstream services on which we have data, with the public sector tending to emerge as strongly favoured (Sykes and Leather, 1997; Wenger, 1999). This represents a marked contrast with evidence on trust and preferences in the other two UK impact studies, and also on qualitative attitudes amongst older people themselves on social support *other than* mainstream social care (see below). This may reflect the outcome of a combination of state-friendly attitudinal conservatism (shaped, not least, by wartime experiences), hostility towards 'charity' due to negative imagery and experiences in the pre-war era (Taylor and Kendall, 1996), and perceptions that weaknesses such as paternalism could be particularly prevalent here (see Section 8.3).

Some recent quantitative evidence on actual service achievements (rather than prior attitudes towards providers) is also relevant to service function comparisons. A PSSRU survey, comparing care homes using the sheltered care environment scale as interpreted by home staff, found that in terms of four out of seven measures – organization, physical comfort, cohesion and self-disclosure – the for-profit sector was rated higher than the voluntary sector – with no significant differences along other dimensions (Netten *et al.*, 1999). Although not a direct measure of quality of care as such, there is some evidence to suggest that, at least for people with dementia, homes which score well on this measure do tend also to have superior welfare outcomes for users (Netten, 2000).

These results could have been affected by the inclusion of 'not-for-profit (ex-SSD) trusts' as part of the voluntary sector in the survey (see Section 8.2 and Box 8.4); their exclusion might have positioned the latter sector differently. To an extent, variations also reflect the difference in average size between the homes, since *ceteris paribus*, the smaller homes which are typical of the for-profit sector also tend to score more highly. However, if we assume that this differential would still have been evident, can it be reconciled with the qualitative data relating to public officials' attitudes and the concentration of lower pay in the for-profit sector discussed above?

One possibility is that it cannot: the hypothesis regarding the link between staff pay and quality of care is simply mistaken, and superior pay and conditions in the voluntary sector have not tended to generate higher quality at all (a possibility endorsed by one for-profit interviewee). A second possibility is that differential enforcement of regulations by registration and inspection authorities under the old (1984–2002) regime, with greater enthusiasm for closing down below-standard for-profit sector than voluntary sector facilities, had left a legacy of poor quality. One for-profit interviewee claimed this had happened because the social work background of many inspectors made them, consciously or otherwise, 'prejudiced' against the profit motive. This was said to have led them to target for-profit homes for closure, while being more tolerant of voluntary sector facilities known to have dubious standards. This would have left more 'bad apples' in the latter case, dragging down average quality in the voluntary sector at the time of the survey (1996), even if a more 'even-handed' approach has now levelled standards up. However, since we also know that in terms of at least one of the easily measurable regulatory standards – the extent of room-sharing – the voluntary sector currently has a better record than the for-profit sector, there are grounds for caution here.

A final possibility is that the SCES was not really an adequate proxy for care quality at all. A high score in terms of dimensions, such as 'organization', may imply an appropriate environment for some users, but not for others. Voluntary sector providers could still have been delivering a higher quality of care overall, but the SCES scale might not have been capturing more subtle dimensions of care quality, especially relevant for people not suffering from dementia.[7] This wider focus on user welfare takes us beyond the confines of 'service provision' as defined here in terms of the three core SSD-financed services, and into a discussion of the 'expressive' function. This can be considered analogous to broadening our remit from 'social care' to 'social care and support' in what follows.

8.3.2 *The expressive function*

Recent qualitative research has underlined the significance of company, contact and a feeling of being treated with respect as components of care and support from the perspective of front-line professionals (care managers) and users themselves. This is relevant for both recipients of mainstream care services, and other older people who receive emotional support from volunteers, but are outside that system (Qureshi *et al.*, 1998; SPRU, 2000; Waddington and Henwood, 1996; Quilgars, 2000a, b).[8] Clearly, these experiences depend on the style of social interaction, as well as on the quantity of formal social care services provided.

Prima facie, because the voluntary sector is the primary formal organized source of volunteers, and involves a disproportionate number of paid staff *not* subject to mainstream contracting and national regulatory controls, it seems to be at a comparative advantage over other sectors in facilitating 'expression'. Strictly speaking, certain conditions must apply. First, the climate in which non-SSD-funded voluntary sector employees contribute to social care and support must be relatively less prescriptive. Second, the existence of volunteer–user relations resulting from involvement with formal voluntary sector organizations must systematically produce friendship-like social bonds, which otherwise would not arise. Third, such friendships must tend to be supportive, effectively generate arenas of intimacy within which identities can be meaningfully expressed.

These assumptions concerning the 'added value' of volunteers compared to paid workers seem to be widely made in practice (Davis Smith, 1998). Volunteering can be mutually understood as meaning the volunteer is there primarily through 'free choice', and could finish involvement with relative ease. The presence of payment in the case of paid employees could be an obstacle to the emotional investment and intimacy involved in friendship, because both understand that that worker is, at least initially, there 'being paid to do a job'. Further, volunteers may be less likely to have formal qualifications and to project themselves as 'professionals' than their paid counterparts, thus opening up the possibility for empathy (Quilgars, 2000a: 2; 2000b: 86 and Chapter 5).

In addition, friendships could flourish with relative ease simply because the volunteers involved in supporting older people tend to be older themselves (Knapp *et al.*, 1995: 18–19). As 'chronological peers', they may be more able to empathize with the user than a paid worker (from a younger generation). Common ground may also be easier to find because older volunteers are relatively time rich (Office for National Statistics, 1999) – and familiarity takes time to develop. Shared situations, modes of thinking and experiences of dramatic life events or crises can also be conducive to empathy and coping strategies, to such a extent that the boundaries between 'recipient' and 'volunteer' essentially dissolve (Wardell and Chesson, 1998: 12; Rochester *et al.*, 2001: 18).

Where user frailty necessitates the delivery of social care in the institutionalized context of residential homes, the voluntary sector may also have particular strengths because of a capacity to retain continuities in relationships, and valued links with the familiar. Particularly traumatic is the actual decision to enter a home, and the subsequent process of adjustment (Social Services Inspectorate, 1999). Although very heavy reliance for care services is placed on paid staff, voluntary sector homes' greater capacity to involve volunteer visitors in a social capacity can potentially make a real difference nonetheless (Kavanagh and Knapp, 1999). Indeed, to the extent that simple boredom is a problem (Hughes and Wilkin, 1987; Oldman and Quilgars, 1999), the expect-ation and experience of interaction with people from outside may be particularly prized because of its scarcity value. At just the moment when institutional-ization threatens to deprive the older person of relational aspects of life (and not infrequently, quite soon after the bereavement of a spouse), personal relationships may suddenly take on a whole new order of significance. Closeness to death and loss of financial or physical assets may make personal relationships relatively more important than in the more materialistic, early phases of life (Counsel and Care, 1997: 21; see also Box 8.6).

Box 8.6 Traditional generalists and the significance of ritual for older people

The traditional generalists who still comprise a significant component of the residential care market may be especially advantaged in facilitating expressive relations for two further reasons. First, it may be more difficult to argue that volunteering in such a context is compatible with volunteers' self-interest and social interaction motivations when the supported user is very frail and living in an institution: there is less *obvious* scope for fun or emotional reward for the volunteer. In such situations, the moral suasion available especially to such organizations may come into its own. Second, such organizations tend to be endowed, by their very nature, with repertoires of resonant rituals. Deprived of the rituals of everyday life (including family rituals, and the rituals that characterize friendships as part of ordinary living), familiar religious rituals and ceremonies can be an especially important source of continuity with the past, as well as providing the more obvious scope for spiritual development and comfort about the future. In general, religious concerns are more significant amongst older people than the population in general (Office for National Statistics, 1999: 40; 2001: 235). Even for people with high levels of mental frailty, the punctuation of their lives with familiar, regular rituals can provide unparalleled opportunities for expression (Counsel and Care, 1997). The majority of residential homes in all sectors, in fact, offer occasional religious services (Myers, 1989; Netten *et al.*, 1999), but the experiences reported in Counsel and Care's 1997 research suggest that there is deeper content and meaning – that is, resonance – to these rituals in denominational homes.

As far as leadership development is concerned, some interviewees offered examples of named individuals who had moved from the voluntary sector into the departments or agencies of central government, or on retirement been rewarded with a place in the House of Lords. All of the public and for-profit sector interviewees had themselves been quite heavily involved in voluntary sector activities in the past, or were still so involved, juggling these commitments alongside their 'day job'. However, as with social housing, what was most striking was the extent to which net movement seems to have taken place from the public to the voluntary sector. A number of our national specialist and nonprofit social entrepreneurship organization interviewees, widely regarded as charismatic leaders, had previously worked in senior capacities as officers in local government. Some had made the move, at least in part, because they felt stifled in that environment and relished the greater freedom to innovate in services or ideas offered in the voluntary sector. It is to the discussion of innovation as a 'function' that we now turn.

8.3.3 The innovation function

An inconsistent and unclear picture of this function emerges from the literature in this policy field (Ferlie *et al.*, 1989; Knapp and Thomason, 2000). Echoing this, discussion of the link between innovation and the voluntary sector in the interviews themselves tended to involve three contrasting forms of reaction, in part linked to their broader analyses of the overall character of the care system (Box 8.3). A first, dismissive reaction, associated particularly with the sceptical view of the current developmental trajectory social care system as a whole, was one of cynicism and disbelief. In this camp were for-profit interviewees, who thought that they tended to have an advantage here over both of the other sectors because of their ability to avoid 'burdensome' committee structures, particularly at the 'small business' end of the sector. Next (not aligned in terms of the dichotomy suggested in Box 8.3) were agnostics indicating that they thought it dangerous to generalize, even in terms of contrasting just one of the 'types' of voluntary sector organizations with public or private sector comparators. Even where such judgements had been made on other functions, there was a reluctance to do so in this particular case. Individual examples were given of what interviewees labelled as 'innovative' voluntary sector projects and practices, but they did not feel able to move beyond anecdote, or to compare. A third group, enthusiasts (who tended also to be from a wider optimist camp), felt that the voluntary sector, or particular types within it, were comparatively innovative, all referring to local authorities as a reference point.

A number of explanations for this tendency were offered by these enthusiasts. The most frequent were in terms of a relative freedom from statutory duties or requirements, a more general lack of rule-boundedness, contrasts in procedures for decision-making in comparison with the public sector, and the ability to avoid engaging in explicit politics. However, in the particular case of innovation on the boundary between housing and social care, as with very sheltered housing, the significance of public grants for innovation in housing, including those available from the Housing Corporation, was also mentioned. These financial opportunities were off-limits for the for-profit sector (see Chapter 7).

8.3.4 The community-building function

In the case of social care, the emergence and fortunes of 'community-building' have long been bound up with those of the 'community social work' tradition (Wistow *et al.*, 1994: 135). A significant component of the grants programmes of local authorities in support of voluntary sector organizations, particularly community groups receiving funding at early stages of development, traditionally had this orientation. As with campaigning, such activities were perceived by some in this field to be under threat in the context of the so-called 'contract culture' (see more generally Chapter 4).

However, the 'joined-up government' and 'democratic renewal' agendas has reawakened interest in this area.[9] For its part, many within the voluntary sector – most visibly, the later generations of organizations identified in our typology – have often explicitly articulated values sympathetic to these ideas. With the new government endorsing such policy aspirations, our interviewees emphasized that many voluntary organizations were now receiving new recognition and legitimacy for goals which they were already pursuing (see too Cameron *et al.*, 2001: 2).

In parallel to this very general Government recognition in policy terms, research has begun to demonstrate the significance that individual older people attach to 'community' or 'social' engagement as an ingredient in their own welfare or quality of life. This is typically assumed to imply involvement with voluntary organizations. In a recent study, 'social participation and involvement' – defined to include not only informal activities, but also 'lunch clubs, day centres, transport facilities and organized activity via voluntary sector organizations' – was rated by many older people as of greater significance than more 'classic' social care interventions (Netten *et al.*, 2000; see Box 8.7).

In a broadly complementary way, but based on research with public and voluntary sector actors at the local level rather than older people themselves, evidence as to the general significance of voluntary activity in the wider goal of 'promoting well-being' through 'prevention' has been gathered (Lewis *et al.*, 1999; and see BGOP Steering Committee, 2000; Hayden and Boaz, 2000). The voluntary sector comes to the fore in a number of ways in this account. It has been argued to be well placed to encourage 'cohesion amongst local players' since 'local people were more involved where there were active representation groups, such as Age Concern'. It could also help people navigate through the complex maze of information on entitlements and service options which is so notorious in this field. Finally, voluntary sector support could have more legitimacy (see also Counsel and Care, 1998). This contrasts markedly with the 'mainstream' service function activities discussed earlier. But reinforcing this point was the perspective of a funder, one of our central government (public sector) interviewees. He indicated that the decision to support local 'outreach'

Box 8.7 Interpreting the voluntary sector's contribution to older people outcomes

~~The PSSRU SCOOP study found that a representative sample of 356~~ older people on average ranked social participation second in importance only to personal care, and ahead of food and nutrition, safety and control over daily life. For older people below 75 years of age and people living with others, social participation was given particular weight, and even ranked above personal care in the case of people living with others. The SCOOP research team concentrate on a medical explanation, suggesting this may be because of the protection from risk such participation offers: it could flow from a health-oriented desire to avoid social isolation because 'the latter is associated with higher levels of morbidity and mortality' (Netten *et al.*, 1999: ii and 50, who refer to a variety of literature to substantiate this link). However, this high ranking could also reflect the importance attached by respondents to needs other than those relating narrowly to physical health – particularly protection from the risk of deterioration of emotional and mental health (see Glass *et al.*, 1999). Indeed, following our earlier discussion, one could go further to suggest that older people may attach particular weight to social participation because of the recognition of self and friendship that it brings, over and above any relevance this has for their medically diagnosed health state.

---

activities via financing the voluntary sector was in part driven by a belief that people reacted 'angrily or deferentially' to official representatives of the state, but more 'naturally' to voluntary sector personnel.

8.3.5 *The advocacy function*

Nationally, public officials' interest here has been heightened on the assumption that receptivity to, and encouragement for, advocacy flows from the 'joined-up government' and 'democratic renewal' agendas noted under 'community-building'. Yet while voluntary sector advocacy for and by older people in the UK has grown in recent years – and has most visibly been manifested by the creation of community care fora and networks in the 1990s – it still seems relatively limited in scope and scale compared to other client groups in Britain, and to older people's advocacy in the US and continental Europe (Ginn, 1996; Walker and Naegele, 1999; Ginn and Arber, 1999; Twigg, 2000). Certainly at the local level, a picture of uneven and haphazard activity emerges from official reports on 'consultation' (Social Services Inspectorate, 2000a, b; Social Services Inspectorate and Audit Commission, 2000). The interviewees confirmed that this was the case, and indicated that those consultation exercises which had taken place, particularly when styled as 'participatory', could often leave those involved annoyed by a sense that 'the real decisions had already been made' and their contributions were not affecting significant change.

However, if we are interested in broad policy influence rather than participation and agenda setting per se, the picture is less clear. There is a long-established tradition in central government of seeking advice from national specialists and nonprofit social entrepreneurs because of their 'technical' knowledge, expertise and experience – whether or not this had necessarily involved the active participation of older people themselves. This takes place in numerous ways, but the Centre for Policy on Ageing's leading role in the design of new country-wide regulations for residential care pursuant to the Care Regulations Act 2000 is a recent good example (see Section 8.2). Our interviewees confirmed that, also at the local level, the voluntary sector's influence was probably felt as much through low-visibility inputs into planning, implementation, research and evaluation processes. High-profile 'campaigning', or involvement with local authority staged 'consultation events', were only one part of the story.

Can a more explicitly comparative perspective, accounting for the three sectors be adopted? In the case of care and support for older people, many studies suggest both services and income maintenance (including pensions) have been underfunded, overinstitutionalization of services has taken place, and insufficient attention has been paid to the development of 'social rights' (for example, see Means and Smith, 1998a; Bornat *et al.*, 1997). The 'blame' has often been placed at the door of politicians and public sector insiders, including civil servants and local government officials. However, to the extent national specialists have long worked closely with such constituencies – and pensioners' groups, lobbying from the outside, have largely failed to have their demands realized – then the state and the voluntary sector are both 'responsible'.

At the same time, a competition for influence in setting agendas and designing policies is also de facto taking place with the for-profit sector too. Nationally, the corporate and financiers' perspective from this sector was strongly pressed in the Royal Commission. Some analysts have characterized for-profits as dominant actors in a residential care 'lobby', with small home owner-managers therefore also entering the stage politically as powerful 'vested' interests to which policy-makers have had to respond (Bernard and Phillips, 1998; Wistow *et al.*, 1996: Chapter 7).

Set against these symptoms of for-profit hegemony, as late as 1996/7, the annual Community Care Plans established as part of the early 1990s reforms were still considerably more likely to reflect inputs from the voluntary sector than the for-profit sector. This was despite the impetus that had emerged from above in the form of a central government *Direction* in 1993, requiring that for-profits be 'fully involved' in their production (Nuffield Institute for Health Community Care Division, 1998: 3). A for-profit interviewee insisted that 'ideological prejudice' was actually quite widespread, and consequently had increasingly sought to enter into coalitions with voluntary sector actors for lobbying purposes where perceptions of interest coincided. However, we have already noted that overt ideology seems to have become less of a differentiating factor in recent years. Reconciling these two positions, one local authority interviewee suggested that policy-makers were still more open to the voluntary sector, but in quite a subtle way. The contrast between for-profit 'self-interest' and voluntary sector 'sainthood' was an oversimplification – but a 'layer of altruism' was said to be more prominent in the latter case, and so a 'different stance' was said to be evident.

8.4 Weaknesses of the voluntary sector in care and support for older people

8.4.1 *Chronic resource problems*

It has been noted that 'underfunding' is often claimed to be a problem for older people's care and support services: it is portrayed as a 'cinderella service', unfavourably treated compared with other social welfare services, such as health, education and perhaps social housing. This could be understood from a theoretical perspective as ultimately a collective action problem: the 'inadequate' advocacy referred to in the previous section, on this account, has failed to secure the state resource commitments which are efficient from a societal point of view.

However, the theoretical reasoning and empirical evidence which might identify the scale of such a shortfall evident in this field has yet to be developed. Instead, what emerges from existing research is that on the ground, the sectors are experiencing, and responding to, resource 'insufficiencies' in different ways, as a reflection of both their contrasting developmental trajectories and current situations. In the case of contracted, mainstream services, compared with the primarily small business for-profit sector, on average, the voluntary sector seems relatively well positioned to take these strains. This is because of its tendency to operate with a relatively diversified portfolio of care, its access to historically accumulated resources, and its ability to access funding schemes not available to the for-profit sector, such as the Community Fund, support from purely private grant-making trusts, and community development and innovation grants from the national and local state.

Yet to the extent these conditions do not hold, then the vulnerability of the voluntary sector is as severe as small, business, for-profit counterparts. For example, in residential care, a significant minority of specialist voluntary sector providers are small-scale, free-standing, and heavily dependent on fees from just one or two local (SSD) public purchasers. The management of these small homes seem to be taking council 'underfunding', and a lack of encouragement and sensitivity to their situations, as badly as their small business counterparts in the for-profit sector (Kendall *et al.*, 2003b). In the case of domiciliary care, in some locales voluntary sector providers are still deliberately treated preferentially via partnership arrangements or grant aid (Ware *et al.*, 2001: 337). But research indicates that when the two sectors are apparently facing similar 'objective' conditions in terms of resources and environmental competitiveness, the voluntary sector may come out significantly worse off in motivational terms. This could be because for-profit operators are used to, and expect, the difficult, competitive and even 'adversarial' conditions that now often characterize the supply of care of this form. For their part, voluntary sector organizations, traditionally used to preferential treatment, seem to be finding it comparatively difficult to adapt to a 'level playing field' (Kendall *et al.*, 2003b). Differences discussed earlier in terms of preferential 'advocacy access' notwithstanding, as ideological hostility to for-profits seems to fade, such competitive 'even-handedness' increasingly characterizes the field, at least as far as independently provided mainstream services are concerned.[10]

In fact, it is voluntary organizations operating primarily outside the main-stream 'system' which have generated the most worries amongst policy commentators in terms of 'insufficiency'. Public funding has increasingly been concentrated on the most dependent older people still living at home, in an attempt to prevent inappropriate admissions to residential care (Office for National Statistics, 2001; Knapp *et al.*, 2001). Groups offering low-intensity care and support for people who have not been identified as at risk of admission, or not classified as addressing priorities (that is, not offering services to people with very high levels of physical or mental frailty) tend to be financed on a precarious basis. If public funding is required to make such services viable, those involved have the task of convincing potential public funders that there is a need for their services at all, and trying to sustain an 'adequate' flow of resources there-after. Organizations of this type operating in locales where councils have a strong 'community development' orientation, and/or deemed by the central state to be in need of additional central support on the grounds of tackling geographically concentrated social exclusion, have considerably more oppor-tunities for securing public funding than others (cf. Chapter 4). Yet even when officials are convinced, resources committed and growth achieved, this has involved juggling public resources from different programmes and tiers of the state precariously, often with insufficient time and skills to build appropriate organizational infrastructure (Alcock *et al.*, 1997; Scott *et al.*, 2000; Lewis *et al.*, 1999; Scott and Russell, 2000).

8.4.2 *Particularism*

As with other policy fields, this second 'weakness' is often interpreted as a strength – to the extent it represents a desirable degree of specialization. Black and minority ethnic elder centres appear to be good examples (Ahmad, 1996; Atkin, 1996; Patel, 1999), as are denominational residential care homes and many community-based activities. Other forms of 'particularism' which are widely welcomed as legitimate 'product differentiation' and 'specialism' are those developed for particular levels of user frailty or dependency, or involving condition-specific services. For example, the nonprofit social entrepreneur organizations interviewed were providing a range of day, domiciliary and residential care for older people with dementia, in the context of local situations in which the public and for-profit sectors had been unwilling or unable to supply such services.

There are, however, further forms of particularism which tend to be widely recognized as actual or potential weakness in this field, reflecting familiar emphases in the British welfare services literature more generally. First, the continued uneven geographical distribution of voluntary sector services, especially where state support for them has been perceived as inadequate, is an enduring theme in the literature (Means and Smith, 1998b). Second, certain 'communities of interest' could also be thought of as 'excluded' to the extent roles other that the mainstream service role involve some groups more than others. For example, with regard to the community-building function, the *Better Government for Older People* pilot evaluations suggested that participation was often dominated by a relatively small group of 'joiners'. There were clear gaps in engagement as far as ethnic minority elders, housebound and frail older people, and people on lower incomes were concerned (Hayden and Boaz, 2000: 37).

Finally, in line with the more general understandings reviewed in Chapter 6, a number of interviewees argued that traditional generalists and national specialists were dominated in terms of supporters and members by people from higher socio-economic groups, at least in some places. Evidence as far as users are concerned is more mixed. A number of interviewees thought that many voluntary sector activities were very clearly geared towards a middle-class clientele. However, we also know that on average, in the residential care case, while voluntary sector homes do have far fewer private payers than the public sector, they are similar to the for-profit sector in this regard (Netten *et al.*, 1999). That a similar balance between publicly funded (and hence, lower private income and wealth) and 'self-funded' clients prevails in each sector is at least suggestive that this distinction should not be overdrawn.

8.4.3 *Paternalism*

Paternalism, the interviewees agreed, was now far less pervasive than it had been historically, when older people were prominent amongst the recipients of traditional charity at its most negative. This could involve dependency, involuntary deference and a sense of powerlessness on the part of the recipient of care (Marshall, 1949; Thane, 2000). The situation changed markedly during the second half of the twentieth century, as the values of newer generations of voluntary organizations with more progressive approaches were put into practice, and some of the pre-war agencies also adapted. However, it is clear too that quite high levels of paternalism have persisted both in the field as a whole and in the voluntary sector within it. The voluntary sector's apparently limited advocacy success referred to earlier has involved a failure to win social rights comparable to those won by some other social care client groups and in other policy fields. For example, two interviewees spontaneously compared social care directly with social housing. They took the view that an expansive repertoire of tenants' rights and entitlements effectively underpinned an enabling, participatory culture in the latter case. In contrast, greater reliance on means testing and professional mediation in the former was taken to be symptomatic of an underdeveloped sense of 'empowerment'.[11]

There are two further reasons why paternalism is also especially pervasive in the voluntary sector. First, the older generation of traditional generalists are still a significant presence here in delivering local services and support. They are certainly proportionately more important than either old agencies in the other sectors within the care and support for older people field, or compared to the social housing field, as noted in Section 8.1. While some have undoubtedly adapted over time, some of our interviewees took the view that many or even most had retained philosophies, or continued to foster practices, of an essentially paternalistic character. Second, if account is taken of volunteers as well as paid employees, then the concentration of older workers by comparison with the for-profit and public sectors is relevant. To the extent that old age and conservatism are correlated, and conservatism tends to involve more paternalistic attitudes, then de facto such attitudes will be necessarily more pervasive here.

8.4.4 Excessive professionalism or amateurism

In the discussion of the quality of care it was noted that some public purchasers had been worried in the 1990s about the managerial competence of some contracted voluntary sector providers. This could be seen as in part a reflection of worries about 'excessive amateurism' in the sense suggested by Ralph Kramer (see Chapter 6). These concerns were not universal, however, and were probably most relevant to relationships with traditional generalists and local affiliates of national specialists, and in only some locales. At the same time, interviewees suggested a virtual consensus as to the 'professionalism' with which relations between national specialists and nonprofit social entrepreneurs, on the one hand, and central government civil servants, on the other, were conducted.

8.4.5 Accountability problems

Diversity quickly comes to the fore when this weakness is considered. At one extreme, very small community groups on the edge of the sector in terms of their degree of formality are not accountable to anyone other than beneficiaries. But moving towards larger-scale activities, arrangements for ensuring accountability for agencies in this field in the current policy context seems to exhibit complexity in extremis. Above and beyond sector-specific requirements such as those of charity law, and regulations regarding the use of volunteers, organizations which are incorporated and employers also have generic company and employment law to contend with (including, for the first time since 1998, European measures on health and safety and working time, and domestically instigated minimum wage legislation).

Agencies providing mainstream social care services to local public purchasers under contract must now comply with the increasingly dense web of contractual and regulatory constraints described at the end of Section 8.2. These have, in theory, been designed – in the regulatory case in particular, with a leading role from national specialist voluntary organizations – to explicitly reflect the interests not only of purchasers, but also of users too. Under the current administration, local contractual regimes are, in turn, subject to central command and control mechanisms through the implementation of 'Best Value' (see Chapter 4) and 'National Service Frameworks' (NSFs), with a user orientation in mind. There is a voluminous NSF specifically for older people. At the furthest extreme, those at the social care-housing interface operating with the support of the Housing Corporation – a situation typified by the many social entrepreneurs who have diversified from social care into housing, or vice versa – have the whole, further array of regulatory requirements discussed in Chapter 7 with which to contend, and our analysis of the issues in that chapter would clearly be relevant to these providers.

Surprisingly, this issue has received relatively little attention in the literature specifically on older people compared with quite involved debates touched upon in the other impact studies, so this section relies particularly on the fieldwork. Asked the deceptively simple question of whether existing arrangements for accountability were appropriate, in the face of this startlingly complex and varied situation, interviewees offered mixed responses. However, it is possible to conclude that while a minority thought the formal status quo as described above did provide an adequate basis for accountability, most were dissatisfied.

First, where public finance was involved, necessary safeguards for accountability upwards ultimately to the electorate as a whole, via the civil service and ministers were judged to be insufficient, echoing Malpass' analysis of social housing (see Chapter 7), with its traditional representative democracy benchmark.

Second, some felt that, despite the existence of a dense web of regulatory and contractual arrangements – supposedly designed to take into account the interests of service users and older people more generally – there remained a significant deficit of accountability downwards. There was a strong sense that there was considerable room to alter the balance of power much further in favour of older people themselves. The very complexity of the system was itself seen as a major obstacle to such accountability (cf. Royal Commission, 1999), and this could be a problem for those seeking access to services in the first place, as well as those receiving mainstream services. As well as a need to change formal structures and develop further existing policy emphases on community-building and inclusive advocacy, the much more intangible, longer-term goal of fostering a participatory culture was also stressed.

8.5 Conclusions

The literature reviewed and expert opinions gathered here provide clear evidence that both functions and weaknesses have salience in this field. There is a relatively rich literature and a range of empirical evidence comparing the voluntary sector with its for-profit and public sector counterparts. Based upon this, we now know a good deal about variations in inputs and structures between sectors. However, to a large extent because of the complexity and opacity that characterizes social care 'production', we cannot reach definitive conclusions on such key questions as comparative efficiency or effectiveness using available data. This is strongly in line with the characteristics of policy argument relating to the voluntary sector which were suggested in the introduction to this part of the book (Chapter 5).

Moreover, and partly symptomatic of this situation, there was considerable variation between experts concerning emphases and interpretations. For example, the 'innovation' function and 'problematic accountability' generated considerable differences of opinion as to their character and content. To a marked degree, contrasts of interpretation were linked to differences in broader, overall evaluation of the current workings and direction of the social care and support system for older people amongst these experts. Thus, those who were essentially optimistic about the system's functioning seemed willing to believe that on balance the voluntary sector was contributing to healthy patterns of innovation, and the weaknesses mentioned, while present, were tolerable, being addressed or at least managed. The pessimism of some was in turn reflected in their very cautious, and often negative, conclusions about the voluntary sector's contributions.

More positively, the weight of evidence reviewed does begin to suggest that under certain conditions, and in some contexts, the sector may have tended to have comparative advantages during the 1980s and 1990s at least. What were these conditions? Whether or not such an advantages arises appears to be contingent on two major factors, both ultimately reflecting the legacy of resources and relationships built up over time. First, the type of care or support in question. In particular, volunteering, a relatively small scale of operation, sector-specific funding programmes, informality and social network connectedness appear to account for the voluntary sector's conspicuous presence and economic strength in day care and support activities. In residential care, where the sector is very much a minority provider, different factors come into play. Economies of scale and scope, historically accumulated resources and proven track record, and (for traditional generalists) access to repertoires of resonant rituals seem to confer economic and social advantages for many older people in this case.

Second, and relatedly, the mix in terms of the type of organizations is also relevant. There is much internal diversity within the sector, which we tried to capture in our simplifying typology at the onset. Each type has a distinctive combination of care and support priorities, tends to be both constrained and enabled by particular historical legacies, and involves different resource capabilities and patterns of relationship with the state. This is associated with different emphases in terms of the functions reviewed – specializing or generalizing to different degrees – and contrasts in the degree to which 'weaknesses' are relevant or significant.

It is important to finish by underlining that what our review does not allow us to do is to reach an overall conclusion that some types of voluntary organization are 'performing better' or producing a 'superior impact' to other types. For example, traditional generalists were often mentioned in interviews as exemplifying 'weaknesses', appear not to have been significantly involved in some important forms of care (such as publicly funded mainstream domiciliary care), and were less recognized by stakeholders as contributing to policy design or community-building. Yet this may in part reflect the fact that such organizations are simply less visible and less engaged with public systems than other types. In particular, the impact of denominational and other religious rooted social care activity is, as Margaret Harris surmises 'quiet' (Harris, 1998). For a range of constitutional, technical and organizational reasons groups may legitimately choose to keep their distance from the state. Such relatively limited engagement as far as some of these functions are concerned does not mean they are necessarily making less 'impact' than counterparts with higher political profiles, such as national specialists and nonprofit social entrepreneurs, but rather that their impact is different in balance and character.

Notes

1 Unfortunately, since 1996, official data collections do not distinguish within the 'independent sector' between voluntary sector and for-profit sector activities.
2 A role as pioneers of new services, claimed particularly by the new generation of wartime and post-war charities, was significantly supported by central government with the instigation of a new grants programme. Under a 1968 Act of Parliament, this was to be available only to voluntary sector organizations, in part under the banner of the encouragement of 'innovation'.
3 The particular institutional form taken by the new policies reflected a mixture of ideological, political and research-based influences. The 'New Right' central government's enthusiasm for markets and consumer-led services was a driver shared with many countries also experiencing social care reform (Forder, 2000). But unique to the UK was the ideological antipathy towards local government's direct services provision already noted in discussing social housing. There was the political imperative of stabilizing the burgeoning independently provided residential care market. And there was perhaps a desire to locate political blame for 'underfunding' and scandals involving client neglect at the door of local government. Research suggesting inefficiencies and failure to meet needs under the previous arrangements was a further factor (Davies and Challis, 1986, 1990; Baldock and Ungerson, 1993).
4 New proposals to replace local authority SSDs with 'care trusts' involving central government health authority and local government joint responsibility for social care and health care could further shift power towards the centre. At the time of writing, care trusts are in a piloting phase only in a small number of locales.
5 This categorization is based mainly upon a service delivery typology suggested in Kendall (2000b), but has been made more inclusive of advocacy roles in particular by drawing on Thornton and Tozer (1994), Wertheimer (1993), Bernard and Phillips (1998), Ginn (1996) and Ginn and Arber (1999).
6 In referring to the 'voluntary sector', it often transpired after further exploration that most interviewees tended to have in mind a limited number of the 'types' identified in Section 8.2 (typically limited to, or including, their own 'type' for voluntary sector interviewees) rather than holding in their minds a generalization or average across these types. Similarly, in the case of 'the for-profit sector', when prompted some

interviewees indicated that their comparator was either really the 'small business' component of the sector, or the 'corporate' element, rather than a generalization or average across these categories. In the case of local authority provision, there is more uniformity in terms of historicity and size, even if considerable variety between locales.

7 Put slightly different, while the SCES may be a reasonable proxy for the quality of social care for this particular group of older people, it may be less adequate for those not suffering from this type of mental frailty. Netten (2000) points out that a high 'organization' score, for example, refers to the importance of order in the home, the extent to which residents know what to expect from their daily routine, and the clarity of rules and procedures. This could clearly involve a highly routinized regime, which could suit people with dementia and perhaps some without, but might be experienced as too constraining, regimented or dirigiste by many others.

8 These sentiments can emerge from bilateral relationships with other individuals, or in the context of social activities involving groups of individuals. We consider the former under the 'expressive' function and the latter under the 'community-building' function.

9 State support for 'community-building' within the care for older people domain can also be traced as originating from above (the 1998 Department of Health White Paper); from the boundaries (policy documents encouraging working across the housing–social care and health–social care interfaces produced by inspectorates and adjacent Whitehall Departments); and from outside (for example, the proposal to import Compact principles into the social care field; Social Services Inspectorate, 2000b).

10 The 'level playing field' policy is supposed to apply across all three sectors – those which are still council owned and run, as much as for-profit and voluntary sector services. However, in practice there seem to be marked differences in the treatment of the former, on the one hand, and the 'independent sector' – voluntary plus private sector as a whole – on the other. It is not clear that these differences are defensible in terms of the 'Best Value' principles which are meant to ensure value for money in local government services (Commissioning and Performance Team, 2002).

11 One respondent, also a 'sceptic' on the scale of innovation in this field, intriguingly linked this 'protective' culture with a perceived absence of innovation, and contrasted this with the social housing field where she argued innovation was pervasive: 'It is perhaps no accident that many of the recent developments in new forms of service provision have arisen from the housing rather than the social care sector: this sector has a different philosophy and a long-standing tradition of tenants' rights and tenant participation, quite unlike the protective culture of much social care'. This analysis is consistent with the suggestion at the end of the previous chapter that users' participation in governance is relatively well developed in social housing.

9 The impact of voluntary sector environmental organizations

- **The voluntary organizations active in this domain share an aspiration to foster an environmental sensibility, and many are especially savvy in media management techniques.**

- **Comparisons with other sectors are largely impressionistic.**

- **The problem of resource insufficiency is perhaps more severe than in social housing but less severe than in social care.**

- **Because of the conspicuously ideological character of the policy debate, 'excessive professionalism' may be seen as more of a problem here than elsewhere.**

9.1 Introduction

This chapter examines the impact of voluntary environmental organizations. This area was chosen as the UK example of a field in which the voluntary sector contributes to society in the sense of 'promoting rights and self-expression'. The 'self-expression' element relates to the means by which environmental goals are pursued by human agency via the activities of formally constituted voluntary organizations. (An increasing amount of environmentally oriented collective action is also undertaken through 'disorganizations', but these are not surveyed in this chapter because they do not meet our defining criterion of formality (see Chapter 1).) This is to interpret 'rights' not in the conventional human sense, but in terms of protecting the Earth from what would otherwise be the (potentially) adverse consequences of economic activities. The development of human rights as the ultimate ends of voluntary action involves the encouragement of a supportive discourse, the promotion of legal instruments, and activities geared towards their enforcement (Klug, 2000). Analogously, the ends we are considering here include the encouragement of an 'environmental sensibility' (Wapner, 1996), the introduction and elaboration of domestic law and international treaties and conventions internationally, and efforts to change or police the legal framework for the benefit of the environment. Environmental voluntary organizations also protect natural resources by other means. For example, as Table 9.1 shows, charities alone now own some 6 per cent of forested land in Britain – almost as much as the public sector (apart from the Forestry Commission). Much land has been acquired specifically to conserve the environment.[1]

Table 9.1 Ownership of forests in England, 1998

Ownership category	Area (000 hectares)	Per cent of forested land
Personal sector (individuals and families)	481	47.1
Business sector (for profit)	154	15.0
Public sector *of which*	311	30.5
Forestry Commission	223	21.8
Local authority	61	6.0
Other	27	2.7
Voluntary (charity) sector	68	6.7
Community ownership, common land	4	0.4
Unidentified	4	0.4
Total	1,023	100

Source: Forestry Commission, 2001: 28, Table 12.

The British environmental sector has an exceptionally rich history (McCormick, 1991), and is unusually large by international standards as measured in terms of expenditures and paid employment (Kendall and Knapp, 1996: 115). The significance of this field as an arena for individuals to express and develop environmental sensibilities is also suggested by data on membership trends. Depending upon the survey which one consults, between one in five and one in eight of the British population are members of environmental groups (compare Johnston, 2001; Citizen Audit, 2002). Recent trends in the best known organizations' situations are shown in Table 9.2.

As will become clear as the sector's 'functions' are reviewed below, many of these people are 'passive' in the sense that their membership does not involve 'hands on' participation in campaigns or protective activity. However, unpublished analysis of British Household Panel Survey (BHPS) data suggest that as many as 56 per cent of environmental group members subjectively consider themselves 'active' rather than 'passive' – a much higher ratio than trade unions, for example (Almond and Kendall, 1998). More conservatively, even if only one in 10 members are seen as 'activists' by the organizations themselves (a figure which has appeared in the literature for one of the organizations listed in Table 9.2), that would still mean that several hundreds of thousands of people are 'actively' engaged nationally.

9.2 The environmental field in comparative perspective: policies and ideologies

Like the other fields examined in this part of the book, there is an extraordinary diversity of organizations to be found, with contrasting historical origins. While modern international 'social movement' organizations founded in the 1960s and 1970s, such as Greenpeace and Friends of the Earth, are clearly prominent,

Table 9.2 Membership of largest British environmental organizations

	1971	1981	1991	1997	1999
National Trust	278	1,046	2,152	2,489	2,643
RSPB	98	441	852	1,007	1,004
Civil Trust	214	–	222	330	–
Wildlife Trusts	64	142	233	310	325
WWF	12	60	227	241	255
NT for Scotland	37	105	234	228	236
Woodland Trust	–	20	150	195	200
Greenpeace	–	30	312	215	176
Ramblers Association	22	37	87	123	129
FoE	1	18	111	114	112
CPRE	21	29	45	45	49

Source: Office for National Statisics, 2001: 31, Table 11.2.

Notes:
RSPB, Royal Society for the Protection of Birds; WWF, World Wide Fund for Nature; FoE, Friends of the Earth; CPRE, Council for the Protection of Rural England.

flourishing yet more obviously (Tables 9.2) are home-grown 'traditional' organiz-ations founded in the nineteenth century, including the Royal Society for the Protection of Birds (RSPB) and the National Trust (Garner, 2000: Chapter 3; Rootes *et al.*, 2000; Lansley, 1996).

Box 9.1 reports briefly on the origins and current publicly expressed purpose of these four organizations: these would certainly be the most significant voluntary bodies in the field on economic and political criteria, with the older bodies leading in membership terms, and the newer agencies in pole position in terms of centrality to policy networks (Rootes and Miller, 2000). Ideology is usually taken as the single most important differentiating factor between groups within this field (Dalton, 1990). Scholars typically distinguish between those towards the 'light green' end of the spectrum which are reasonably happy to work, as 'conservationists', within existing social, political and economic systems. This would include the National Trust and RSPB. In contrast, 'dark green' groups are assumed to espouse a more fundamentalist 'ecological' version of anticapitalist environmentalism, supposedly with a greater taste for 1960s and 1970s style drama, protest and confrontation. This latter 'type' has traditionally been assumed to include Friends of the Earth and Greenpeace. In fact, while this ideological distinction still had sufficient currency for us to use it at the time of our fieldwork, it is admittedly only a crude shorthand.

Unlike the two preceding chapters, no attempt is made at this point to present a distillation of an overarching 'policy legacy' within which to situate our discussion. The very idea of 'environment policy' in terms of protecting the environment in its own right – rather than as a reactive response to particular industrial negative side-effects like pollution, or as a 'spillover' from areas such as public health or agriculture – is relatively recent. We have seen that Acts of Parliament systematically delineating sector public responsibilities for social housing and social care were first put on the statute books in the first half of the

---

Box 9.1 Public faces of the four economically largest/politically connected environmental voluntary organizations

Friends of the Earth, founded in 1970, is the largest international network of environmental groups in the world; one of the leading environmental pressure groups in the UK; with 90 per cent of income from individual donations. Associated with it is the Friends of the Earth Trust which commissions detailed research and provides extensive information and educational materials.

Greenpeace, founded in 1971, is an independent nonprofit global campaigning organization that uses creative confrontation to expose global environmental problems and their causes, researching the solutions and alternatives to help provide a path for a green and peaceful future. It does not solicit or accept funding from governments, corporations or political parties nor . . . donations which could compromise its independence, aims and objectives.

The National Trust was founded in 1895 by three Victorian philanthropists concerned about the impact of uncontrolled development and industrialization. It cares for 612,000 acres of countryside, 600 miles of coastline and 200 buildings and gardens of outstanding interest. It is a registered charity and completely independent of government, therefore relying heavily on the generosity of subscribing members and other supporters.

The Royal Society for the Protection of Birds was founded in 1889 and is Europe's largest wildlife conservation charity, with more than a million members. While its original campaign to end the plumage trade was successful, it has widened its sphere of influence to include a huge range of issues that affect both wildlife and habitats.

Source: Each organization's website.

---

twentieth century. These have been built upon subsequently, albeit less systematically that many commentators have felt appropriate, particularly in social care (see discussion of 'insufficiency' in Chapter 8). But an equivalent process did not even begin to take place until relatively recently with environmental protection.[2]

The adoption of the language of 'sustainable development' – the idea that development that the needs of the present should be met 'without compromising the ability of future generations to meet their own needs' was not widely accepted until the late 1980s (World Commission on Environment and Development, 1987: 43). Indeed, a significant amount of voluntary sector campaigning activity in the second half of the twentieth century has been geared towards getting this topic per se on the agenda as a 'problem' in the first place, and hence justifying a consolidated policy response from the state. In this sense at least, a coherent 'policy legacy' as a backdrop for each sector's roles is only just beginning to take shape.

This chapter also differs from the others in this part of the book in its approach to comparison. Data on land ownership aside, there seems to be no comparative data on each sector's contribution in the sense of their relative scale of activity or mobilization of resource inputs, let alone comparison of processes or outcomes. This may in part be a symptom of belated policy recognition, with this situation yet to be diagnosed as an issue worthy of sustained attention, and yet to prompt serious research enquiry. It is probably also the case that the activities undertaken by each sector are often so different in content that outputs and outcomes – including quality – may be hard to compare, and relative economy measures will therefore also be difficult to interpret meaningfully.

More generally, there is a relative paucity of empirical evidence on both non-service functions and drawbacks comparing the sectors directly. Moreover, our focus group participants and interviewees found it more difficult than in other cases to compare sectors, in part because in fulfilling a number of roles there was often simply not readily identifiable 'equivalent' activity in the public or for-profit sector. This may be inherent in the choice for our research of a policy field in which agenda setting activity is so central. Needs are being constructed and shaped within the voluntary sector in an ongoing discursive process – being converted from 'conditions' into 'problems' in Kingdon's (1995) terms. As such, they may have yet to be formulated as discrete 'demands' on the behalf of 'the environment' in a form to which markets or the political arena could respond. Or they may be so complex that such mechanisms (which have to standardize and simplify problems for marketing or packaging purposes) cannot grasp them. In addition, voluntary organizations in this field are often acting as specialists in such particular 'niches' that there is often only room for one provider, a situation evident in other fields, but perhaps not quite so pervasive. Furthermore, precisely because these organizations have been uniquely placed in offering diagnoses of problems, they may have a 'first mover' advantage and tend to operate in comparative isolation even if the activities in question could conceivably be economically or politically profitable.

In this context, this chapter is partly based upon the perspectives which our interviewees and focus group participants did feel able to offer – necessarily derived primarily from their personal experiences and expertise, rather than systematic surveys or other conventional comparative research (see Appendix 2). At the same time, in order to keep a comparative dimension as prominent as possible, this chapter does include some more speculative, macro-theoretical material that is to be found in the other chapters in this part of the book. For example, the chapter draws upon Beck's rarefied account of the nature of risk, uncertainty and the role of the media, with the added twist that it gives particular attention to the possible implications of the dominance of for-profits in this domain. Writers like Beck have been more concerned with the functioning of macro-political systems than the minutiae of sectors' capabilities, but in examining much broader issues, they have incidentally pointed to distinctive voluntary sector contributions in the environmental sphere. While this combination of sources seems to offer interesting arguments, it must be stressed that it is more impressionistic and less firmly grounded in systematic empirical enquiry than the material presented on social housing and social care for older people. This situation has also meant that the quasi-Delphi review process, whereby drafts of earlier versions of this chapter were reviewed and adapted, was particularly important. The arguments around comparison developed here, while necessarily developed at quite some remove from day to day experiences, are therefore at least known to be reasonable and resonant from the perspective of the 'experts' chosen.

9.3 Functions of environmental voluntary organizations

9.3.1 *The service provision*

The most obvious way in which these groups fulfil a 'service' function is through the management of land. Forest ownership can be compared (Section 9.1), but we also know that in the mid-1990s, 1.3 million acres or 2.7 per cent of the land area of the UK was in the ownership of 'conservation, amenity and recreation trusts' (Dwyer and Hodge, 1996). The very largest 'light green' agencies account for a good deal of this property, with 600,000 acres in the hands of the National Trust, and 230,000 managed by the RSPB. The network of local wildlife trusts are also prominent. Surveys further testify to the significance of land use to voluntary organizations more generally.[3]

Much of this land has been reclaimed from private sector agricultural use, although urban land environmental development by the sector has also grown in recent years (Marshall and Patterson, 1996). In the former case, the National Trust, for example, dedicates a significant proportion of such land to the preservation of flora and fauna (Harvey, 1985). This is highly unlikely to be a priority if it were to be farmed commercially under current regulatory arrangements. Farmers wishing to generate profits have an incentive to use intensive modern methods which are deeply damaging to the environment, and even if more environmentally friendly approaches may become commercially viable (as consumer tastes and technology develops), there are large sunk costs in existing patterns of production. Moreover, current regulations involve only voluntary arrangements policed by relatively weak state conservation advisory agencies in place to fill the vacuum left by an absence of local planning controls (see Garner, 2000: 156–62). In urban environments, existing local government controls are skewed towards commercial development. While plans for land use must be open to consultation from all sectors, only developers have the right to appeal against decisions. The sector's land acquisition efforts can therefore be thought of as a response to the combination of externality-related market failure (an insufficient framework for internalizing environmental damage costs) confounded by various public regulatory failures associated with the *status quo ante*.

Land use by the sector can also be understood as a response to failures in public sector directly provided services. Dwyer and Hodge (1996), in particular, argue that national government schemes, whilst having made important contributions to environmental protection, have generally been designed centrally and are therefore standardized. Of course, sensitivity to local conditions could also be achieved, in theory, through local government provision, and indeed this tier of the state does have a wide range of environmental roles above and beyond the land use planning responsibilities already mentioned (Morphet, 1998). However, local authorities have increasingly sought to create 'independent trusts' to circumvent their own poor images and bureaucratic constraints (Dwyer and Hodge, 1996); or to discharge these statutory responsibilities through subcontracting with an existing organization.

The significance of cost considerations as a factor in deciding to 'contract out' local authority responsibilities in recent years has been suggested in a recent case study, which found that Torbay, in response to pressures to cut its countryside management budget, was looking to 'use local green space groups for volunteer labour and management skills' (Pennington and Rydin, 2000: 247). Amplifying and generalizing on the quality aspect, one of our experts asserted:

> A lot of the good land management practices in terms of physical land conservation have been done through specific dedicated projects that have been 'subbed' (subcontracted) out to wildlife trusts. They undoubtedly represent value for money and a level of service that would be beyond the competency and capability of the local authority in their own right.
>
> (Local authority interviewee)

The second crucial service function, which is bound up with the awareness raising and campaigning dimension of the sector's activities described below, is the provision of information and education. Again, its general significance can be underlined with reference to survey evidence.[4] Concretely, this role includes the collecting and processing of primary environmental data (ranging from the RSPB's or the Butterfly Society's mobilization of volunteers and paid contract researchers to undertake national fauna surveys; to the collection and analysis of data by local groups as part of Biodiversity Action Plans (see Box 9.2); to the practice of directly employing professional scientists adopted by FoE and Greenpeace[5]), the packaging and presentation of information largely or wholly collected by others; and conducting environmental audits and providing advice on a consultancy basis to for-profit companies or the public sector.

As with land management activities, the relative importance of this role can be theoretically understood to a significant degree as stemming from the limitations to the market and the state in the dissemination of information. Our interview and focus groups suggested the voluntary sector's superiority over the advice-giving (public sector) quangos was in part simply because the latter were 'strapped for cash'. In this context, there were seen to be specialist areas in which voluntary sector dominance was particularly appropriate. As one respondent

---

Box 9.2 Biodiversity Action Plans and environmental organizations

Biodiversity Action Plans were introduced from 1996 onwards in the UK as part of the Government's response to the 1992 Rio 'Earth summit' (this also led to 'Local Agenda 21', discussed under 'community-building'). One of the summit's conclusions had been that biodiversity – variety and variability of living organisms – should be protected and strengthened as a matter of local and national environmental policy (Cahill, 2001: Chapter 2). Local and national environmental organizations have been heavily involved in developing and implementing these plans – and indeed, according to Young (2000a), have 'shouldered most of the implementation process'.

---

commented, 'if you want to know about the conservation of a particular bird species, you would go to the RSPB. You wouldn't necessarily go to English Nature [an environmental quango]'. It is certainly the case that the combined budgets of the relevant organizations exceed those of these quangos (Rawcliffe, 1998). Factoring in the volunteering contributions mentioned above would further deepen the divide between the sectors in terms of human resources.

The voluntary sector is also involved in a 'mixed economy of persuasion', involving a competition between sectors in which arguments and ideas are promoted and 'sold'. In situations where all three sectors are directly 'competing' to provide the 'authoritative' or at least most convincing account of an environmental problem, surveys of public opinion have revealed a preference for voluntary organizations over their for-profit and public sector counterparts. MORI polls showed that, in 1996, confidence in scientists was significantly higher if they are 'working for environmental groups' (75 per cent of respondents having 'great or fair confidence in what they have to say about environmental issues'), compared with those working in industry (45 per cent) or for government (just 32 per cent).

It is unclear whether this reflects each sector's 'performance' in responding to recent scientific controversies, or more enduring factors (see Box 9.3). Lamb has claimed that FoE 'won respect' through 'telling the truth about global warming long before government' and this explains why they are 'far more trusted as a source of objective information' (Lamb, 1997). For his part, Ullrich Beck sees the situation as more to do with other sectors' failures. He has argued that the public sector is inherently prone to chronic untrustworthiness, developing 'polished routines for concealing and denying hazards' in response to the conditions of 'risk society' in which the control of environmental hazards has spun out of control (Beck, 1997). As for the for-profit sector, employed scientists (see Box 9.4) could face pressures to misrepresent information opportunistically where this yields commercial advantages. Such pressures could be especially problematic in the UK (Neale, 1997: 9 and 21).

Box 9.3　Interpreting trends in each sector's environmental reputations

For all sectors, including voluntary sector environmental groups, recent figures on level of confidence are lower than in previous years, leading the premier analyst of public opinion to conclude that 'there have been no winners from the scientific controversies of recent years' (Worcester, 1997: 170). He cites the behaviour of industry (i.e. Shell) at the time of the Brent Spar incident and the Government's bungled handling of the BSE affair ('mad cow disease') as 'probably' the most significant factors. However, it seems unlikely that such events will have indiscriminately affected each sector's credibility to the same degree. In the short term, presumably the Brent Spar incident had negative repercussions for Shell or the wider for-profit sector's position. Greenpeace was later revealed to have made exaggerated and inaccurate claims that could have affected that organization and the voluntary sector more adversely in the longer term (Edwards, 1999, 2001). These effects would have affected these sectors differently at different times. As far as the BSE affair is concerned, it is hard to see how that could have undercut the voluntary sector's reputation, since the implicated individuals and institutions were in the public and for-profit sectors (Millstone and van Zwanenberg, 2001).

Box 9.4　Environmental scientists in the for-profit sector

Specialist resource development companies, and private consultancies have proliferated to offer advice on a wide range of environmental matters, from environmental audits to advice on how companies can best respond to the 'green consumer'. There has also been a growth of research capacity and the employment of professional scientists in-house by large companies, or industrial associations representing them, in energy and resource utilization industries, such as nuclear energy and fossil fuels. 'Corporate responsibility units' now form part of the bureaucratic apparatus of some of the larger companies, and for those active in environmentally relevant industries, prominent personnel often include those with backgrounds in environmental science.

Finally, Grove-White (1997) has argued that voluntary environmental organizations are treated with more confidence by the public because they are able to connect with 'deeper cultural anxieties'. By this account, it is their presentation of environmental problems in a holistic and cumulative way, in contrast to the 'reductionist' and 'positivist' approaches which dominate elsewhere, which lie behind such attitudes. However, it is not clear that this necessarily implies the public's blanket rejection of 'positivist' science. Indeed, many voluntary organizations seem to be implicitly rejecting this interpretation when they argue that being seen to be conducting 'good science' is crucial for their public reputations (Rootes *et al.*, 2000).[6]

9.3.2 *Advocacy function*

The *raison d'être* of many groups has been to heighten environmental sensibility.[7] But as well as seeking to shape public opinion very generally, significant numbers of organizations choose to affect specific changes in particular policies (at the stages of agenda-setting, decision-making and implementation) by deliberately targeting the politically and economically powerful: that is, advocacy or as it is universally labelled in this field, campaigning. As Michael Jacobs notes, 'even though now adopted by government and business, the discourse of environmental policy . . . comes directly from the green movement's conceptual framework and ethics' (Jacobs, 1997: 2).

Rootes and Miller's (2000)'s survey has revealed the extent to which most national organizations concentrate on 'conventional' and 'respectable' activities. After leafleting, lobbying, press conferences, the publication of scientific reports and petitioning are the most pervasive actions. Mass demonstrations, boycotts, stunts and direct action are very rarely undertaken. Our for-profit and public sector interviewees confirmed that the vast bulk of their experiences of pressure from voluntary environmental organizations involved dialogue and debate, rather than confrontation or conflict.

The role of the media has been crucial. During the 1990s, in the absence of a significant Green political party and limited attention to green issues by the mainstream political parties, the media routinely relied on voluntary organizations simply to keep the environmental agenda alive (Porritt in Lamb, 1997). As part of their media-oriented efforts, some organizations pursued dramatic, high public profile strategies and have been particularly successful in grabbing headlines, and this sometimes secured policy change. Greenpeace's successful bid to reverse a policy of a transnational corporation, Shell, is perhaps the best known example. In the 'Brent Spar incident', the companies plans to dispose of an oil platform were challenged and reversed by a combination of superior news management skills, clever use of information technology, and the mobilization of 'green consumer' power.

However, the relationship between the voluntary sector, other sectors, and the media is far from straightforward. One interviewee claimed that voluntary organizations basically had to play to the latter interests, rather than the other way round. There was 'Tio Pepe diplomacy, the sector follows the media-made agenda, by and large'. As with information and education more generally (see above), the voluntary sector could be seen as involved in a struggle to project ideas other than those which the profit motive might otherwise tend to favour.

In the printed media in particular, with raw circulation targets for financial gain increasingly seeming to trump the values of professional journalism, there could be strong pressures to trivialize, oversimplify or just plain ignore what are complex and challenging issues (Hannigan, 1995; we return to this theme in the following section).

Beyond helping to create the discourse of environmentalism and fostering a climate of awareness which has to some extent changed public opinion and been reflected in the media, how influential has all this activity been in terms of public policies? One major example suggested to us in our interviews was organizations' influence on biodiversity policy, as initiated with the 1981 Wildlife and Countryside Act. The RSPB had shaped that original act's content, but in its implementation a wide range of local and national agencies were involved particularly in the protection of sites of special scientific interest (Wildlife and Countryside Link, 1997). Almost immediately after this legislation was adopted, these organizations began to build up a body of evidence on their implementation experiences, with suggestions for making the legislation more effective. Subsequently, the Countryside Act 2000 directly reflected many of the revisions suggested in these voluntary organization authored reports (Young, 2000b). At the European level, a significant example in the biodiversity field has been the leading role of the RSPB in the shaping and monitoring of the Birds and Habitats and Species Directives (Dixon, 1998).

However, even with these apparent successes, in some respects the results more generally have been disappointing both procedurally and in terms of outcome. There are numerous examples where environmental campaigning has failed to achieve its goals, particularly at the domestic (rather than European) policy level under the previous, Conservative administration (Hannigan, 1995: Chapter 7; Hajer, 1995). The two most recent, comparative and wide-ranging reviews by political scientists of the relative impact of these organizations on UK environmental policy in general have reached largely negative conclusions. They suggest that 'the successful campaigns of the national groups have only been one, often small, part of the pressure for policy change', and consequently 'the environmental lobby does not seem to have made much impact' (Rawcliffe, 1998: 221; Garner, 2000: 211, respectively). Based on a number of closely argued case studies, they conclude that the for-profit and government sectors have been much more influential. The lobbying of business interests (including, for example, farmers in the case of agriculture and polluters in the case of pollution control, and power generators and suppliers in the case of the energy policy community) has tended to trump that of environmental groups.

Following the US lead, a 'wise-use' business movement has begun to emerge specifically to argue against the priorities of environmental groups in the public domain (for example, through arguing for the continuation of some pollution practices regarded by the relevant organizations as always unacceptable). But the most consequential pressures from business are exerted quietly behind the scenes, and on a distinct policy community by policy community basis (i.e. separately for agriculture, transport and so on). Business has been largely successful in fostering the belief that, only by protecting their interests – largely on their terms – can jobs be safeguarded and economic success guaranteed. This can influence policy-makers even without being stated explicitly because of their awareness of businesses' 'structural position' in the economy (Lindblom, 1977).

As far as the public sector is concerned, it is true that environmental organizations have fostered increasingly intimate relationships with the Department of the Environment and its relabelled successors (Osborne, 1997; Sharpe, 1998). However, many environmentally relevant public policy decisions are ultimately controlled by more powerful 'economic' departments of state, in particular the Department of Trade and Industry, and the Treasury (Voisey and O'Riordan, 1997; Long, 1998). Civil servants here do not have a background in environmental matters, and their political masters have tended to side with business in their cornucopian interpretations of economic development. They have remained resistant to arguments for environmental protection, and have tended only to approve policies in line with their own economic aspirations for growth and public revenue generation (as with the retrospective labelling of VAT on fuel as a 'green tax').

9.3.3 The innovation function

Where voluntary organizations have succeeded in raising awareness as noted above, this represents an 'innovation' in terms of how people in general view their environments, and sight should not be lost of this diffuse influence. However, innovation is more usually understood as the purposive introduction of changes in 'production' involving a sharp discontinuity with existing practices (see Chapter 6's definition). Neale (1997) argues that innovation is most significant when concrete changes in resource use, technology applications or patterns of institutional relationships – actually take place. It is precisely an emphasis on practical solutions, rather than in highlighting problems, which emerged as an innovation from a number of our interviews: not merely objecting, but offering feasible alternatives for adoption (Byrne, 1997).

Innovation in land use has been a particular feature of the activities of the light green family of conservation organizations. For example, the National Trust has tested new ways of farming on its properties and examined its effects on different habitats, while the RSPB has purchased and run farmland specifically to explore how efficient farming methods can best be combined with the preservation of particular species. For darker green organizations, the most often cited example over recent years has been Greenpeace's 'Greenfreeze' technology, a refrigeration system which eliminates the need for fluorocarbons (the chemical emission shown to damage the protective ozone layer). Other well-established examples include recycling schemes, the fitting of pioneering solar houses, developed renewable energy technology and photovoltiac energy (Millais, 1996).

Another form of innovation highlighted by a number of our interviewees was the creative use of information technology as both a tool for campaigning, a method of recruiting new members and a facilitator of coalition-building. A simple but important example was the downloading of template protest letters, cutting the time costs of mail-based campaigning to individual activists, but many organizations had also put sophisticated interactive technology to good use – probably more so than the for-profit sector, according to at least one respondent. Certainly the skilled use of information technology was an important ingredient in Greenpeace's successful bid to confront Shell and reverse its oil rig disposal policy in the 'Brent Spar incident'.

A final form of innovation which seems salient in the environmental field has been organizational innovation in the sense of developing new sets of external relationships. Most controversial has been the development of sustained and systematic links with the public and business sectors. To a significant extent, the controversy stems from the strongly felt aspiration to retain – and be seen to retain – autonomy and avoid 'incorporation' or 'co-option': the strong ideological basis of beliefs make this a pervasive concern in this field. Since government and business are both seen to be deeply implicated in the environmental damage which many are seeking to reverse, this suspicion is hardly surprising, and darker green groups are naturally more predisposed to avoid 'collusion' with 'the enemy' at all costs. Yet what is new is that even the most high profile of the darker green groups, Greenpeace and FoE, while still not actively developing financial links with the public and for-profit sectors as potentially 'corrupting' in principle, have now accepted funds for specific purposes, and more generally sought to foster relations in nonfinancial respects (Garner, 2000: 122).

There are a number of reasons why even darker green organizations' are now more willing to work with business and the public sector. First, the shift to a solutions-based approach has to a certain extent made such relations unavoidable. For example, because the for-profit sector largely controls the input and output markets in energy technologies, Greenpeace has had to work with it to understand how existing technologies function, in order to find ways of moving beyond them. Similarly to promote its recycling solutions, FoE has clearly had no option but to develop links with local government to establish the feasibility and desirability of their preferred recycling methods, because the latter has statutory responsibility for handling refuse.

Second, there is a belief that, while business and government can be environmentally destructive, the changing climate of public opinion, and the increasing repertoire of regulatory and fiscal requirements used to control those sectors, has meant that it is now more often in those sector's 'enlightened self-interest' to operate 'responsibly' from an environmental point of view. The 'greening' of individuals' tastes has forced business and government to move in this direction to avoid being branded 'environmental pariahs' (Porritt, 1997: 66), and thus lose custom and votes. To the extent that the dominant 'story-line' in policy circles is now that of 'ecological modernization', business and government must at least appear to take environmental concerns seriously , or lose face (see Box 9.5). Third, the willingness to build relationships with other

---

Box 9.5 Ecological modernization

'Ecological modernization' is the doctrine that apparent conflicts between economic and environmental objectives are often illusory. This is so because it is said to be in firms' and governments' own interests to develop the modern technology and techniques needed to boost efficiency and foster economic growth in an environmentally friendly way (see Hajer, 1995; Young, 2000b: 4–28).

---

sectors has increasingly not been seen as simply a black and white matter to be approached uniformly, but as a possibility which can be considered on an informed, case-by-case basis. Thus, for-profits seen as appropriately green are thought of as worthy partners; others are branded as 'environmental pariahs', and avoided or challenged as adversaries.

How do environmental groups compare the public and for-profit sectors in terms of their ability to innovate? One interviewee speculated that 'economists and scientists [employed by voluntary groups] come up with the new solutions: if we waited for government scientists to come up with solutions we would be waiting until the end of time!' The extent to which environmental organizations have at least the potential to be relatively innovative is implied by examples given above, but there seems to be little or no direct comparative evidence. Most of our informants did not feel able to make such general claims, and aside from the single Greenpeace–Shell information technology example, we were unable to find a specific basis for direct comparison. Even here, one voluntary sector interviewee stressed the extent to which many voluntary organizations remained extremely wary of, and averse to modern technology, implying that the for-profit sector was basically the primary conduit for new ideas of this sort. Moreover, a for-profit interviewee suggested that Greenpeace's apparent ability to outwit Shell in its use of information technology and news management techniques with the Brent Spar incident was something of an isolated example. The company had learned a lot from the 'shock', and was now at least as adept at managing information flows to present its own case.

9.3.4 The expressive and leadership development function

As emphasized in Section 9.1, ideology plays a central role for many environmental organizations. The literature does emphasize the part played by strong convictions, and in some cases, almost mystical enthusiasm. Burgess (2000), reflecting on 20 years involvement in the UK environmental movement, refers to its 'aesthetic' tendency as evidenced by 'an inclination towards mysticism and spiritualism within the romantic tradition which can be readily found within current environmentalism' (*The Independent*, 4 August 2000). This was underlined by interviewees, where it was suggested that 'the environmental movement is an alternative to a religious movement. People are very opinion-ated and ideologically driven'; and that these organizations 'filled a spiritual gap'.

Relevant recent research evidence on motives for engagement concerns activist members and volunteers involved with Greenpeace and FoE. Carroll and Harris (1998), interviewing local Greenpeace campaign volunteers, found that while 'instrumental' human and social capital goals were important, actions were also saturated with emotional meaning. They thought of their organization as combining 'passion' with 'professionalism' (with varying degrees of success), involving 'the Greenpeace ethic . . . a desire to confront what they perceive to be wrong, a desire to effect immediate change, and a commitment to non-violence' (p. 2). Jordan and Maloney (1997), reporting on FoE members' reasons for joining, similarly argue for the relevance of incentives which are not 'material'. Respondents 'joined because they believed they were backing a good group/cause' (p. 142). Commercial activities have been developed providing material rewards too, but these are claimed to be of less importance here in terms of underlying motivation (but see next section).

As far as leadership development is concerned, there are several well-known individual examples of influential and often charismatic public figures who have spent a considerable number of their 'formative years' working in the voluntary sector, while simultaneously or subsequently being employed in important capacities in the public sector in particular as with Tom Burke or Barbara Young. Given the ideological concerns noted earlier, such movements, especially from the darker green end of the spectrum, can generate cries of 'poacher turned gamekeeper'. But most controversial of all for this reason have been the movements of personnel from the darker green end of the voluntary sector into business. This phenomenon has only recently reached the mainstream media spotlight when very high profile figures have moved in this way, as with the decision of Greenpeace's long-standing director, Lord Melchett to take an advisory position in public relations company Burson-Marsteller (*The Observer*, 13 January 2002, *Business*, p. 8). But one of our for-profit interviewees stressed that this had been happening in a low visibility way for decades. Many of the first large wave of graduates in environmental science in the 1970s, who had often also been active in such groups, were now working in a wide range of capacities for corporations (cf. Box 9.4).

9.3.5 The community-building function

Conceptually, Szerszynski (1997) has asserted not only that local voluntary organizations can make significant contribution to the development of a 'sustain-able society', but that they can do so better than the public sector. The latter is portrayed negatively as the carrier of a 'bureaucratic monoculture'. But there are also three positive advantages intrinsic, it is claimed, to the voluntary sector. First, their 'natural rootedness in public concerns and enthusiasms [position them] much better . . . to generate environmental and quality of life objectives which will align with people's own everyday experiences and concerns' (p. 151). Second, following Putnam's more general thesis (see Chapter 6), environmental organizations are theorized to be crucial for 'encouraging the cultural conditions of trust and public-spiritedness, not just because it makes possible the practice of shared, deliberative judgement, but also because it encourages moral habits' (p. 155). This is contrasted starkly with 'deep suspicions' towards public sector institutions. Third, stress is put on the process of participation involved in local activity, which is argued to enhance citizen's quality of life 'as an end in itself'.

In terms of policy, the British Government has recently imported the language of 'social capital' into environmental policy, and explicitly linked this to the voluntary sector at the local level (see Box 9.6). Prior to this, the notion was implicit, as evidenced in the UK's response to international environmental policy initiative. Relevant research has focused on the contributions of the voluntary sector in implementing Local Agenda 21, put in place after the Rio Earth summit (see Cahill, 2001: Chapter 3). This initiative has had a mixed track record in terms of voluntary sector involvement (Church and Young, 2000), but it did give the public sector at local level a significant impetus to consult the sector in pursuing sustainable development goals. Young stresses the extent to which the process of participation and 'visioning' (agenda setting and policy design) associated with the implementation of Local Agenda 21 could sometimes create a genuine sense of ownership or stakeholding. This has been the priority in part as 'an influx of people from the NGO world with detailed ideas about how to promote partnership' and in part from a growing consensus from within local authority officers that 'top down schemes . . . did not work' (p. 141). He also suggests that such schemes' restriction on profits distribution are important: 'the contrast with [conventional for-profits] is important . . . capital is free to move, but [there is] a close link to place, to improving conditions where their members and stakeholders live' (Young, 1997: 145; see also Church and Young, 2000: 14).

Box 9.6 Social capital and environmental policy

In a 2001 White Paper on local government, under the heading 'Delivering Sustainable Development', it is asserted that 'strong community leadership means developing social capital by supporting civic engagement and networks of neighbourhood organizations. It means enhancing environmental quality by reducing waste, energy use and air pollution and improving public space. And it means safeguarding the interests of future members of the community'.

Source: Smith and Geerts, 2002, p. 64.

A number of our interviewees interpreted the role of the voluntary sector in the spirit of these policy aspirations and academic accounts. The importance of allowing local people to be involved in 'visioning' was argued to generate a sense of community ownership, with one suggesting that it was the combination of nonprofit and nonpublic status which allowed them to operate as effective 'honest brokers' in communities. The significance of practical, hands-on involvement as volunteers (who might or might not be members) in actual implementation was also emphasized:

> A group that is interested in wildlife because of the locality may cut across socio-economic dimensions of people in that area. They can build bridges and make connections that the government never could.
>
> (Local authority interviewee)

> By enhancing the full potential of the sites in a local area local people suddenly feel more driven to protect it and look after it . . . many people are alienated and they look around and see they can make a difference in a local areas and that can really empower people.
>
> (Voluntary sector interviewee)

However, other focus group research has been suggestive of the limitations of voluntary sector-led solutions as far as some local private and public sector actors are concerned. One local study has reported that while NGOs often believe that small-scale 'nuts and bolts' projects involving such activities as habitat creation and recycling initiatives could generate real feelings of ownership and 'make a difference' environmentally and socially, 'there was more scepticism from public and private sector representatives. Restructuring of the national economy [and adverse local economic conditions] meant small-scale, community-led projects could not address the wider issues of achieving sustainable development on a city-wide scale (Burgess *et al.*, 1998: 1,452–3).

9.4 Weaknesses or drawbacks of environmental voluntary organizations

9.4.1 *Chronic resource insufficiency*

Section 9.3 showed that environmental voluntary organizations can be thought of theoretically as a response to the limitations and failures of other sectors. Yet a difficulty of under-allocation of resources to the voluntary sector itself exists where 'public goods' and 'externalities' are concerned. Environmental activities ranging from pollution control, to habitat preservation and environmental information and education are classic examples of 'goods' of this type. They are nonexcludable, so that noncontributors will benefit from their existence and some – such as information – can be nonrival, wherein one person's 'consumption' does not prevent others from doing likewise (cf. Chapter 1, Box 1.1). In such cases, it is axiomatic to rational choice reasoning that, absent coercion, too few resources will be allocated from a societal perspective. This is the so-called 'free rider' problem (Olson, 1965).[8]

As previous chapters have underlined, public funding can be one response to those situations where voluntary resources are lacking. But in this field, ideological factors have traditionally blocked the cultivation of such links – although in discussing innovation, we noted this situation is changing. Yet despite the significant and increasing overall amount of statutory resources channelled into environmental groups in this way, as a share of total income, income from public sources for this field remains disproportionately small by comparison to both the voluntary sector as a whole, and to our other impact cases. Most discussed in the literature in this field is organizations' turn to commercial techniques, rather than government sources, as a way to overcome perceived shortfalls. Some national groups have now developed expansive and aggressive marketing ploys to boost 'supporter' or 'member' numbers, private giving (particularly through legacies) and sales (particularly through catalogue products, to supplement the more traditional 'commercial' revenue source, charging for access to nature reserves and heritage sites). Using the empirical examples of Friends of the Earth and Amnesty International as prototypical, Jordan and Maloney (1997) have argued that the membership recruiting and retention strategies of the largest groups have, to an extent, 'solved' the theoretical free rider problem by unrelenting and purposeful 'supply-side' manipulation of how potential members frame and calculate their decisions to contribute.

More generally, Rootes has suggested that despite these developments, organizations in this field 'remain minnows by comparison with the government and corporations whose initiatives they challenge' (2002: 7). However, as the comparison of the budgets of quango and the voluntary sector cited earlier in discussing information and education, much will depend on the definitions involved, and which aspects of environmental action are considered in scope. Certainly in our interviews, the problem of quality in funding – in terms of a tendency to be short term and insecure – was a more pervasive concern that the quantity of funding. There certainly seemed to be no sense that the environmental voluntary sector should necessarily aspire to compare in size to government and business on economic measures.

The economic cycle problem is also relevant here. To the extent that private individuals' motivation for contributing is 'post material' (Inglehart, 1990; Worcester, 1997; see below), then it could tend to fall by the wayside at times of economic recession. Given the centrality of awareness-raising for these organizations, the negative impact of economic recession on the amount and quality of attention devoted by the mass media to environmental problems is also a concern. Not only do human needs become more obvious and acute at such times, but newspapers may feel (rightly or wrongly) they have to respond to any heightened sense of insecurity amongst their readership by privileging stories about economic life and its casualties over environmental ones. In this sense, the media may amplify and aggravate any existing tendency for citizens to become 'desensitized' to environmental 'needs' when economic hardship bites.

The same could also hold true of the political elite who rely heavily on the mass media for their understanding of environmental matters (Beck, 1997; Jordan, 2000, cited in Smith and Geerts, 2002: 65).

Set against this, however, could be the counter-cyclical nature of the problems themselves. For example, when economic activity contracts, industrial pollution and environmentally insensitive commercial land development will decline, leading to a lessening of the 'need' for countervailing environmental action. Counter-cyclical spending by the Government could also be relevant, although in a much more opportunistic sense than the other cases reviewed: for example, some voluntary organizations have benefited in the past from central government's training schemes, which were seen as an opportunity to pursue environmental ends even if the state's goals were more to do with responding to unemployment (Lamb, 1996; Marshall and Patterson, 1996).[9]

9.4.2 Particularism

Our interviews and focus groups largely saw particularism as a strength, under-lining the extent to which diversity in this field is expressed through its marked degree of specialization (cf. Lowe and Goyder, 1983). One interviewee claimed the large national organizations had a sensibly complementary relationship to the smaller, more specialized local groups, commenting that 'from my direct experience, small players often add a particular and useful element to the nationwide efforts of FoE, the RSPB and the Wildlife Trusts – as with many plants, butterflies, bats and local plants'. FoE, Greenpeace and the WWF were found by Rootes and Miller (2000) to be the most important co-operators, at least from the perspective of other national groups. According to these authors, as a result they 'are more likely to be sensitive to intra-movement criticism than more specialized organizations that do not have direct competitors for a constituency. Thus FoE has been especially responsive to the demands and criticisms of others in the movement not only because of its participatory ethos and centrality to the networks that are the movement, but also because of the breadth of its concerns' (Rootes and Miller, 2000: 18).

But FoE's claimed sensitivity is only one part of the story. Rawcliffe suggests smaller species-specific groups have prospered in recent years, sometimes making in-roads into the membership of the largest generalist groups (Rawcliffe, 1998: 77). It is argued that this could bring problems of 'fragmentation', to the extent that the former seem to be less well embedded in organizational networks, and thus may not be able to communicate or develop so effectively. Specialist organ-izations could either miss opportunities for constructive joint working, or some-times undertake inefficient duplication where agendas overlapped (Rawcliffe, 1998: 25).

A second issue flows from what is in many ways a defining feature of this field: the very particular nature of their human constituency. Whole bodies of sociological theory, developed to explain why the environmental movement grew so extensively in the late twentieth century, have been built around the empirical observation that their supporters are, by and large, professional middle-class people. They have tended not be be the poor people, including many from ethnic minorities, who are actually disproportionately affected by environmental problems. Amongst the arguments made are that only the former and particularly the post-war generation, are sufficiently 'post material', with interests which predispose them to take environmental protection seriously (Cotgrove, 1982; see Hannigan, 1995: 24–8, for a review and critique).[10] Most inactive seem to be people from ethnic minorities. At best, they have been de facto omitted from recruitment drives because of their socio-economic status. Subsequently, some groups have specifically been formed to meet the needs of ethnic minorities, and links have been forged with sympathetic existing national organizations (Taylor, 1993). All our interviewees and focus groups acknowledged this situation, although the extent to which it was seen as a 'problem' was limited.[11]

A third potential problem of particularism in this field relates directly to the balance of environmental priorities addressed, rather than the composition of their membership. Organizations have been accused of concentrating unduly on causes and issues for which it is easy to raise funds, but which are relatively unimportant as far as the real needs of conservation or the environment are concerned. This is especially the case for the larger 'generalists', who might be in a position to cross-subsidize 'unprofitable', but needed activities because of high current income, or accumulated reserves. While what former FoE director Richard Sandbrook refers to as 'charismatic megafauna', such as whales, dolphins, birds and seals secure protection, neglected may be other 'significant' species, from an instrumental biodiversity perspective or a more radical eco-centric position (see Fox, 1995: 164, cited in Garner, 2000: 50). Land management choices have also been criticized. For example, the National Trust has been accused of preferring 'fashionable' and already well-protected landscapes in Devon and Cornwall to the rather remote, but more threatened County Durham coastline; and 'dramatic cliffs' to 'mud flats and marshes' (Hobson, 1999: 116).

Environmental issues which are diffuse, complex and involve disputes between the scientific community, policy-makers and scientists – such as genetic modification, global warming and nuclear power use – may also be relatively neglected if left to voluntary initiative, because these very features make them hard to 'market' and 'package' to mass memberships, the public and the media alike (Hannigan, 1995). Along this line of argument, Rawcliffe (1998: 46) suggests that 'particular events, and, notably, "eco-disasters"' may have received disproportionate attention, while one of our for-profit interviewees suggested that voluntary organizations 'over-simplified', implying a failure to adequately discharge the information and education role referred to earlier. For this interviewee, this was linked to a more general lack of 'responsibility' (see discussion of 'accountability' below). Another interviewee, from within the sector, saw this as ultimately a problem of the resources on which voluntary groups were forced to depend in their research. Despite its growing professional infrastructure, the sector lacked the long-term research programmes of other sectors. Much research was necessarily short-term and limited, and could therefore be dismissed as ' biased green wash!' by unsympathetic commentators.

9.4.3 Paternalism

Neither our interviews nor focus groups regarded paternalism as a significant issue, and it does not appear to be as pervasive a theme in the literature as the other weaknesses discussed here. However, a conspicuous exception is Mitchell's (1999) colourful polemic against the conservation activities of London- and Edinburgh-based national charities in the Hebrides (also see Hobson, 1999: Chapter 3). These organizations are cast not only as undemocratic – traits increasingly remarked upon by other writers more generally (see below) – but as oppressive colluders with the public sector (Scottish heritage quangos), threatening the way of life of indigenous crofters and farmers. According to this author, the latter were excluded from decision-making over land use in the late 1990s, thanks to the apparently underhand strategies of these charities. This aggravated existing resentments based upon the way in which local people more generally had felt that their economic livelihoods were not given sufficient weight when the activities of local distilleries had been undermined by RSPB land acquisition (Young, 2000a). Unfortunately, however, the book did not really report on how the organizations themselves have viewed these developments. [12]

9.4.4 Excessive amateurism or professionalism

As Rootes *et al.* (2000) remark, 'the strongest story line in recent discussions of the environmental movement in Britain is that of institutionalisation . . . for mainstream [organizations], a measure of institutionalisation is an accomplished fact' (pp. 2–3). Rawcliffe has noted how from the late 1980s, 'the national environmental groups evolve into corporate organizations with large memberships and sponsorship income, management structures and networks, scientific research capabilities and sophisticated public relations and campaign machines . . . the increasing professionalism of the British environmental movement' (1998, p. 72).

The increasing use of paid professional staff by these organizations has been perhaps the most important mark of such institutionalization.[13] Why might this be 'excessive'? Most fundamentally, if such professionals are chosen without any reference to their environmental experiences or empathy with and commitment to environmental causes, they are likely to be little different in their overall value orientation and world-views from their counterparts in the for-profit and public sectors. According to Diani and Donati (1999), this has increasingly been the case across Europe in recent years, and movement between the three sectors has grown amongst 'top officials' which may be symptomatic of this development. In the UK, too, the largest national bodies now involve a core of campaigners surrounded by 'departments of specialists, who, it is claimed, often have no particular reason to work for an NGO than for any other company' (Rawcliffe, 1998: 97–8).

To the extent such 'uncommitted' specialists exert influence and authority over their committed campaigning and other co-worker counterparts, which the latter in turn resist and resent as inappropriate or unprincipled from an organizational or movement perspective, a problem of 'excess' could emerge. Different writers imply that this is a danger with regard to the impact of different groups of professionals, but two categories tend to be of most concern. First, for those who are in principle hostile to the epistemological claims of orthodox natural science, particularly to the extent it is 'excessively positivist', the growth in employment of 'the wrong sort' of professional scientists raises real problems (Beck, 1997; Hajer, 1995).

Second, another group of professionals whose increased deployment has caused concern are marketing, fundraising and media specialists. In this regard, some aspects of the specific problem of particularism are often alluded to explicitly in the literature, or at least implied. This includes the tendency to focus attention on 'charismatic megafauna' and 'cherry pick' for attention in fundraising and campaigning causes which are more easy to dramatize and package in an undemanding way at the expense of more difficult issues. There is also the problem of their role in the aggravation of the narrow existing social base of members and supporters alluded to under that heading too (Jordan and Maloney, 1997; Mitchell, 1999).

A further difficulty associated with professionalism, examined in most detail with respect to the campaigning function, has been that of sunk costs and associated vested interests. Many national groups successfully built up specialist campaign teams on particular issues during the 1980s, but these became 'entrenched baronies' with their own budgets and investments in expertise to protect, making it harder to initiate new campaigns (Rawcliffe, 1998: 100–1).

Our interviews and focus groups recognized these tensions as real, and significantly, on balance, held the view that 'excessive' professionalism was much more of a problem than 'excessive' amateurism. This view was not universal, however. One interviewee claimed that some organizations viewed their volunteers as 'a nuisance'. Another tied together the unwillingness or inability of some local organizations to move towards the solution-led campaigning discussed earlier with a continued dominance of 'unprofessional' approaches to knowledge by some campaigners:

> People come to a problem and demand that it is solved or stopped without any real understanding of what it means and how you would stop it, what the options are, what the economic and social costs of following it up are and how they might be out of touch with the local populace.
>
> (Local authority interviewee)

9.4.5 Problematic accountability

The nature of accountability is as complex in this policy field as in others. Other than for the smallest and simplest of participatory organizations on the edge of formality, there is a much wider range of stakeholders to take into account than only members' interpretation of the immediate interests of the environment. These include, current users (such as tenants in land management), and statutory funders and regulators (including the Charity Commission in the case of registered charities, Companies House for agencies with corporate status).

Organizations with inherited properties or legacies must act in line with the wishes of testators in the uses to which these resources are to be put. Moreover, with environmental organizations in particular, there may also be a sense of responsibility to future generations of human kind, as well as acting as 'stewards' for nature or the environment more generally. Depending on the nature of the organization, the 'experts' thought to be qualified to make such judgements will vary. For example, in light green organizations, scientific and land-owning interests may be seen as the legitimate source of authority; while in dark green organizations, trust may be vested in activists with the right ideological and experiential credentials. Conflicts of interest can and do arise between the different demands or needs of these constituencies (Lansley, 1996; Hobson, 1999: Chapter 3).

In growing national organizations, as noted earlier, a tension can emerge between their traditional 'committed' activist or elite core, and an expanding generic professional periphery (Jordan and Maloney, 1997; Maloney and Jordan, 1997; see also the polemic of Mitchell, 1999). Mass memberships – or more accurately, perhaps, 'supporters' – have played a supporting background role in this developing drama. This is far from saying that the views of mass memberships are irrelevant, but rather to stress that their influence is typically perceived as a latent and indirect constraint on policy, and most often revealed through carefully controlled in-house market research style surveys, and the threat of (passive) exit. As Maloney and Jordan surmise, however, this situation is apparently broadly accepted within these bodies: for them, to note their 'anticipatory oligarchic' tendencies 'is not a direct criticism of the groups . . . they do not see themselves as being vehicles for participatory democracy, nor do their members . . . in the market for political activism, individuals are prepared to contract out the participation task to organizations' (Maloney and Jordan, 1997: 117–18).

However, if account is taken of external stakeholders' concerns about legitimacy more generally, then the situation of these organizations does emerge as a much more critical issue. Picking up on our earlier discussion of one aspect of particularism, for-profit corporations have increasingly challenged their 'responsibility' when they feel environmental groups are sensationalizing, over-simplifying or misrepresenting complex issues with an economic dimension to the public and the media. Most famously, this proved to have been the case after the event with the Brent Spar incident noted earlier. A for-profit interviewee claimed they could more generally be 'decadent', and that it was 'too easy to be critical of the world of commerce' without the latter's responsibilities, partic-ularly those associated with employing very large numbers of people. A recent *Times* leader also focused on 'responsibility', and crystallizes such concerns. It drew on the critique of 'maverick' ex-Greenpeace member Bjorn Lomborg that environmental damage has been 'grossly exaggerated', and Leadbetter's (2002) assertion that the movement are key actors in an overly pessimistic coalition of global 'doom-mongers'. It is claimed that a 'scare-story mentality' has been fostered 'irresponsibly' by the voluntary sector, downplaying apparently encouraging evidence of the world's flourishing biodiversity, and stressing 'excessively' negative trends.[14]

Greenpeace has responded to criticism that it is 'unaccountable' and 'sensationalist' with reference to its members and its media prominence: 'it is accountable because it relies on their donations for its existence . . . we only have success if the public support us. If we say things are wrong then they get pointed out under the public spotlight' (*The Independent on Sunday*, 24 September 2000). This deeply contested debate is likely to increase in intensity, particularly at the international level. The countervailing 'public sector' apparatus that they face at the UN or EU, for example, is much weaker than at the national level (Held *et al.*, 1999), and in a sense environmental groups indeed therefore bear an exceptionally heavy burden of public responsibility. Moreover, their perspective is not only contested by the media and corporate interests; some commentators from developing countries have interpreted the claims of transnational Northern-based environmental groups, including those with British affiliates, as implying a disregard for the legitimate needs and demands of the South (Garner, 2000: Chapter 5; Wapner, 1996: Chapter 6; Yearley, 1996a, b).

9.5 Conclusion

This chapter has shown that while the sector's expressive and advocacy-for-change roles nationally are as significant as expected when we chose this field to exemplify those functions. But organizations are also engaged in a less visible array of service delivery and community-building roles at the local level. They are emerging as key actors in policy implementation. As Young has emphasized, in many cases these roles have often worked in tandem; for example, 'involvement in the detailed Rio implementation process gave organizations insights into how to amend policies in all sorts of tiny ways, generating a feedback loop back into the design stage' (Young, 2000a).

However, this field differs from the others reviewed because there is only a small body of quantitative evidence relating to how the sectors compare. Our attempt to offer a comparative sector perspective within this field has had to be speculative therefore, and we have found it impossible to be conclusive on most issues. Moreover, it terms of the qualitative evidence gathered, there was no sense of 'consensus' or even a dominant viewpoint to match that evident on some key points in the previous chapters. This may in part reflect the relative immaturity of this area as a consolidated policy field. But also important may be the intensity of ideological divisions that persist, even if these are now less stark than analysts have claimed in the past. If our conception of the policy process and the evaluative evidence it generates as complex and indeterminate is correct, as more comparative evidence emerges in years to come, organizations' ideological agendas will continue to affect the way they interpret it, and influence the rhetoric with which they respond. For example, if studies comparing each sector's contributions to environmental innovation were to apparently reveal the for-profit sector to be relatively successful, this would by no means close the debate. Dark green criticisms would be anticipated to challenge the evidence, to the extent that they believed it might be used to justify policies which they found incompatible with their values. The expressive role, as interpreted in this chapter, after all involves strong a priori commitments by voluntary environmental activists, a core of beliefs which acts to filter evidence rather than be revised in the light of it (Sabatier and Jenkins-Smith, 1993).

If sector comparisons within the field have been and will be especially hard to draw, this area is also distinctive in other ways too. It involves a strong international dimension, as well as local and national activities, as environmental problems have increasingly been understood as global concerns (Yearley, 1992, 1999; Rootes, 1999a). The emergence of tangible policies on these issues has been strongly influenced by transnational environmental organizations active at both international and EU levels (Garner, 2000: Chapter 5; Lowe and Ward, 1998). The sheer complexity of issues and problems, and the range of possible options for dealing with them, is increasingly seen to demand a pluralistic approach which can draw upon the resources of the environmental voluntary sector (Rawcliffe, 1998: 6).

In addition, environmental organizations have achieved an exceptionally high degree of public visibility. The media-centricity, particularly of some 'darker green' organizations, has seen them develop remarkable skills in constructing perceptions of environmental risks through increasingly sophisticated news management (Hannigan, 1995). This seems to be unmatched by other parts of the sector. However, as our closing discussion on accountability underlined, this new prominence is increasingly accompanied by intense critical scrutiny by the media itself, for-profit corporations, and social commentators more generally. Critics are now ready to charge at least some organizations with irresponsibility, exaggeration, sensationalism or distortion, potentially undermining the trust upon which they have traditionally relied.

Notes

1 Aside from environmental organizations, the three other major voluntary sector landowners in Britain are probably housing associations; educational institutions (particularly the famously landed Oxbridge colleges and elite public schools); and the churches, in particular the Church of England (if that is not considered part of the state).

2 It now seems clear that the 1981 Wildlife and Countryside Act was something of a landmark, but this was focused quite narrowly as its title suggests. More broadly, in 1990 the White Paper *This Common Inheritance* was presented by the Government as a major policy statement. Although unified with the language of 'sustainable

development' (World Commission on Environment and Development, 1987), this was still criticized by most informed commentators in terms of substance as being essentially an ad hoc, piecemeal list of disparate existing measures, rather than a purposive coherent statement of intent, or willingness to adopt new responsibilities. New Labour has portrayed itself as 'greener' than all previous administrations and invested in an unprecedented level of institution-building, but commentators hold mixed views as to whether it can be said to have transformed the landscape to the extent its rhetoric suggests; for example, see Smith and Geerts, 2002: 56–66.

3 Pinner *et al.* (1992) found that half of their national and local environmental organization respondents registered 'land use, open spaces and buildings' as a significant activity; Rootes *et al.* (2000) covering national organizations, established 'wildlife habitats' to be the single most often cited 'thematic concern' (for 40 per cent of their respondents), with 'nature conservation' the second most important 'field of action' (55 per cent).

4 Rootes *et al.* (2000) found that 'information' was the most often cited 'activity' amongst their national respondents (49 per cent), while 'environmental education' was found to constitute the single most frequent 'main field of action' for 61 per cent.

5 Environmental voluntary organizations have traditionally also benefited from the voluntarism of professional scientists who they do *not* directly employ but who are sympathetic to their goals. The for-profit sector has had to pay 'generously' for equivalent advice, and recognition of this situation has been seen as a major rationale for financial support at the EU level (Rootes, 1999c, d: 1–2).

6 It could be claimed that the public believe 'good science' involves 'holistic' approaches to environmental problems. However, the examples in the literature seem to equate 'good' with orthodox natural science techniques, and lay understandings of science probably tend towards this interpretation.

7 Simple awareness seems to be crucial for many groups. One survey found that 85 per cent of respondents reported that limited public awareness of their organization, and 75 per cent reporting that limited public awareness of environmental issues, were important problems for them (Pinner *et al.*, 1993: 24). A survey of national voluntary environmental agencies found that simple leafleting, presumably to raise awareness, is the single most frequent activity (Rootes *et al.*, 2000).

8 Pennington and Rydin (2000) point out that this problem tends to be more severe with some environmental activities than others. For example, in the case of air quality, there is relatively little voluntary sector involvement in local environment policy networks, which seems to be linked to the diffuse nature of the problem, and the large numbers of those affected but with few clear incentives to act. In contrast, land management is a case where voluntary sector involvement is, as already shown in the previous section, extensive. At the local level, with green spaces, this may reflect a more spatially limited user group with more high-powered incentives to take action 'in terms of the visual amenity benefits from the space and to a lesser extent in terms of recreational use'. It may be easier to form and sustain the relevant social networks in these cases, and apply social sanctions to overcome free riders (Pennington and Rydin, 2000: 243).

9 The more recent involvement of voluntary organizations in New Labour's New Deal environmental task force, while oriented towards unemployed people, is evidently not a 'counter cyclical' public expenditure programme because it has been introduced during a period of macroeconomic growth and falling unemployment.

10 The propensity to convert 'anxiety into action' may be 'a side effect of the generally enhanced levels of personal efficacy that flow from education and/or social status' (Rootes, 1997: 322). Whatever its origins, the marketing approaches adopted by many of the larger groups exaggerate this effect, because they involve targeting mailing and advertising efforts on those higher socio-economic groups which have already demonstrated their interest in environmental protection (Jordan and Maloney, 1997).

11 One rationalized the status quo somewhat defensively, noting that 'We are accused of not involving ethnic minorities, since we tend to focus on traditional users of the countryside – it is easy and does not require huge resources to do it'. However, most expressing a view claimed to be 'making concerted efforts', with approaches to date including translation of literature, and there has been an active recruitment drive in the Asian and black communities by at least one national organization (*The Times*, 1999a). However, the impact of these or other similar efforts has yet to be catalogued.

12 A journalistic review of the book remarks that 'In the end, one senses a lack of balance. The picture he paints is so bleak as to be almost suspicious – surely they cannot be quite as bad as that?' (*The Times*, 1999c; see also *The Times*, 2000)

13 The main professions represented will of course depend upon the balance of functions and activities undertaken, but marketing and fundraising personnel, media and dissemination specialists, lobbyists and policy analysts, land management professionals, lawyers and natural scientists (such as graduates with higher degrees in ecology and environmental sciences), as well as a plethora of support and administrative staff, have probably all increased in number. This trend in the UK seems to be part of a wider European one (Diani and Donati, 1999). Professionals have also made increasing inputs from outside as paid consultants and contract workers, and, in the case of committed professional scientists, voluntarily, particularly to trans-European environmental networks (Rootes, 1999b).

14 'The greatest casualty of such campaigning is the cause of responsible conservation. By painting the sky so dark, the green gloom-mongers forfeit trust and encourage a sense of hopeless decline . . . there is still a need to recognize that biodiversity is threatened in certain, specific circumstances but an effective focus on those areas where despoliation is occurring is obscured by the bleak panorama painted by the green gloom-mongers', *The Times*, July 2002.

Part III

Summary and conclusion

10 Summary and conclusion

Comparative perspectives on the monster

- **The voluntarism which is a central characteristic of much voluntary sector activity means that these organizations are 'awkward' customers. They cannot be steered by fiat or finance to the extent that state entities or for-profit organizations respectively can.**

- **In Britain, the centralized apparatus of the state, and the history of problematic relations within it, strongly shape the possibilities for voluntary sector policy development.**

- **Rival world-views provide contrasting ways of thinking about the voluntary sector's evolving relations with the state sector.**

10.1 Introduction and summary

This book has attempted to advance our understanding of the 'loose and baggy monster' that is the voluntary sector in Britain as a comparative phenomenon.[1] It has approached the topic from a number of angles. This final chapter proceeds by summarizing some of the main themes of the foregoing discussion, and points to the overall conclusions that can be drawn concerning the voluntary sector's comparative impact. The following two sections then situate the discussion of impact in a broader political economy context. Section 10.2 notes why the relationship between voluntarism and policy is considerably more fragile than it at first appears. Section 10.3 compares and contrasts rival views as to the desirability of the current relationship between the state and the voluntary sector that is taking shape. Section 10.4 concludes by relating these normative accounts to the approach taken in this book.

10.1.1 Summary of main themes and findings

The British voluntary sector is a major part of the economy. It now contributes a significant share of paid employment, although unpaid labour – through volunteer contributions – still accounts for most of this sector's work. This sector in the UK has grown significantly from a comparative perspective. In the first half of the 1990s, it expanded more rapidly than its counterparts in other countries. In absolute terms, most paid employment growth has been concentrated in for-profits and public agencies in recent years, but the voluntary sector has witnessed a *proportionately* larger increase from a low base.

An important driver of this expansion has been financial support from central and local government. This has been an important factor in a number of policy fields, but has been particularly prominent in social care and social housing, involving both central and local government. The overall situation is unique internationally to the extent it involved, especially from the 1990s onwards, a new order of financial dependence on the state. While the voluntary sector in many other countries, particularly in Europe, is also dependent upon public sector support, elsewhere such patterns represent continuity with long-term historical financial settlements. Consequently, and because of the associated policy turbulence, it is very difficult to classify the UK voluntary sector 'case' as similar to other countries. It shares some similarities with its US cousin and some with its European neighbours.

In the early 1990s, despite the voluntary sector's exceptional growth and the significance of the state as a catalyst for this development, levels of recognition in the then Conservative administration's rhetoric was limited. The policy discourse was dominated by references to the strengths of the market and the weaknesses of the state. However, from the mid-1990s onwards, based on policy foundations laid in previous years, space has systematically and consistently been found for the voluntary sector in policy rhetoric and proposals for the first time under New Labour. Soon after coming to office in 1997, the rapid adoption of a 'Compact', the allocation of significant additional resources to foster development, and the initiation of and follow through to major Treasury reviews have all been symptomatic of this step change.

No single factor explains the emergence of this situation. Rather account must be taken of the joint influence of a number of factors which came together to make significant policy change possible. These influences included specialist institutions long nurtured, but previously with very limited policy visibility; New Labour's aspiration to differentiate itself from 'statist' Old Labour; and the promotional activities of policy entrepreneurs with a stake in the sector, spanning the worlds of both research and politics. It is noteworthy that while ideational connections in policy and research are increasingly being made between the voluntary sector, social capital and social exclusion, this process has really only gathered momentum after mainstreaming had already taken place.

New Labour has now begun to implement the 'mainstreamed' agenda through a range of new 'horizontal' policies. These have included attempts to foster a 'bigger role' via national and subnational Compacts and allied institutions; extensive involvement of the sector in New Deals, including the New Deal for young people; and new initiatives at the local level, involving local government.

Existing evidence did not allow us to gauge whether such voluntary sector engagement has contributed to substantive policy outcomes such as end-user welfare gains or increased community sustainability. However, the new institutions seem to have widened access to the policy process; offered groups resources and hence new opportunities to meet needs; and led to constructive new relationships in some cases. To this extent, it was concluded that they represented an advance from the perspective of the beneficiary organizations. At the same time, there were also major difficulties, some of which seem to involve the recurrence of problems familiar from the previous administration. These include a failure to involve groups as extensively as many had expected in policy design; the imposition of inappropriately narrow performance measures where politically expedient; and a range of barriers to implementation at the local level.

The fraught and frustrating experiences of actual implementation were found to contrast dramatically with the smooth and rapid agenda mainstreaming process. Reasons for this divergence were identified as necessary reliance on a much wider range of stakeholders at multiple levels; conflicts in perspectives on the intent and meaning of policy goals, only coming to the surface in the process of delivery ('devils in the detail'); contrasts in understandings of appropriate time scales and levels of bureaucracy; and unrealistic expectations stemming from each sides' miscalculation as to the other's capacity to 'deliver'. This partly reflected overoptimistic understandings of the possibilities for change prior to implementation.

In Part II, the book moved from consideration of inputs and processes to outcomes. A range of discipline-based approaches to the 'impact' of the voluntary sector were noted. These include economic cost–benefit analysis, management science approaches, and financial accounting-based comparisons. However, the approach used here differed in being eclectic. It drew on evidence and argument from a range of disciplines. One element was multidisciplinary international third sector theory, suggesting a range of sectoral 'functions'/strengths and 'failures'/weaknesses. 'Functions' reviewed included service provision, advocacy, innovation, expression/leadership development, and community-building; while weaknesses involve insufficiency, particularism, paternalism, excessive amateurism or professionalism and problematic accountability.

It was argued that it is important to understand impacts against the evolving political and policy background. Policy legacies were identified as a significant component of this context. As had been emphasized at the onset, this partly reflects general characteristics of economic institutional life. But they are also relevant in the voluntary sector case in particular because of the associated public good properties, inherent complexity and (for charities) the legal environment's co-ordinating tendencies, as well as because of more general attributes of public policy institutions.

The 'functions' or strengths attributed to the third sector in the international theoretical literature were found to be familiar from the 'horizontal', sector-wide UK research literature. At the same time, informed reviews of the research evidence suggest that at least some of these claims do not always stand up to critical scrutiny, and sometimes have a quality akin to myths. The most dramatic change in recent years has been the adoption of the language of 'social capital'. This has involved a rediscovery of the role of the voluntary sector in fulfilling the 'community-building' role, giving new prominence to themes long established in British 'community development' and allied discourses. Recognition of failures or weaknesses are also strongly evident in the British research case. Prominent amongst the diagnosed difficulties are patchiness in terms of geographical distribution; lack of involvement for people from lower socio-economic backgrounds, and some minority ethnic groups; and problematic human resource or personnel practices in the case of many agencies which employ paid staff.

Political rhetoric has been selective in drawing upon the body of research evidence in recent years. This has tended to accentuate positive contributions and downplay failures, or attribute them to factors beyond the control of the voluntary sector. There has therefore a 'motherhood and apple pie' flavour to much contemporary political debate. However, beneath the apparent near consensus amongst ministers and parliamentarians that the voluntary sector is essentially 'a good thing', lie significant fault lines. First, disagreement on means between those, including the current Government, who enthusiastically endorse proactive state horizontal policy as conducive to a 'healthy' voluntary sector; and those who do not. Second, conflicting perspectives on ends. This has been most evident between those who attach paramount weight to an 'efficient' service provision role; and those who give particular importance to the sector's expressive contributions, including higher implied tolerance of inefficiencies. It is unclear where the Government is currently situated regarding the relative importance it attaches to these roles.

Chapters 7, 8 and 9 reviewed the impact situation in three fields which have been of particular economic and political significance over the past decades: social housing, social care and support for older people, and environmental protection. The voluntary sector's growing prominence in social housing could partly be explained by the limitations and failures – or at least, perceptions of limitations – of other sectors. However, the current balance and content of social housing activities between the voluntary sector, the public sector and the for-profit sector was also argued to strongly reflect unplanned historical eventualities. In particular, the attractiveness of its housing portfolio significantly follows from its 'late starter' status in mainstream policy terms compared with most parts of Europe.

Significant variation between housing associations in terms of performance was in evidence. On average, however, this sector was compared favourably with other sectors in the delivery of social housing services in certain important respects. Aside from 'inherited portfolio' effects, this situation seems to have reflected a combination of such factors as superior patterns of specialization, greater access to financial and human resources, and the avoidance of 'distortions' caused by party political control. Comparative evidence regarding the discharge of other functions was less extensive, but distinctive emphases include the involvement of volunteers in advocacy; innovations associated with diversification into adjacent policy fields, including social care; and distinctive capabilities in community-building, reflecting sensitivity to local needs, and involving practices such as local labour clauses. Regarding 'weaknesses', a remarkable feature of voluntary sector social housing has been its situation of resource abundance, rather than resource insufficiency. This followed directly from generous central government investment, particularly in the 1970s and 1980s. The most salient weakness to emerge was problematic accountability, although there was no expert consensus as to whether recent elaborations of the current complex institutional infrastructure have been sufficient to rectify any perceived deficit.

The next field reviewed was care and support for older people. The policy environment which organizations in this field inhabit was shown to have evolved in a particularly complex and piecemeal way since the mid-twentieth century. Partly as a result of this inheritance, the supply-side is especially diverse. While a range of 'types' of organization are recognizable, no single 'type' dominates, with groups prominent in certain functions and forms of care less involved or conspicuous in others.

In mainstream service delivery, particularly publicly funded social care, the voluntary sector is now less significant than the for-profit and public sectors. It is known to mobilize significant volunteer inputs, offer services at lower prices and involve certain care possibilities not offered by other sectors in certain situations. But in other situations, it does not do so. Partly as a result, the evidence that is available on comparative economy and quality of care is inconclusive and liable to a range of plausible interpretations.

Outside mainstream service delivery – in low-intensity social care, and support activities – the advantages of voluntarism have long been recognized by policy-makers. Recent research on user outcomes has underlined the relevance of voluntary social support activities, and this prominently reflects the expressive role in the sense of fostering friendships and sociability. Other functions were evident, although it is less clear that they have been discharged effectively, sometimes for reasons beyond the control of the organizations themselves. A wide range of failures or 'weaknesses' were suggested by a body of evidence and argument in this field. However, it was very difficult to distinguish between problems attributable to the field and problems attributable to the voluntary sector in particular within it. In addition, the significance of variety again came to the surface, with different types of organizations and policy situations apparently being characterized by failures to a greater or lesser degree. Consequently, it seemed to be very difficult to conclude either that one sector is 'performing' better than others, or that within the voluntary sector, particular types of organization were making more overall 'impact' than others.

The final field for 'impact' review was environmental policy. This has relatively recently taken shape as a consolidated field. The voluntary organizations active in this domain are diverse, but share an aspiration to foster an environmental sensibility, or raise environmental awareness and many are noticeably savvy in their media management techniques. Two varieties seemed to be particularly prominent nationally: 'light green' organizations, the largest of which are 'conservative' and date back to nineteenth-century philanthropic traditions;

and 'darker green' groups, the most visible of which originate in the 1960s and 1970s, and whose more 'progressive' orientation has traditionally seen them labelled as 'new social movements'.

The activities of these groups could be seen as a response to the cumulative failures of other sectors, including externality-related market failure, public regulatory failure and perceived failures in public ownership. But comparisons with other sectors were largely impressionistic, in part because the sectors less evidently discharge comparable roles to the extent this occurs in the other fields reviewed. However, the sector does seem to have enjoyed a trust premium, and to be carving itself an increasingly significant niche as an implementer of environmental policy, in addition to its higher profile campaigning role. At the same time, the extent of influence of its advocacy efforts is contested, with the most recent wide-ranging reviews tending to suggest that corporations and unsympathetic interests within the state have often been in the ascendant in policy terms.

The discharge of functions, like other fields, was found to be accompanied by weaknesses or failures too. The problem of resource insufficiency was perhaps more severe than in social housing but less severe than in social care, to the extent that sophisticated marketing and sales approaches had ameliorated the free rider problem. In addition, in part because of the conspicuously ideological character of the debate, 'excessive professionalism' was more conspicuous here than elsewhere, as a core of committed activists has struggled to retain control over an expanding periphery of professionals.

10.1.2 Diversity, complexity, distinctiveness and ubiquity

Viewing the sector through the heuristic lens provided by international third sector theory should help encourage a more informed debate regarding the voluntary sector's contributions. The review bears witness to the diversity and complexity of the voluntary sector which those involved with it sense, and experience with both fascination and frustration. We have seen that public officials, for example, have routinely misconstrued the 'nature of the beast' as they have sought to involve it in new implementation programmes.

It can also be concluded that, taken in the round, the voluntary sector is different from the public and for-profit sectors. Like those sectors, it contributes to society in ways that most or all people would perceive as positive; it exhibits failures and weaknesses as well, often closely related to its positive roles. And some of its features are viewed as strengths by some, but weaknesses by others, as with some aspects of particularism.

On a 'function by function' comparative basis, overall (Chapter 6) and vertically (Chapters 7–9) numerous ways in which the voluntary sector's contribution is distinctive have been reviewed. Viewing the functions cumulatively within a field, or looking at the same function across fields, suggests to an extent not really made apparent before, the ubiquity of voluntary action and its importance to the fabric of the lives of the majority of the population, and minorities alike. It enriches social and political life, has and continues to set and develop agendas which otherwise would not have been set, and meets diverse, variegated and idiosyncratic needs which otherwise would not have been met. On the surface, that was already going to follow from the way we have defined it. But we have managed to dig a little below that level to reveal how the criteria of definition employed have significance and meaning for those involved. With the notable exception of social housing, where the sector's 'nonprofit' character and 'nonstate' status have been the most 'active ingredients', it is its 'voluntarism' which emerges as the most distinctive criterion.

Once the (almost tautological or circular) assumption that voluntarism is characterized by a lack of financial reward or conscious coercion has been made, it become difficult to generalize about impacts or social consequences. Recognition of the complexity and diversity which characterizes this field is not an argument for not undertaking reviews of evaluative evidence of the sort attempted in Part II of this book. Rather, it implies the need to develop more sophisticated approaches to evaluation better able to capture and account for outcome complexity; variation between organizations in terms of size, type and historical origins; and contrasts with respect to policy field, social conditions and political conditions at the level of fields and subfields.

However, such evaluations must constitute just one part of the research agenda, which can help to inform the decision-making process and ultimately allow political choices to be made on a firmer empirical basis. The remainder of this conclusion will underline the need to situate the voluntary sector in the worlds of policy and politics more broadly. The understanding of these organizations from a comparative perspective will be deepened partly by pursuing ever more specific impact and other evaluative exercises sensitive to variation and complexity. Our account of policy legacies suggests that, even within a quite narrow evaluative frame of reference, historical eventualities across and within policy fields are central in shaping the outcomes that are observed. But it is also important to stand back from these minutiae and try to locate the voluntary sector within the broader political economy.

10.2 The monster in policy context: an awkward (but valued) customer

We have here defined the sector as involving independent, nonprofit distributing, voluntary formal organizations, while acknowledging that for certain purposes narrower definitions are apposite. Broadening our 'case' to the monster *in situ* involves raising the question of what is distinctive about the voluntary sector as a policy actor? What is distinctive about the voluntary sector in Britain as a policy actor? And what is distinctive about the voluntary sector in Britain as a policy actor now, under a New Labour administration? The following section briefly considers each in turn.

10.2.1 Voluntarism

One useful way of approaching the first, most general of questions is to consider the implications of our definition. Voluntarism seems to emerge as the crucial central ingredient in understanding functions and weaknesses alike. While voluntarism can be found in the state and for-profit sectors too, it is in the voluntary sector that its formally organized expression tends to be concentrated.[2] As pointed out in earlier chapters, there are therefore limits to the extent to which the state can use fiat or financial incentives to 'steer' policy outcomes in the desired direction. Monetary approaches may be used diplomatically – but if they dominate, and are seen to dominate, then the very voluntarism which may be the point of the policy engagement in the first place will have been undermined. This external relational implication of voluntarism for state–voluntary sector relations mirrors the internal situation which Diana Leat's (1995) exploratory research began to highlight. In seeking to organize both unpaid volunteers and those of its employees who feel themselves to be making a salary sacrifice, voluntary sector managers have often been flummoxed to find themselves unable to use rewards and sanctions to the same extent as they were able in the for-profit sector.

In engaging with organizations characterized by voluntarism, the state then has a more restricted repertoire of policy tools at its disposal than it does if dealing with market organizations, components of its own structure, or classically corporatist institutions. Often, it will be the voluntary sector itself which seeks to initiate public policy actions. In other cases, needs will be jointly diagnosed. But when it is the state which is seeking to lead, it must persuade, coax and convince its potential policy partners as to the coincidence of agendas and aspirations. This is in the knowledge that if it fails to do so, it cannot simply resort to sanctions or cash to secure compliance. Policies which are too obviously premised on the application of perceived or actual coercion will likely be shunned, as the state has found out, particularly on the case of training and employment programmes. Cash could be acceptable if mutually understood as 'covering costs' or 'paying for [legitimate] expenses', perhaps explicitly compensating for mutually recognized voluntary insufficiency. This arrangement is certainly reflected on an ever greater scale in many countries through grants, service level agreements and contracts with public authorities.

Disproportionate reliance on persuasion means disproportionate reliance on the full range of strategies for persuasion. Rhetoric, as well as evidence-based reasoning, will all tend to loom particularly large, therefore, in voluntary sector policy-making.

10.2.2 Voluntarism in Britain

Are there underlying political institutional arrangements which set Britain apart from other countries, and which need to be taken into account if the intention is to rely increasingly on voluntarism for policy purposes? Voluntary sector commentators have traditionally emphasized the continuities flowing from the ancient tradition of charity, and the regulatory apparatus that supports and constrains it in England and Wales (Thomas and Kendall, 1996).[3] This clearly remains an important factor, although at the time of writing it is not known which proposals for reform of the relevant institutions will be taken forward (Strategy Unit, 2002).

It was decided not to focus on charity law and the Charity Commission (perhaps to become the Charity Regulatory Authority) per se here for the reasons mentioned in Chapter 1. But in the case of charities (which account for a significant share of the voluntary organizations considered in scope for this study), it was found appropriate to bring into our analysis of impact that institution's regulatory role for two reasons. First, it has been significant in controlling entries into and exits from (what charity law defines as) 'public benefit' services. In discouraging the provision of similar services by more than one provider, by encouraging co-ordination via co-operation and collaboration (within and across sectors) rather than competition, and by protecting assets from changes in use, it has significantly shaped activities in the public sphere. Second, and more widely discussed in the literature, it has sought to promote a particular legal version of accountability. As such, it has overlain a wide range of other institutions also geared towards this goal (whose precise configurations we have seen vary in scope and relevance according to organizations' size, activities and policy field).

The state's apparatus for regulating charity is not, however, the only significant public institution with consequences for the voluntary sector's 'cross-cutting' policy environment. As the voluntary sector in the UK increasingly engages with the state, for the purposes of legal regulation but also in the process of accessing financial and other official forms of support, the broader architecture of constitutional design comes to be seen as of more obvious relevance. It then becomes crucial to recognize that the relevant policies are ultimately a reflection of Britain's unique parliamentary system, and to recognize the relative concentration of policy power in the centre that this involves. In North America and much of western Europe, a more balanced relationship between the levels of the state has been the constitutional backdrop against which voluntary sector welfare responsibilities have evolved. Local and regional tiers of the state in these countries have developed there multifarious engagements with voluntary organizations relatively free of central regulation (see 6 and Kendall, 1997).

To a significant extent, the exceptional growth trajectory of the British voluntary sector that has been outlined in this book reflects this institutional inheritance. The formative social housing legislation from the 1960s onwards, and the social care legislation of the 1990s, which have been shown to be so critical in underpinning the voluntary sector's recent aggregate development, were themselves products of this system. Each involved the state exercising its legal prerogative, legitimated by Parliament to steer strongly from the centre. It is interesting to reflect that in most other countries, were policy elites also to wish to foster such significant breaks from their pasts in terms of patterns of ownership in social welfare domains, constitutional settlements would tend to act as more significant constraints on their ability to do so.

Of course, intra-state linkages in the UK have been famously frayed by international standards (Carter and John, 1992). The shift from council housing to housing associations in social housing can of course be read as in part a consequence of precisely this distrust (alongside distrust of the for-profit sector). But even in the primary field of welfare in which local government has taken the lead in developing direct relations with the voluntary sector – social care – the amount of background control exercised from the centre is atypically high (and rapidly increasing) by comparison with other countries.

10.2.3 *Voluntarism in Britain under New Labour*

Local government remains the primary statutory port of call for the voluntary sector in Britain. The current central administration asserts that it has moved, as 'partners' with this tier of the state, beyond the adversarial relationships of the past. It certainly needs to do so if it is to foster the horizontal institutions at local level which it believes will help support voluntary sector development. But the evidence reviewed earlier (particularly that presented in Chapter 4) seems to suggest that it has yet to win the trust to which it aspires in voluntary sector-relevant policy domains. Local government typically feels insecure and apprehensive about its own future in the context of heavy government demands and an unprecedented barrage of targets and initiatives from the centre.

Under these conditions, it is not clear that it is as enthusiastic about sharing its role with the voluntary sector in local public service delivery as central government would like. Apparently even less evident is the conviction that it can or should embrace the voluntary sector – if given more support in so doing – in the pursuit of 'democratic renewal'. In many ways, this is not surprising. If generalization is possible, and there really is a siege mentality at the local government level, then politicians and officials within it are as likely to feel threatened by, as to wish to ally themselves with, the voluntary sector as a participatory policy actor.

10.3 The monster's welfare: five diagnoses and five prognoses

Whether the evolving situation outlined in this book is considered as healthy or dysfunctional will depend ultimately on our view of the nature of the state. Accordingly, the final section of this chapter presents some stylized alternative normative characterizations which offer us rival views on the state and its relationship with the voluntary sector.

Table 10.1 offers an (oversimplified) schema which seeks to compare and contrast the most influential and theoretically developed 'world-views'. These are set alongside the author's own view, shaped by the process of writing this book, and tentatively labelled a 'contingent realist' perspective. It is important to stress that this final column is meant to act as a suggestive comparative marker only (hence the use of quotation marks to differentiate it from the fully developed analytic approaches). The purpose of this study has certainly not been to develop or test an alternative general theory of the state, and no general conclusions can be drawn with regard to that topic. However, some of the features of the policy process which were argued to be consequential for understanding voluntary sector policy and voluntary sector impact themselves involve a way of thinking about the nature of the state in Britain. Because this does not really correspond to any single one of the five developed frameworks of existing analyses shown, it is important to try and draw out the different emphases that it entails, and this is the purpose of Section 10.4.[4]

For now, in Section 10.3 the analysis proceeds by comparing the content of the five established approaches.[5] Table 10.1 refers to respective sectoral policy capabilities and intentions; the character of sector relationships, and the policy environment associated with that relationship; and from that diagnosis, coupled with their contrasting theoretical underpinnings, ascertains different prognoses about the likely future path of development. Note that the explicitness of the theoretical content varies – least explicit in the social democratic optimist position, and most explicit in the fatalist and determinist views – but that none of them can be said to be 'atheoretical', to the extent that all carry assumptions and expectations about the way the world works.

Reading from left to right across the table involves shifting from rather general theoretically rarefied and abstract accounts towards those which would claim to be more pragmatic and grounded in style. Moving from top to bottom involves first of all thematizing the state's assumed starting orientation; then specifying the implications for the voluntary sector as the monster whose welfare is to be diagnosed; and then suggesting what each perspective may be willing and able to assert about future developments.

First, an interesting account has been developed by Jon Morison, inspired by Michel Foucault, and is portrayed here as 'Foucauldian fatalist'. Under this account (Morison, 2000), the imperative of 'governmentability' which is taken to characterize all modern societies involves the development of disembodied social control. Thus, the source of power which shapes the voluntary sector's policy environment neither follows from the economic system, nor from a historically contingent focus on electoral gain and deliverables (see below).

Morison interviewed a range of participants involved in the process of developing Compacts, and concluded that the voluntary sector organizations thus involved (especially intermediary bodies) were necessarily contributing to a newly restrictive and enervating policy situation for the sector as a whole. Contemporary pressures for 'governmentability' acts as the underlying driver. The process as smooth, uniform and invidious, rather than uneven, openly contested and spatially uneven.

The second approach also emphasizes predictability, but following a different logic. This neo-Marxist, determinist model was developed by Jennifer Wolch, an American scholar who sought to compare the British and US situations at the end of the 1980s. (This is the only approach of those listed which has not been explicitly articulated in a 1990s context.) While Marxist approaches are hardly in vogue, the approach is worth mentioning here because it represented a

Table 10.1 The voluntary sector monster as policy actor in modern Britain: diagnoses and prognoses

Worldview → / Implications ↓	Foucauldian fatalist	Neo-Marxist determinist	Civic conservative pessimist	Liberal sceptic	Social democratic optimist	'Contingent realist'
Reason for initial attempts at consolidation of public policy towards the voluntary sector	'Governmentibility' pressures generate 'enclosures' whose construction is possible due to modern technologies of control	Functional needs of capital: alliance of business and subservient state	Pressures from alliance of state insiders and 'unproductive' interest groups	Unwise and myopic faith in centrally-led public policy as instrument of social progress	Legitimate process of 'need' diagnosis led by well-informed experts, with supporting input from organized civil society	*Horizontal* Initiation: Conjuncture of macro-political stream dynamics and policy entrepreneurship *Vertical* No dominant motive can be inferred. Varies, reflecting net effect of interaction of inherited and emergent policy community dynamics with wider national political structures and overall *zeitgeist*.
Current dominant motives for state's public policy engagement	Not relevant: inherent tendencies to control and economize as part of broader social processes	Serving the needs of capitalism	Arrogant assumption of 'knowing best' combined with continued pressure group self-interest	Well-intentioned, but misguided 'obsession' with 'deliverables'	Not uniform, varies by policy field but tends to be benign	Key attributes of national political structure include unitary nature of the State (see below) and evolving horizontal institutions (see above)
Distribution of power	Ubiquitous, invidiously present in all sectors	Concentrated in corporate for-profit sector; expressed in social welfare through the state on behalf of capitalism	Tendency to concentration in the state (whatever state's rhetoric)		Mixed across and within policy fields, but intelligent state tends to be legitimately authoritative	Emphasises constitutional capacity for British unitary state to concentrate power. But reliance on persuasion in context of complex horizontal and vertical infrastructure limits overall state capability

Leitmotif for contested state interventions	'Control' or 'surveillance'	'Para state' or 'shadow state incorporation'	'Over regulation', 'colonization' or 'infiltration'	'Interference'	'Support', 'regulation', 'collaboration'	No a priori label; will reflect design process
Extent of policy relevant choice facing voluntary organizations	Illusory	Downplayed, unless stay 'pure' meaning 'agitators' or 'radicals'	Downplayed, unless stay 'pure' meaning 'apolitical'	Limited, once engaged beyond minimalist relationship	Extensive and real	Contingent upon net outcome of horizontal and vertical interactions. Choices can be extensive in some situations, limited in others
Metaphor for current situation of the monster	Unknowingly doped and then caged	Healthy→ schizophrenic→ passive (tamed)	Already restricted by existing institutional landscape: institutions have undermined by 'colonization'	In process of being restricted by emerging institutional landscape	Roaming quite free in benign (but risky) institutional environment	None. In some situations learning to adjust to highly complex environment with mixed results; in others experiencing indifference or hostility
Case of past or anticipated 'golden age'	Pre-modern era when extensive control technologies not available	Interlude of local 'rainbow alliances' in London in early 1980s	Heyday of Victorian philanthropy (Whelan) or situation pre-1940s social welfare legislation (Willetts)	Implicit: Pre-ongoing elaboration of new central institutional infrastructure	A future where current rhetoric of 'partnership' is systematically followed through	None
Overall prognosis	Inevitably trapped (under any modern political settlement)	Almost inevitably poor health (under actual existing capitalism)	Inevitably poor health (under misguided social democracy)	Tending towards poor health	Despite risks, tending towards good health	Not possible to predict on the basis of existing mixed symptoms, uncertainty on future Government practices

pioneering attempt to explicitly theorize the complex political economy of this field. Wolch (1990) treated the Thatcher Government's then recent destruction of the Greater London Council and the network of 'radical' organizations that it had been supporting as symptomatic of a predictable process of dysfunctional intervention and manipulation by the central state on behalf of capital.

The language of 'dynamics' and 'dialectic' portray the possibility of variation in central–local relations with some sensitivity, seeming to suggest alternatives local patterns could unfold. However, in the end, Wolch ultimately sees state–voluntary sector relations as following a predetermined path (in the absence of economic systemic transformation). The 'radical' local government–voluntary sector alliance was always going to be a relatively isolated and temporary pocket of resistance. It would find it impossible not to bow – albeit perhaps after wrestling with an episode of 'schizophrenia', as simultaneously a creature of the (necessarily conflicting) interests of 'local community' and the 'state' – to the pressures of the latter as mediator of for-profit corporate interests (Wolch, 1990).

What are we to make of these analyses? While theoretically elegant, both of these approaches seem to rest on a number of conceptual ambiguities and implausible assumptions. The fatalist account seems too vague to be useful concerning the sources of power and to be unhelpful to the extent it resists specifying if, or under what conditions, the state, on the one hand, and the voluntary sector, on the other, have particular roles to play in the exercise of power. To argue that the relevant written codifications are capable of generation and invidious imposition whatever the state and the voluntary sector's intentions and modus operandi seems to assume rather than explain the observed situation. As far as the neo-Marxist account is concerned, I have suggested elsewhere a number of problematic aspects. These include that approach's use of the concepts of autonomy and efficiency, its conflation of intentions with actual practices, and its exaggerated claims regarding the central state's omniscience (Kendall, 1992).

The remaining accounts of the monster's health share a reluctance to a priori specify the direction and pattern of development, and find increasing room for contingency moving rightwards. But they differ in their interpretations of the monster's presented symptoms, and hold contrasting expectations about how well the creature is coping, and will be able to cope, with the changing institutional landscape.

'Civic conservatism' is the first of these less deterministic accounts. Chapter 6 noted that in parliamentary debates, Conservative politicians have tended to be acquiescent regarding most aspects of the current administration's 'support' for the voluntary sector. But a principled opposing position, in keeping with the previous Conservative administration's rejection of the proposed Concordat as not 'desirable', is implicit in David Willetts' (1994) philosophical essay (for the broader context, see also Green, 2002: Chapter 9). Indeed, Willetts explicitly criticized even the relatively modest reforms to charity law that had then taken place under his own administration to the extent they were 'imposing heavy new burdens' and involving the 'pernicious effect of heavy-handed regulation'. The analysis has been developed most recently by writers from the Conservative think tank, the Institute of Economic Affairs, with an eye to critiquing the extension of state–voluntary sector financial relationships outlined in this volume (see in particular, Green, 1996; Whelan, 1999). The theory of the state involves portraying the public sector as at best necessarily a blunt, inefficient and centralizing policy instrument 'captured' by unproductive interests. At worst, the state's actions are argued to be fundamentally corrosive of moral life. Either through directly funding or providing, statutory interventions premised on political decisions are assumed to crowd out or distort the otherwise responsible and community-sensitive actions of the voluntary sector. Given this expectation, tax breaks are assumed to be inappropriate for state-funded organizations. Voluntary organizations are urged to stand wholly apart from the state as 'apolitical' practitioners, and get on with meeting the local needs which only they, it is argued, can authentically diagnose and address.[6]

Civic conservatism seems to share with the other approaches discussed so far an extraordinarily expansive view of the reach and uniformly penetrative capacities of the modern state. Of course the contrast is that, in this case, unhealthy influence is assumed to be wielded by different actors and processes. Now, the problem lies with an alliance of self-interested, state-funded professionals and pressure groups, rather than with for-profit corporations or invidious technology. But unlike those accounts, this is implicitly taken to be salvageable and reversible if only a government with the correct ideological credentials were to be elected!

An obvious point here is that the monolithic, predatory image of the state involved in civic conservatism is at odds with the variegated situation portrayed in earlier chapters, and the account below will draw out distinctions in more detail. But the argument also seems implausible for other reasons. Clearly, a portrayal of the state as always and everywhere the cause of decline and decay – and a voluntary sector funded by independent means as necessarily developing in the opposite direction – is too simplistic a portrayal of historic or current voluntary sector–state relations. The suggestion that politics can somehow be avoided by fostering a residual state and expansive voluntary sector also seems naive unless an extremely narrow view of political life is adopted. Moreover, if in spite of these difficulties, a move towards this world-view were to form the basis for a 'policy' in this domain, it would undoubtedly face enormous difficulties of political feasibility. As with Knight's (1993) proposals, it would face general resistance from charities standing to lose tax advantages. In addition, the significant build up of bureaucratic infrastructure that has accumulated in recent years around the horizontal agenda would itself be a formidable barrier to any attempt to foster the systemic switch to essentially private institutions that this approach prefers.

The final two perspectives are associated with two observers whose perspectives have commanded more attention than all others, not least because their proponents have been more obvious and directly active participants in the policy process itself. The prototypical liberal sceptic view, as represented by Lord Dahrendorf, is represented through contributions in the House of Lords, and a recent, much cited lecture (Dahrendorf, 2001). This position is more nuanced than it is sometimes portrayed, and does not argue for the wholesale rejection of state–voluntary sector engagement. What it does do is point to emerging tendencies which, it is argued, could lead to a world in which what we have referred to as the 'expressive' and 'innovation' functions in particular are severely constrained – even if well-meaning politicians have the opposite outcome in mind. Essential scepticism about the wisdom of extensive state involvement, so different from Deakin's active endorsement, was initially revealed through Dahrendorf's comment on the Deakin Commission report as 'recommending too much co-ordination and central organization for my liking' (Hansard, 27 November 1996, column 315).

More recently, the 2001 lecture acknowledges the Chancellor's rhetorically expressed intention to 'loosen control of the state apparatus and give control back' (2001: 4). But *despite* these intentions, for Dahrendorf, the dead hand of the state is always in the background as a threat to liberty. At this particular moment in time, imperatives of electoral 'delivery' seem set to generate an 'over controlling' state 'not because ministers are control freaks but because public–voluntary promises otherwise lead to an impasse' (Dahrendorf, 2001: 10).

Finally we can characterize the position of Nicholas Deakin, revealed through his leadership of the Commission on the Future of the Voluntary Sector (see Chapter 3) and expressed subsequently (Foreword to Plowden *et al.*, 2001; Deakin, 2002), as that of a social democratic optimist. General 'optimism' is evident in the willingness to lead the independent Commission, and offer the 'Concordat' proposal as a meaningful way of shaping future relations. But in Deakin (2001), a particular perspective on the current situation with New Labour's welfare reforms is also expressed: for him, this administration's track record demonstrates that 'major welfare problems are capable of being tackled' with the input of voluntary organizations.

Second, while the other writers reviewed emphasize the tendency for the central state to act as a concentrator of power (via contrasting institutional processes, depending on the particular world-view espoused), this author is quick to point to countervailing possibilities. For Deakin, alliances between the local state and voluntary organizations (and potentially the newly strengthened tier of regional government now being introduced) can and should endure and proliferate as healthily obstructive barriers to control from the centre. Third, reflecting long-held social democratic values (cf. Deakin, 1994) there is a faith in the state as a constructive source for the good, willing and able to adapt to changing needs and demands. Specifically on the implications for the voluntary sector, Deakin's Foreword in Plowden *et al.* (2001) portrays the combination of state and voluntary sector as responsive to changing progressive societal needs and demands, implicitly in spite of wider 'systemic' imperatives. For example, self-help groups involvement in public services are argued to have shaped a much greater client group orientation that prevailed heretofore.

10.4 The monster's welfare: future unknown?

For this author, taken together, the Deakin and Dahrendorf analyses collectively involve a higher degree of plausibility than the other three approaches examined To a significantly greater extent those other perspectives, their accounts seem to resonate with the materials reviewed in the course of writing this book. Each could point to aspects of the evidence that has been assembled here in support of their diagnosis. For example, a liberal sceptic could point to the ways in which horizontal implementation has sometimes involved real and enduring tensions between electoral imperatives and the more measured and gradualist approaches that are often characteristic of organized civil society. Imperatives to be seen to 'deliver', and quickly, have clearly trumped voluntary sector aspirations for more inclusiveness, time and closer attention to detail. The sceptic could also align themselves with those who point to claimed deleterious effects on the voluntary sector's social capital, following the development of linkages with the state which are perceived to represent dysfunctional institutionalization. At the vertical field level, most ammunition for his worries about an overbearing and centralizing state would be found by pointing to the accounts of those experts we already labelled as sceptics in social care. There is an apparent affinity with their concerns about the implications of escalating institutional and regulatory elaboration, and its supposedly deleterious effects on innovative and expressive roles. From a comparative perspective, ultimately the British constitutional settlement has, of course, made these policy shifts easier.

A welfare optimist, by contrast, would take heart from positive aspects of the experiences of the implementation process reviewed in Chapter 4, pointing to unprecedented input into the policy process; and refer to the upbeat interpretations of the consequences of the state's involvement with the voluntary sector in fostering social capital favoured by some political scientists. He would also take comfort from the evidence on the voluntary sector's countervailing power which emerged from the field level impact studies, for example in the case of environmental protection – at least from the perspective of some environmental policy analysts and on some aspects of policy. The comparativist optimist could – and does – also point to those aspects of ongoing constitutional reform which seem to shift power away from the centre. Finally, from a sectoral point of view, the optimist might also look with approval on the essential 'awkwardness' of voluntarism suggested in Section 10.2 as an important and healthy obstacle to the malleability of the voluntary sector as a policy actor.

Each account, therefore, would be consistent with one selective reading of the evidence. The final, 'contingent realist' position that is tentatively identified in Table 10.1 sets out how the author's overall position, which tries to offer balance and nuance, differs from both these accounts and the others presented earlier. A heavy price is clearly paid in terms of elegance and parsimony by the attempt to accommodate more systematically the full range of evidence and argument reviewed in this book. But certain features of the voluntary sector, and the evolving relations between the state and the voluntary sector while necessarily adding layers of complexity seem to be simply too consequential to sidestep if the goal of the analyst is to begin to understand the richness and diversity of the current situation.

First and most obviously, the account is 'realist' in pointing to the failures as well as the strengths of the voluntary sector – in the context of a realization of the failures and strengths of other sectors too. Implicit in the attempt to systematically survey the impact of this sector from a comparative perspective has been the goal to present voluntary organizations in as balanced a light as possible. Existing approaches have been too hasty to portray the state in either a uniformly positive light or in a universally negative light (especially those to the left of Table 10.1) – and too reticent to point to the limitations of voluntary action, particularly in the 'pure' state, or under the 'golden age' conditions, to which they refer.

Second, received approaches have not adequately come to terms with another aspect of diversity: the highly variegated nature of the modern state in Britain, and consequently the multiplicity of relationships at stake. Of the perspectives reviewed above, the neo-Marxist account and social democratic optimist analysis move furthest in this direction. Each acknowledges the significance of central, local and (now) regional state differentiation, and points to the relevance of inter-sectoral alliances as a countervailing source of influence to the concentration of power in the unitary British state.

However, the analysis presented here has pointed to a number of further sources of highly relevant intra-state complexity. Recognition of this situation was indeed one of the rationales for distinguishing the approach taken in this book from others reported in the international third sector literature in Chapter 1. The argument was further developed because of its relevance to understanding voluntary sector impact in Chapter 5. Sources of variation within and between policy fields, it will be recalled, have included contrasting policy legacies (including unintended consequences); differences in the intra-state balance of policy responsibilities; and the contrasting priorities of different actors within the state, particularly politicians, on the one hand, and bureaucrats, on the other. These were elaborated in some detail not just for expository purposes, but because they have had real consequences for the recent and current development of voluntary sector policy. These field-specific temporal and internal dimensions of intra-state differentiation are as important, this book suggests, as spatial factors.

The adjective 'contingent' used by the author to distinguish the perspective taken in this book from the others reviewed here is in part a reflection of this belief about how little we actually know about the current and recent applications of power in this Byzantine institutional landscape. It is also a useful marker when we are considering what we can and cannot say about the monster's prognoses. It underlines the essential relevance of a theme which has permeated this book: diversity and variation. It is the case that all but the fatalist account recognizes the significance of the internal diversity of the voluntary sector, at least at certain points of development, and count this as valuable in its own right. But this consideration is not really adequately built into the actual theoretical frameworks deployed. The contingent approach, however, sees diversity as fundamental. By distinguishing between vertical and horizontal policy, and by attending systematically and explicitly to the co-existence of a wide range of varieties of organization, the goal has been to keep this feature at the centre of analysis throughout.

Moving from diagnosis to prognosis is therefore treated as deeply problematic by this account. Yet at this moment caution is reinforced by an additional difficulty: the lack of clear parameters for future policy content. At the time of writing, the central state's 'horizontal' intentions are evident in very broad recommendations from the Strategy Unit and the Treasury for reform. Not unnaturally, the thinking expressed there could be said to be most in line with that set out here as social democratic optimist. However, the actual political decisions concerning which of these recommendations will be put into practice are yet to be made, and the crucial minutiae of institutional design have yet to be settled. It will only be when key political decisions pursuant to these reviews have been taken, and when those in positions of authority within the state begin to reveal their true colours through how they actually interpret and implement those political decisions, that we will get a better sense of what the 'horizontal' future really holds.

Notes

1 The idea of labelling the voluntary sector in this way came from Colin Rochester, one of the editors of the volume in which the author jointly contributed a chapter analysing voluntary sector definitions and typologies (Kendall and Knapp, 1995). The source of the original expression is unclear, but was coined by novelist Henry James in describing the modern novel, while also featuring in children's nursery rhymes.

2 As noted above, in the latest year for which comparative data are available (1995), we know that voluntary sector volunteers were still outnumbering their paid counterparts in full-time equivalent terms under a broad definition. Under a narrow definition, the distribution is yet more skewed towards the former. Furthermore, in all other formal sectors, paid employees completely dominate, even if there is a significant amount of volunteering in particular activities. (In the public sector case, this would most prominently include volunteering in maintained school governance, hospital support, via local authority social service departments, and the local magistracy (Davis Smith, 1998).) Finally, there is financial voluntarism. While we have seen that private donations are no longer the voluntary sector's primary source of income according to the definitions used here, they are proportionately more significant than in the public sector or the for-profit sector (Glennerster, 2003).

3 Although of course the principles of charity law have been adopted by many countries with historic ties to Britain, they have been adapted according to national circumstances. Charity law in England and Wales in turn has evolved in its own direction since its 'export' to other countries. Thus, there are significant differences in the policies and practices of charity law between charity law and common law inheritance countries, as well as the better known contrasts which can be drawn

between this group of countries, on the one hand, civil law countries, on the other, and mixed cases (see Salamon and Toepler, 2001).

4   I am grateful to Perri 6 for suggesting that I set the assumptions deployed in this study alongside the explicit theories of the state identified – a comparison I had initially resisted as incommensurate given the different levels of analysis involved. However, all approaches necessarily involve assumptions, and it is important to be as explicit as possible about what is involved. I have stopped short, however, of following Perri's further recommendation that prognoses be developed based upon the contingent realist analysis. This reluctance partly reflects limitations of space, but also follows as a consequence of the approach itself. As will be emphasised below, the extraordinary variety and complexity exposed by this book's analysis cautions against general prediction. In addition, at the time of writing there is a lack of clarity regarding the concrete future intentions of central government, and a deeply problematic relationship between such intentions and actual implementation practices.

5   The attentive reader may notice that the only theoretical perspective that appears in both Table 10.1 and the international third sector theories referred to in Chapter 1 (Box 1.1) is Wolch's neo-Marxist approach. Hansmann's approach does not seriously attend to the role of the state (other than as background enforcer of the nondistribution constraint). The other approaches make heroic simplifications which portray the state inappropriately, if the aim is to understand the richness of voluntary sector–state relations (rather than deductively simplify for modelling purposes). In particular, Weisbrod (1975) and James (1987) implicitly treat the state as a passive aggregator of voter and interest group pressures, and Ben-Ner and Van-Hoomissen (1993) seem to carry these assumptions over in their theoretical synthesis. Salamon and Anheier (1998) read voluntary sector–state relations as essentially the stable outcome of strategic bargaining between classes over welfare state design, and we have already pointed to numerous difficulties with that approach in the opening chapter. The Salamon (1987) approach comes closest to accommodating the complexity in which we are interested, but verges on the Panglossian, tending to portray voluntary sector–state relations as likely to evolve constructively and to mutual advantage.

6   Only those not receiving any financial support at all from the state, Green and Whelan argue, deserve tax breaks at all. Social progress should be fostered by a renewed 'publicly spirited habit' expressed by participation in such independently funded organizations, rather than public policy per se. Organizations should not look to the state for more than the most minimal basic standards of transparency and probity. Rather, it is argued, they should form a self-financed movement seeking to foster a new version of citizenship, fostering the 'right' habits of mutual respect and practical help (Green, 1996: 137–41).

Appendix 1 Quantitative statistical sources for country comparisons

The statistical estimates relating to the BNS, BVS and the NVS were established primarily through secondary analysis of a wide range of large datasets at the Personal Social Services Research Unit, London School of Economics and Political Science. In each case, detailed re-analysis of data collected for other purposes was undertaken, and careful account was taken of the varying approaches to coverage and definition. Two of the most important sources, which were exhaustively and comprehensively examined, were:

- Surveys of registered charities conducted in 1992/3 and 1995/6, and subsequent analyses of registered charities' accounts, conducted by the National Council for Voluntary Organizations (NCVO) on behalf of the Office for National Statistics (ONS). This survey, with the sample stratified according to size of total income, has been used by the ONS as its primary source for constructing estimates in the national accounts relating to the economic contribution of what are referred to as 'general charities', in turn defined as part of the wider 'nonprofit sector serving households' set of entities within the personal sector. The most recent survey involved a gross sample size of 4,038, generating 1,271 useable returns. For further details, see Hems and Passey (1998).
- The UK Labour Force Survey, undertaken by ONS, which is the primary source of labour market data in the UK. Pooled data for 1995 relating to around 2,000 people who (on a subjective definition) were employed in the voluntary sector (out of a total sample of 96,000 households included overall) were analysed. For a detailed account of the first attempt to compare and contrast employment in the voluntary, public and private sectors using pooled data for 1995 to 1997 from this source, see Almond and Kendall (2000). A less extensive report on trends in voluntary sector employment between 1993 and 1997 using data from this survey involving the ONS's own tabulations is Zimmeck (1998).

In addition, a special re-analysis of a major survey of volunteering undertaken in 1997 by the National Centre for Volunteering was conducted on behalf of PSSRU by BMRB. This survey (Davis Smith, 1998) yielded data on 1,598 individuals, drawn from a random sample of 3,276 postal addresses. Data were grossed using 1995 UK population data for compatibility with the other sources used.

These data fed into estimates across a number of fields of voluntary activity in a variety of ways. In addition, specialist data sources were used in developing estimates for particular fields. Some of the most important of these were the Museum and Galleries Commission's DOMUS database; published and unpublished data from the Department for Education and Employment, the Higher Education Statistical Agency, the Further Education Funding Council, and the Office for Science and Technology; data reported in Laing's Review of Private Health Care (Laing and Buisson, 1996); and the Housing Corporation database. Where these databases only provided data on England, or England and Wales, equivalent data were sought for Scotland, and for Northern Ireland (with the help of the Northern Ireland Council for Voluntary Action (NICVA)) through a range of official and other sources, in order to build consolidated UK estimates.

It was possible to construct estimates of income, expenditure, paid employment and volunteering by creatively combining these and other sources of information in all fields, with the exception of financial and paid employment estimates for recreation (part of the wider category culture and recreation). To estimate the scale and scope of activity in this field, special surveys were undertaken of sports and social clubs in three locales: Kent (the basis for estimates in Great Britain, apart from London); London; and Northern Ireland (undertaken by NICVA). In total, survey questionnaires were sent to some 2,800 organizations identified through a combination of court petty sessional divisions (licensed clubs registered under section 40 of the Licensing Act, 1964), *Yellow Pages*, and local intelligence. After follow-up, the surveys yielded returns from just over 300 organizations – a low response rate, but in line with our realistic expectations for this type of organization.

Finally, the only subcategory identified in the ICNPO not fully covered in our estimates was political parties. These organizations' paid staff and volunteers are included for the category 'law, advocacy and politics' for the BNS in 1995, using the sources referred to above. However, it was not possible to include their income and expenditure in the financial estimates.

Appendix 2 Interviews and focus groups in specific fields

Field of activity	Qualitative evidence base: stakeholder types
Social housing (Chapter 7)	Interviews were undertaken in 1997. Included were a senior policy officer from the Housing Corporation; a senior officer from a London borough public sector housing authority; a founding member of a group campaigning for tenants' rights; a spokesperson from housing associations' representative body; the chief executive of a large, well-established Northern housing association; and a London-based for-profit supplier of social housing. Our focus group (led by LSE housing) comprised representatives of central government (DETR); a Northern public sector housing authority; a professional housing institute; and senior officers from a large generalist housing association; a homeless people campaigning organization representative; and a historically pro-poor London-based housing association. Additionally, as part of the quasi-Delphi review process, many of these participants commented on an earlier draft of this chapter.
Care and support for older people (Chapter 8)	Interviews were conducted in 1999, and involved two 'experts' currently working predominantly in the public sector; three in the for-profit sector; and six in the voluntary sector. In the language of the types identified in Box 8.2, this included three older people service and policy specialists; two nonprofit social entrepreneurs; and one pensioner's group representative. This balance was adopted in an attempt to complement what was known from the extensive corpus of existing research. A report was drafted based upon this fieldwork and circulated for comment and feedback in 2001. Chapter 8 draws heavily upon that report and the 'quasi-Delphi' review process.

Environmental action (Chapter 9)	Stakeholders interviewed in 1998 included, from central government, senior officers from the Environment Agency and the Countryside Commission; from local government, a senior officer responsible for consultation with the public and the development of Local Agenda 21 in a south east of England borough council; and four expert interviewees currently in, or with exceptional experience of, voluntary sector environmental organizations. Two focus groups took place in November 1998, with the assistance of the Centre for the Study of Social and Political Movements, University of Kent. The first involving an officer with responsibility for land management contracts and the development of Local Agenda 21 in a county council, and two senior representatives from the voluntary sector. The second included representatives from three mainstream voluntary sector organizations, and one direct action activist. Additionally, in the quasi-Delphi review process, many of these participants commented on a draft of a report upon which this chapter is based. Note that three of the 'Big 4' organizations described in Box 9.1 were represented in interviews and/or focus groups. The main omission at the interview and focus group stage was the for-profit sector. However, as part of the quasi-Delphi review, two respondents from the corporate for-profit energy and natural resources sector were interviewed, and commented on the draft report. Their views have been taken into account in the final version of this chapter.

Bibliography

Active Community Unit (2002) Personal communication, November 2002.

Addy, T. and Scott, D. (1987) *Fatal Impacts? The MSC and Voluntary Action*, Manchester: William Temple Foundation.

ADSS and National Centre for Volunteering (2001) 'At one with volunteers: joint statement on volunteering in social services', Association of Directors of Social Services, National Centre for Volunteering, Community Service Volunteers, National Volunteer Managers Forum, London: the Home Office and Department of Health.

Ahmad, W. (ed) (1996) *'Race' and Community Care*, Buckingham: Open University Press.

Alcock, P., Harrow, J., Macmillan, R., Vincent, J. and Perarson, S. (1999) *Making Funding Work: Funding Regimes and Local Voluntary Organizations*, York: South Yorkshire Community Foundation/Joseph Rowntree Foundation.

Aldridge, S., Halpern, D. and Fitzpatrick, S. (2002) 'Social capital', draft discussion paper, London: Performance and Innovation Unit (now Strategy Unit), downloadable from http://www.strategy.gov.uk/2001/futures/attachments/socialcapital.pdf

Allen, I., Hogg, D. and Peace, S. (1992) *Elderly People: Choice, Participation and Satisfaction*, London: Policy Studies Institute.

Almond, S. and Kendall, J. (1998) 'Unpublished analysis of trends in passive and active membership based upon the British Household Panel Survey', London: Personal Social Services Research Unit, LSE Health and Social Care.

Almond, S. and Kendall, J. (2000a) 'Taking the employees' perspective seriously: an Initial United Kingdom cross-sectoral comparison', *Non-Profit and Voluntary Sector Quarterly*, 29(2): 205–31.

Almond, S. and Kendall, J. (2000b) 'Paid employment in the self-defined voluntary sector in the late 1990s: an initial description of patterns and trends', Civil Society Working Paper Number 7, London: Centre for Civil Society, London School of Economics and Political Science, downloadable from http://www.lse.ac.uk/collections/CCS/pdf/CSWP_7_final.PDF

Almond, S. and Kendall, J. (2001a) 'Low pay in the UK: the case for a three sector comparative approach', *Annals of Public and Co-operative Economics* 72(1): 45–76.

Almond, S. and Kendall, J. (2001b) Quality of UK third sector employment in comparative perspective, paper presented at the 29th Annual Conference of ARNOVA, New Orleans, November.

Almond, S. and Kendall, J. (2002) 'Trends in third sector employment, 1995–2000', Centre for Civil Society Working Paper 22, London: Centre for Civil Society, London School of Economics and Political Science, downloadable from http://www.lse.ac.uk/collections/CCS/pdf/CSWP_22_final.PDF

Amin, A. (2002) *Placing the Social Economy*, London: Routledge.

Anheier, H.K., Glasius, M. and Kaldor, M. (eds) (2001) *Global Civil Society 2001*, Oxford: Oxford University Press.

Anheier, H.K. and Kendall, J. (eds) (2001) *Third Sector Policy at the Crossroads: An International Nonprofit Analysis*, London: Routledge.

Anheier, H.K. and Kendall, J. (2002) 'Trust and voluntary organizations: three theoretical approaches', *British Journal of Sociology* 53(3): 343–62.

Anheier, H.K. and Seibel, W. (2001) *The Nonprofit Sector in Germany*, Manchester: Manchester University Press.

Atkin, K. (1996) 'An opportunity for change: voluntary sector provision in a mixed economy of care', in W. Ahmad (ed.) *'Race' and Community Care*, Buckingham: Open University Press.

Baldock, J. and Ungerson, C. (1993) 'Consumer perceptions of an emerging mixed economy of care', in A. Evers and I. Svetlik (eds) *Balancing Pluralism: New Welfare Mixes in Care for the Elderly*, Aldershot: Avebury.

Banks, J. and Tanner, S. (1997) *The State of Donation: Household Gifts to Charity, 1974–1996*, Institute for Fiscal Studies Commentary 62, London: Institute for Fiscal Studies.

Banks, J. and Tanner, S. (1999) 'Patterns in household giving: evidence from UK data', *Voluntas* 10(2): 167–78.

Barclay, L. (1982) *Social Workers: Their Roles and Tasks*, London: National Institute for Social Work and Bedford Square Press.

Barker, D. (1993) 'Values and volunteering', in J. Davis Smith (ed.) *Volunteering in Europe: Opportunities and Challenges for the 1990s*, Voluntary Action Research Second series Paper No. 4, Berkhamsted: The Volunteer Centre.

Barlett, W. and Le Grand, J. (1993) *Quasi-Markets and Social Policy*, Basingstoke: Macmillan.

Batsleer, J. (1992) 'Remuneration policies and employment practices: some dilemmas in the voluntary sector', in J. Batsleer, C. Cornforth and R. Paton (eds) *Issues in Voluntary and Non-Profit Management*, Wokingham: Addison Wesley.

Batsleer, J. (1995) 'Management and organization', in J. Davis Smith, C. Rochester and R. Hedley (eds) *An Introduction to the Voluntary Sector*, London: Routledge.

Bauld, L., Chesterman, J., Davies, B., Judge, K. and Mangalore, R. (2000) *Caring for Older People: An Assessment of Community Care in the 1990s*, Aldershot: Ashgate.

Beck, U. (1997) 'Global risk politics', in M. Jacobs (ed.) *Greening the Millenium*, London: Blackwell.

Beckford, J. (1991) 'Great Britain: voluntarism and sectoral interests', in R. Wuthnow (ed.) *Between States and Markets: The Voluntary Sector in Comparative Perspective*, New Jersey: Princeton University Press.

Beder, S. (1998) *Global Spin: The Corporate Assault on Environmentalism*, Totnes: Green Books.

Ben-Ner, A. and Van Hoomissen, T. (1993) 'Nonprofit organizations in the mixed economy: a demand and supply analysis', in A. Ben-Ner and B. Gui (eds) *The Nonprofit Sector in the Mixed Economy*, Michigan: University of Michigan Press.

Bernard, M. and Phillips, J. (eds) (1998) *The Social Policy of Old Age: Moving Into the 21st Century*, London: Centre for Policy on Ageing.

Beveridge, Lord (1948) *Voluntary Action*, London: George Allen & Unwin.

BGOP Steering Committee (2000) *All Our Futures: The Reports of the Better Government for Older People Programme*, Wolverhampton: Better Government For Older People Programme.

Billis, D. (2001) 'Tackling social exclusion: the contribution of voluntary organizations', in M. Harris and C. Rochester (eds) *Voluntary Organizations and Social Policy in Britain: Perspectives on Change and Choice*, Basingstoke: Palgrave.

Billis, D. and Glennerster, H. (1998) 'Human services and the voluntary sector: towards a theory of comparative advantage', *Journal of Social Policy* 27(1): 79–98.

Bines, W., Kemp, P., Please, C. and Radley, C. (1993) *Managing Social Housing*, London: HMSO.

Birchall, J. (2001) *The New Mutualism in Public Policy*, London: Routledge.

Blackmore, A. (2000) 'Local government reform and the voluntary sector', in *Dimensions 2000 Volume 1: Income from Government Sources*, West Malling: Charities Aid Foundation

Blackmore, A. (2002) The Added Value of the Voluntary Sector: A Discussion Paper, prepared for seminar 8 April, London: National Council for Voluntary Organizations.

Blair, T. (1998) *The Third Way: New Politics for the New Century*. Fabian Pamphlet 588, London: Fabian Society.

Blair, T. (2002) 'Foreword' by the Prime Minister in Strategy Unit, *Private Action, Public Benefit: A Review of Charities and the Wider Not-for-Profit Sector*, London: Cabinet Office Strategy Unit, downloadable from www.strategy-unit.gov.uk

Bloor, K. (no date) 'Comparing national compacts', Working Paper 2: 'Evaluating local compacts', Brighton and Lincoln: Health and Social Policy Research Centre, University of Brighton and Policy Studies Research Centre, University of Lincolnshire and Humberside.

Blunkett, D. (2001) *Politics and Progress: Renewing Democracy and Civil Society*, London: Politico's Publishing.

Bornat, J., Johnson, J., Pereira, C., Pilgrim, D. and Williams, F. (eds) (1997) *Community Care: A Reader*, 2nd edn, Basingstoke: Macmillan Press in association with the Open University.

Brenton, M. (1985) *The Voluntary Sector in British Social Services*, Harlow: Longman.

Bridgewood, A. (2000) *People Aged 65 and Over*, London: Office for National Statistics, London.

Broady, M. and Hedley, R. (1989) *Working Partnerships: Community Development in Local Authorities*, London: Bedford Square Press.

Brown, G. (2000) *Civic Society in Modern Britain: The 17th Arnold Goodman Charity Lecture*, London: The Smith Institute.

BTCV (no date) 'People working for a better environment: the strategy to the millennium 1996–2000', London: British Trust for Conservation Volunteers.

Buckle, M. and Thompson, J. (1996) *The UK Financial System: Theory and Practice*, 3rd edn, Manchester: Manchester University Press.

Bulmer, M. (1987) *The Social Basis of Community Care*, London: Allen & Unwin.

Burgess, G. (2000) 'Questioning the motives of environmentalism', Podium: from a talk given by the environmental activist and wind-pump manufacturer to the Bath Philosophical Society, *The Independent*, 4 August.

Burgess, J., Harrison, C.M. and Filius, P. (1998) 'Environmental communication and the cultural politics of environmental citizenship', *Environmental and Planning*, 30: 1445–60.

Byrne, P. (1997) *Social Movements in Britain*, London: Routledge.

Cabinet Office (1999) *Modernising Government*, Cm. 4310, London: The Stationery Office.

Cabinet Office Performance and Innovation Unit (2000) *Winning the Generation Game: Improving Opportunities for People Aged 50–65 in Work and Community Activity*, London: Cabinet Office.

Cahill, M. (2001) *The Environment and Social Policy*, Eastbourne: Gildredge.

Cameron, H. (2001) 'Social capital in Britain: are Hall's membership figures a reliable guide?', London: Centre for Civil Society, London School of Economics.

Cameron, L., Harrison, L., Burton, P. and Marsh, A. (2001) 'Crossing the Housing Divide', *Foundations report*, York: Joseph Rowntree Foundation.

Caritasdata (2001) *The Top 3000 Charities 2000*, London: Caritasdata.

Carroll, M. and Harris, M. (1998) 'Actions speak louder: volunteer participation in campaigning agencies', Working Paper 21, London: Centre for Voluntary Organization.

Carrington, D. (2002) 'The Compact – the challenge of implementation', paper prepared for the Voluntary and Community Research Section, Home Office, tabled at third annual Compact review meeting, House of Commons, 29th April, downloadable from http://www.thecompact.org.uk/ and at http://www.homeoffice.gov.uk/acu/compmeet.htm

Carter, C. and John, P. (1992) *The New Accord: Promoting Constructive Relations Between Central and Local Government*, York: Joseph Rowntree Foundation.

Cartwright, A. and Morris, D. (2001) 'Charities and the "New Deal": compact relations?' *Journal of Social Welfare and Family Law* 23(1): 65–78.

Casey, T. (no date) 'Social capital and regional development in Britain', undated working paper.

Centre for Housing Research (1989) *The Nature and Effectiveness of Housing Management in England: a Report to the Department of the Environment*, Glasgow: Centre for Housing Research, University of Glasgow.

Charities Aid Foundation (2000) *CAF's Top 500 Fundraising Charities: Dimensions 2000, Volume 2*, West Malling: Charities Aid Foundation.

Chesterman, M. (1979) *Charities, Trusts and Social Welfare*, London: Weidenfeld and Nicolson.

Church, C. and Young, S. (2000) 'The future of Local Agenda 21 after the Local Government Act of July 2000: a discussion paper', EPRU Paper No. 1/00, Manchester: European Policy Research Unit, Department of Government, University of Manchester.

CIRIEC (2000) *The Enterprises and Organizations of the Third System: A Strategic Challenge for Employment*, International Center for Research and Information on the Public and Cooperative Economy, Liege: University of Liege.

Citizen's Audit (2002) http://www.shef.ac.uk/~pol/citizenaudit/findings.htm

Compact Working Group (2002) 'Futurebuilders fund: proposals for boosting sector's public service delivery capacity (6 November)', London: Compact Working Group, downloadable from http://www.thecompact.org.uk/

Commissioning and Performance Team (2002) 'Degrees of separation: are local authorities changing their commissioning behaviour?' PSSRU Research Summary 24, July, London: Personal Social Services Research Unit, LSE Health and Social Care.

Commission on the Future of the Voluntary Sector (1996) *Meeting the Challenge of Change: Voluntary Action in the 21st Century*, the Report of the Commission on the Future of the Voluntary Sector chaired by Nicholas Deakin (the 'Deakin Commission'), London: NCVO Publications.

Comparative Nonprofit Sector Project (2002) http://www.jhu.edu/~cnp/

Cooke, S. (2000) *Welfare to Work: A Voluntary Sector Perspective*. London: National Council for Voluntary Organizations.

Cope, H. (1999) *Housing Associations: Policy and Practice*, Basingstoke: Macmillan.

Cotgrove, S.F. (1982) *Catastrophe or Cornucopia: The Environment, Politics and the Future*, Chichester: John Wiley.

Counsel and Care (1997) *The Fullness of Time: How Homes for Older People Can Respond to their Residents' Need for Wholeness and a Spiritual Dimension to Care*, report written by D. Regan and J. Smith, London: Counsel and Care.

Counsel and Care (1998) *Older People in Control*, report written by L. Bright, J. Hollands and J. Smith, London: Counsel and Care.

Craig, G. and Warburton, D. (2001) 'Willing partners? Voluntary and community associations in the democratic process', paper presented at the Social Policy Association Conference, Belfast, July.

Craig, G., Taylor, M, Wilkinson, M. and Bloor, K with Monro, S. and Syed, A. (2002) *Contract or Trust? The Role of Compacts in Local Governance*, Bristol: Policy Press.

Cunningham, I. (1999) 'Managing employee relations in the voluntary sector – a difficult case for personnel', paper presented at a conference 'Human Resources for Development: People and Performance', Hume Hall, University of Manchester, June.

Cunningham, I. (2000) 'Prospects for union growth in the UK voluntary sector: the impact of the Employment Relations Act 1999', *Industrial Relations Journal* 31(3): 192–205.

Cutt, J. and Murray, V. (2000) *Accountability and Effectiveness Evaluation in Nonprofit Organisations*, London: Routledge.

Dahrendorf, R. (2001) *Challenges to the Voluntary Sector*, London: 18th Arnold Goodman Lecture.

Dalton, R. J. (1990) *The Green Rainbow: Environmental Groups in Western Europe*, New Haven: Yale University Press.

Davies, B. and Challis, D. (1986) *Matching Resources to Needs in Community Care: An Evaluated Demonstration of a Long-Term Care Model*, Aldershot: Gower.

Davis Smith, J. (1998) *The 1997 National Survey of Volunteering*, London: Institute for Volunteering Research.

Deakin, N. (1994) *The Politics of Welfare: Continuity and Change*, Hemel Hemstead: Harvester Wheatsheaf.

Deakin, N. (1995) 'The perils of partnership', in J. Davis Smith, R. Hedley and C. Rochester (eds), *Introduction to the Voluntary Sector*, London: Routledge.

Deakin, N. (2001) *In Search of Civil Society*, Basingstoke: Palgrave.

Deakin, N. (2002) 'Public–private partnerships: a UK case study', *Public Management*, 4(2): 133–47.

Deakin, N. and Edwards, J. (1993) *The Enterprise Culture and the Inner Cities*, London: Routledge.

Dekker, P. and van den Broek, A. (1998) 'Civil society in comparative perspective: involvement in voluntary associations in North America and Western Europe', *Voluntas* 9(1): 11–38.

Department for Work and Pensions (2002) 'First release: New Deal for young employed people and long term unemployed people aged 25+: Statistics to March 2002', Sheffield: Information Centre, Analytical Services Division, Department for Work and Pension.

Department of Environment, Transport and the Regions (1998) *SRB Challenge Fund Guidance Manual*, London: DETR.

Department of Environment, Transport and the Regions (1998) *Modern Local Government. In Touch with the People*, London: DETR.

Department of Health and Social Security (1981) *Growing Older*, London: HMSO.

Department of Health (1999) *The NHS Plan: The Government's Response to the Royal Commission on Long Term Care*, Cm, 4818–II, London: The Stationery Office.

Department of National Heritage (1996) *Raising the Voltage: The Government's Response to the Deakin Commission Report*, London: Department of National Heritage.

Dewson, S. and Eccles, J. (2000) *The New Deal for Young Unemployed People: Final Report*, London: National Council for Voluntary Organizations.

Diani, M. and Donati, P. (1999) 'Organizational change in western European environmental groups: a framework for analysis' *Environmental Politics* 8(1): 13–34.

Dixon, J. (1998) 'Nature conservation', in P. Lowe and S. Ward (eds) *British Environmental Policy and Europe: Politics and Policy in Transition*, London: Routledge.

Douglas, J. (1983) *Why Charity? The Case for a Third Sector*, Beverly Hills and London: Sage.

Driver, S. and Martell, L. (1997) 'New Labour's communitarianisms', *Critical Social Policy* 52: 27–46.

Driver, S., and Martell, L. (1998) *New Labour: Politics After Thatcherism*, Cambridge: Polity Press.

DTZ Consulting (1998) *Rents in Local Authority and Registered Social Landlord Sectors*, London: Report to the Local Government Association and National Housing Federation.

Dunn, A. (ed.) (2000) *The Voluntary Sector, the State and the Law*, Oxford: Hart Publishing.

Dwyer, J.C., and Hodge, D. (1996) *Countryside in Trust: Land Management by Conservation Recreation and Amenity Organizations*, Chichester: Wiley and Sons.

Edwards, M. (1999) *Future Positive: International Co-operation in the Twenty-First Century*, London: Earthscan.

Edwards, M. (2001) *NGO Rights and Responsibilities: A New Deal for Global Governance*, London: Foreign Policy Centre.

Ehrenberg, J. (1999) *Civil Society: The Critical History of an Idea*, New York: New York University Press.

Emsley, I. (1986) *The Development of Housing Associations with Special Reference to London*, London: Garland Publishing.

Etzioni, A. (1995) *The Spirit of Community: Rights, Responsibilities and the Communitarian Agenda*, London: Fontana Press.

Evandrou, M., Falkingham, J. and Glennerster, H. (1990) 'The personal social services: everybody's poor relation and nobody's baby', in J. Hills (ed.) *The State of Welfare*, Oxford: Clarendon Press.

Evandrou, M. and Falkingham, J. (1998) 'The personal social services', in H. Glennerster and J. Hills (eds) *The State of Welfare: The Economics of Social Spending*, Oxford: Oxford University Press.

Evans, R. (1998a) *Innovation and Good Practice; Grants Available from the Housing Corporation*, Source Advice 3, London: Housing Corporation.

Evans R. (1998b) *Housing Plus and Urban regeneration: What works, How, Why and Where?* London: Institute for Urban Affairs in association with the Housing Corporation.

Evans, M., Glennerster, H. and Hills, J. (1998) *The State of Welfare II: The Economics of Social Spending*, Oxford: Oxford University Press.

Evers, A. (1995) 'Part of the welfare mix: the third sector as an intermediate area between market, economy, state and community', *Voluntas* 6(2): 159–182.

Ferlie, E., Challis, D. and Davies, B. (1989) *Efficiency-Improving Innovations in Social Care for the Elderly*, Aldershot: Gower.

Forder, J., Kendall, J., Knapp, M., Matosevic, T., Hardy, B., Ware, T. and Wistow, G.

(2000) *Prices, Contracts and Domiciliary Care*, unpublished report from PSSRU and Nuffield Institute to the Department of Health, filed internally as DP 1609/2, London: PSSRU at LSE, London School of Economics.

Forestry Commission (2001) *National Inventory of Woodland and Trees England*, Edinburgh: The Forestry Commission.

Foster, V. (2001) *The Price of Virtue: The Economic Value of the Charitable Sector*, Cheltenham: Edward Elgar.

Fox, W. (1995) *Towards a Transpersonal Ecology: Developing New Foundations for Environmentalism*, Totnes: Resurgence.

Garner, R. (2000) *Environmental Politics: Britain, Europe and the Global Environment*, Basingstoke: Macmillan.

Gaskin, K. and Davis Smith, J. (1995) *A New Civic Europe? A Study of the Extent and Role of Volunteering*, London: Volunteer Centre UK.

George, V. (1996) 'The future of the welfare state', in V. George and P. Taylor-Gooby (eds.) *European Welfare Policy: Squaring the Welfare Circle*, Basingstoke: Macmillan.

Gerard, D. (1983) *Charities in Britain: Conservatism or Change*, London: Bedford Square Press.

Giddens, A. (1998) *The Third Way: The Renewal of Social Democracy*, Oxford: Polity Press.

Ginn, J. (1996) 'Grey power: Age-based organizations' response to structured inequalities', in D. Taylor (ed.) *Critical Social Policy: A Reader*, London: Sage.

Ginn, J. and Arber, S. (1999) 'The politics of old age in the UK', in A. Walker and G. Naegele (eds) *The Politics of Old Age in Europe*, Buckingham: Open University Press.

Glass, T.A. de Leon, C.M., Marottoli, R.A. and Berkman, L.F. (1999) 'Population-based study of social and productive activities as predictors of survival of elderly Americans', *British Medical Journal* 319: 478–83.

Glennerster, H. (2003) *Understanding the Finance of Welfare: What Welfare Costs and How to Pay for It.* Bristol: Policy Press.

Green, D. (1996) *Community Without Politics: A Market Approach To Welfare Reform*, Choices in Welfare No. 27, London: Institute for Economic Affairs.

Green, E.H.H. (2002) *Ideologies of Conservatism: Conservative Political Ideas in the Twentieth Century*, Oxford: Oxford University Press.

Grenier, P. and Wright, K. (2001) 'Social capital in Britain: An update and critique of Hall's analysis', paper presented at 30th Annual Conference of ARNOVA, November–December.

Grove-White R, (1992) 'GrossBritannien', in C. Hey, U. Brendle and H. Weinber (eds), *Umweltverbande und EG*, Frienburg: EURES – Institut fur Regionale Studien.

Grove-White R. (1997) 'Environment, risk and democracy', in M. Jacobs (ed.) *Greening the Millenium*, London: Blackwell.

Hague, W. (2000) 'Values in the twenty-first century', speech to a policy forum with Britain's faith communities, 1 November, Emmanuel Centre, London, retrieved 2 November 2000 from the internet http://www.conservatives.com/newspeeches.cfm?article_id=30

Hajer, M.A. (1995) *The Politics of Environmental Discourse: Ecological Modernisation and the Policy Process*, Oxford: Clarendon Press.

Halfpenny, P., and Lowe, D. (1994) *Individual Giving and Volunteering in Britain: Who Gives What . . . and Why?*, 7th edn, Tonbridge: Charities Aid Foundation.

Hall, P.A. (1999) 'Social capital in Britain', *British Journal of Political Science*, 29(3): 417–61.

Hannigan, J.A. (1995) *Environmental Sociology: A Social Constructionist Perspective*, London: Routledge.

Hansard, parliamentary, debates on the voluntary sector in the House of Commons and House of Lords (1996–2000) 'Voluntary sector ' (House of Commons, 26 July 1996, col 205 et seq.); 'Voluntary work' (House of Lords, 27 November 1996, col 314 et seq.); 'Charities' (House of Lords, 4 March 1998, col 1213 et seq.); 'Voluntary sector' (House of Commons, 15 June 2000, col 273 WH et seq.) downloadable from http://www.parliament.the-stationery-office.co.uk

Hansmann, H.B. (1980) 'The role of nonprofit enterprise', *Yale Law Journal* 89: 835–98.

Hardwidge, C. (2002) 'Jobs in the public and private sectors', *Economic Trends* 583: June, 39–52.

Harris, M. (1998) *Organizing God's Work: Challenges for Churches and Synagogues*, London: Macmillan.

Harris, M. and Rochester. C. (eds) (2001) *Voluntary* Organizations *and Social Policy in Britain: Perspectives on Change and Choice*, Basingstoke: Palgrave.

Harrison, M. (1998) 'Minority ethnic housing associations and local housing strategies: an uncertain future?' *Local Government Studies* 24(1): 74–89.

Harrison, M., Karmani, A., Law, I., Phillips, D. and Ravetz, A. (1996) 'Black and minority ethnic housing associations: an evaluation of the Housing Corporation's black and minority ethnic housing association strategies', Housing Management and Research Division Research Report No. 16, London: Housing Corporation.

Harvey, H.J. (1985) 'The National Trust and nature conservation: prospects for the future', *Biological Journal of the Linnean Society* 56: 231–48.

Hayden, C. and Boaz, A. (2000) *Making a Difference: Better Government for Older People Evaluation Report*, Warwick: Local Government Centre, University of Warwick.

Hedley (1995) 'Inside the voluntary sector', in J. Davis Smith, R. Hedley and C. Rochester (eds), *Introduction to the Voluntary Sector*, London: Routledge.

Held, D. McGrew, A., Goldblatt, D. and Perraton, J. (1999) *Global Transformations*, Cambridge: Polity Press.

Hemmington Scott (1994) *The Henderson Top 2000 Charities 1994*, London: Hemmington Scott Publications.

Hems, L. (2001) 'The organizational and institutional landscape of the UK wider non-profit sector', background paper prepared for Strategy Unit (2002) *Private Action, Public Benefit: A Review of Charities and the Wider Not-for-Profit Sector*, Cabinet Office Strategy Unit, London, downloadable from http://www.strategy-unit.gov.uk/2002/charity/background/OrganizationalandInstitutionalLandscape.pdf

Hems, L. (2002) Personal communication relating to the Institute for Philanthropy's UK Compact Research Programme, May, London: Institute for Philanthropy, Faculty of Laws, University College London.

Hems, L. and Passey, A. (1996) *The UK Voluntary Sector Statistical Almanac 1996*, London: NCVO Publications.

Hems, L. and Passey, A. (1998) *The UK Voluntary Sector Statistical Almanac 1998/9*, London: NCVO Publications.

Henderson. J. and Karn, V. (1985) 'Race, class and allocation of public housing in Britain', *Urban Studies* 21: 115–28.

Henderson. J. and Karn, V. (1987) *Race, Class and State Housing: Inequality and the Allocation of Public Housing*, Aldershot: Gower.

Hennessy, P. (2000) *The Prime Minister: The Office and Its Holders Since 1945*, London: Penguin.

Hennessy, P. (2001) *Whitehall*, 2nd edn, London: Pimlico.

Hills, J. (1989) 'The voluntary sector in housing: the role of British housing associations', in E. James (ed.) *The Non-Profit Sector in International Perspective*, New York: Oxford University Press.

Hills, J. (1998) 'Housing: a decent home within the reach of every family?' in H. Glennerster and J. Hills (eds) *The State of Welfare: The Economics of Social Spending*, Oxford: Oxford University Press.

Hills, J., Le Grand, J. and Piachaud, D. (eds) (2002) *Understanding Social Exclusion*, Oxford: Oxford University Press.

Hirshmann A.O. (1970) *Exit, Voice and Loyalty: Reponses to Decline in Firms, Organizations and States*, Cambridge, MA: Harvard University Press.

Hirshmann, A.O. (1986) 'Rival views of market society', in *Rival Views of Market Society and Other Recent Essays*, Harmondsworth: Viking Penguin.

Hirst, P. (1994) *Associative Democracy: New Forms of Economic and Social Governance*, Cambridge: Polity Press.

HM Treasury (1999) *Consultation Document: Review of Charity Taxation*, March 1999, London: HM Treasury.

HM Treasury (2002a) *The Role of the Voluntary and Community Sector in Service Delivery: A Cross-cutting Review*, London: Her Majesty's Treasury, downloadable from http://www.hm-treasury.gov.uk/media//AFFOO/CCRVolSec02.pdf

HM Treasury (2002b) *Service Delivery Technical Paper*, downloadable from http://www.hm-treasury.gov.uk/media//70AEC/Service%20delivery%20tech%20paper.pdf

Hobson, D. (1999) *The National Wealth: Who Gets What in Britain*, London: HarperCollins.

Home Office (1990) *Efficiency Scrutiny of Government Funding of the Voluntary Sector*, London: Home Office.

Home Office (1993) *The Individual and the Community: the Role of the Voluntary Sector*, London: Home Office and Central Office for Information.

Home Office (1998) *Compact: Getting it Right Together*, Cm 4100, London: The Stationery Office.

Home Office Research, Development and Statistics Directorate (2001) *Central Government Funding of Voluntary and Community Organizations: 1982/83 to 1999/2000*. London: Home Office.

Hood, C. (1998) *The Art of Rhetoric: Culture, Rhetoric and Public Management*, Oxford: Clarendon Press.

Housing Today (1999) 'Associations told not to go too far with new freedom', No. 121, 18 February 1999.

Hudson, B. (2000) 'Conclusion: "modernising social services": a blueprint for the new millennium?', in B. Hudson (ed.) *The Changing Role of Social Care: Research Highlights in Social Work 37*, London: Jessica Kingsley Publishers.

Hughes, B. and Wilkin, D. (1987) 'Physical care and quality of life in residential homes', *Ageing and Society* 7(4): 399–426.

Hutton, W. (1995) *The State We're In*, London: Jonathan Cape.

Inglehart, R. (1990) *Culture Shift in Advanced Industrial Society*, New Jersey: Princeton University Press.

Jacobs, M. (1997) 'The quality of life: social goods and the politics of consumption', in M. Jacobs (ed.) *Greening the Millenium*, London: Blackwell.

James, E. (1987) 'The nonprofit sector in comparative perspective', in W.W. Powell (ed.) *The Nonprofit Sector: A Research Handbook*, New Haven: Yale University Press.

Jas, P., Wilding, K., Wainright, S., Passey, A. and Hems, L. (2002) *The UK Voluntary Sector Almanac 2002*, London: NCVO Publications.

Johnston, M. (2001) *Social Capital in Britain, Europe, and the United States: Recent Evidence and Continuing Questions*. Hamilton, New York: Department of Political Science, Colgate University.

Jordan, G. and Maloney, W. (1997) *The Protest Business? Mobilizing Campaign Groups*, Manchester: Manchester University Press.

Kavanagh, S. and Knapp, M (1999) 'Cognitive disability and direct care costs for elderly people', *British Journal of Psychiatry* 174: 539–46.

Kendall, J. (1992) 'Review of Jennifer R. Wolch: the shadow state: government and voluntary sector in transition', *Voluntas* 3(2): 247–56.

Kendall, J. (2000a) 'The mainstreaming of the third sector into public policy in England in the late 1990s: whys and wherefores', *Policy and Politics* 28(4): 541–62.

Kendall, J. (2000b) 'The voluntary sector and social care for older people', in B. Hudson (ed.) *The Changing Role of Social Care: Research Highlights in Social Work* 37, London: Jessica Kingsley Publishers.

Kendall, J. (2001) 'Of knights, knaves and merchants: the case of residential care for older people in England in the late 1990s', *Social Policy and Administration*, 35(4): 360–75.

Kendall, J. and Anheier, H.K. (2001a) 'Conclusion: the nonprofit sector at the crossroads? Social, political and economic dynamics', in H.K. Anheier and J. Kendall, (eds) *Third Sector Policy at the Crossroads: An International Nonprofit Analysis*, London: Routledge.

Kendall, J. and Anheier, H.K. (2001b) 'The third sector and the European Union policy process: an initial evaluation', in H.K. Anheier and J. Kendall (eds) *Third Sector Policy at the Crossroads: An International Nonprofit Analysis*, London: Routledge.

Kendall, J. and Knapp, M.R.J. (1995) 'A loose and baggy monster: boundaries, definitions and typologies', in J. Davis Smith, R. Hedley and C. Rochester (eds), *Introduction to the Voluntary Sector*, London: Routledge.

Kendall, J. and Knapp, M. (1999) 'Evaluation and the voluntary (nonprofit) sector: emerging issues', in D. Lewis (ed.) *International Perspectives on Voluntary Action: Reshaping the Third Sector*, London: Earthscan.

Kendall, J. and Knapp, M.R.J. (1996) *The Voluntary Sector in the UK*, Manchester: Manchester University Press.

Kendall, J. and Knapp, M. (2000) 'Providers of care for older people: the experience of community care', in M. Harris and C. Rochester (eds) *Voluntary Organizations and Social Policy in Britain*, Basingstoke: Macmillan.

Kendall, J. and Knapp, M.R.J. (2000) 'Measuring the performance of voluntary organizations', *Public Management* 2(1): 106–32.

Kendall, J. and 6, P. (1994) 'Government and the voluntary sector in the United Kingdom', in S. Saxon-Harrold and J. Kendall (eds) *Researching the Voluntary Sector*, 2nd edn, London: Charities Aid Foundation.

Kendall, J., Anheier, H.K. and Potucek, M. (eds) (2000) 'Ten years after: the third sector and civil society in central and eastern Europe', *Voluntas* (special issue) 11(2).

Kendall, J., Knapp, M. and Forder, J. (2003a) 'Social care and the nonprofit sector in the Western developed world', in W.W. Powell and R. Steinberg (eds) *The Nonprofit Sector: A Research Handbook*, 2nd edn, New Haven: Yale University Press.

Kendall, J., Matosevic, T., Forder, J., Hardy, B., Knapp, M. and Ware, P. (2003b) 'The motivations of domiciliary care providers in England: New concepts, new findings', *Journal of Social Policy*, 32(3), forthcoming.

Keynes, J.M. (1947) *The General Theory of Employment, Interest and Money*, London: Macmillan.

Kingdon, J.W. (1995) *Agendas, Alternatives, and Public Policies*, New York: HarperCollins Publishers.

Klug, F. (2000) *Values for a Godless Age: The Story of the United Kingdom's New Bill of Rights*, Harmondsworth: Penguin.

Knapp, M. (1984) *The Economics of Social Care*, Basingstoke: Macmillan.

Knapp, M. (1990) 'Time is money: the costs of volunteering in Britain today', Vountary Action Research Paper No. 3, Berkhamsted: Volunteer Centre UK.

Knapp, M. and Missiakoulis, M. (1982) 'Inter-sectoral cost comparisons: day care for the elderly', *Journal of Social Policy* 11: 335–54.

Knapp, M. and Thomason, C. (2000) *Voluntary Sector Activity and Public Sector Support in Care in the Community for People with Long-Term Care Needs*, Report to the Economic and Social Research Council, London: PSSRU, London School of Economics.

Knapp, M., Robertson, E. and Thomason, C. (1987) 'Public money, voluntary action: an economic examination of public sector support of the voluntary sector', Report to the Voluntary Services Unit of the Home Office, PSSRU Discussion Paper 500, Canterbury: Personal Social Services Research Unit, University of Kent at Canterbury.

Knapp, M., Robertson, E. and Thomason, C. (1990) 'Public money, voluntary action: whose welfare', in H.K. Anheier and W. Seibel (eds) *The Nonprofit Sector: International and Comparative Perspectives*, Berlin: de Gruyter.

Knapp, M., Koutsogeorgopoulou, V. and Davis Smith, J. (1995) *Who Volunteers and Why? The Key Factors Which Determine Volunteering*, Volunteer Centre third series paper 3, London: Volunteer Centre UK.

Knapp, M., Koutsogeorgopoulou, V. and Davis Smith, J. (1996) 'Volunteer participation in community care', *Policy and Politics*, 24(2) 171–92.

Knapp, M., Hardy, B. and Forder, J. (2001) 'Commissioning for quality: ten years of social care markets in England', *Journal of Social Policy* 30(2): 283–306.

Knight, B. (1993) *Voluntary Action*, Ovingham and London: CENTRIS.

Kramer, R. (1981) *Voluntary Agencies in the Welfare State*, Berkeley: University of California Press.

Kramer, R., Lrentzen, H., Melief, W. and Pasquinelli, S. (1993) *Privatization in Four European Countries: Comparative Studies in Government–Third Sector Relationships*, New York: M.E. Sharpe.

Krishnamurthy, A., Prime, D. and Zimmeck, M. (2001) *Voluntary and Community Activities: Findings from the British Crime Survey 2000*, London: Research, Development and Statistics Directorate, Home Office.

Labour Party (1997) *Building the Future Together: Labour's Policies for Partnership between Government and the Voluntary Sector*, London: Labour Party.

Laing and Buisson (1996) *Laing's Review of Private Health Care*, London: Laing and Buisson.

Laing and Buisson (2002) *Laing's Review of Private Health Care 2002*, London: Laing and Buisson.

Lamb, R. (1997) *Promising the Earth*, London: Routledge.

Lansley, J. (1996) 'Membership participation and ideology in large voluntary organizations: the case of the national trust', *Voluntas* 7(3): 221–40.

Lane, J. (1993) *Charities in Recession: A Survey from CAF*, Tonbridge: Charities Aid Foundation.

Leach, G. (1999) *The End of Altruism? Institute of Directors Economic Comment*, London: Institute of Directors.

Leach, S. and Wilson, D. (1998) 'Voluntary groups and local authorities: rethinking the relationship', *Local Government Studies* 24(2): 1–18.

Leach, R. and Percy-Smith, J. (2001) *Local Governance in Britain*, Basingstoke: Palgrave.

Leadbetter, C. (1997) *The Rise of the Social Entrepreneur*, London: Demos.

Leadbetter, C. (2002) *Up the Down Escalator: Why the Global Pessimists are Wrong*, London: Viking.

Le Grand, J., Robinson, R. and Propper, C. (1992) *The Economics of Social Problems*, Basingstoke: Macmillan.

Le Grand, J. and Bartlett, W. (eds) (1993) *Quasi-markets and Social Policy*, Basingstoke: Macmillan.

Leat, D. (1993) *Managing Across Sectors: Similiarities and Differences Between For-Profit and Voluntary Non-Profit* Organizations, London: VOLPROF.

Leat, D. (1995) *Challenging Management: An Exploratory Study of Perceptions of Managers Who Have Moved from For-Profit to Voluntary* Organizations, London: VOLPROF.

Levin, P. (1997) *Making Social Policy: The Mechanisms of Government and Politics and How to Investigate Them*, Buckingham: Open University Press.

Lewis, H., Fletcher, P., Hardy, B., Milne, A. and Waddington, E. (1999) *Promoting Well-Being: Developing a Preventive Approach with Older People*, London: Anchor Trust.

Lewis, J. (1999) 'Reviewing the relationship between the voluntary sector and the state in Britain in the 1990s', *Voluntas* 10(3): 255–70.

Lewis, J. and Glennerster, H. (1996) *Implementing the New Community Care*, Buckingham: Open University Press.

LGMB (1997) *Independent Sector Workforce Survey 1996*, London: Local Government Management Board and Central Council for Training and Education in Social Work.

Lindblom, C. (1977) *Politics and Markets*, New York: Basic Books.

Long, T. (1998) 'The environmental lobby', in P. Lowe and S. Ward (eds) *British Environmental Policy and Europe: Politics and Policy in Transition*, London: Routledge.

London Research Centre (1998) *Housing Update* No.18 June, London.

Lowe, P. and Goyder, J. (1983) *Environmental Groups in Politics*, London: Allen & Unwin.

Lowe, P. and Ward, S. (eds) (1998) *British Environmental Policy and Europe: Politics and Policy in Transition*, London: Routledge.

Lowndes, V. and Wilson, D. (2001) 'Social capital and local governance: exploring the institutional design variable', *Political Studies*, 49: 629–47.

MacGillivray, A., Conaty, P. and Wadhams, C. (2000) *Low Flying Heroes: Micro-Enterprise Below the Radar Screen*, London: New Economics Foundation.

Maier, C.S. (editor) (1987) *Changing Boundaries of the Political: Essays on the Evolving Balance Between the State and Society, Public and Private in Europe*, Cambridge: Cambridge University Press.

Majone, G. (1989) *Evidence, Argument and Persuasion in the Policy Process*, New Haven: Yale University Press.

Maloney, W. and Jordan, G. (1997) 'The rise of protest businesses in Britain', in Jan van Deth (ed.) *Private Groups and Public Life: Social Participation, Voluntary Associations and Political Involvement in Representative Democracies*, London: Routledge.

Maloney, W., Smith, G. and Stoker, G. (2000) 'Social capital and urban governance: adding a more contextualised 'top-down' perspective', *Political Studies* 48: 802–20.

Maloney, W., Smith, G. and Stoker, G. (2001) 'Social capital and the city', in B. Edwards, M.W. Foley, and M. Diani (eds) *Beyond Tocqueville: Civil Society and the Social Capital Debate in Comparative Perspective*. Hanover, London: University Press of New England.

Malpass, P. and Murie, A. (1999) *Housing Policy and Practice*, 5th edn, Basingstoke: Macmillan.

Malpass, P. (2000) *Housing Associations and Housing Policy*, Basingstoke: Macmillan.

Malpass, P. and Mullins, D. (2002) 'Local authority housing stock transfer in the UK: from local initiative to national policy', *Housing Studies* 17(4): 673–86.

Mannion, R. and Smith, P. (1998) 'How providers are chosen in the mixed economy of care', in W. Bartlett, J.A. Roberts and J. Le Grand (eds) *A Revolution in Social Policy: Quasi-Market Reforms in the 1990s*, Bristol: Policy Press.

Martin, S. (2000) 'Implementing "best value": local public services in transition', *Public Administration* 78(1): 209–27.

Marshall, T.H. (1949) 'Voluntary Action', *Political Quarterly* 25–36.

Marshall, R. and Patterson, J. (1996) 'The role of the voluntary sector in urban nature conservation in Britain', *Local Environment* 1(3): 323–8.

Marshall, T., Woodburn, S. and Miller, J. (1997) 'Comparing the areas LOVAS SWEEP 1: Variations in size of sectors, volunteering, staff and income', LOVAS Paper 3, Local Voluntary Activity Surveys, London: Home Office, Research and Statistics Directorate.

Matosevic, T., Knapp, M., Kendall, J., Forder, J., Ware, P. and Hardy, B. (2001) *Domiciliary Care Providers in the Independent Sector*, London: Personal Social Services Research Unit, London School of Economics.

Mayo, E. and Moore, H. (2001) *The Mutual State: How Local Communities Can Run Public Services*, London: New Economics Foundation.

Mayo, M. (1994) *Communities and Caring: The Mixed Economy of Welfare*, Basingstoke: Macmillan.

McCormick, J. (1991) *British Politics and the Environment*. London: Earthscan.

Means, R. and Smith, R. (1998a) *Community Care: Policy and Practice*, 2nd edn, Basingstoke: Macmillan.

Means, R. and Smith, R. (1998b) *From Poor Law to Community Care: The Development of Welfare Services for Elderly People 1939–1971*, 2nd edn, Bristol: Policy Press.

Michael, A. (1995) 'The Labour promise to the voluntary sector', *Unity Trust Bank Financial Briefing* 7(1): 1.

Mill, J.S. (1867) *On Liberty*, Harmondsworth: Penguin.

Millais, C. (1996) 'Greenpeace solutions campaigns – closing the implementation gap', *ECOS*, 17(2).

Millstone, E. and van Zwaneberg, P. (2001) 'Politics of expert advice: lessons from the early history of the BSE saga', *Science and Public Policy*, April, 99–112.

Mitchell, I. (1999) *Isles of the West: A Hebridean Voyage*, Edinburgh: Canongate Books.

Mocroft, I. (2000) 'The survey of local authority payments to voluntary and charitable organizations', in Charities Aid Foundation *Dimensions 2000 Volume 1: Income from Government Sources*, West Malling: Charities Aid Foundation.

Moon, J. and Richardson, J. (1984) 'The unemployment industry', *Policy and Politics* 12: 391–411.

Morison, J. (2000) 'The government–voluntary sector compacts: governance, govermentability, and civil society', *Journal of Law and Society* 27(1): 98–132.

Morphet, J. (1998) 'Local authorities', in P. Lowe and S. Ward (eds) *British Environmental Policy and Europe: Politics and Policy in Transition*, London: Routledge.

Morris, D. (2000) 'Charities in the contract culture: survival of the largest?' *Legal Studies* 20(3): 409–27.

Morris, R.J. (1990) 'Clubs, societies and associations', in F.M.L. Thompson (ed.) *The Cambridge Social History of Britain, 1750–1950: Volume 3: Social Agencies and Institutions*, Cambridge: Cambridge University Press.

Mulgan, G. (1999) 'Government and the third sector: building a more equal partnership', in H.K. Anheier (ed.) *Third Sector, Third Way: Proceedings of a Policy Symposium*, organised by the LSE Centre for Civil Society, Report No. 1, Centre for Civil Society Report Series, London: Centre for Civil Society.

Mulgan, G. and Landry, C. (1995) *The Other Invisible Hand: Remaking Charity for the 21st Century*, London: Demos.

Mullins, D. (1999) 'Managing ambiguity: merger activity in the nonprofit housing sector', *International Journal of Nonprofit and Voluntary Sector Marketing* 4(4): 349–64.

Mullins, D. (2000) 'Social origins and transformations: the changing role of English housing associations', *Voluntas* 11(3): 255–76.

Mullins, D. (2002) Personal communication, November.

Mullins, D. and Riseborough, M. (2001) 'Non-profit housing agencies: "reading" and shaping the policy agenda', in M. Harris and C. Rochester (eds) *Voluntary Organizations and Social Policy in Britain*, Basingstoke: Palgrave.

Mullins, D., Latto, S., Hall, S. and Srbljanin, A. (2001) *Mapping Diversity: Registered Social Landlords, Diversity and Regulation in the West Midlands, Housing Research at CURS Number 10*, Birmingham: Centre for Urban and Regional Studies, University of Birmingham.

Murie, A. and Walker, B. (2002) 'State of the art review of evaluating performance of social landlords: final report to the Office of the Deputy Prime Minister and Her Majesty's Treasury', Birmingham: Centre for Urban and Regional Studies, University of Birmingham.

Myers, B. (1989) *Religious Services in Retirement Homes*, London: Marc Europe.

NCVO (1990) *Cause and Effect*, London: National Council for Voluntary Organizations.

NCVO (1992) *On Trust: Increasing the Effectiveness of Charity Trustees and Management Committees*, London: National Council for Voluntary Organizations.

NCVO (2000) 'Coming apart – or coming together? New findings on social participation and trust in Britain', *Research Quarterly* 11, London: National Council for Voluntary Organizations.

Neale, A. (1997) 'Organising environmental self-regulation: liberal governmentality and the pursuit of ecological modernisation, in Europe', *Environmental Politics* 6(4): 1–24.

Netten, A., Bebbington, A., Darton, R., Forder, J. and Miles, K. (1999) *1996 Survey of Care Homes for Elderly People: Final Report*, Discussion Paper 1432/2, Canterbury: Personal Social Services Research Unit, University of Kent.

Netten, A., Ryan, M., Smith, P. Skatun, D., Healey, A., Knapp, M. and Wykes, T. (2000) *The Development of a Measure of Social Care Outcome for Older People*, Discussion Paper 1690, Canterbury: Personal Social Services Research Unit, University of Kent at Canterbury.

Netten, A. (2000) Personal communication, May.

Newman, J. (2001a) *Modernising Governance: New Labour, Policy and Society*, London: Sage.

Newman, J. (2001b) 'The new public management, modernization and institutional change: disruptions, disjunctures and dilemmas', in K. McLaughlin, S.P. Osborne and E. Ferlie (eds) *New Public Management: Current Trends and Future Prospects*, London: Routledge.

Newton, K. (1997) 'Social capital and democracy', *American Behavioral Scientist* 40(5): 575–86.

NHF, National Federation of Housing Associations (1995) *People First: Housing Associations Caring in the Community*, London: NFHA.

North, D.C. (1990) *Institutions, Institutional Change and Economic Performance*, Cambridge: Cambridge University Press.

Nuffield Institute for Health Community Care Division (1998) 'Inter-agency collaboration: community care plans and planning', Update Issue 5, Leeds: Nuffield Institute for Health.

Obler, J. (1981) 'Private giving in the welfare state', *British Journal of Political Science*, 11: 17–48.

Offe, C. (1984) *Contradictions of the Welfare State*, London: Hutchinson.

Office for National Statistics (1997) *Labour Force Survey Historical Supplement 1997*, London: Office for National Statistics.

Office for National Statistics (1998) *Social Trends 1997*, London: Office for National Statistics.

Office for National Statistics (1999) *Social Focus on Older People*, London: The Stationery Office.

Office for National Statistics (2001) *Social Trends No. 31*, London: The Stationery Office.

Office of the Deputy Prime Minister (2002) *Housing Statistics Summary Number 13*, retrieved 11 December 2002 from: http://www.housing.odpm.gov.uk/statistics/publicat/summaries/013/03.htm

Oldman, C. and Quilgars, D. (1999) 'The last resort? Revisiting ideas about older people's living arrangements', *Ageing and Society* 19: 363–84.

Olson, M. (1965) *The Logic of Collective Action*, Oxford: Oxford University Press.

Olson, M. (1982) *The Rise and Decline of Nations: Economic Growth, Stagflation and Social Rigidities*, New Haven: Yale University Press.

Osborne, D. (1997) 'Making environmental policy', in M. Jacobs (ed.) *Greening the Millenium*, London: Blackwell.

Osborne, S.P. (1998) *Voluntary Organizations and Innovation in Public Services*, London: Routledge.

Osborne, S.P. (2000) 'Reformulating Wolfenden? The roles and impact of Local Development Agencies in supporting voluntary and community action in the UK', *Local Government Studies* 26(4): 23–48.

Owen, D. (1964) *English Philanthropy 1660–1960*, Cambridge, MA: Harvard University Press.

Page, D. (1993) *Building for Communities: A Study of New Housing Association Estates*, York: Joseph Rowntree Foundation.

Palmer, P. and Randall, A. (2002) *Financial Management in the Voluntary Sector: New Challenges*, London: Routedge.

Parsons, W.W. (1995) *Public Policy: An Introduction to the Theory and Practice of Policy Analysis*, Cheltenham: Edward Elgar.

Patel, N. (1999) 'Black and ethnic elderly: perspectives on long-term care', in S. Sutherland (chair), *With Respect to Old Age: Long-Term Care – Rights and Responsibilities*, Research Volume I, Cm 4192–II/1, London: HMSO.

Patel, R., Manchanda, S. and Smith, G. (1999) *Competitiveness and Social Inclusion – Investing in Third Sector Skills Development*, London: Greater London Enterprise.

Patel, R. and Elgar, J. (1999) *Partnerships for the New Deal: Playing an Active Role, A Guide*, London: National Council for Voluntary Organizations.

Paton. R. (1992) 'The social economy: value-based organizations in the wider society', in J. Batsleer, C. Cornforth and R. Paton (eds) *Issues in Voluntary and Non-profit Management*, Wokingham: Addison Welsey.

Paton, R. (2003) *Managing and Measuring Social Enterprises*, London: Sage.

Pattie, C., Seyd, P. and Whiteley, P. (2002) 'Citizenship and civic engagement: attitudes and behaviour', paper presented at Political Studies association Annual Conference, University of Aberdeen, 5–7 April.

Pennington, M. and Rydin, Y. (2000) 'Researching social capital in local environmental policy contexts', *Policy and Politics* 28(2): 33–49.

Perkin, H. (1989) *The Rise of Professional Society*, London: Routledge.

Pharoah, C. (2002) 'How much do people give to charities, and who are the donors', in C. Walker and C. Pharoah with P. Jas, A. Passey and C. Romney-Alexander (eds) *A Lot of Give: Trends in Charitable Giving in the Twenty First Century*, London: Hodder & Stoughton.

Pharoah, C. and Smerdon, M. (eds) (1998) *Dimensions of the Voluntary Sector 1998*, London: Charities Aid Foundation.

Pickard, L., Wittenberg, R., Comas-Herrera, A., Davies, B. and Darton, R. (2000) 'Relying on informal care in the new century? Informal care for elderly people in England to 2031', *Ageing and Society* 20, 745–72.

Pierson, P. (1994) *Dismantling the Welfare State? Reagan, Thatcher and the Politics of Retrenchment*, Cambridge: Cambridge University Press.

Pierson, P. (2000a) 'Not just what, but when: timing and sequence in political processes', *Studies in American Political Development* 14: 72–93.

Pierson, P. (2000b) 'Increasing returns, path dependence and the study of politics', *American Political Science Review* 94(2): 251–67.

Pinner, J., Kendall, J., Knapp, M., Fenyo, A. and 6, P. (1992) *The Voluntary Sector and the Environment: Scope, Contributions, Issues*, PSSRU Discussion Paper 864/2, University of Kent at Canterbury.

Plowden, W., Kearney, J., Williamson, A., Burt, E., Taylor, J., Green, C. and Drakeford, M. (2001) *Next Steps in Voluntary Action*, London: Centre for Civil Society, London School of Economics.

Policy Action Team 9 (1999) *Report of the Policy Action Team on Community Self-Help* (chaired by Lord Fittall), London: Active Community Unit.

Porritt, J. (1997) 'Environmental politics: the old and the new', in M. Jacobs (ed) *Greening the Millenium*, London: Blackwell.

Posnett, J. (1993) 'The resources of registered charities in England and Wales – 1990/91', in J. Kendall and S. Saxon-Harrold (eds), *Researching the Voluntary Sector*, Tonbridge: Charities Aid Foundation.

Power, A. (1993) *Hovels to High Rise: State Housing Since 1850*, London: Routledge.

Power, A. (1997) *Estates on the Edge: The Social Consequences of Mass Housing in Northern Europe*, Basingstoke: Macmillan.

Price Waterhouse (1995) *Tenants in Control: An Evaluation of Tenant-led Housing Management Organizations*, London: HMSO.

Prince's Trust and Employment Policy Institute (1998) *What Works: The New Deal for Young People*, London: The Prince's Trust.

Prochaska, F. (1990) 'Philanthropy', in F.M.L. Thompson (ed.) *The Cambridge Social History of Britain, 1750–1950: Volume 3: Social Agencies and Institutions*, Cambridge: Cambridge University Press.

Putnam, R. (1993) *Making Democracy Work: Civic Traditions in Modern Italy*, New Jersey: Princeton University Press.

Putnam, R. (2000) *Bowling Alone: The Collapse and Revival of American Community*, New York: Simon & Schuster.

Quilgars, D. (2000a) *Low Intensity Support Services: A Systematic Literature Review*, Findings, Ref 640, York: Joseph Rowntree Foundation.

Quilgars, D. (2000b) *Low Intensity Support Services: A Systematic Review of their Effectiveness*, Bristol: Policy Press.

Qureshi, H., Patmore, C., Nichola, E. and Bamford, C. (1998) *Outcomes in Community Care Practice Number 5: Overview: Outcomes of Social Care for Older People and Carers*, Social Policy Research Unit, University of York.

Randall, A. (1998) 'Taxation in charities – the way ahead', in *Baring Asset Management Top 3000 Charities 1998*, London: CaritasData limited.

Rawcliffe, P. (1998) *Environmental Pressure Groups in Transition*, Manchester: Manchester University Press.

Renshaw, J., Hampson, R., Thomason, C., Darton, R. Judge, K. and Knapp, M. (1988) *Care in the Community: The First Steps*, Aldershot: Gower.

Rentoul, J. (1995) *Tony Blair*, London: Little Brown.

Richardson, L. and Mumford, K. (2002) 'Community, neighbourhood, and social infrastructure', in J. Hills, J. Le Grand and D. Piachaud (eds) *Understanding Social Exclusion*, Oxford: Oxford University Press.

Richards, D. and Smith, M.J. (2001) 'New Labour, the constitution and reforming the state', in S. Ludham and M.J. Smith (eds) *New Labour in Government*, Basingstoke: Macmillan.

Riddell, P. (1997) 'The end of Clause IV, 1994–5', *Contemporary British History* 11(2): 24–49.

Riseborough, M. (1995) 'Housing associations: voluntary, charity or non profit bodies? An analysis of blurred boundaries', paper presented to second NCVO Researching the Voluntary Sector conference.

Robson, P., Locke, M. and Dawson, J. (1997) *Consumerism or Democracy? User Involvement in the Control of Voluntary Organizations*, Bristol: Policy Press.

Rochester, C., Hutchison, R. with Harris, M. and Keely, L. (2001) *Realising the Value of Older Volunteers? An Evaluation of the Home Office Older Volunteers Initiative*, Roehampton: Centre for Nonprofit and Voluntary Sector Management, University of Surrey, Roehampton.

Rootes, C. (1997) 'Environmental movements and green parties in western and eastern Europe', *The International Journal of Environmental Sociology*.

Rootes, C. (ed.) (1999a) *Environmental Movements: Local, National, Global*, London and Portland: Frank Cass.

Rootes, C. (1999b) 'The Europeanisation of environmentalism', revised version of paper prepared for conference L'Europe des Interets: Lobbying, Mobilisations et Espace Public Europeen, Masion Francaise and Nuffield College Oxford, October.

Rootes, C. (1999c) 'Acting globally, thinking locally? Prospects for a global environmental movement', in C. Rootes (ed.) *Environmental Movements: Local, National, Global*, London and Portland: Frank Cass.

Rootes, C. (1999d) 'Environmental movements: from the local to the global', in Rootes, C. (ed) *Environmental Movements: Local, National, Global*, London and Portland: Frank Cass.

Rootes, C. (2002) 'The transformation of environmental activism: an introduction', unpublished manuscript, Canterbury: University of Kent.

Rootes, C. and Miller, A. (2000) 'The British environmental movement: organizational field and network of organizations', paper presented to the workshop Environmental Organizations in Comparative Perspective, ECPR Joint Sessions, Copenhagen, April, corrected May.

Rootes, C., Seel, B. and Adams, D. (2000) 'The old, the new and the old new: British environmental organizations from conservationism to radical ecologism', paper presented to the workshop Environmental Organizations in Comparative Perspective, ECPR Joint Sessions, Copenhagen, April, corrected May.

Royal Commission on Long Term Care (1999) *With Respect to Old Age: Long Term Care – Rights and Responsibilities*, Cm 4192, London: The Stationery Office.

Russell, L., Scott, D. and Wilding, P. (1995) *Mixed Fortunes: The Funding of the Voluntary Sector*, Manchester: Department of Social Policy and Social Work, University of Manchester.

Sabatier, P. (editor) (1999) *Theories of the Policy Process*, Colorado: Westview Press.

Sabatier, P. and Jenkins-Smith, H. (1993) (eds) *Policy Change and Learning: An Advocacy Coalition Approach*, Boulder: Westview Press.

Salamon, L.M. (1987) 'Partners in public service: toward a theory of government-nonprofit relations', in W.W. Powell (ed.) *The Nonprofit Sector: A Research Handbook*, New Haven: Yale University Press.

Salamon, L.M. (1995) *Partners in Public Service*, Baltimore: Johns Hopkins Press.

Salamon, L.M. (2001) 'The nonprofit sector at a crossroads: the case of America', in H.K. Anheier and J. Kendall (eds) *Third Sector Policy at the Crossroads: An International Nonprofit Analysis*, London: Routledge.

Salamon, L.M. and Anheier, H.K. (eds) (1997) *Defining the Nonprofit Sector: A Cross-National Analysis*, Manchester: Manchester University Press.

Salamon, L.M. and Anheier, H.K. (1998) 'Social origins of civil society: explaining the nonprofit sector cross-nationally', *Voluntas* 9(3): 213–48.

Salamon, L.M., Anheier, H.K. and associates (1999) 'Civil society in comparative perspective', in L.M. Salamon, H.K. Anheier, R. List, S. Toepler, S.W. Sokolowski and associates (1999) *Global Civil Society: Dimensions of the Nonprofit Sector*, Baltimore: Johns Hopkins Center for Civil Society Studies, downloadable from http://www.jhu.edu/~ccss/pubs/books/gcs/

Salamon, L.M., Hems, L.C. and Chinnock, K. (2000a) 'The nonprofit sector: for what and for whom?' Working Papers of the Johns Hopkins Comparative Nonprofit Sector Project 37, Baltimore: Johns Hopkins Center for Civil Society Studies, downloadable from http://www.jhu.edu/~ccss/pubs/cnpwork/index.html.

Salamon, L.M., Sokolowski, S.W. and Anheier, H.K. (2000b) 'Social origins of civil society: an overview', Working Papers of the Johns Hopkins Comparative Nonprofit Sector Project 38, Baltimore: Johns Hopkins Center for Civil Society Studies, Baltimore, downloadable from http://www.jhu.edu/~ccss/pubs/cnpwork/index.html

Salamon, L. and Toepler, S. (2001) 'The influence of the legal environment on the development of the nonprofit sector', Centrer for Civil Society Studies Working Paper 17, Baltimore: Johns Hopkins University Press.

Saxon-Harrold, S. and Kendall, J. (eds) (1995) *Dimensions of the Voluntary Sector*, London: Charities Aid Foundation.

Saxton, J. (2002) 'Love in a warm climate: are the public turned off by charities?', unpublished paper, London: Future Foundation.

Schmitter, P.C. (1979) 'Still the century of corporatism?' in P.C. Schmitter and G. Lehmbruch (eds) *Trends in Corporatist Intermediation*, London: Sage.

Scott, D., and Russell, L (2000) 'Contracting: the experience of service delivery agencies', in M. Harris and C. Rochester (eds) *Voluntary Organizations and Social Policy in Britain*, Basingstoke: Macmillan.

Scott, D., Alcock, P., Russell, L. and Macmillan, R. (2000) *Moving Pictures: Realities of Voluntary Action*, Bristol: Policy Press.

Seebohm, F. (1968) *Report of the Committee on Local Authority and Allied Social Services*, Cmnd 3703, London: HMSO.

Seibel, W. (1990) 'Organizational behaviour and organizational function', in H.K. Anheier and W. Seibel (eds) *The Nonprofit Sector: International and Comparative Perspectives*, Berlin: De Gruyter.

Sharpe, R. (1998) 'Responding to Europeanisation: a governmental perspective', in P. Lowe and S. Ward (eds) (1998) *British Environmental Policy and Europe: Politics and Policy in Transition*, London: Routledge.

Shore, P., Knapp. M., Kendall, J., Fenyo, A. and Carter, S. (1994) 'The local voluntary sector in Liverpool', in S. Saxon-Harrold and J. Kendall (eds) *Researching the Voluntary Sector, volume 2*, Tonbridge: Charities Aid Foundation.

Smith, R. and Geerts, F. (2002) 'The eco-management and audit scheme in Britain', in H. Heinelt and R. Smith (eds) *Sustainability, Innovation and Participatory Governance: A Cross-National Study of the EU Eco-Management and Audit Scheme*. Aldershot: Ashgate.

Social Policy Research Unit (2000) *Outcomes and Assessment with Older People*, Research Works Research Findings from SPRU, York: University of York.

Social Services Inspectorate (1999) *Choice in Residential Care for Older People*, Social Care Group, London: Department of Health.

Social Services Inspectorate (2000a) *Modern Social Services: Commitment to People, the 9th Annual Report of the Chief Inspector of Social Services*, London: Department of Health.

Social Services Inspectorate (2000b) *Towards a Common Cause – 'A Compact for Care'*, *Inspection of Local Authority Social Services and Voluntary Sector Working Relationships*, report written by Ann Barwood, London: Department of Health.

Social Services Inspectorate and Audit Commission (2000) *Promising Prospects: Joint Review Team Fourth Annual Report 1999/2000 English Regions*, London: Audit Commission Publications.

Strategy Unit (2002) *Private Action, Public Benefit: A Review of Charities and the Wider Not-for-Profit Sector*, London: Cabinet Office Strategy Unit, downloadable from www.strategy-unit.gov.uk

Sykes, R. and Leather, P. (1997) *Grey Matters: A Survey of Older People in England*, London: Anchor Trust.

Szerszynski, B. (1997) 'Voluntary associations and the sustainable society', in M. Jacobs (ed.) *Greening the Millenium*, London: Blackwell.

Taylor, D.E. (1993) 'Minority environmentalist activism in Britain: from Brixton to the Lake District', *Qualitative Sociology* 16(3): 3–5.

Taylor, M. (2001) 'The new public management and social exclusion: cause or response', in McLaughlin, K., Osborne, S.P. and Ferlie, E. (eds) *New Public Management: Current Trends and Future Prospects*, London: Routledge.

Taylor, M. and Kendall, J. (1996) 'History of the voluntary sector', in J. Kendall and M. Knapp, *The Voluntary Sector in the UK*, Manchester: Manchester University Press.

Taylor, M. and Lansley, J. (1992) 'Ideology and welfare in the UK: the implications for the voluntary sector', *Voluntas*, 3(2): 153–74.

Taylor, M., Wilkinson, M., Craig, G., Monro, S., Parkes, T. and Warburton, D. (2001a) 'From protest to partnership: voluntary and community organizations in the democratic process', paper presented at the ARNOVA conference, Miami, November/December.

Taylor, M., Craig, G. and Wilkinson, M. (2001b) 'Co-option or empowerment? The changing relationship between the state and the voluntary and community sectors', Brighton: unpublished manuscript, HSPRC, University of Brighton.

Taylor-Gooby, P. (1994) 'Charities in recession: Hard times for the weakest?' in S. Saxon-Harrold and J. Kendall (eds) *Researching the Voluntary Sector*, 2nd edn, Tonbridge: Charities Aid Foundation.

Thane, P. (1986) *Foundations of the Welfare State*, London: Longman.

Thane, P. (2000) *Old Age in English History: Past Experiences, Present Issues*, Oxford: Oxford University Press.

Thomas, G. and Kendall, J. (1996) 'Legal position of the voluntary sector', in Kendall, J. and Knapp, M. (1996) *The Voluntary Sector in the UK*, Manchester: Manchester University Press.

Thornton, P. and Tozer, R. (1994) *Involving Older People in Planning and Evaluating Community Care: A Review of Initiatives*, York: Social Policy Research Unit, University of York.

The Times (1999a) 'Ramblers aim to attract blacks and Asians', 30 June (Valerie Elliott).

The Times (1999b) 'Invasion of the bureaucrats', 23 December (Magnus Linklater).

The Times (2000) 'A flight of fancy and little more', 13 May, Weekend section (Ian Mitchell).

The Times (2002) 'Green and pleasant: doom-mongers cannot prevent the flowers blooming', leading article, date untraced.

Timmins, N. (2001) *The Five Giants: A Biography of the Welfare State*, 2nd edn, London: HarperCollins.

Tonkiss, F. and Passey, A. (1999) 'Trust, confidence and voluntary organizations: between values and institutions', *Sociology* 33(2): 257–74.

Twigg, J. (2000) 'The changing role of users and carers', in B. Hudson (ed.) *The Changing Role of Social Care: Research Highlights in Social Work 37*, London: Jessica Kingsley Publishers.

United Nations Statistical Division in co-operation with the Center for Civil Society Studies (2002) *Handbook on Nonprofit Institutions in the System of National Accounts*, New York: United Nations Statistical Division.

Vincent, J. (1998) '"Head and Heart" vs. "Meeting the Challenge of Change": the Scottish and English "Commissions on the Future of the Voluntary Sector" compared', Volume 2, Conference proceedings of the 4th Researching the Voluntary Sector Conference, 9–10 September, Loughborough University, Loughborough.

Voisey, H. and O'Riordan, T. (1997) 'Governing institutions for sustainable development: the United Kingdom's national level approach', *Environmental Politics Special Issue: Sustainable Development in Western Europe: Coming to Terms with Agenda 21*(61): 24–53.

Waddington, E. and Henwood, M. (1996) *Going Home: Report on an Evaluation of the British Red Cross Home from Hospital Scheme*, London: British Red Cross.

Walker, A. and Naegele, G. (eds) (1999) *The Politics of Old Age in Europe*, Buckingham: Open University Press.

Walker, R, Jeanes, E. and Rowland, R. (2001) *Managing Public Services Innovation: the Experience of English Housing Associations*, Bristol: Policy Press.

Walker, C., Pharoah, C. with P. Jas, A. Passey and C. Romney-Alexander (eds) (2002) *A Lot of Give: Trends in Charitable Giving in the Twenty First Century*, London: Hodder & Stoughton.

Wapner, P.K. (1996) *Environmental Activism and World Civic Politics*, Albany, NY: State University of New York Press.

Wardell, F. and Chesson, R. (1998) 'Volunteering: a healthy choice?' *Elderly Care* 10(6): 12–13.

Ware, A. (1989) *Between Profit and State: Intermediate Organizations in Britain and the United States*, Cambridge: Polity Press.

Ware, A. and Goodin, R. (1990) *Needs and Welfare Provision*, London: Sage.

Ware, P. (1997) 'Independent domiciliary services and the reform of community care', unpublished PhD thesis, Sheffield: Department of Law, University of Sheffield.

Ware, P., Matosevic, T., Forder, J., Hardy, B., Kendall, J., Knapp, M. and Wistow, G. (2001) 'Movement and change: independent domiciliary care providers between 1995 and 1999', *Health and Social Care in the Community* 9(6): 334–40.

Warner, Lord (chair) (1999) *Giving Time, Getting Involved: A Strategy Report by the Working Group on the Active Community*, London: Active Community Unit, Home Office.

Webb, S. and Webb, B. (1912) *The Prevention of Destitution*, London: Longman.

Webb, A. and Wistow, G. (1987) *Social Work, Social Care and Social Planning: The Personal Social services Since Seebohm*, London: Longman.

Weisbrod, B.A. (1975) 'Toward a theory of the nonprofit sector', in E. Phelps (ed.) *Altruism, Morality and Economic Theory*, New York: Russell Sage.

Weisbrod, B.A. (1996) 'Evaluating the nonprofit sector: needs, obstacles and approaches in Washington DC: measuring the impact of the independent, not-for-profit sector in society, independent sector', Working Papers from Carnegie Conference Center, 5–6 September.

Wenger, C.G. (1999) 'Choosing and paying for care', *Health and Social Care in the Community*, 7(3): 187–97.

Wertheimer, A. (1993) *Speaking Out: Citizen Advocacy and Older People*, London: Centre for Policy on Ageing.

Whelan, R. (1996). *The Corrosion of Charity: From Moral Renewal to Contract Culture*, London: Institute of Economic Affairs.

Whelan, R. (1999) 'Involuntary action? How voluntary is the voluntary sector?', in *Involuntary Action? How Voluntary is the 'Voluntary Sector'?*, Choices in Welfare No. 52, London: Institute of Economic Affairs.

Wilcox, S. and Rhodes, D. (1998) *All Tenure Guide to Local Rents 1997*, Centre for Housing Policy, University of York, Housing Corporation Research 27, London: Housing Corporation.

Wildlife and Countryside Link (1997) *The Role of the Agencies*, London: Wildlife and Countryside Link.

Wigglesworth, R. and Kendall, J. (2000) 'The impact of the third sector in the UK: the case of social housing', Centre for Civil Society Working Paper 9, London: Centre for Civil Society, London School of Economics.

Willetts, D. (1994) *Civic Conservatism*, London: Social Market Foundation.

Williams, S. (1998) 'The cost of charity tax relief to the Exchequer', in L. Hems and A. Passey (eds) *The UK Voluntary Sector Almanac 1998/99*, London: NCVO publications, 139–141.

Wilson, D.C. and Butler, R.J. (1985) 'Corporatism in the British voluntary sector', in W. Streeck and P.C. Schmitter (eds) *Private Interest Government*, London: Sage.

Wistow. G., Knapp, M., Hardy, B. and Allen, C. (1994) *Social Care in a Mixed Economy*, Buckingham: Open University Press.

Wistow, G., Knapp, M., Hardy, B., Forder, J, Kendall, J. and Manning, R. (1996) *Social Care Markets: Progress and Prospects*, Buckingham: Open University Press.

Withers, P. and Randolf, B. (1994) *Access Homelessness and Housing Associations*, London: NFHA.

Wittenberg, R., Pickard, L., Comas-Herrera, A., Davies, B. and Darton, R. (2001) 'Demand for long-term care for older people in England to 2001', *Health Statistics Quarterly* 12, 5–17.

Wolch, J. (1990) *The Shadow State: Government and Voluntary Sector in Transition*, New York: The Foundation Center.

Wolfenden, Lord (1978) *The Future of Voluntary* Organizations, London: Croom Helm.

Worcester, R. (1997) 'Public opinion and the environment', in M. Jacobs (ed.) *Greening the Millenium*, London: Blackwell.

World Commission on Environment and Development (1987) *Our Common Future: The Report of the Commission Chaired by G.H. Brundtland*, Oxford: Oxford University Press.

Yearley, S. (1992) *The Green Case: A Sociology of Environmental Issues, Arguments and Politics*, London: Routledge.

Yearley, S. (1996a) 'Campaigning and critique: public-interest groups and environmental change', in F.O. Hampson and J. Reppy (eds) *Earthly Goods: Environmental Change and Social Justice*, Ithaca and London: Cornell University Press.

Yearley, S. (1996b) *Sociology, Environmentalism, Globalization: Reinventing the Globe*, London: Sage.

Young, S.C. (1997) 'Local Agenda 21: The renewal of local democracy?', in M. Jacobs (ed.) *Greening the Millenium*, London: Blackwell.

Young, S.C. (2000a) Personal communication, October.

Young, S.C. (2000b) 'The origins and evolving nature of ecological modernisation', in S.C. Young (ed.) *The Emergence of Ecological Modernisation*, London: Routledge.

Zimmeck, M. (1998) *To Boldy Go: The Volluntary Sector and Voluntary Action in the New World of Work*, London: Royal Society for the Arts.

6, P. (1993) 'Innovation by nonprofit organizations: policy and research issues', *Nonprofit Management and Leadership* 3(4): 397–413.

6, P. (1997a) Editorial statement, *Nonprofit Studies* 1(1): 1–6.

6, P. (1997b) *Holistic Government*, London: Demos.

6, P. and Kendall, J. (eds) (1997) *The Contract Culture in Public Services: Studies from Britain, Europe and the USA*, Aldershot: Arena, Ashgate.

6, P. and Leat, D. (1997) 'Inventing the British voluntary sector by committee: from Wolfenden to Deakin', *Non-Profit Studies* 1(2): 33–46.

6, P., Leat, D., Seltzer, K. and Stoker, G. (1999) *Governing in the Round: Strategies for Holistic Government*, London: Demos.

6, P., Leat, D. and Stoker, G. (1999) *Governing in the Round: Strategies for Holistic Government*, London: Demos.

Index